CLOSING THE GAP

Inner Views of the Heart, Mind & Soul of the Honorable Minister Louis Farrakhan

Conducted & Compiled by
Jabril Muhammad

FCN Publishing, Co.
Chicago

 Published in the United States by FCN Publishing Company, Chicago, Illinois.

All photos by Jabril Muhammad unless otherwise noted.

ISBN: 1-929594-99-2

Printed in the United States of America

First Edition

First printing, October, 2006

TABLE OF CONTENTS

J F E I

Minister Louis Farrakhan
NATIONAL REPRESENTATIVE OF THE HONORABLE ELIJAH MUHAMMAD
AND
THE NATION OF ISLAM

IN THE NAME OF ALLAH, THE BENEFICENT, THE MERCIFUL.

My Dear Brother Jabril,

May this letter find you in the best of health and spirit. I'm writing this letter to personally thank you, and all those with you, for this wonderful book *Closing the Gap*. I am sincerely hoping that those who would read this book will become enlivened by the spirit that motivated such a book.

To the readers of this wonderful book, Brother Jabril has been my personal friend, brother, companion and confidante for 51 years of my Islamic life. He has dedicated the better part of his life to the constant study of the word that Master Fard Muhammad gave to the Honorable Elijah Muhammad, as the means of the resurrection of an entire people and, as a force that would close out an old world of evil and form the foundation of a new world of righteousness, freedom, justice and equality where all who live on this planet will live in peace and harmony; not for a day, a month or a year, but for an eternity.

I thank Brother Jabril for the questions that he asked of me and more importantly, I thank Allah for forming the answers in my head and heart even as he was asking the questions.

I thank Allah for putting it into your heart, Brother Jabril, to ask me these questions. I thank Allah for helping me to answer these questions in such a way that it might serve the purpose of closing the gap between the followers and their leader; but more importantly, in closing of the gap between us and Allah (God). It is misunderstanding, distrust, and suspicion that have made the gap. It is understanding and the purification of the heart, through trials, that will allow the mind and the heart, to read the words of this book and close the gap between us and Allah (God), and by so doing close the gap between us and his servant, and close the gap between one another.

May Allah bless those who read these words. May Allah guide the hearts and minds of those who read these words, that we might successfully come through this ever darkening period, into the dawn of a brand new day.

4855 South Woodlawn Avenue CHICAGO, ILLINOIS 60615

Page 2

So, to my Brother Jabril and to all of those who helped him in a great or a small way, to get this book published, I say thanks, thanks, thanks.

May Allah reward each of you who helped, and each of you who read, with a place in the Hereafter, which is the true goal of every Muslim (the righteous.)

Thank you for reading these few words.

I am your Brother and Servant,

Louis Farrakhan

Louis Farrakhan
September 27, 2006

FOREWORD

For years human beings have attempted to identify, quantify and improve the quality of all of their relationships. Yet, by the words of the leading experts and scientists, in every field imaginable—economics, medicine, politics, ecology and others —the effort to accomplish the full identification, quantification and perfection of relationships remains undone. Some of these men and women who are described as being on the cutting edge or most knowledgeable in this effort are searching for what has been loosely referred to as "A Theory of Everything." It is, in other words, that which would explain everything about life, the universe, and their relationship(s), unifying the currently separate disciplines of the sciences of this world.

A Black man born in Georgia, in the 19th century–first named Elijah Poole, then Elijah Karriem, and finally Elijah Muhammad—said and wrote publicly that he was taught the wisdom—and its root—that explained every significant thing about life, the universe and their relationship(s.) He stated on many occasions that what he was taught was not a theory. He said that theories were essentially "guesses" that could not be proven. Everything he taught—he stated firmly—could be proven. He physically taught in the public and through others, in a special way, for a time period that touched five different decades (the 1930s, 1940s, 1950s, 1960s and 1970s) of the 20th century. But he never claimed to be the originator of that which he shared with others. He said that he was the *witness* of another.

The Honorable Elijah Muhammad taught that he learned what he did from another human being whom he referred to most directly in the public, by the name of Master Fard Muhammad. Master Fard Muhammad, he taught, was a man born, also in the 19th century, to a Black father and a White mother, in the holy city of Mecca, Arabia. The Honorable Elijah Muhammad also said that he met Master Fard Muhammad in Detroit, Michigan, in the United States of America and that Master Fard Muhammad had been coming in and out of the United States for twenty years before beginning to teach Black people in Detroit, on July 4, 1930. Their *relationship,* in a most profound way, "began" in their meeting, in that very city, on the night of September 22, 1931. That night, the Honorable Elijah Muhammad recognized that the words and actions of this man corresponded to certain words contained in the Bible regarding the coming of a human being who would have the power to permanently change life as we all know it, and for the better. Their meeting—characterized by the realization of the identity of one man (Master Fard Muhammad) by another (the Honorable Elijah Muhammad), provides the definitive reference point for those looking for the birth date of what is now known as the Lost-Found Nation of Islam in the West, more commonly referred to as The Nation of Islam.

The meeting between Master Fard Muhammad and the Honorable Elijah Muhammad in 1931 and the evolution of their *relationship* was part of a chain reaction of events that eventually included the attendance and participation of a young man—a brilliant and talented entertainer from Boston, Massachusetts, named Louis Eugene Walcott—at a Nation of Islam event in February of 1955, celebrating the birthday of Master Fard Muhammad. That annual event was called Saviour's Day (it continues today as Saviours' Day). Although they did not physically meet in the usual sense of that word on that day (that would happen in 1957) the nature of the *relationship* between the Honorable Elijah Muhammad and the man to whom he would later give the last name of "Farrakhan," was clearly defined.

In that very same year, 1955, another young man, three years Minister Farrakhan's junior (and born in the very same Bronx, New York hospital as Minister Farrakhan)—a brilliant student, talented athlete and gifted musician, whose first name was "Bernard"—would also enter into a *relationship* with the Honorable Elijah Muhammad, as one of his followers. In January 1955, months after first attending Temple #7 in 1954 to hear the teachings of the Honorable Elijah Muhammad, he became a registered member of the Nation of Islam.

Later that same year, while this young man "Brother Bernard" was working in a restaurant run by the Nation, he would meet, or see, for the first time, this other young man, known at the time, simply as "Brother Louis." The two would become instant friends. That *relationship*, although neither young man knew it at the time, would evolve and grow, in a certain way, for twenty-two years, and be punctuated by a most significant meeting between these two, yet again, in a restaurant, but this time, on the other side of the United States of America—in Hollywood, California.

It is September 1977, and both men have lived what many might consider "full lives" in the Nation of Islam. The "Brother Louis" who joined the Nation of Islam twenty-two years prior, became Minister Louis Farrakhan of Temple #7 of New York City, serving a publicly recognized eight year period (1967 to 1975) as the National Representative of the Honorable Elijah Muhammad—functioning as his leader's spokesperson, in his leader's physical presence. He is now 44 years old, and seriously considering going back into the entertainment industry, while simultaneously realizing an emerging desire to rebuild the work of the Honorable Elijah Muhammad, which has now been destroyed. The "Brother Bernard" who joined the Nation of Islam twenty-two years prior in New York, eventually went west, and became Minister Bernard Cushmeer of Temple #32 of Phoenix, Arizona—living for six years in the home of the Honorable Elijah Muhammad (1965 to 1971)—receiving direct training as a theologian from him, and even writing a book about his leader, *This Is The One* (interestingly Minister Farrakhan wrote a song by this same name in 1957 and sang it for the Honorable Elijah Muhammad at his 60th birthday celebration on October 7, 1957), bearing *witness* to his leader, in his leader's physical presence. He is now

41 years old and seriously considering how to best help Minister Louis Farrakhan realize, even deeper than he ever had before, the unique nature of the Minister's special relationship to the Honorable Elijah Muhammad.

The two men have not seen each other since December of 1974 in New York City and they have not spoken to one another since February of 1975 when they last had a telephone conversation. A lot has happened since December of 1974.

The Nation of Islam, as they and the public knew it, is no more—taking on a change, after the rise to leadership by the Honorable Elijah Muhammad's son, Wallace Muhammad, now known as Imam Warith Deen Mohammed. The Honorable Elijah Muhammad is no longer present, and it has been announced that he died on February 25· 1975. Many who once followed him are confused about the aim, purpose and meaning of what he taught. Some believe that the physical son of the man that they once lovingly referred to as "The Messenger" has represented a properly guided new direction, not a fall, but an increase, an evolution, if you will, of the teachings and organizational structure established by his father. There are others who believe and boldly claim that their own relationship to the Honorable Elijah Muhammad has qualified them to take a leadership position in representing him and in achieving the fulfillment of some of his desires and what appears to remain unfinished of his great work. Still others believe that there is no unique person, no special individual who is qualified to do any such thing, and that the Honorable Elijah Muhammad never designated any one person to sit in his seat after him. These persons believe that the teachings of the Honorable Elijah Muhammad and the work that remains of his mission can best be performed by, and is left to, the numerous individuals who, as a mass, have followed him and studied his words. And, there are more—some who believe that Minister Louis Farrakhan, above anyone else, has been best qualified, or even designated by his teacher, to lead an effort to carry on the work of the Nation of Islam. But there are differing views as to whether or not a window of opportunity for him to take a stand exists, and whether or not it has already closed.

One of the hundreds of thousands of those who have followed "The Messenger" and who are living in and through this controversial and dangerous period of swirling emotions, thoughts, and actions, is Minister Bernard Cushmeer. He is convinced that the nature of the *relationship* between the Honorable Elijah Muhammad and Minister Louis Farrakhan is so critical, intimate, important, and prophetic in nature, that he does not believe for one minute that it ended in 1975, in the way that many did. Nor does he believe that the Nation of Islam's assignment—which the Honorable Elijah Muhammad taught involved an expanded aspect of his work among Black people, Mexicans, Native and Aboriginal people, and others, in the Western Hemisphere and around the world—was completed in 1975. Nothing seems to weaken his conviction regarding the role he believes Minister Farrakhan is pre-destined to serve, as the prime Minister leading the rebuilding of the Nation of Islam in the name of the Honorable Elijah Muhammad. In 1976 he even witnesses to some—who believe *they* should lead the way—that it is Minister Farrakhan and no one else who has this tremendous job to do. He even asks them to be patient and wait on the Minister to take his stand. That same year he also turns down an offer of a home and financial support, courtesy of some in California, if he—Bernard Cushmeer—would assume the responsibility of lifting the name of the Honorable Elijah Muhammad, and lead the rebuilding of the work of the Nation of Islam.

He knows it is *Minister Farrakhan*, and not he, who has that job to do.

So, now, in September of 1977—as part of his effort to help a man he believes to be his "Big Brother" and superior officer—Minister Bernard Cushmeer has an opportunity to give Minister Louis Farrakhan, the National Representative of the Honorable Elijah Muhammad, an important book. It is a book that Minister Bernard began writing in 1972 as a result of a telephone conversation he had with the Honorable Elijah Muhammad. He completed in 1973. In the latter part of 1974 a combination of events settled his mind on just what he was to do with the book. He realized that he was not to publish *this* book publicly, but that, rather, in fact, he had written this book *for* Minister Farrakhan and he was to give it to him at sometime in the future.

Thirty-five months after he realized for whom he had ultimately written this book, Minister Bernard Cushmeer was finally giving it to the intended recipient, Minister Louis Farrakhan. Indeed, Minister Farrakhan read the book, which was hundreds of pages in length, doing so over a three-day period. After finishing his reading of the book, while on the twelfth floor of a hotel in Hollywood, Minister Farrakhan informed Minister Cushmeer of the impact his writing had on him—using language from the Bible—and asked his younger Brother to join him in prayer. Then, both men went downstairs so that Minister Farrakhan could attend a scheduled meeting with the famed Black actor, Brock Peters (who passed away in 2005.) In that meeting the Minister informed Mr. Peters of his decision to rebuild the work of the Honorable Elijah Muhammad.

Now, it is 2006, and all of those reading this book, ***Closing The Gap***, in one way or another are becoming familiar with the Honorable Minister Louis Farrakhan or have been affected by the impact he has had on the United States of America and the world since he arose to rebuild the work of the Honorable Elijah Muhammad twenty-nine years ago. Some may not fully realize it but that statement, just made, is the same as stating that all of us reading this have been affected by the relationship that began between Master Fard Muhammad and the Honorable Elijah Muhammad in September of 1931, and the relationship that began between the Honorable Minister Louis Farrakhan and the Honorable Elijah Muhammad in February of 1955.

In the normal sense of the word we do not, as a mass of people, have access to all of the forms of communication with Master Fard Muhammad and the Honorable Elijah Muhammad that we might enjoy today with many of our family and friends, for example. Nor have we had regular access to a widely disseminated, non-stop flow of communication about the Honorable Elijah Muhammad or his Teacher, directly from themselves, identical to what we might receive from celebrities and public figures through this world's media—whether broadcast, television, or Internet.

The same cannot be said about the other third member of this significant relationship, the Honorable Minister Louis Farrakhan.

Through speaking events, written letters, dinner table talks, webcasts, telephone conversations, meetings, appearances, and other engagements and settings, many of us have an opportunity to learn much directly through the words and actions of Minister Farrakhan as part of his active and open physical presence among us.

And then there are *interviews*—those unique opportunities where we get to see, hear or read Minister Farrakhan respond to the thoughts and feelings of others expressed to him in the form of direct questions.

What makes the interview such a powerful vehicle for learning and communication is that in a direct manner, an individual is placed in a position of being presented with concepts, ideas, and arguments of varying intelligence and emotional content and given an opportunity to express what they think and how they feel about what has been placed before them. Another critical aspect of the interview process is that an individual has the opportunity to speak about their view of themselves in relation to persons, ideas, institutions and events.

But *what kind of interview* yields the most information and learning and produces the greatest impact on others? It is that interview where the interview subject is the most candid in answering the most informed, important, and consequential questions, while speaking deeply *into* that which is of the greatest consequence, motivated by love, the deepest respect for the Truth, and concern for what is most appropriate for those who are listening.

This book, ***Closing The Gap***, represents the very best of interviews. For the first time, in one handy reference, we have Minister Farrakhan's clearly expressed views about himself; the roots of what he teaches; his relationship with the Honorable Elijah Muhammad; his growth in the Nation of Islam—as both a Believer and Laborer; and his thinking across an exceptionally wide range and variety of disciplines, individuals, institutions and events.

As these interviews clearly show, Minister Louis Farrakhan is as much a servant as he is a leader—interested first and foremost with the deepest education of all of us into the best of ourselves and our proper connection to one another and the Ultimate Reality. In other words, he is facilitating proper and right *relationships* between all of the human family, the universe, and its Creator. His answers to the questions placed before him in ***Closing The Gap*** are informative, sobering, stimulating, and inspiring, and also cast light on the international implications of his function as a reconciler, by humanity.

It is on this divine function of the Honorable Louis Farrakhan where I will place a concluding focus and emphasis.

Consider that the chain of events connected to the beginning of a relationship on September 22, 1931 continue today. As there has been an expansion from Master Fard Muhammad to the Honorable Elijah Muhammad and from the Honorable Elijah Muhammad to the Honorable Minister Louis Farrakhan, there is now an expansion from the Honorable Minister Louis Farrakhan to a body of people, and then beyond, in a very special way.

Two points related to this subject of a chain of events—all loaded with implications, immediately come to mind. I hope that they stimulate serious questions and the deepest kind of thought in answering them and further *introduce* ***Closing The Gap***.

Here is what comes to my mind:

First, during his historic *Theology of Time* lecture series of 1972, the Honorable Elijah Muhammad indicated that on occasion he had been asked by the leadership of the nations of Africa to leave or spend less time with his own people—the Black Man and Woman of America—in order to teach on that continent. The African leadership expressed to him that he would have greater success abroad than he was having at home. The Honorable Elijah Muhammad stated, with great humility and confidence, that he declined such offers. He said clearly that one day, in the future, once he got his own people up to a certain level, it would be *they*, and not he, who would come and teach abroad. He explained a certain order of things—a chain reaction that over time would represent an expanded relationship between he, his earliest followers, a larger group of followers who would come later, and the rest of humanity.

Question: Over what period of time do you think the full chain reaction and expanded relationship is to take place?

Secondly, in an article written in 1963 which also appears in the book, *Message To The Blackman*, the Honorable Elijah Muhammad wrote that *one day* the Nation of Islam would make an effort to reach, teach and unite all of the original people of the Western Hemisphere. His words make it very clear, that as of the time of that writing, the Nation of Islam had not yet undertaken that specific activity.

Questions: Did such an activity take place in between 1963, when this article was written, and 1975, when the Honorable Elijah Muhammad departed from among us? And, who are the original people of the Western Hemisphere?

So, now, finally—*what is the relationship between the actual rise of Minister Farrakhan and the rebuilding work of the Nation of Islam since September 1977, and **all** of the points and questions I have raised in the previous two examples?*

In my humble opinion, this wonderful book, ***Closing The Gap,*** suggests, points to, and provides a powerful, glorious and convincing answer to this question and the others I have posed.

Let us all read this book with the disposition and attitude best suited for receiving and learning from another—that of the child, student, and seeker of truth.

And may we all—regardless to race, belief system, social status, language, and nationality—benefit from its contents.

Remember, we are all potentially witnesses *of*, and participants *in*, a very special *relationship*.

Cedric Muhammad
September 25, 2006

Introduction

Every student's dream is to be close to his or her teacher. So close that he or she is considered the favorite; and even closer, that one day, the student hopes to be "like" or "equal" to the one teaching.

Any good student yearns for the day when his teacher calls upon him; because he takes pleasure in showing the teacher he got his lesson. He takes pleasure in being pleasing his in the teacher's sight.

Not only is it the student's desire, to be "like" the teacher, or to one day become a teacher, it is the aim and purpose of the teacher, that the student one day equals and even surpasses him. This is what fuels any good teacher. It is his driving force, it is also what gives him patience with the student, for he sees and knows the power that is active in the teacher lays dormant in the student. So it is the teacher's aim to ignite the energy that is potential and turn it to kinetic.

So the teacher will perform all kinds of "stunts" (if you will) to get the attention of the student, to show the student what is inside of him. But, often times, instead of the student(s) taking hold of the truth of the witness of his teacher as a sign of his own attributes; all the teacher gets is more accolades, claps, cheers, tears and salutes. But, that's not what he (the teacher) is after. In fact, he wants none of that; his greatest desire, that in which he came into the world for, and that which he will give his life for; is for his student(s) to become what he or she already "is."

The Honorable Elijah Muhammad stated that "the ultimate aim and purpose" of Master Fard Muhammad was/is to make "each one into a God." If that is His purpose, and The Honorable Elijah Muhammad wouldn't have a purpose, except for the purpose of the Master; and Minister Louis Farrakhan wouldn't have a purpose, except for the purpose of the student of the Master; then it is safe to say, that the ultimate aim and purpose of Minister Louis Farrakhan is the same as the Master, to make each one of "us" into a God.

"For this cause I have come into the world," said Jesus; ultimately to be the bridge that connects and binds man back to his original state; where there is no gap in thought, where there is no separation between man, and God. This couldn't be achieved by Jesus or any of the Messengers of Allah, unless they themselves went through the "process" or actually stood "in the gap" between man and God.

Well, where exactly is the gap? It was put like this in the Old Testament: "My thoughts are not your thoughts and neither are my ways your ways. Mine are from above while yours are from beneath." Then it went on to say, "that as the rain falls down from heaven, so shall my word be, that cometh out of my mouth, it shall not return unto me void, but shall accomplish what 'I will' and prosper whereunto I send it."

It's clear by this statement that someone is operating or "thinking" on a higher level and therefore able to "do" greater things and accomplish more than the one who is operating beneath. So there forms a gap or difference in the results of a person whose thoughts are from above, and the person's whose thoughts are from beneath. The gap exists in the "thought consciousness." And if the gap exists in "thought," then the gap can be closed by "thought."

Faith is the substance of things hoped for; the evidence of things not seen. What is the "substance?" The Honorable Elijah Muhammad taught us that thought can be measured; it travels at the speed of 24 billion miles per second. Is "thought" substance? And if thought is substance, how do we transfer that substance into material evidence?

We are told in the scriptures that "as a man or woman thinketh in his heart, so is he." At no time does man ever manifest or experience anything that he is not conscious of being. Try as you might to fight the circumstances, situations, or people; it is like shattering a full-body mirror. You are only fighting the "image" not the "source" of the image; which is your consciousness. Everything in your life, from the way your furniture is arranged to the way your life events play out, is a direct result of the sum total of your thoughts.

We war not against flesh and blood, but against principalities and spiritual wickedness in high places. The high place is your mind. The scriptures say, Jesus went up on the mountain to pray, and there Satan tempted him. Well, where was Satan? In his mind? Jesus went "up," and in his attempt to reach higher levels of awareness of his self, he found a devil; a contrary thought/opposition. I heard a great R&B singer say about his climb to the top, "on every level, there's another devil."

There is a process to closing the gap between you and the object of your desire. It involves raising your awareness. There is no escape except through "consciousness." You must assume the "consciousness" of that which you seek, if you are to see that desire fulfilled in your life. In order to become anything, you have to "be" the thing desired.

If we look a little closer at the life and times of Jesus, we see that in the beginning of his ministry, he submitted himself totally to the Father. He loved and spoke "of" the authority of his Father. He said, "I can of myself, do nothing. ... The Father doeth the work. ... No man cometh unto me, except by the Father."

But, as Jesus grew in his ministry and mission, he continued in obedience to "the" authority, then, he began to perform miracles and carried out the will of The Father. We saw a merging of the mind of Jesus (son of a carpenter) and "Christ consciousness" (the son of God). Then, we heard the same man, begin to speak differently.

When his disciples or followers asked him, "when will we see the Father?" Jesus showed major disappointment with them. He said things like, "how long must I suffer with you? All these miracles I have shown you, yet you still don't believe." Then, toward the so-called end, we heard Jesus speak "from" the authority, "When you see me you see the Father. For I am in Him, and He is in me." Then he said, "I Am The Resurrection and The Life."

What happened? The more Jesus yielded to the higher power, the more access he had to "The Source of Power." The higher power was never something outside him; The Father, was and is his own "consciousness" of being.

Those who witnessed, kept asking, "Is this not the son of Joseph, the son of a carpenter?" And the people were divided over him. But, Jesus said unto Peter, "Who do you say I am?" And Peter answered and said, "Thou art the Christ." Jesus said, 'flesh and blood has not revealed that to you. But, Peter, your consciousness has been pricked and the scales have been removed from your eyes. When you look at me, you don't see a mere man, you see the "divine spirit" in a human being operating at its Full Potential. You see God.

What irritated Jesus most wasn't the fact that they (followers/students) didn't recognize him, for the sake of recognizing him. It wasn't vanity. His concern was that if they never saw him, for whom he was/is; if they never saw him transform into Christ, they would never see themselves properly and never "press-out" the essence of their beings. And that is what made him groan in his spirit; that they marveled at what they saw him do, but failed to really see that he was trying to show them a picture of themselves.

He was upset with them, that they weren't getting the lesson. When someone needed healing, they brought the person to Jesus. It was okay in the beginning; he had to show forth the force and power that was in him, that they might believe. But, they kept clapping, and clapping, and bringing the people to Jesus.

The only thing that separated them from him was their awareness of being. The rich man, poor man, saint or sinner are not different minds, but different arrangements of the same mind. Think of it like this; a piece of steel when magnetized differs not in substance, from its demagnetized state, but in the arrangement and order of its molecules.

"A single electron revolving in a specified orbit constitutes the unit of magnetism. When a piece of steel or anything else is demagnetized the revolving electrons have stopped. Therefore, the magnetism has not gone out of existence. There is only a re-arrangement of the particles, so that they produce no outside or perceptible effect. When particles are arranged at random, mixed up in all directions, the substance is said to be demagnetized; but when particles are marshaled in ranks so that a number of them face in one direction, the substance is a magnet.

Magnetism is not generated; it is displayed. Health, wealth, beauty and genius are not created; they are only manifested by the arrangement of your mind—that is your concept of yourself."

Jesus closed the gap between his consciousnesses of being man and became God, which he already was; for no man can express that which is not conscious of being.

The Honorable Elijah Muhammad said he would be gone for three years. He departed in February, 1975. In the first week of September of 1977, in a hotel in California, the man who was/ is considered, The Honorable Elijah Muhammad's best student, The Honorable Minister Louis Farrakhan, was given a word, in a book form; that helped to change to course of his life and the lives of countless others, not to mention the course of American and world history. He is the example of the perfect love of a student for his teacher.

It's similar to when a woman loves a man, she submits herself totally to him. She desires to be "*with*" him at all times; so much that she devotes her life to his life. She wishes she could be apart of his very genetic makeup. This is the Divine Love. The Divine Love is one of service. The pain of being without the loved one is so unbearable, that she begins to take on the characteristics of the object of her love and affection. She becomes one with him.

I guess we can say that the story of The Honorable Minister Louis Farrakhan is a true love affair. A man in love with his teacher, The Honorable Elijah Muhammad, in love with his God, Allah, Who Came in the Person of Master Fard Muhammad; and in love with his people and humanity. What better love than this;

than a man would lay down his life for his friend?

As you read, this book, *Closing The Gap*, you are literally taken on an intimate journey into the heart, mind and soul of a man. His destiny, didn't start when he met the Honorable Elijah Muhammad, it began in his mother's womb. In fact, when he heard that God had raised a messenger for our people, he was a little upset, asking God, "Why didn't you choose me, you know I love my people." And the Honorable Elijah Muhammad almost had to whip him, to get him to see, that he, The Honorable Elijah Muhammad didn't make him; he said, Allah made Farrakhan for him.

> *"Every time you look into the face of a Black man/woman, you are looking at God."*
> *— The Honorable Elijah Muhammad*

> *"Is it not written in your law? Yea are all gods"*
> *— Jesus, The Christ*

"The spiritual journey does not consist in arriving at a new destination where a person gains what he does not have, or becomes what he is not. It consists in the dissipation of one's own ignorance concerning one's self and life, and the gradual growth of that understanding, which begins the spiritual awakening. The finding of God is a coming to one's self."

— Aldous Huxley

P.S. I must mention this, as it is so relevant to this book and the work of the Honorable Minister Louis Farrakhan. One of the main impediments to truly becoming one with the teacher/leader's mind is found in attachments. Attachment is actually death; and is a sign of insecurity. Since a Muslim is one who has been made secure and Allah is Sufficient; then, if Muhammad is slain, killed or taken; will you turn back on your heels? You will if you are attached to Muhammad, then your life begins and ends with Muhammad. But, if your life begins and ends with Allah, and He was with you in the womb of your mother, and Allah is Eternal;

than as long as you are one with Allah, the only Source; you can never die.

This is why Jesus, said, it's expedient that I go. I go to prepare a place for you, that where "I am," there you shall be also. Where "I am" where? Where "I am" in consciousness. In other words, as long as I am among you; you are so attached to me, the personality; but, if I'm no longer in your presence perhaps, just maybe, you will remember the principles by which I lived my life. And perhaps; just maybe, you will grow into the maturity of the meaning of my life. And perhaps; just maybe in your desire to "see" me again; in your intense longing to "be with" me again; you will pick up those principles that I taught you and carry them into action; and then, through your obedience and acts of devotion to me (principles that I represent); You Will See Me Again. You will See My Face Coming Across Your Face. Then you can say, like me, "I and My Father Are One!"

With great love, all things are possible
Sister Latonja Muhammad
July 7, 2006

The Meaning of this Book's Cover

I sent the Minister what I thought was a beautiful photo of himself for the cover of this book. He turned it down. Then we agreed that I would send him three or four other photos of himself and we would work together to pick one of them. A day or so later, I was in a situation where I was rushing to get an important package off to him. I saw that I did not have enough time to make the photographs that I had in mind. I would have to make them later.

So, I decided to send him photographs of himself, which I already had made where he was with others, in a happy mood. These were photos that I don't think he had ever seen. This was not long after the 1st of September.

He called me the next day to share with me what he immediately saw in the photograph, that now is the cover of this book. He saw deeply. He told me that what he saw in this photograph that it was symbolic of this book, these times, and our condition; a condition, which he hoped his words would help to heal.

He mentioned that the setting of the sun, in the photograph, reminded him of the words of the Honorable Elijah Muhammad during his last address to us, on February 26, 1974 when he was at the close of the first phase of his assignment. In that address he stated, "The sun is setting. But it will rise again."

Minister Farrakhan told me that the scene in the photograph reminded him that he and we are now at the setting of the sun of this phase of his work. I mentioned to him that the photograph was of himself and Minister Akbar Muhammad.

He said to me that he recognized himself but not the other person. But *before* I informed him of who the other person was he had already thought of this scene and that other person as symbolic of the Nation's condition in terms of a gap. I informed him that when I took the picture we were close to the juncture of the merging of the Blue and the White Niles (Rivers) at Khartoum, Sudan. He seemed to already know that and commented on the teachings in the Holy Qur'an concerning *Moses and the Wise Man* and what led to the parting between the two (Surah 18; Section 9 and 10.)

He spoke a few more words on the gap between us and himself. And expressed his desire that this book might be used by Allah to close the gap that he so beautifully and clearly explains in this book, and clearly explains how this gap can be closed.

I then mentioned to Minister Farrakhan that generally photographs are taken for three purposes. They are taken to record something; to report something; or to make a statement about someone or something or some event.

I took that picture without thinking much about where we were. Of course, I didn't have this book in mind. (Smile) But what I did see in that scene, which I tried to capture, was; "Friends." That was the title that I gave that image, from then 1995 to now.

I'll now attempt to blend the significance of our thinking, of the significance of this photograph for the cover of this book, in but a few words. If we work, according to the will and purpose of Allah, we can *close the gap* and become that which Allah desires us to become; "Friends" with Him; "Friends" with the Honorable Elijah Muhammad; "Friends" with the Honorable Minister Louis Farrakhan; "Friends" with each other and "Friends" with ourselves—thus becoming completely what He desires us to be, to serve our people and the people of the world!

Jabril Muhammad
September 27, 2006

This book is being translated into Spanish by Bro. Mustapha Muhammad of Upland, California. Arrangements are presently being made to have this book translated into French.

Section 1

FARRAKHAN: THE TRAVELER
For The FINAL CALL
Vol. 18; No. 24

In Phoenix, Arizona, on Easter Sunday April 17, 1987, the Honorable Minister Louis Farrakhan opened his speech with certain words. Please read them carefully, even slowly. He began:

"In the Name of Allah, the Beneficent, the Merciful. I bear witness there is no God but Allah, and I bear witness that Muhammad is His Messenger.

"My beloved Brothers and Sisters, once again it is my great pleasure to have this opportunity to speak with you on the basis of the teachings of the Honorable Elijah Muhammad.

"Today is a very important day in the Christian world. For this day that is called Easter revolves around the glorious resurrection of Jesus Christ which represents a victory; not only a victory over physical death, but a victory over all the impediments that keeps man from oneness with God.

"This important day in the life of Christians is also important in the life of a Muslim only from a different perspective. There is no Muslim who does not believe in the resurrection of the dead.

"In fact, all Muslims traditionally believe that they will see the return of Jesus. And of all of the men of God that have ever lived and worked on behalf of the righteousness of God among the people—of all of these men—the Muslims only believe that one man will return. And that man, of course, is Jesus.

"So there is a similarity between the belief of the Muslims and the belief of the Christians. But today, by the help of Almighty God if you are willing to reason, we want to hopefully clarify our—what I would call—immature understanding of one of the most profound events in religious history.

"Now, as you notice Christianity does not take it's beginning from the birth of Jesus; nor from the ministry of Jesus. But Christianity takes it beginning from the most painful and critical aspect of his life. It begins on the basis of his passion under the judicial decree of crucifixion.

"Isn't that interesting? You would think that a religion would base its beginning, or start its calendar, from the birth of a great man or from the beginning of his ministry. But Christianity takes its beginning in the most sad and sorrowful, painful and trying time of the so-called Christian era when Jesus was being crucified, and his friends were leaving him.

"Its disturbing to see this powerful human being in a state where it appeared as though he had no power to save himself. But this is the beginning of Christianity. Islam is somewhat similar.

"Islam does not start its calendar from the birth of prophet Muhammad, peace be upon him. Nor does Islam begins its calendar from the first revelation of God to Muhammad. But Islam begins its history, its calendar with a death plot against the life of the prophet from which he escapes and fled from his enemies.

"So, when you hear the Muslim calendar given—this is the year 1406, I believe—1406 AH, after the hegira, or after the flight of Muhammad on the heels of a death plot.

"So here is a critical time in Islamic history, and a critical time in Christian history where these religions take their calendar from.

"Now, what should we learn from that? There's a lesson here.

"That in our darkest hour, an hour when you think you should give up because the forces arrayed against you are so mighty; so powerful; and they look as though they have totally overwhelmed you, it is in *that* hour that your greatest opportunity for triumph is in you.

"And it is in *that* hour that most people give up the struggle and they never come to victory over the forces that are now apparently overwhelming them.

"So, this is to be taken personally by you and me—that the life of these two great religious movements in the world begins from an apparent tragedy.

"And you know what? Your and my great beginning as a people has started from the tragedy of slavery. Where we think that our slavery; and our suffering; and our total destruction as a people is a cursing, underneath what appears to be a cursing, is a great blessing; for a new history begins on the basis of a tragedy."

I intend no insult to anyone with what follows. But, let me repeat these words of his: "Now, what should we learn from that? There's a lesson there.

"That in our darkest hour, an hour when you think you should give up because the forces arrayed against you are so mighty; so powerful; and they look as though they have totally overwhelmed you, it is in *that* hour that your greatest opportunity for triumph is in you."

Haven't you either seen or heard of instances in these last twenty or so years when *the hand of the Lord,* working through Minister Farrakhan, has turned what appeared to be defeat into victory, again and again and again and again? Haven't you? If you are so "new" to this hopefully others, who have been around for a while, will share with you what I am writing about.

This expression, "the hand of the Lord," appears in thirty-six different verses in *The King James Bible*. In *The Old Testament*, the word "hand," in this phrase, appears thirty-three times, and is from a Hebrew word, which is transliterated, "yad," and is pronounced, "yawd." It refers to the hand of man. However, in the figurative sense it essentially means: "the strength and the power of God."

In the three places in *The New Testament,* where "the hand of the Lord" appears, the word "hand," is from the Greek word, "cheir" and pronounced "khire."

It means, "by the help or agency of any one, or by means of any one." In the figurative sense, and as applied to God, it symbolizes, "His might, activity, and power in creating the universe; in upholding and preserving."

The expression, again means, in essence, that "God is present protecting and aiding one; or in punishing; or in determining and controlling the destinies of men."

Study this expression, "the hand of the Lord." That same idea is expressed in the Holy Qur'an, but in somewhat different words. Look at how it is used, in the scriptures, regarding men and woman of God; through whom Allah was working His will.

If we do, we will see—if we have enough of the spirit of Allah—that the hand of the Lord was/is will ever be with Minister Farrakhan all through his health problems and beyond. This is written!

More next issue, Allah willing.
Jabril Muhammad
April 6, 1999

On May 7, 2006, **the Honorable Minister Louis Minister Farrakhan** appeared on "The Open Line Show" on 98.7 KISS FM in New York, N.Y., which is hosted by **James Mtume**. The following are brief excerpts from that interview.

James Mtume: Could you give us your summation of your trip to Cuba [in March 2006], as you explain the need for Black people in America to globalize and (that) we don't have to depend on people necessarily here in America?

Minister Farrakhan: In the Book of Genesis, when Adam was made by God, he was told to eat of all of the fruit of all of these trees except one. Today, we are in the Genesis of the birth and rise of Black people all over the world. We were fed from a tree of good mixed with evil, of lies mixed with truth and it has poisoned the bloodstream of the Black family. So we are filled with self-hatred and self-destructive behavior. But we are a global people, we are an international people and there are many trees of knowledge all over the world that we should be willing to at least taste the fruit of.

After Hurricane Katrina, which unmasked the naked racism and ineptitude of government and the non-caring attitude of government toward the suffering of Black people, we decided that since Cuba was only 90 miles from the shores of America—under a blockade for 47 years with a leader who has withstood over 670 assassination attempts—Cuba has been mobilized for 47 years to withstand disaster. There have been Category 5 hurricanes that hit that island and not one life was lost.

At the 10th Anniversary of the Million Man March, which we call the birth of the Millions More Movement, we said that we can no longer depend on government to look after us, but we must set up those instrumentalities that would allow us, to look out for ourselves. So we wanted a Ministry of Health, a Ministry of Education, a Ministry of Defense, a Ministry of Foreign Affairs, a Ministry of Science and Technology, a Ministry of Art and Culture and the people that were on that Mall agreed that we should set up these types of ministries, gathering the Talented Tenth that W.E.B. DuBois talked about and with a programmatic thrust to work to lift the masses of our people.

So as the Ministry of Defense, we wanted to go to Cuba to see how they defended themselves and their people against hurricanes, against natural disaster. It was one of the greatest learning experiences that we had—and that is a tree that I believe we all can eat from and the fruit of that tree will not poison us.

James Mtume: Many people do not understand what your image and relationship are with world leaders. Could you elaborate on that?

Minister Farrakhan: In Cuba, we documented with a videographer everything that we saw and we saw much. Every word is being transcribed and we are bringing from that transcription a document that we desire to share with our Brothers and Sisters, church leaders and organizational leaders because disaster is going to strike America. It is written in the Holy Qur'an that Allah (God) will bring one calamity after another until the enemy is laid low. So Hurricane Katrina is only one, but there are many more to come. We, as suffering people in America and the poor of America, must be prepared to save ourselves and our people. So what we learned, we want to share it through churches and organizations to Black, Native American and Chicano families. We also want to work with city, state and federal government so that when these disasters strike, as they will, we can make sure that there is not the loss of life, that tremendous loss of property and dislocation that we saw with Hurricane Katrina.

As far as the global effects, I want to say to Bob Law, Viola Plummer and all of the wonderful Brothers and Sisters here in New York, Reverend Herbert Daughtry and others who helped make the Million Man March such a great success—this was certainly not a one-man show. It took many, many, many wonderful people to turn out nearly two million Black men on the Mall.

All the news media was there, so it was an event that was seen around the world. When the world saw these Black men in peace and unity, demonstrating love for one another, the outside world saw Black America as hope for them. They knew that, if we unite, we could form a political base of power that could change not only domestic policy, but also influence foreign policy.

So when I went around the world after the Million Man March, we were met with leaders that literally praised Black people in America for such a demonstration. People lined the streets and cheered us from the airports into the cities. There was no head of state or government that did not receive us with honor and now the doors to the world are open to us.

But we must be prepared for when these doors open, to go in and take advantage of the fact that we are an international people, a global people. We are not a minority. We are the majority on the Planet and the whole world is looking to Black America because we grew up in the world leader.

We understand them better than anyone outside of America. We get nearly a trillion dollars out of this economy and we are the best-educated Black people on the earth, but what we need is a knowledge of self that will give us self-love, self-determination and a desire to do for self. Then, the whole world is not our playground, but our garden, where we can eat the fruit from all of the trees except the one that's in the midst of the garden, the Tree of the Knowledge of Good and Evil.

The Honorable Minister Louis Farrakhan appeared on **Cliff Kelley** radio program, in the WVON Studios. The title of the specific program was, "The State of Black America," and "The Covenant," on May 2, 2006, in Chicago, Illinois. At one point **Minister Farrakhan** said: "... wonderful, wonderful demonstration yesterday of our Hispanic family.

"I was so very proud of them; to see them standing as they have never stood before to shake America; to let America know that, 'we're here.' No matter how we got here, we are here.' And although America likes to call them 'aliens,' maybe they don't see themselves as 'aliens.' Maybe they see themselves as coming home to what was once theirs that by clever designed was taken from them—Arizona, Texas and California.

"The Mexicans that are coming into the country, they say, 'illegally,' many are doing jobs that we wouldn't do. But there are many that are doing jobs that we would be happy to do—mainly in the building trades; in the road and construction business. But the powers that are controlling this want cheap labor to build their bottom line, but they don't want us, because we are union—they forced use to become union. Now they don't want us because they would have to pay us. And then the racial thing is deep.

"I went to the movie the other day to see the picture *Sentinel*. It was interesting to me that in one of these rich homes, when you opened the door it would usually be a Hattie McDaniel type. If you saw the butler, it would be one of us. If you peeped in the kitchen it would be one of us. But when the door opened [now], it was a Hispanic woman and the cook was Hispanic and the butler was Hispanic.

"So, actually Pharaoh has let us go. The job opportunities that are there for us are the highly skilled jobs and even there we're suffering. But the masses are being herded into criminal activity that we might fill the jails and institutions of this country. They have really let us go."

Question from radio audience: Minister Farrakhan, Brother I've been following you for a number of years. I have the utmost respect of you. I thank God for WVON. I thank God for you and I pray to God that He keep you with us many, many more years. I think that if more of us in the Black community, as well as the politicians of City Hall, Springfield and in Washington: if they would follow your lead, I think we, as a people would be much better off.

As far as the job situation with the Hispanics verses us, granted, we do have skills in our community as well as in other communities, they have their skills too. But I do know of instances, Minister Farrakhan, where there have been requests that Hispanics are hired over Blacks. I do know of three instances—and these are personal experiences—that I've had that Hispanics are hired over Black people.

One other thing Minister Farrakhan, in order to become a citizen in this United States, does not one not have to enter this country illegally?

Thank you for your time Brother and I appreciate listening to you.

Minister Farrakhan: Well... there is a big question as to whether we have ever been real citizens. See if you go and study, according to what the Honorable Elijah Muhammad taught us, the ancient dictionaries of "what is an American?" – "An American are those of European descent. An American truly cannot be any member of the Aboriginal people of the earth" of which we are. That's the original definition of what an American is.

So they have always treated us as un-American. That's why we were called "second class citizens." Respectfully Brother, yes they want to hire the Mexican over you. They want to create hatred between two elements of the poor community. They (Mexicans) are a part of an indigenous population as we are. So (they) pit us against each other.

But if we could find ways to strategically ally, then we can work very well to end a lot of the suffering that we have.

INTERVIEW OF THE HONORABLE MINISTER LOUIS FARRAKHAN
BY JABRIL MUHAMMAD
PHOENIX, ARIZONA
JUNE 23, 2006

Jabril Muhammad: Brother Minister, you have quoted the Honorable Elijah Muhammad as saying that: "A good Christian is a good Muslim and vice versa." Please explain.

Next, an Aztec Brother asked for a better understanding of the phrase: in a Lesson a registered Muslim receives: "...with the two million Indians." He wanted a deeper understanding of "with" in the Lesson. He also mentioned the fact that the Bible teaches that, eventually, God is going to cause each nation of people to go unto their own vine and fig tree. He wanted to understand how this fits with the "with" concept in the lesson.

Minister Farrakhan: If we understand Christ and the definition of what a Muslim is as the Honorable Elijah Muhammad taught us, and the scholars of Islam agree that, "A Muslim is one who submits his or her will to do the will of God." By so doing, one is made secure because this one has entered into peace with God.

If we understand Jesus Christ, he never asked the people to worship him. He demanded of his followers to follow him.

In the book of John, I believe it says, "God is a spirit and those who worship Him must worship Him in spirit and in truth for such the Father seeketh."

Jesus was, according to what the Honorable Elijah Muhammad told me, the most perfect man in obedience to the law given by Moses. Perfect in obedience means perfect in submission. *The New Testament* bears witness to this of Jesus for he said, "I can do nothing of myself, but whatsoever the father commanded me to do that I do. Whatsoever the father commanded me to speak that I speak."

He was so perfect in his obedience to Allah, God, called in scripture "the father," that he became one with the Father. He was so much in unity with the will of the father that he became a perfect reflection of the father, so that he could say, "When you see me you see the father. For I am in the Father and the Father is in me."

So the Honorable Elijah Muhammad said, "A good Christian is a Muslim," using the definition of what is a Muslim. A good Christian, who is following Christ, in perfect obedience to God, is a Muslim. A good Muslim is a Christian, because he is also in perfect obedience to God, in oneness with God, through His Christ or His Messiah or His Messenger.

So this destroys the artificial barrier that separates Muslims and Christians from each other. In a time such as this, where Muslims and Christians are at war with each other, over their misunderstanding of the word, such a simple phrase or sentence by the Honorable Elijah Muhammad, if properly understood, and carried into practice, would then unify Muslims and Christians in a bond of love and Brotherhood. Then both would be in complete submission to the will of God, which is righteousness. Righteousness will destroy hatred. Righteousness will produce love, harmony and peace.

Now, if I say to you Brother Jabril, "I am planning a trip to Houston. I would like you to be with me;" *with* could mean accompanying me on some journey, or agreement on some goal, or objective. But, "*with*" could be even deeper. I want you to be *with* me; meaning in total agreement *with* me in what I am saying or doing or planning.

Now, let's understand the seventeen million, "*with,*" the two million Indians. What God is after is for the Native Americans to accompany the Black man as members of the original family in a pilgrimage. The Honorable Elijah Muhammad taught us that the Native Americans were exiled for breaking the law of Islam, over 16,000 years ago. They were exiled to this part of the planet, which was at that time, a wilderness. It is the law of Islam that was broken. The law of Islam is obedience.

When you have a thought of an idea that causes you to disobey the will of God then you have broken the law of Islam. We are descendents of the tribe of Shabazz that also broke the law of Islam.

Our father Shabazz, as the Honorable Elijah Muhammad taught us, wanted to go down into the jungle of East Asia, as it is now called Africa, to make a people close to nature. He was one of the major scientists of the 24. When he brought his idea before the rest they disagreed with him. Naturally, if the majority disagrees with you, submission is required of you. But Shabazz did not agree with the other scientists. So they said, "Well you cannot make your man here." So he went out into the jungle of East Asia as we now call it Africa, where he would be free to make his man.

I was very upset with the scientists, one day as I was studying. I wrote the Honorable Elijah Muhammad a letter rebuking the scientists for leaving us in that condition in the jungle of East Asia going into savagery; losing the knowledge of our high civilization that we once had. I was angry with the scientists for sending so many prophets to the Caucasian people and not sending anyone to raise us from our condition.

Well, when I met with him, he told me, "Don't send any letter like that again through my secretarial staff, but approach me directly." Then he said, "Well God could say it like this, 'I didn't put him out there' in words, 'He went out there. He disagreed. He rebelled. So I'm not under any obligation after he rebelled to go after him.' "

So here you have the Caucasian, bringing the children of a rebel, Shabazz, out of Africa coming to a land of another rebel, the Native American. The Native American rebelled and broke the law of Islam. So you have three rebels now. You have the Caucasian, who has rebelled against God. You have Shabazz's people who rebelled. You have the Native Americans, who did the same.

Now we're in the time of the coming of God, the Most Merciful of those who show mercy. He comes now to retrieve what is lost and to bring it again to its once high position with Himself. He wants the Native American to go along with the original man to be reconciled again to that high position.

So, "*with.*" means accompany us in the process of resurrection. "*With,*" means being in harmony with God and *with* us in our desire to be resurrected and reconciled to God Thus we can reclaim the original position that we, and they, had with God. "*With*", means to be in harmony, to be in agreement, to be in accord, to be "*with*". With, here means, not just to go along for the ride, but be in absolute unity "*with*" the spirit of the journey.

Seventeen million "*with*" the two million Indians—well, if every man will go unto his own, and find refuge under his own vine and fig tree, then the question that must be asked is what is his own?

The Native American, what is his own? The Original Black man, what is his own? His own is Islam, the nature made by God in which He has created the human being. So that's the vine and the fig tree that each of us will go to so that we will not only go to that vine and fig tree, we will go together to that vine and fig tree. We'll find joy and peace under that vine and fig tree, which is Islam, the nature of God and the nature in which He created both the children of the tribe of Shabazz and the Native people, who were exiled over 16,000 years ago to this part of our planet.

Brother Jabril: How does this apply to Mexicans and Latin Americans in general?

Minister Farrakhan: If you visit Mexico and Latin America you see remnants of the Spanish, the Portuguese, British and the Dutch, who have colonized and ruled in the western hemisphere, mixing their blood with the indigenous people, even as they mixed their blood with us, producing these various shades and colors.

As you go into Mexico you see the lighter Mexican, who are more akin to Spain, ruling those who are darker. In Brazil, you see the lighter Brazilian, ruling those more akin to the darker Portuguese. The masses of Mexico are dark in hue. You can see that they are akin to the indigenous Native people who were exiled to this part of the hemisphere and went down from East Asia through Alaska, down the west coast and across Canada and to the east coast, then down into Mexico; down into Central America; down into South America.

Everywhere you look in there you find kinship to the Native people who are called Indians. It is not that they are Indians,

Photo: Carlos Muhammad

Jabril Muhammad (*left*) presents Steven Muhammad (*center*) with a draft of *Closing The Gap*. Phoenix, AZ-based Bro. Steven recommended Upland, CA resident Mustafa Cajeme Muhamad (*right*) to translate the manuscript into Spanish for future publication.

but they're called that because poor Columbus wanted to find a new route to India. He ended up in the West and he had no better name to give the people than to call them after his misjudgment.

But the Native people don't accept his misjudgment. They are the original people of the earth. So they have a part in this journey. The journey is for them as well as it is for us. This is why we see the Native people rising. We see the indigenousness people of the western hemisphere rising against white supremacy. They are already showing they are with the movement.

The movement was created by the presence of God, and His revealed word. That started the movement. Now we are all moving toward a goal. Some know what the goal is and others don't know what the goal is. Those who do not know the goal are being pushed along by the motion of the masses. Ultimately all will be with God and with the original man for they are the descendents of the original people of our planet.

The Honorable Elijah Muhammad said to me that his Teacher, Master Fard Muhammad, Whom he represented to us as God in person, revealed to him that the Native American people originated in Asia. They broke the law of Islam and were exiled to this part of the earth, which was and still is considered by God and the prophets a wilderness.

In *Message To The Black Man* and in the *Muhammad Speaks* and elsewhere, the Honorable Elijah Muhammad wrote much on the Native American and their rise to divine prominence, along with the Black man. He did much too. For example, he placed a part of his family in Mexico. He established at least five Temples, or places where his teachings were delivered in Mexico. More about this, in another forum.

FARRAKHAN: THE TRAVELER
FOR THE FINAL CALL
VOL. 25; NO. 31

"We know that in all things God works for the good of those who love him, who have been called according to his

purpose. For those God foreknew he also predestined to be conformed to the likeness of his Son, that he might be the firstborn among many brothers. And those he predestined, he also called; those he called, he also justified; those he justified, he also glorified."

— NIV Romans 8:28-30

In 1974 I wrote an article for *The Black Scholar* that refuted a position taken by many intellectuals, both black and white, that perverted the truth of the mindset and motives out of which the majority of the followers of the Honorable Elijah Muhammad were attracted to and joined him. Moreover, they exaggerated the importance of their perversion, thus setting up a "straw-man argument" in their efforts to discredit the Honorable Elijah Muhammad and the Nation of Islam.

From *Wikipedia*, the free encyclopedia, we read that the "straw-man argument" is this: "Present the opponent's argument in weakened form, refute it, and pretend that the original has been refuted. Present a misrepresentation of the opponent's position, refute it, and pretend that the opponent's actual position has been refuted. Present someone who defends a position poorly as *the* defender, refute that person's arguments, and pretend that *every* upholder of that position, and thus the position itself, has been defeated. Invent a fictitious persona with actions or beliefs that are criticized, and pretend that the person represents a group of whom the speaker is critical."

It was a lengthy article.

A fundamental part of my answer was that whether or not one grew in their adherence to the teachings of the Honorable Elijah Muhammad, was whether or not they grew in their acceptance and understanding of his self-concept. I went on to show that this was ultimately irrelevant to the truth of himself and his ultimate success.

Whether or not one became a follower of his, and increased in their commitment to him, is in direct proportion to the maturity, of their growth in their understanding and acceptance of his self-concept and theirs too.

That article included the identity of the source of his self-concept.

I never sent it.

Years later, with the permission of the Honorable Minister Louis Farrakhan, I interviewed him on January 10, 1996 in Phoenix, Arizona.

The purpose of my question, in that interview, was to get from Minister Farrakhan a short but comprehensive response to my question that involved how he saw himself—in terms of his mission—in relation to the mission of his teacher.

It was a one-question interview. His answer is presented below.

Brother Jabril: Brother Minister, on the night of June 4th, right after your Phoenix speech in 1995, you spoke to a little over 40 of us, at your dinner table, about the relationship between the mission of the Honorable Elijah Muhammad and your mission, with your mission coming out of his mission. You spoke of your mission and his mission as being mutually compatible and complimentary. Would you please elaborate?

Minister Farrakhan: If a man is to be a helper of another man, the question becomes what help does he need? And based upon that necessity, persons are probed. Persons are sending their resumes. Persons are interviewed and persons are selected to help in whatever phase of the work or assignment that the main man has.

The Honorable Elijah Muhammad, like Moses, desired a helper. That desire was in him from the time he started his mission. He knew that he needed a helper, but not for the reason that he thought. It would later come to him, as he grew in understanding his assignment, exactly what kind of help he would need. So he scanned the persons that surrounded him. And he measured them based upon his knowledge of the scripture and the help (in persons) that God gave to former prophets that shared the assignment of those prophets. In Surah 20 entitled "*Taha*," Moses asks God for a helper. The first thing he says is, "Expand my breast for me and ease my affair. And loosen the knot in my tongue that they may understand my words. And make him to bare of my burden or an aider to me."

Now if we look at those words, "Expand for me my breast..." well, that could mean when your breast is expanded you can take in more oxygen. The more oxygen you take in, the more power you have taken in, to give your body more power. For the energy of life is in the oxygen that we breathe into ourselves.

So this also goes for the spiritual world and these words mean, "Expand my breast for more inspiration, more understanding that would give me more power to do a greater work." Again, since in the chest cavity, or in the breast cavity, there is the lungs and the heart, then he's asking God to grant him broader compassion; broader sensitivity; a greater love coming from his expanded breast for an expanded mission.

As you may recall, the mission of Moses was one in the West, then in the East. So his breast had to be expanded; for first he had to deal with a savage people in the hills and cave-sides of Europe and later, according to the scriptures, deal with another type of sickness in Egypt. So he has two assignments. One West; one East.

So the Honorable Elijah Muhammad has an expanded assignment. He has an assignment in America. He has an assignment in the Caribbean. And he has an assignment that covers the whole of the children of both the first and the second Adam. So his breast has to be expanded to fit that requirement.

Well it takes time to expand your breast. It takes time to open you up to the depth of understanding of your mission. He said that he had come to fully understand the last aspects of his mission at the time that he was to leave.

He was given 40 nights. Thirty and then he was given ten more. He then calls his helper and says to his helper, "Take my place among the people and follow not the way of the mischief maker." So the helper is not to look exactly like the person he is helping, but the helper helps in the expanded version of the mission of the Master who preceded him and laid the foundation for him.

When the master leaves, with his fully developed understanding of the depth and the breadth of his mission, he can now guide the servant who works in the expanded aspects of the mission, to help him in an expanded way. Thus, his work compliments the initial work that was done by the master.

In the scriptures Jesus' focus at one point, was exceedingly narrow. He told his disciples, "Go ye not in the way of the Gentiles. Go ye not in the way of the Samaritans. But go ye to the lost sheep of the house of Israel." But then at another point he says, "Go ye into all the worlds and preach this gospel to every nation, kindred and tongue."

Well those disciples who preached the gospel only to the lost sheep—how would they be prepared to preach the gospel to the ends of the earth except their breast was expanded; their understanding was expanded?

JABRIL MUHAMMAD
APRIL 30, 2006

FARRAKHAN: THE TRAVELER
FOR THE FINAL CALL
VOL. 25; NO. 32

"And certainly We sent Noah to his people: 'Surely I am a plain Warner to you, to serve none but Allah. Verily I fear for you the chastisement of a painful day.

But the chiefs of his people who disbelieved said: 'We see thee not but a mortal like us, and we see not that any follow thee but those who are the meanest of us at first thought. Nor do we see in you any superiority over us; nay, we deem you liars.' "

— Holy Qur'an 11:25-27

"He said: 'My Lord, help me against their calling me a liar.' So We revealed to him: Make the ark under Our eyes... and speak not to Me in respect of those who are unjust; surely they will be drowned."

— Holy Qur'an 23:26-27

The Honorable Minister Louis Farrakhan continues his answer to my question in an interview on January 10, 1996, in Phoenix, Arizona.

Minister Farrakhan: Now, let's look at the quality of the persons with whom the master first dealt. What was their condition? They were totally in the dark. They were a very ignorant people. Master Fard Muhammad, to Whom praises are due forever, taught them in a language that was the way you teach babies. You teach babies using words that conjure pictures. The picture is not the truth. But the truth is contained in the picture. But as long as the picture remains in the brain, as you mature in understanding, then you can reach into the picture and extract the principle of truth that lies therein.

The Honorable Elijah Muhammad was teaching me this lesson one day, as he was spanking me for reciting the history of Jesus as he taught it 40 years earlier. He said, 'I don't want you to teach it like, I said it, 40 years ago. I want you to give the meaning of the history.'

Thus when he said, 'And loosen the knot in my tongue... ', tongue here represents the language of revelation. God's grace to him came in the words that He gave him, which was a complement to the Qur'an. It was an opening or a key to unravel the depth of the Qur'an. But the lessons themselves had to be unraveled over time.

We must remember that the Honorable Elijah Muhammad said that baby language should not be used by us. Now, we thought at one time that baby language meant profanity and certainly that is baby language. But baby language means an immature understanding of the word that Master Fard Muhammad brought. We must remember that the Honorable Elijah Muhammad gave the answers to the Lessons when he was three and a half years old. That is a baby. Therefore, he said, 'Oh, if I could answer those questions now, I would answer them so much deeper, with so much breadth and depth.'

So when he said, 'Loosen the knot in my tongue... ,' it meant

unravel the wisdom that is contained in the message that Master Fard Muhammad brought, that the expanded helper working in the expanded dispensation or aspect of the mission of the Honorable Elijah Muhammad would be a more mature representation of the message of Master Fard Muhammad. And that more mature message would allow him to speak to all humanity.

The work of his helper is an outgrowth of his—the Honorable Elijah Muhammad's, work and it complements his work and his work lays the foundation for the work of his helper.

I would conclude by saying this, that I heard the Honorable Elijah Muhammad say once that two thirds of the Qur'an were for him and one third was for some other man, and I would let that other man worry about his part. Well, he said the book that the Savior gave him was the Qur'an, but two thirds of it, which deals with faith *that* would be established before he departed. But the other third would be established under his guidance from another place in which he would be.

He said that he was like a guided missile that God was off in a secret place guiding him. He's a guided man. Well now, he has grown up into that kind of power where he can be where he is and guide his man in the fulfillment of his third. So this helper doesn't really have to worry about his part. All he needs to do is to reach up into his brain for the guidance that the Honorable Elijah Muhammad will continue to give him.

In my conclusion, on this subject in 1972, when he stood the Minister up before the followers and said, "This is one of my greatest preachers in the bounds of North America." Then he said, "When you see him, look at him. When he speaks, listen to him. Wherever he bid you to go, go. Wherever he bid you to stay from, stay from." Then he said how, "This Brother would get you across the river on his shoulders. And when he gets you safely across to the other side he will not say, look what I have done. He will say, look what God has done, for he is a humble man."

Well Jesus said, "Take my yoke upon you." But you can't do it unless you learn of me. Learn my spirit. Learn the nature of me; the inside of me that makes me who and what I am. If you learn of me you will learn that I am meek and lowly of heart and you will find rest in your soul.

His helper has learned of him and is meek and lowly of heart. Therefore, his soul is at rest, because he knows he is being guided to fulfill the work and mission of his father. So in leaving, the Honorable Elijah Muhammad also said, and "... his preaching is a bearing of witness of me and so continue to hear my Minister Farrakhan."

Well, what did he mean, "Continue to hear my Minister?" He meant that his followers should continue to listen to me, for my teaching would bear witness of his being alive; of his continued growth into power; of the great commission that God had given him.

He also said in his *Theology of Time* lectures, "If you continue to listen to me," he said, "I will have you so smart that you will have the devil around your finger as a little string, and you would not even know that he was present."

Well, what did he mean, "If you continue to listen to me?" If you continue to hear my servant, whom I am continuing to guide and grow, then you will grow out of the thought that the enemy is any burden to you, any more than a piece of string on your finger would not be a burden to impede you in doing anything that you desire to do.

Yakub's grafted man may be a burden to you if you refuse to allow yourself to grow up into the wisdom of God. You cannot do that unless you continue to hear his Minister Farrakhan and his witness of his master and teacher, the Honorable Elijah Muhammad.

Brother Jabril: Thank you Minister Farrakhan.

Minister Farrakhan: You are welcomed.

How does his view of his mission involve ours, as a member of God's kingdom? How does his self concept involve our self concept?

JABRIL MUHAMMAD
APRIL 30, 2006

FARRAKHAN: THE TRAVELER
FOR THE FINAL CALL
VOL. 25; NO. 33

In commissioning His prophets with His message for the people, Almighty God, Allah, always equips them with the knowledge of how to advocate, prove and defend His message.

Jews expect the Messiah to arrive when God establishes His kingdom on earth. Establishing eternal peace on earth, God must remove Satan from the earth. Jews believe that the prophets are signs of the Messiah.

The Jews do not believe that the Messiah was here 2,000 years ago, but he is yet to come.

Christians believe the same broad sketch I gave of the Jews except that they believe that the Messiah, whom they also refer to as the Christ, appeared in the person of Jesus, who was here 2,000 years ago. They also believe he has been with God in heaven ever since. They believe that he is to return to earth to destroy Satan while participating with God in establishing His eternal reign.

Christians believe that the prophets were signs or types of Jesus.

Muslims believe that all of the prophets of Allah, Who is God, were signs of Prophet Muhammad. They do not expect him to return to participate in erasing this evil world. They do expect the appearance of the Great Mahdi, Whom they believe is to establish justice and equity throughout the earth. They also believe that He is to be accompanied by Jesus, whom they expect to return. Together, in short, they are to make right all that is wrong on this earth forever.

What I've just sketched is just that; the barest kind of sketch of the position of these three groups. However, there are certain critical areas upon which all three groups agree. They all agree that we're living under the rule of Satan. All agree that rule is to be destroyed. All three groups believe that the Messiah is definitely involved in the destruction of this evil world and in the permanent establishment of God's kingdom. Increasingly, members of all these groups either already believe, or are coming to believe, that we're living at the end of Satan's time. What compels them to believe this? It's the correspondence between what they see and hear of the circumstances of the inhabitants of the earth, to what was written in the scriptures in which they believe. Either they already believe, or are coming to believe, that the condition of the lives of humanity fulfills or is fulfilling what was written in the scriptures.

Furthermore, it's easy to hear and/or read of many Jews, Christians and Muslims pointing to this or that person as being the Messiah, or in some way profoundly connected to him, if not outright representing him. Their following occupies varying degrees of respect by other Jews, other Christians and Muslims who don't follow them.

So we could spend a great deal of time studying the teachings of the leaders and the supporters of many of these groups. No doubt they all put forth some or many truths, which they believe to be the solutions to the bad circumstances of their people and of humanity. But if they too believe that we are at the end of this wicked world and the establishment of the kingdom of God is at hand; then does their teaching contain the ultimate solutions to the problems of humanity?

Now, if their messages contain teachings of the ultimate solution to the problems of humanity; on a permanent scale; then one of their leaders would have to be, the Supreme Being, or have been taught by the Supreme Being. All the others, who present truths of the problems of humanity, may be respected for their truthful insights, but that's where it end.

It certainly does not seem that this world will remain too much longer. It would seem ridiculous to believe that he is yet to be born, grow up and go through his final preparation before presenting himself to the world. So all Jews, Christians and Muslims, so it seems, must believe He is present in the world right now.

We who follow the Honorable Elijah Muhammad, under the leadership of the Honorable Minister Louis Farrakhan, see the former as the Messiah and the latter as his National Representative. We see the former as having met the Supreme Being, in Person, and was commissioned by Him, to work as he did from the early 1930s until his departure in February 1975. We also see Minister Farrakhan as the divinely designated person who was/is to continue the Messiah's work, under his direct guidance, right up to the end of this world's power to rule.

In the last two articles we read Minister Farrakhan's brief conception of the relation between his mission to that of his teacher's mission. It grows, in part, out of his self-concept and his grasp of his teacher's self-concept and the relation between the two. Their self concepts are part of their teachings of God's Self-concept and His perfect conception of the true identity of the "despised and rejected" or "a people who are no people" (as the scriptures refers to Black people of America.) This also includes their teachings of God's conception of humanity as a whole and the nature of the times in which we all live.

So, whenever God Almighty sent representatives of Himself, generally called prophets, He sent them with His teachings for the people among whom they were raised. He taught them how He wanted them to present His message. He taught them how to defend that message from every conceivable attack and how to convince even the wisest of the people that they were telling the truth.

Our position is that Minister Farrakhan has presented what God and the Messiah wanted him to present. Further, he has presented the most cogent and compelling arguments, with other forms of proofs, to the truth of that message he was given to teach. Furthermore, God has provided proofs, which are in abundance, that Minister Farrakhan has taught the truth to Black people of America, to White America and to the nations of the earth; that he represents the Messiah, and is backed by him and God Himself.

At the end of the 45th chapter of *The Fall of America,* the Honorable Elijah Muhammad wrote: "God has given to me a very strong and invincible truth that will defend, protect and prevent you from falling victim to the arch-deceiver." This is what Minister Farrakhan has taught and is teaching.

I am among those who heard the Honorable Elijah Muhammad say, "It is not what we say from our mouths, but what we could prove that people should lay hold to."

Please, read the interviews I've conducted with Minister Farrakhan. These articles show something of the superb depth and range of his wisdom. They provide evidence, leading to the proof of his identity, and of his Backers, of his truthfulness, and the truth of his message. They also allow us to enter into the heart, to some extent, of this great lover of God, his people and of humanity.

JABRIL MUHAMMAD
MAY 17, 2006

SECTION 2

CLOSING THE GAP
PART I:
THE ORIGIN AND EVOLUTION OF GAPS

MAY 17, 1998
PHOENIX, ARIZONA

Brother Jabril: Brother Minister, this first question concerns a universal phenomenon, which affects the relationship between a leader and his staff and followers—divine leaders in particular.

From time to time, gaps develop as the leader moves ahead and the followers work to keep pace. There has been a degree of misunderstanding among some with respect to certain moves Allah (God) has directed you to make in the fulfillment of the mission of the Honorable Elijah Muhammad. Among them involves the way you have come to relate to the broad community, including the Caucasian race. Please comment.

Minister Farrakhan: The first thing I shall do is analyze "*why*" gaps appear between leaders of consequence, particularly divine leaders, and their followers at given times in the growth and development of them in their mission.

Whenever a leader is chosen by Allah (God), he is chosen ofttimes thousands of years before he comes to birth. He is formed in his mother's womb under certain circumstances, which make him fit for the specific job he is to do, by equipping him with the basic material at birth. As he comes into the knowledge of his assignment, or mission, the next and greatest need for him is to find the adequate and proper help to fulfill the mission that Allah (God) has given him. This is where the problem begins.

First, he has to grow to understand his mission. In the course of his growth, persons come to help him at every stage of his evolution. As people do not always evolve with the leader, some fall off when the leader is in the seminal stage. Some fall off when the leader is a clot. Some fall off when the leader is embryonic. Some fall off when the leader is in the fetus stage and some fall off when the leader is a child in understanding. Some others fall off as he begins to mature.

There are those who think they fully know him and his teachings when they became acquainted with him in the clot stage. However, such people lose sight of him as he evolves and they go out thinking they fully know him and his teachings. They teach what they know, but a gap develops and widens between them and the leader as he goes through the clot stage; the embryonic stage; the fetus stage; the child stage; and finally becomes the mature man.

What can prevent this? His help has to evolve with him. All of his help may not necessarily have been formed under the unique circumstances that led to his evolutionary development from before he was actually in physical form even while that which produced him was being formed. So, now he comes into the world constitutionally fit for his mission, but his helpers may or may not have that base; that brilliance; that insight; that foresight which comes from being divinely prepared.

So, his helpers, at best, come according to their own understanding of this man, his mission, and his teachings, at the moment in time when they first encounter him. But as he continues to grow and evolve, change and mature, perhaps they will not see him in the same way in the next phase of his development as they saw him in the stage when they first came to help him. Why? Because he sufficed a particular need that was very personal and individual for them. When that need is met, they claim him as their leader. As he evolves more and more, if they do not grow with him, a gap develops. Therefore, Allah (God), gives His servant helpers from Himself. That help is the best help because these persons grow along the same lines [the servant] grew. They are formed in the same way he is formed; their hearts are formed in the same way his heart is formed. Therefore, these helpers see into this man what other helpers may not see, because the latter were not made from Allah (God) to be his helpers, in the same way or degree, as the former.

However, they (the latter) accept the role of a helper. Nevertheless, if they don't stay in constant submission; in constant obedience; in constant study; and in constant growth; then gaps will develop between the teacher and the student that will lead the student (sometimes) to be critical of the teacher when the teacher grows beyond the particular need of that helper that motivated that helper to first want to help. That is the way I would answer that question.

PART II:
EVOLUTION OF THE DIVINE MESSAGE

Minister Farrakhan: With respect to your question about changing attitudes toward the Caucasian people: In the 1970s, the Honorable Elijah Muhammad advised me, as his National Representative, to stop using the term *"devil,"* but to use the term *"Satan;" "the enemy;"* or the *"slave - master's children,"* in describing Caucasian people, at least in describing some aspects of Caucasian people and their work.

I never asked the Honorable Elijah Muhammad why he would ask me, as his National Representative, to stop using the term *"devil,"* since that term had been used from the '30s into the '70s. His directive to me comes now, 40 years into his work, he is telling me, "don't use that term anymore."

Well, I never asked him, '"why." But as I matured in the teaching, I saw this:

First, Master Fard Muhammad, the Great Mahdi, was born from a white mother and a black father. We were taught that Master Fard Muhammad's father "cleaned up" or "purified" His wife from the Caucasus Mountains, so that she could give birth to this very special human being.

What means and methods did He use to accomplish the "cleaning up," or as the *Bible* puts it, the *"casting out of seven devils?"* Did He alter the nature of this human being? Or did He destroy the inclination toward the teachings of Yakub that was responsible for the making of *"devil?"* The Holy Qur'an teaches us that "evil" is a bad name after faith. If the mother believed in Allah and submitted her will to do His will, then, in her obedience to Allah, how could she be given a nickname or an evil name after faith?

Then I looked again and deeper at the Honorable Elijah Muhammad's Teaching that white people could be our brothers and sisters in faith, though not by nature. I then compared the way of life, of the descendants of the whites who were in the Middle-Eastern area and did not go into the hills and cave sides of Europe 6,000 years ago, to the descendants of the whites, who were rounded up and driven out of that part of the world.

The Lessons teach us that we rounded up all we could find, which means there were some we could not find, as they were hidden by some of our people. Those whom we could not find married into the original family, grew up under Islam, and knew nothing of Yakub and his teaching of lying, stealing and how *to* master the original man. So these are white people, or Caucasian people, who grew up under the influence of the nature of Islam.

Well, if that is so, and it is, why did the Honorable Elijah Muhammad tell me not to use the term "*devil?*"

Secondly, as I studied more, I learned that the term "*devil*" applied to them (Caucasian people) all right enough, but it also applies *to any human being who devotes the essence of* his *or her life to rebellion against God, and leading others* in *that rebellion.* This makes any person who does that a devil.

Of course, we learned from the Honorable Elijah Muhammad that the essence of "*devil*" is in the nature of the original man. If the original man, gives into the weakness of self; or the rebelliousness of self; then that person, no matter what the color, that gives into the weakness and rebelliousness of self, against the wisdom and will of the eternal God, they make themselves not only fools by rejecting and rebelling, but they make themselves "*devils*" as well.

He told me to use the term "*Satan.*" "*Satan*" is a *devil maker.* "*Satan*" is an arch-deceiver who uses the skill and wisdom of *right* in a way to lead those who would seek *right* into the doing of *wrong.* This is much different than a "*devil.*"

A *devil* is a person that can give into the weakness of themselves and rebel and do acts in rebellion against Allah (God). But *Satan* is an enemy that is a sworn enemy; a knowing enemy. *Satan* is a wise enemy who not only started as a little devil, but grew up in devilishment to become a master of evil and then leads others into evil and rebellion against Allah (God).

So now who are these? Who is the *Satan?* The Honorable Elijah Muhammad gave us Lessons outlining the 85%, the 10% and the 5%. What does this have to do with *devil, Satan, enemy, slavemaster's children?* As I studied that, it means to me that the 85% are the ignorant, who are poison-animal eaters; who don't know the living God; who are unaware of the law of cause and effect; and who have been made to believe in a mystery god.

He deals with 85% because this has nothing to do with color. It has to do with *Satan's* reach to master the entire planet and its people and he has gotten 85% of them. So, this *Satan* has to be the 10% who know the Living God and teach the contrary. *Satan* is a knowing arch-deceiver who is mastering the 85%, by keeping them in ignorance and fighting against anyone who would bring them knowledge; that he might continue his wicked rule over them; that he might live in luxury by sucking the blood of the poor and ignorant.

The 5% are those poor righteous teachers who also know the Living God, but do not wish to be satanic or devilish, and desire to take the 85%, out of the control of the 10%, by making manifest the wickedness of the 10%.

As I grew into this kind of knowledge, you cannot reform a

devil, therefore, *devil* must be destroyed, I began to gain a deeper understanding of what was meant by: *"Why does Muhammad and any Muslim murder the devil?"* If Allah (God) is to survive in us, we have to murder that in ourselves, which sets up associate gods with Allah, which would lead us contrary to the will of Allah (God).

In my increased understanding of this, I began to see that the *devil* is not only a product of physical grafting, but a product of spiritual grafting. This altered my thoughts, not concerning the nature of white people as they are, but deepened my understanding of the nature of human beings. The question of how to murder the *devil* effectively, whether that *devil* is in a white man, a yellow man, a brown man, a black man, a Muslim, a Christian, a Jew or Buddhist, the *devil* is a universal factor. Therefore, if the *devil* is to be slain, he must be slain by a universal knowledge of God, a universal knowledge of self and a universal knowledge of the *devil.*

A knowledge of the *devil* must not just be the rudimentary knowledge that we learned of the grafting of white people or the birth control methodology that was used to bring white out of black, but we also must understand how a *devil* is made by grafting—on all levels—what does that mean? *By knowing how to make a devil, in the deepest sense, you also know how to kill the devil.*

Brother Jabril: Please comment on the response you made to Brother Rodney in Boston, many years ago, when you first heard the concept from him, that the white man was the devil. What is the relationship between that and the very wide mission the Honorable Elijah Muhammad put you on before he left, when he said, *"Through you,* I *will get all of* my *people."*

Minister Farrakhan: While I knew that white people were evil, and I hated the evil that they had done to all of us, I was not ready to concede that they were the source of all evil actions. So I raised this question to the Brother: "If I came home and found another man in bed with my wife; both of them have committed adultery and if I, in passion, murdered my wife and the strange man, then, I committed murder." So I asked him "where was the white man in that sin?" He could not answer.

The Honorable Elijah Muhammad taught us that Master Fard Muhammad was born of the two people that He could give justice to both people. So it is not only that the *Mahdi* has to give justice to Black; He has to give justice to white. Well, then, what is justice for black and what is justice for White?

Many of us would feel that justice for [white people] is the complete slaughter of them; and justice for us is paradise. In a simplistic sense, in a very infantile look at justice, we might think that. But as we mature in the principle of justice, we would better understand the Honorable Elijah Muhammad. In his last speech to us, he gave us a more mature look at the principle of justice. He said, *"Allah didn't raise us up to be mockers of anybody. You can call him the devil, but he could easily say, 'I didn't make myself you made me."*

So, who is responsible, the clay or the potter? That is another mature aspect of growth into the principle of justice for both. Unless we mature in the process of understanding the root of *devil* and the root of evil, we will never be able to give justice to ourselves, our people and we will never be able to give justice to the Caucasian.

Brother Jabril: How does this apply to the statement of the Honorable Elijah Muhammad, that through you he would get all of his people, especially now, in the light of your three world tours.

Minister Farrakhan: The Honorable Elijah Muhammad signed *off* on his articles, *"Elijah Muhammad, Messenger of Allah to you all."* Well, who is *"you all?"* Since the book is titled; *Message to the Blackman in America,* does *"you all"* mean all Black people in America? Why then did he plant a part of his family in Mexico? When they asked what teaching would he give to the Mexicans, he answered that Mexicans should be given the same teachings that he gave us.

Messenger to *"you all"* then, has to mean to the whole human family. If I am answering your question correctly, all of his people are certainly Black people. But all of his people are certainly the *righteous,* wherever they are, and from whatever people they come, they belong to Allah, and they belong to the Messenger of Allah, or the Christ, or the Messianic figure.

This is why understanding the Honorable Elijah Muhammad as Messiah, or as Christ; understanding the body of Christ, or the Messianic mission makes you outgrow looking for all of God's people to come out of one people. You look for all of God's people to come out of the human family that exists on earth.

Brother Jabril: So there is a relationship between that and the Biblical statement, or words from the mouth of Jesus, "I *have other sheep that are not of this fold."*

Minister Farrakhan: Yes, and it also relates to Joseph's coat of many colors; *"Come and see, they, all will come* to *thee."* And *"Surely* I *will clothe you with them all."* All who? Who is this all?

Brother Jabril: *"And even the Gentiles shall come..."*

Minister Farrakhan: "...to *the brightness of thy rising."*

Brother Jabril: There are those who have criticized your moves with respect to this world's political system. How would you respond?

Minister Farrakhan: My answer will be based on a natural law and scripture. Daniel prophesied that a stone would be hewed out of a mountain without hands, it would roll down a mountain, and it smote an image, and then became a mountain that would fill the entire earth.

When a baby is conceived, it is conceived in a system that is already working. It feeds from that system as it is developing an independent system. It takes from a system already in existence. Through the placenta, it purifies as much as it can to feed on to grow itself into a new creation coming from that system. But now, it is developing an independent system that will take on a life of its own. I believe we are to grow like that.

We live in America. We have no other nation to go to. We live in the world leader. We pull whatever we can and filter it through the placenta, or the blood of the teachings of the Honorable Elijah Muhammad, that forms around us as a protection for us. What we draw from this satanic mother is filtered through this screening system called Actual Facts; Student Enrollment; Lesson No.1; Lesson No.2; the Problem Book and English Lesson #C1. The wisdom in these Lessons is the filter, so that through this filter we can take what we need from the larger system, as we develop our own system, hopefully somewhat free of that which is corrupting and destroying the larger system or body.

Brother Jabril: How would you react to those who still criticize you for teaching in the Christian churches?

Minister Farrakhan: I say to them, as the Honorable Elijah Muhammad said to the Arabs who criticized him, *"You don't have my mission. You don't have my assignment."*

I believe that Master Fard Muhammad's coming and work is the initial fulfillment of what was prophesied of the coming of the Messiah of the Jews, and the Christ of the Christians. I believe His coming was the fulfillment of the coming of the Mahdi of the Muslims.

Master Fard Muhammad gave a demonstration of the first phase of the Messianic or the Jesus mission, which the Honorable Elijah Muhammad was to fulfill. If all these churches are named after our man, Jesus, and have his title on their door, should I not go into a house that represents such a man and help them to understand him and truly live by his eternal message?

Any house that has the name of Jesus or Christ on it, I feel is my house. I have every right to enter and give its inhabitants, or congregation a better understanding of the Jesus Christ that they have come to love and now improperly worship.

Brother Jabril: What would be your response to those who criticize you for holding out an olive branch to Jews?

Minister Farrakhan: First, as a student of the *Bible* and the *Holy Qur'an particularly,* the *Holy Qur'an* Allah, Himself, holds out an olive branch to the members of the Jewish community when He says, *Those who are Jews, and those who are Sabians, those who believe in Allah and the Last day, they have their reward from their Lord."*

He, Allah (God), holds out an olive branch to a community that He sent prophet after prophet after prophet to, and our father, the Honorable Elijah Muhammad, told us to study Israel, for they are a sign of us; should I not respect the sign of us and appeal to that sign to come into the wisdom and behavior that would bless them and their children? Of course I should.

Regardless of what people think of me, I am doing exactly what Allah (God) would want me to do, not what the emotional instability of our people would have me to do. I must offer them the olive branch; as time goes on, they will come to see that I am the representative of the Messiah and a little messiah myself. They have been looking for me for a long, long time. I am here now and through me they can access the big Messiah, Allah's (God's) forgiveness and a place with Allah (God). Why should I not then offer them a way that Allah (God) has made me to offer?

Brother Jabril: Where are we now with respect to our relation to the Jewish people?

Minister Farrakhan: I think it is moving as Allah (God) would have it to move. Slowly, but gradually, they are beginning to see me more, and more, and more. As they see me more, and more, and more, they are going to become more and more divided over me. Some say, *"Kill him,"* others say, *"Leave him alone. He is our passport to heaven.* "

Brother Jabril: How would you summarize the response of the Muslim world to you, during your last world tour and since?

Minister Farrakhan: The response of the Muslim world has been marvelous. I was well received everywhere I went, as a *son* of Islam, s-o-n—and a *sun* of Islam, s-u-n—or a star in the jeweled crown of Islam; a hope for our brothers and sisters in the Islamic world.

They see Brother Farrakhan in a spiritual sense like they saw Muhammad Ali years ago in a physical sense. They take pride in my strong stand and fight for Islam, and for justice in America against the wickedness of the U.S. Government, and against Zionist manipulation of the Government and they praise Allah (God) for me.

I believe as time goes on, their arms will open wide, as the Honorable Elijah Muhammad said to us, *"at a certain point, we will flee out of America into the open arms of the Muslim world."* I do not know how those arms could open for us, unless they came ultimately to see us as true Muslims and lovers of Prophet Muhammad (peace be upon him). Also, they would come to see the Honorable Elijah Muhammad, not as a prophet, but as one whom Allah (God) has raised up to establish Islam in America and to revive the faith of Islam in the hearts of Muslims throughout the world.

Brother Jabril: In your speech during this past Saviours' Day Convention (1998), you made it very plain that you would seek to unite with Imam Warith Deen Muhammad, a long time critic of yours. How would you respond to critics of your stand with respect to the Imam—that you would seek to unite with him for the cause of Islam?

Minister Farrakhan: One of the prophets said: *"Look and see. They will come* to *thee."*

The Honorable Elijah Muhammad said, before his departure *"You **all** will leave me."* And when that sunk in, great pain came into our hearts, and into the expression on our faces. *"But,"* he then said, *"You all will return."* He said, *"All* the bones will live."

One night, in the 1960s, at his table, the Honorable Elijah Muhammad accused me of stealing a play written by Mother Tynnetta Muhammad and putting my name on her play to steal credit from her. He beat me, and beat me, and beat me, and beat me, and I bowed to my Messenger. Finally, h*e exonerated me.* However, he did this after he tried me. At the end of the evening, he pulled me off to the side and said to me, *"You and my son, Wallace, go and mop up the wilderness."*

We must consider this carefully.

I believe, Insha' Allah, that ultimately we will be together for the good of Islam; for the rise of our people and for the universal truth of Islam.

PART III: THE PROCESS TOWARD PERFECTION

June 21, 1998
Phoenix, Arizona

Brother Jabril: Brother Minister, this is three points, or three questions in one. It is based on what you said yesterday in response to my most recent articles *(Final Call Newspaper,* Vol. 17, No. 35 and 36). It i s about your forward motion; the need for the believers to keep pace with you; forward motion is designed and directed by Allah (God) Himself. It is also about the crucial need for patience among the believers—with yourself in particular, and with themselves, in general.

The third part of this question is integrated into the above part of this compound question. As you already know, the Honorable Elijah Muhammad said that it takes 75 years to learn how to live. What is your response to all of this and to his words?

Minister Farrakhan: A period of transition is the most difficult period in human development, for during periods of transition the life that is in transition is not where it was, and it is not where it is intended to be. So such periods of time are always very dangerous for the life that is in transition.

When we speak of Messengers of Allah (God) or men and women who are involved in a divine work guided by Allah (God), we must always keep in mind that the first verse of the *Holy Qur'an* is, *"Praise belongs only* to *Allah, the Lord,* N*ourisher, Sustainer, and Evolver of all of the worlds."*

Some of the scholars of language say *"Rabb"* or *"Lord"* means *"He who makes a thing attain stage after stage until it reaches its eventual perfection."*

Whenever a life is in transition from imperfection toward perfection, there is a constant process of change, growth and transition; stage two, change and growth and transition; stage three, change, growth and transition. We are constantly in stages of growth, and between each stage is a transitional stage. This is the most dangerous part of the journey, because many things can get lost in transition.

This life we are living during the last 6,000 years is called a *transitory life.* This is a life, which, gets us from the infinity of time before this limited time period to the infinity of time after this life. This time period a *transitory life* is a life that is dangerous for those who are involved in it, and it could be dangerous for those who judge life that is in this transitory stage.

Now, I say that to say, the Minister and the Nation are evolving toward perfection. Jesus said, "Be ye therefore perfect, even as your Father which is in heaven is perfect." (*Matthew 5:48)* If Jesus is telling a disciple to be perfect, it means he is Lord and Master of the evolutionary process that will lead the disciple to where the Master is. When the disciple is in transition and the master is hidden, but the master's hand is on the disciple, then, the disciple is in a period that is considered *dangerous.*

Peter started to evolve the message of Jesus and feed it to the Gentiles, while before, the message was exclusively toward the Jews. The Jews felt that Peter was stepping out of line of where he should go, but Peter was the transition to Paul. Praise Be to Allah.

So it is with Brother Farrakhan. I am not what I was. I am not yet what Allah

(God) desires me to be. The Nation, in following me, is not what it was, and it is not what it is destined to be. So the Minister and the Nation are in transition. During this period of transition, those who watch the man in transition may have a tendency to be judgmental. They are not sure of where he is. They are not sure of where he is going.

The only thing they understand is where they were, and the level of comfort they had where they were. This can sentence them to stand where they were, then misjudge the man in transition before he gets to where Allah (God) wants him to go. This disallows them to travel with the man who is in transition. Therefore, they stop in the process of growth toward perfection and the process of death begins for the individual or the group.

Therefore, the Honorable Elijah Muhammad, during his *Theology of Time* lecture series, when I was sitting in the audience, looked directly in my face, and quoted these words from the *Holy Qur'an: "Seek assistance through patience and prayer."* Why patience? Because if we are impatient with a man in transition, we will make a judgment, and if we are locked into that judgment by our emotional attachment to our own sense of what is correct, or what is right, based upon what we believe we understand of the divine message, then, *our judgment will sentence us* to *death.*

With reference to what is in the 18th Surah of the *Holy Qur'an,* about Moses traveling with the wise man, the Honorable Elijah Muhammad said, *"This* is *not Moses it* is a type *of the way his followers follow him. They follow him in doubt and with suspicion."* These two things, doubt and suspicion, are the enemies of faith and the mother of hypocrisy.

Faith will allow you to have patience where you do not understand exactly what you are looking at or are not aware of what you are looking at, which is in transition.

The demand by Allah (God) for the believer is that the believer acquires the virtue and the characteristic of *patience.* The only thing that will give us patience is greater and greater faith.

The Honorable Elijah Muhammad openly started the process of transition in 1974 with his last message to us. Imam Warith Deen took the message of transition and did what he thought was in *sync* with the Honorable Elijah Muhammad's guidance toward the perfection that the Honorable Elijah Muhammad desired for his Nation. Unfortunately, the Nation fell, fulfilling the Honorable Elijah Muhammad's words, that the Nation would fall, but it would rise and never to fall again.

Now, we picked up from the message *before* 1974, then, bringing us *to* the message of 1974 that set the process of transition toward the message that would ultimately take us into the hereafter. So, the command that the wise man gave to Moses, according to the *Holy Qur'an,* was *"You cannot have patience with me because you do not have a comprehensive knowledge."*

If a person does not have a comprehensive knowledge, yet is full of faith, he or she can make the journey with the wise man. But, not having comprehensive knowledge, and then not having faith—following in doubt—and in suspicion—there had to be an eventual parting of the ways between the follower and the leader and teacher.

The teacher told the student: "You cannot have patience with me." So whatever the wise man did, the student made a judgment. The student never questioned the wise man in the proper spirit: "Why did you do this?" To seek a greater understanding. Instead, he made a judgment. "This is terrible what you have done. This is awful."

Once he made the judgment, his mind and whole being were wrapped up in this judgment, which came out of his own sense of morality, his sense of what is proper, his sense of what is correct, and his sense of what he understood of life. Therefore, it was difficult for him to have patience with that of which he had no comprehensive knowledge. In the end, after three failures, which came after three serious misjudgments that he made of the wise man, there had to be a parting of the way.

I am under the control, by the Grace of Allah (God), of the Honorable Elijah Muhammad. I cannot say I know tomorrow. I only understand to the degree that Allah (God) gives me to understand the day I have come through. I know where I am. I know it is connected to where we were. I know that it is definitely the link to lead us where Allah (God) wants us to go.

But those who are watching me in transition - if they are following in doubt and in suspicion and have not faith nor patience—then they will judge me based upon their misunderstanding, or their thought or idea of their understanding of the teachings of the Honorable Elijah Muhammad. They will judge me based upon their understanding of morality; their understanding of what is good; based upon their life experiences; based upon what they were taught and based upon what they understand of what they were taught.

So, the Holy Qur'an says, *"Do not malign me as you maligned Moses."* The journey in the wilderness was a 40 day journey that took the children of Israel 40 years, because they followed in doubt and suspicion.

The Honorable Elijah Muhammad, in *The Theology of Time* lecture series said, *"I have done nothing wrong or improper. You just do not understand what a fulfiller looks like."*

People were judging this and that aspect of his life. But they judged improperly because they did not have a comprehensive knowledge and understanding of that out of which he acted; that out of which he acted was that which was written of him thousands and thousands of years before he came onto this planet.

Therefore, if we who claim to be Muslims will not study the scriptures; will not study the *Holy Qur'an;* will not study the *Bible;* and will not study our *Lessons* that will give us keys to the past, present and future—then, we will misjudge the transitional stage and end up wrapped up in our egos; or judgment made by what we perceive of knowledge; what we perceive of reality; what we perceive of morality, based upon our limited knowledge and our limited life experience. We will then find a parting of the ways with us and Allah (God) and the man that we claim to follow to Allah (God) and His Christ.

Remember, it is written in the Bible, "I *will lead them by a way that they know not."* Again, it is written, *"My ways are not your ways. My thoughts are not your thoughts.* I *am from above while you are from beneath."*

PART IV: CHARACTERISTICS OF A REDEEMER

DECEMBER 12, 1998

Brother Jabril: Brother Minister, several times in the 1960s and the early 1970s, the Honorable Elijah Muhammad, at his table, both in Chicago and in Phoenix, he spoke about *mud.* Sometimes he would talk about *mud* as that which the wicked put on him. On other occasions, He would talk like Allah (God) was putting the *mud* on Him.

He would use the word *mud* in very interesting ways. He said and wrote that he was to live, for a time, the life that we live and he explained the reasons why this had to be.

The implications of his words are that certainly after he met Allah (God), he would live a life seemingly like us, in some respects, but with Wisdom Allah (God) would have by then brought to him and would later lift him up from this life. Please comment.

Minister Farrakhan: When the Honorable Elijah Muhammad met with Master Fard Muhammad, he said he was so deep in the *mud* that only his eyeballs were out of the *mud.* This means to me that he was covered with *mud.*

He talked about his people being in the mud of civilization. Well, what is *mud? Mud* is earth that is full of water, it is not firm. If you stand on it, you will sink.

He said the people threw *mud* at him, then you said he said sometimes Allah (God) put *mud* on him. The thought that came to me was an *ayat* of the *Holy Qur'an, "Betake yourself to the mud."* In that state, when you place *mud* on your skin, allow it to dry and then take it off, it becomes a means of purification. That means to me, enemies who look for things to *muddy* your reputation—if they throw enough mud on you and you survive it—it will be a means of your own purification. So *mud-slinging,* in the cheap sense, is when people throw things at each other that they know of one another's weakness or fault or sin. That is called *mud-slinging.*

Why did the Honorable Elijah Muhammad say, *if they took out full-page ads and cursed him out, word for word and line by line, they would only be helping him?* His whole attitude toward *mud* was different from one who is like a child playing in *mud.* The child comes in and gets *mud* all over the floor and all over the furniture. This enrages the mother because she has to clean it up. The Honorable Elijah Muhammad's attitude toward *mud* was that no matter what they slung at him, it only ended up being a means of his purification, which was also a means of his elevation.

Since that was his attitude, what should our attitude be? It should be the same as his; for he is taking us from the *mud* and if *mud* is slung at us there has to be truth in it, because water is in the *mud.* So, whenever somebody is throwing *mud,* there is truth in it that is a means of purification.

Brother Jabril: The other night you talked about gross blindness and you spoke on the Honorable Elijah Muhammad's words about certain kinds of minds that were so dark no light would get in. Then we discussed this in relation to a certain history and a certain phenomenon in nature. Please comment.

Minister Farrakhan: I think I was talking about the law that Moses brought; a law that disciplined the members of the body, but, did not necessarily discipline the mind.

If the law is that a person is guilty of fornication or adultery and that person should be stoned to death, then in carrying *out* that law we take up a stone and throw it at the person who is guilty of this act. For every action there is an equal and opposite reaction. By our stoning the person who is guilty of that act, we are, in effect, stoning the thought in ourselves to commit such an act, which then is a preparatory stage for helping us to deal with the origin of sin.

Now, some of the people who followed Moses, loved the law. David said, "The law is a lamp unto my feet. I delight in that law." But, there are others who do not delight in the law; their minds are against the law, but they fear to break the law because of the consequences.

Seventeen hundred years from the birth of Moses, Nimrod was born. Nimrod gave freedom to those who were rebellious and those whose hatred of the law was in their hearts. Evidently, the majority of the people who were living under that law hated that law. So, when Nimrod freed them from the law, which is light, they could only go into darkness. As they reveled in their rebellion against the law, they added darkness upon darkness; the darkness of their thoughts; the darkness of their deeds; the darkness of consequences and all that it goes for, lying and trying to get around consequences, they added darkness to darkness.

Jesus was born into the world to take Israel out of their fall to a level of spiritual growth never before attained, by trying to get the people to see that sin starts in the mind. They were in gross darkness and he came with light, but they were so in love with the darkness, they hated the light. So that poor man who carried the light had to suffer because of the gross darkness of the people's minds.

What I was attempting to say the other night, was that the Honorable Elijah Muhammad gave us a law. Oft-times we obeyed the law, not out of love for the law, but out of fear of the consequences of being put out of society and being rejected by our peers. But that did not stop us from lusting after a female or fantasizing to do this or that which was against the law.

When the Nation fell, the law was literally vacated and this gave rise to all of the evil of our hearts the law appeared to suppress. Then, this evil was free to burst forth. The law was like a dam holding back the torrent of evil that was in the hearts of the people, but when the dam was removed the torrent broke forth. It was destructive of the house; destructive of the families; destructive of our marriages and ultimately, destructive of our lives. So the process of rebuilding or resurrecting starts with enticing people to come to the truth and to have love and respect for the law.

In the truth is the law. But, in the truth is not necessarily the love of the law. That has to come from the heart, when it is connected to Allah (God). When the heart is connected to Allah (God) it sees the law as a blessing from Allah (God) to give order and regularity to our lives and to discipline our affairs, then, we grow in love with Allah (God) and in love with the law. When we love Allah (God) and love the law, we outgrow the need for the law. So, then, love is the end of the law.

Brother Jabril: The next question is based on a few verses from both the Bible and the Holy Qur'an. It all deals with the same subject you just touched on. The Holy Qur'an says, *"Repel evil with what* is *best."* Then it teaches that you can return the like of that with which you've been treated, but it would be better if you were patient.

2 *Peter* 3:9 says, *"The Lord* is *not slack concerning his promise"* (some say the word "slack" also means dull of mind) *"but is long suffering to us and not willing that any should perish, but that all should come* to *repentance."*

Psalms 32:1 says, *"Blessed* is *he whose transgression* is *forgiven whose sin is covered." Proverbs 10:12* reads: *"Hatred stirs up strife but love covers all sins."* Of course, this is put in various ways in different translations.

1Peter 4:8 says this: *"And above all things have fervent charity [love] among yourself for charity [love] shall cover a multitude of sins."*

And then of this last part, I want to give more of the context because of how it involves the name Elijah. It is from the *Book of James 5:16-20: "Confess your faults one* to *another and pray for one another that you may be healed. The effectual fervent prayer of a righteous man availeth much. Elijah was a man subject* to *like passions as we are. And he prayed earnestly that* it *might not rain. And* it *rained not on earth by the space of three years and six months. And he prayed again and the heaven gave rain* and *the earth brought forth her fruit.*

Brethren if any of you do error from the truth and one converts him, let him know that he which converteth the sinner from the error of his way shall save a soul from death and shall hide a multitude of sins."

Of course, these passages impact many, aspects of our duties including our "fishing" (bringing people to the Mosque) and helping us gain strength, as well as the selling of *The Final Call.* These passages revolve around the same point you made earlier, and with what you just said, as well as what you said the other night, about the process and the price of redemption. Please comment.

Minister Farrakhan: The person who is given the task of redemption is a person who is willing to pay the price of redemption.

What is the price of redemption? The price is that your love must approach the love of Allah (God), that you may be long suffering. Because without long suffering, you interrupt the process by which people are redeemed.

Consider the quality of being slow to anger. Well, you could return like for like. But, if you are a redeemer, or if you are following a redeemer, returning like for like would not be sin, but it would injure the process by which the sinner would eventually come to redemption.

Since the sinner is by nature of God, but the nature of God in the sinner is thoroughly impacted with evil, we have to get past the layers of evil to contact the nature of God in the human being to affect redemption.

Master Fard Muhammad, in His coming, made a demonstration for His servant for three years and four months of long suffering; of taking abuse to show him the price of redemption. Then, on leaving, He tells His servant, *"Take plenty."* He wanted him to be long-suffering so that all may come to life.

He did not want one to perish. We may think that one is so ugly, so terrible, we would want that one to die, because in our judgment, he has earned death. Yet, He said He would pull some out of the fire that have done no good at all. My Lord!

In the 13th chapter of *1st Corinthians* are these words: *"Though* I *speak with the tongue of...angels...though* I *have the gift of prophecy...though* I *give my body* to *be burned...if I have not charity or love, I am nothing."*

In this dispensation, it is *love* that makes you something in the eyes of Allah (God). Because it is only *love* of Allah (God) and *love* of the truth and *love* of the purpose for His coming and *love* of the people for whom He came that would cause you to have value in His sight. *Love* is not proud. *Love* is long suffering. *Love* endures all. It hopeth all. This has to be the spirit, the attitude of a person that has been called by Allah (God) to act as a redeemer. The price he must pay is to be all but completely selfless. Because, wherever the self is, the ego is, and the desire to retaliate is, and the nature of vindictiveness is, and the unwillingness to suffer is.

Allah (God) has to make you selfless, and, only when you are selfless, are you not offended by the wickedness of those whom you have come to save. I do not say you are unaffected in that it does not hurt you, but, you cannot respond as a natural man/woman; you must respond according to the nature of *love* and the nature of yourself as a redeemer.

"For Allah (God) so *loved the world that He gave His only begotten son."* He Gave. He sacrificed him, and the son was willing to be sacrificed. I have no life of my own. My life is for the redemption of a people, and that is pretty hard. However, that is the necessary requirement to affect resurrection, redemption, restoration and reconciliation of the soul that is lost.

In concluding, when a person is like that, he has no sin. He has shortcomings, for sure, and he may commit sin, but by his long-suffering and continuing to pull on the good nature of Allah (God) in the people to make them better and better and better, Allah (God) just wipes away sin that he has and throws it in the sea of forgetfulness and covers his sin, because of the work that he does of redemption. This is why Jesus is looked at as absolutely perfect and sinless.

PART V: SPIRITUAL BLINDNESS

Brother Jabril: Here we have President Clinton. We were talking the other day about the hearings involving President Clinton. Among the points you brought up, one had to do with the general self-righteousness of the Republicans and their staffs, and how they are tearing up the country and are blinded by the bent of their minds (bent on going in *that* direction) how this was ill affecting the country and at the same time they were ignoring the will of the majority.

Your observances were different than those of the reporters and the commentators. It has a direct bearing on us; the Nation of Islam. It included the source of the spirit of these people and their alienation from the mind of Allah (God). I don't remember all the details of what you said at this moment.

Minister Farrakhan: I don't either, Brother (Both laugh).

Brother Jabril: I know you dealt with the bent of their minds. It is a blindness rooted in self-righteousness. I think that may have been a factor leading to the blindness and the gross darkness of the minds of the people, which the prophets spoke of coming to a people, at a certain time.

Minister Farrakhan: I think I was talking about the United States Constitution and the founding fathers and words on pages written by men who loved this country and wanted to preserve and protect this country from the things they knew historically and had, themselves, experienced in Europe.

They wanted to make a new nation that was free of the ills that caused the continuous rise and fall of the nations in Europe.

So they wrestled with each other, with themselves, with history and with wisdom, to formulate a constitution that I literally believe was guided by Allah (God). But to look on words and the intent of the writer, those words are now subjected to the interpretation of the intention of the writer and the words he wrote.

If the intent is different from the intent of the writer, yet, the person believes in his or her own heart and mind that he or she is in *sync* with the writer, then, in their blindness, they persist on a course that could be destructive to the very thing that they say they desire to uphold.

Now, I am looking at the Honorable Elijah Muhammad, a man who wrote hundreds of thousands of words and spoke millions of words – some of which we know, some of which we don't know – but enough of what he wrote and said, we do know. When that man is no longer here, his words are subjected to how we evaluate, perceive, interpret and then carry into practice his words, based upon our perception.

The *Holy Qur'an* teaches, *"We take Allah's colouring and Allah is best at colouring."* That is a very powerful statement. But who is the *"We?* If you take Allah's (God's) colouring, then you see things through His eyes. When you see things through the eyes of Allah (God), you cannot see wrongly, because you see as He sees. But, if you see things through the eyes of your vanity; if you see things through the eyes of your perversity; if you see things through the eyes of desire; then, you can misperceive what you are looking at. Because you feel you are right, and believe you are right, you go forward with power in a wrong direction, thinking you are right, and you end up possibly destroying the very thing you say you desire to uphold.

Such is the case of those followers of the Honorable Elijah Muhammad who see his words through the eye of vanity. *"I am this person.* I *am the son of man.* I *am this."*

If you see yourself as that (more than what you really are) what does your self-perception do to your perception of the Honorable Elijah Muhammad; the words of the Honorable Elijah Muhammad; the intent and motivation of the Honorable Elijah Muhammad? From that you get a splintering. From that you get sects and parties. From that you get the destruction of the unity that was present when the principal party was present. From that you get variations on the theme and teachings of the Honorable Elijah Muhammad, or Prophet Muhammad, Moses, or Jesus.

So it is today with the Constitution. I think you have 535 members of Congress (the Senate and the House of Representatives) all of whom are sworn to uphold the Constitution of the United States. Some are ill prepared for such a task. Some ran for governmental office for the sake of vanity, not for the sake of being a protector of the real aim and intention of the founding fathers of this Republic. Some run for public office as a job. Some run for public office and spend inordinate sums of money so that through that office, and the corruption of that office, by big business, they can double, triple and quadruple what they spent to become *that.*

No one should run for public office in the United States of America, without a profound understanding of the struggle of the founding fathers to write a constitution, that they are going to take an oath to defend and protect against all enemies, foreign and domestic. No one should attempt to become a leader, on the basis of the teachings of the Honorable Elijah Muhammad, without the willingness and the effort to enter into a profound study of the man, his message and his motives; and the history of the Nation; lest we get into a position where our sight is colored by desire or vanity or ego. Of course, every follower must enter into that study to effectively follow and benefit from following the Honorable Elijah Muhammad.

And so, it appears to me that the Republicans so bent on a narrow construction of the rule of law, have not really listened to the arguments of the Democrats, which have fundamental soundness, in that they are trying to interpret the will of the founding fathers on what *they* meant by high crimes and misdemeanors. But on the Republican side, they are looking at it, as it appears to me, a very narrow view of perjury; a narrow view of the President's lying. And it seems as though their desire to get Clinton is more important than what the intention of the founding fathers was and the will of the American people is. So their bent of mind is, "We *must* do this *regardless!*"

It appears to me they are oblivious to the damage it is doing first, to the country, and second, to the party they represent. The anger of the people now grows greater and greater against the Congress, against the Government, and the militia movement gets stronger. The people's malaise and feeling that government does not represent them gets stronger. Dissatisfaction gets stronger.

So their honest perception, (and I do not think they are all dishonest, they are just blinded by desire should cause us to stop a moment and reflect on our father, the Honorable Elijah Muhammad, and his intent, to make sure that when we interpret his word, our mind is in *sync* with his mind and our mind is in sync with the mind of Him who came and raised the Honorable Elijah Muhammad. Then, we know we are on a right course.

I believe that is why the Honorable Elijah Muhammad said, "*I want your mind. I want you* to *line your mind* up *with* my *mind, that there* be one *mind.*" That is what I believe creates the value in the brother and what the brother is attempting to do for all of us and humanity.

I am seeing, by the help of Allah (God), not out of desire, but out of trying to understand the intent of our father that I may properly interpret him. This is what I meant in Washington (October 17, 1998) when I talked about Beethoven. I talked about being in *sync* with Beethoven's mind and spirit as he wrote, so that when you play Beethoven, every nuance is brought out because you have become one with his mind and spirit. Beethoven is on one level. Allah (God) is on another.

When you become one with Allah (God), then you know Him in a hint. You know Him in a sign. You hear His word. You see His word and you bring things out of the word that maybe others cannot see, because of the quality of your heart and its closeness to Allah (God).

Brother Jabril: The other night we dealt with the relationship between the attitude that certain Congressmen and women have, which manifests self-righteousness, because that's obviously the blinding factor.

Minister Farrakhan: Well, that is the blinding factor.

Brother Jabril: Right. Of course, that applies in our own overall situation, for as your book, *A Torchlight for America,* is written for them, it is also written for us. So here we have this huge study in front of us to further plumb.

Minister Farrakhan: They are showing us how to destroy our government in a few easy lessons. Some are talking falsely about Farrakhan wanting to overthrow the government. They are overthrowing their own house. *"If Satan cast out Satan how then can his Kingdom stand?"*

PART VI: DETERMINING THE QUALITY OF OUR PERCEPTION

Brother Jabril: Brother Minister, I want to begin with the concept of mood and how mood affects our perceptions and our understanding of the critical word of Allah (God). You commented yesterday on this subject with reference to a recent Farrakhan the Traveler article, which included the bearing our moods have on our efforts to learn the word of Allah (God). Please give us the benefit of your comments.

Minister Farrakhan: What we bring to whatever we look at is what gives us our perception of that which we are looking at. Knowledge influences perception. However, if we do not know what we are looking at, then, the perception we have of that at which we are looking is not as full or complete as it could be, or would be, if only we had knowledge and further understanding.

In the Holy Qur'an, there is a verse that reads, "We take Allah's colouring, and Allah is best at colouring." I believe it means we take Allah's (God's) view and how Allah (God) views His own creation is how the believer views Allah's (God's) creation. But we cannot see His creation without His help. His help comes by introducing the knowledge to us of that which He created, and, the deeper aspect of perception is understanding the purpose for which He created what He created. It is only when we understand the purpose for the creation of the thing, we are looking, and the lessons He intended in it, that we can say we have taken fully Allah's (God's) coloring.

There is, however, something that alters perception. As you wrote in one of your articles (Vol. 17, No. 41) recently, "mood" can disallow one to perceive properly. Sometimes mood is not able to be controlled because of the things that happened in the course of a day that can alter one's mood. That altering of mood from happy to sad, from peaceful to agitated and irritated can cause us to misperceive the reality of that at which we are looking.

I was with the Honorable Elijah Muhammad one day, and he had just finished reading a letter from his nephew, the son of his brother, Kallatt. He said, the night before he was laying in his bed reading his nephew's letter and he had a negative view of that letter and the person who wrote it. But the next morning he read it again, and he perceived that letter totally different than he did the night before. What altered his perception? It was that "*mood,*" that was created by the daily work of the Honorable Elijah Muhammad; the negatives of that day influenced his perception.

So I would imagine that in order to perceive anything correctly, we must first check the state of mind we are in, then ask ourselves, how much we do know about that at which we are looking at? How deep is our knowledge of this thing? How deep is our understanding of its purpose? And when we can answer those questions properly, then we can say whether we perceive or misperceive reality.

I do not know how anyone can perceive reality properly without Allah (God). The God-conscious individual is less likely to misperceive reality, than one who forsakes Allah (God). When we forsake Allah (God), we forsake Him who is the only reality and the creator of that which we are trying to perceive.

So only through the eyes of the only reality can we really perceive reality. One must, therefore, study the word of Allah (God) in order to perceive the reality of life better. One must study the word of Allah (God) to come into the proper mood and attitude for understanding.

Note: Minister Farrakhan went on to cite another occasion while he was at the dinner table of the Honorable Elijah Muhammad. The Honorable Elijah Muhammad dismissed one of the believers who went to sleep at the table. Minister Farrakhan recalled that the Honorable Elijah Muhammad then said: "If you are talking to someone, and they don't seem to be receptive to what you are trying to teach, it limits your will and desire to try to teach."

Minister Farrakhan continued, in our interview, with these words: "So, the attitude of receptivity is the precondition for perceiving and receiving the word."

Brother Jabril: We know that one day the Honorable Elijah Muhammad said to you that you did not have to study. You have said to some of us that this puzzled you. I bring this up in relation to your appointment of Sister Minister Ava Muhammad as a minister over a mosque in the Nation of Islam. Please comment.

Minister Farrakhan: As I came to understand the words of the Honorable Elijah Muhammad, I came to see not that I should not study, but what he is going to bring through me and from me is that which is revelation. If it is revelation, I cannot study it, because I have no knowledge of what it is until it comes. After it comes through, then we can study it more deeply to understand and interpret it for those who believe.

I said that with respect to the appointment of Sister Minis-

ter Ava Muhammad as minister of the mosque, it was an act of inspiration. I had another person in mind. As I was sitting at the table, knowing I was going to make a change in Atlanta, I looked at Sister Ava, and in an instant, it came to me that she should be the one.

In order to explain my moves to others who might not understand, I said I am not an individual who sits in contemplation and meditation in planning the next step for the Nation's development. Everything we have done has come from inspiration that comes in an instant. I do not know when its coming, or in what context it is going to come. I only know that it comes, and when it comes, I am convinced almost instantly that it is something I should do.

Sometimes after I say it or do it, there are some reservations, there are some "misgivings," if that is a proper word. But they are quickly dispelled, because the reservations and the misgivings come out of a fear, sometimes, of a consequence for the revelation, an inspiration that has been acted upon. Then, Allah (God) confirms me, so that fear or anxiety over what He has inspired me to say or do goes away. Then, I go forward with zeal and strength and total commitment, knowing that Allah (God) is with me in what I am about to do.

Brother Jabril: That happened in the process of the idea of the Million Man March.

Minister Farrakhan: Absolutely. The Million Man March came as a moment of inspiration in the middle of a speech. After it left my lips, I looked at it. I could not believe that this was coming out of my mouth and that we were going to do such a thing. Then I had reservations, not just for a moment, but I had reservations for a little time; *"Oh, maybe I should put it off for a year or two. Maybe I should plan it better."*

Then I came to realize, more deeply, that my life is already planned. The best planner has planned my life through to the end and the plan was written long before I was born. So I need not sit around and plan. I just have to wait *for* aspects of His plan to be given to me to be carried out.

PART VII: THE WOMAN IN THE NEW MILLENNIUM

Brother Jabril: At some point in your Atlanta speech, when you were installing Sister Minister Ava Muhammad, you spoke about the woman being kept in. Would you say that there is a connection between that fact and the woman coming out now? How does this relate to the fact that prior to 6,000 years ago, as we have been taught, there was no "mosque" as such. The establishment of "mosque" is a relatively recent development where we have edifices here and there, throughout the earth and that one day the whole earth would be a mosque. What is the relationship between these two sets of issues?

Minister Farrakhan: Before the coming of the wicked, our whole activity of life was an activity of worship. I am sure that prayer, as a principle, was always a part of our life. Charity, fasting, struggle against human weakness, in order to be obedient to Allah (God), was always a part of the principles of our daily activity.

However, it was seen in the beginning of this 25,000 year cycle, that in the year 8,400 one would be born from among us who would bring in a world contrary to the nature of Allah (God) and the nature in which He created creation. The scientists agreed that such one should come, which they could have altered, or the Judge of that cycle could have altered. But He, in His wisdom, said, *"Let it be."* So this one was coming by the permissive will of Allah (God) to act as the god of this world.

In order to keep this new people from using our ancient wisdom to build his world, we started the process, then, of preparing for the arrival of the god of this world. Part of that act of preparation was to cover up the signs of the wisdom of the original man in the earth. We could not cover up the signs of the original people in the heavens, and the new man would take many, many, many, years before he could even begin to read the wisdom of the Originator in the heavens. But, we could keep him from reading our science in the earth by burying our ancient civilizations under the sea, under the sand and under forests. So the new man came to build his contrary world.

Knowing that the female is the critical part of the building process—that one cannot bring in a new civilization until and/or unless one affects the way the female thinks. So in the wisdom of God, He pulled our women in, and part of the discipline of salvation for us was that our woman should be kept in the house. Not that this is permanent, but, this was an act of protection. The man would go out and meet the new people, while his woman was kept behind the door.

We did not have churches. We did not have mosques, tabernacles or cloisters, because the way of Allah (God) was practiced freely and naturally by the original people wherever they lived. But, when an enemy was coming, whose way of civilization would be so contrary to God, we had to set up a particular house where the people of God could go in remembrance of God, to be instructed in His way, that they might struggle against the way of civilization, that was to hold sway over humanity until the coming of God at the end of their time of rule.

So Moses was commanded to build a tabernacle. Then we had, in the Christian era, churches and in the Muslim era, mosques. These are houses of repair. They are like an automobile repair shop that you go out of the world to mend what is broken, that you may go out on the bumpy highway of life to see how well you do until you need a place of repair again. The mosques, the churches and the tabernacles were called places where we repair; we go to mend a broken spirit. We go to restore a soul. We go to be reminded of the way of God.

So the woman, generally, was kept out of the affairs to keep her from getting entangled in the wicked way of civilization that was to hold sway. She was kept out of government. She was kept out of Church affairs. She was kept out of everything, but home affairs, because Satan was going to rule church affairs, government affairs, and all other affairs.

Allah *(God)* did not want her entangled in Satan's way, because the more she is entangled in such way, the more difficult it would be for Allah (God) to bring forth, out of her, a new civilization.

It is written of Mary in the Holy Qur'an that the angels argued over who would take charge of the life of Mary. If you look at Mary, she was put in a place where she could not be contaminated with the wickedness of the world. She grew up under the care of Zacharias, a righteous man, and grew up in the temple under the Law of God. She was a purified female through whom God would bring forth a man-child who would become, "The Power" that would end the world of Satan. Allah (God) needed a good woman, uncontaminated by the world, through whom He could bring the Messiah.

This is why we kept women in the house, or we tried to (smile). Many of them got out, because they felt this was against the nature of the woman to not be involved. So they kept sneaking out, or being let out, and, of course, when the wicked conquered the man, then they could go in the house and take his woman out of the house and spoil her. But he never got to Mary. So it is through Mary that a new world would come.

One day Master Fard Muhammad told the sisters that a time would come when they would let the devil into their living rooms and entertain him. Little did we know that when the television was made and we put it in our living rooms that the wicked ideas of a satanic mind that governs this world would come into our homes and spoil our women and children.

Sister Minister Ava Muhammad's appointment as a minister over a mosque to head the mosque in teaching and administration is a sign now of new ruler-ship. This is a sign that it is becoming time now for the female to come out into Allah's (God's) new world, as well as to master the home to bring forth a brand new civilization. It is also a sign of the irreversible will of Allah (God) that nothing Satan can do will alter the establishment of Allah's (God's) will. The woman can come out now because Satan's power over her is waning.

All over the world, women are crying out for freedom; crying out for justice. Allah (God) is inspiring their cry and He will answer their cry and make them a party to and a partner with the new Adam in bringing about a very functional family, and a very functional nation on the basis of proper male-female relationships and partnerships in serving the will of Allah (God). She will be His helpmeet.

Brother Jabril: Brother Minister, would you say that warfare has had the effect of liberating the woman?

Minister Farrakhan: Yes. That has contributed toward her total liberation. In World War II, when the men were called to fight, the presence of women in factories to produce the weapons or ordinance of war showed that women could do effective work outside of the home. Women's suffrage in the last century has contributed to her coming out and becoming a partner in society. That push for her liberation has begun and it continues.

Brother Jabril: What is the relationship between a man honoring his mother and a man honoring women in general?

Minister Farrakhan: Mother is next to Allah (God) and the Messenger of Allah (God), who brings the word of Allah (God) and is the example of how that word should be carried forth into life. Next to those two, nothing supersedes mother.

When a man learns to honor and respect his mother and perceives her in accordance with Allah's (God's) will and purpose for her creation, then it flows from that perception (of his mother) and understanding that all women who are mothers potentially should be given the same honor and respect that one would give to one's mother.

When you see your sister, a potential mother, you honor your sister. You protect your sister, as you would protect your mother, your aunt, and your cousin. This flows from the proper perception of mother, from which comes the proper perception of women.

PART VIII: THE TIME WARP

Brother Jabril: How would you relate the fact that so many are in a *"time warp,"* to the parable of Jesus, given in *Matthew* 25, about the talents? How, in your view, does this parable relate to helping us out of time warps, and coming fully into the present to be in accord with Allah's (God's) will for this time period-from 1975, or from whatever time period of the past?

Minister Farrakhan: There is a saying, "the *only thing that* is *permanent* in *creation* is *change."* As long as we live, we are engulfed in an eternal process of change. Sometimes, however, we get locked into an era of time that gives us great comfort, because in that era of time we became possessors of a certain knowledge that acquits us in that time period and we become successful.

Success, in any period of time, means the mastery of difficulty. The success that demonstrates the mastery of difficulty produces the ease that comes after difficulty. When the ease comes we are in a position of danger, the *Holy Qur'an* warns those of us who live the easy life, because the life of ease takes the struggle out of life.

When one does not have to struggle to know; when one does not have to struggle to become successful; when one does not have to struggle, then in *that* stage of development, one becomes comfortable. But another stage is coming, which will cause us to *face* difficulty again. And, it is the refusal to *face* the difficulty that accompanies change that leaves those in ease unwilling to struggle again. They get involved or caught up in a time warp, which then sentences them to death.

So it is when prophets come into the world bringing revelation. Every new aspect of knowledge produces a new challenge. Those in the older aspect of knowledge who have mastered that aspect of knowledge and have found ease, then, the struggle of life is gone for them, and they are more unwilling to accept the challenge of a new revelation, which demands struggle, which demands change, which furthers their evolution toward perfection.

Ease makes a person not want perfection. They say: *"I'm happy where I am; don't disturb me."* So when the new knowledge comes, the people that oppose it most are the people who live the easy lives, or who have become comfortable in their understanding of their revelation (Torah, Gospel, and Qur'an). This is why Jesus said, *"It would be easier for a camel* to *go through the eye of a needle than for a rich man* to *enter the Kingdom of God."*

Why? Because the Kingdom of God demanded a new knowledge; that new knowledge demanded, of those who had previously acquitted themselves greatly with the old knowledge, that they become as a child to learn the new. That became difficult for the arrogant and the lofty. So they got lost in a time warp.

In order for us to continue the evolutionary journey toward perfection, we must remain humble and know that nature and life is critical. History shows that there is difficulty, and, after you've mastered the difficulty, there is ease. When ease comes, a new challenge is going to be presented. If we can accept the discomfort of the new challenge and rise to that challenge to struggle to overcome the difficulties presented by that challenge, then we will have ease again. As the *Holy Qur'an* teaches, *"In the alternation of the day and the night, in this are signs for those who reflect."*

Brother Jabril: The *Holy Qur'an* says Allah (God) straightens the means for whom He pleases. He's not trying to destroy the person. Please comment.

Minister Farrakhan: There are some of us whom God keeps in struggle, that He may teach them lessons through struggle and allow them to teach others through their struggle.

The *Holy Qur'an* teaches, *"He straitens the means of subsistence for whom He pleases and He amplifies* it *for whom He pleases."* In both instances, the human being is being tried. If your means are straitened, how would you react to that, where Allah (God) is concerned? If your means are amplified, how will you act toward Allah (God), Who has amplified your means? In both instances, the human being is under trial. How we react under both circumstances determine how Allah (God) will favor us in the next season.

Brother Jabril: So, in each instance He is advancing each person towards that which pleases Him and His pleasure is in bringing us closer to Himself.

Minister Farrakhan: Absolutely. His pleasure is really the pleasure of the faithful. This is why Job was so beloved of God. No matter what it pleased God to do to Job (which was really *for* Job) Job would *never* curse God. His words are there, according to the Bible, *"I will wait until my change comes."*

This meant that he was patient and long suffering. It meant that he knew his change was coming. It did come. Although the story ends with Job in great wealth, what he learned through the time of the straitening of his means of subsistence was complete reliance on Allah (God). So that when he came into wealth, the wealth never altered his perception of God and great became the character that was developed in him through the struggle to survive when he lost everything.

Brother Jabril: Now, Brother Minister, last night you shared with us information that provides us with deeper insight into the relationship between getting out of the "time warp" and tying it in with the talent. Please comment.

Minister Farrakhan: To capsule it. It is a picture of the day of judgment. Each human being will be called to account for what that human being has done with what that human being has been given. In the parable of the talents, there is a man who was going away to a far country. At the time when that parable was spoken, the means of transportation were such that if a man was going away into a far country, it would take that person an awfully long time to go and return from a far country.

I think the parable was trying to tell us that the person would be gone for a while. The absence of that person was a test for the servants of that person. So, he calls them before he goes and he gives to each talent. One he gives five; one he gives three; one he gives one.

In those days, a talent was money. The man that he gave five increased it to ten. The man that he gave three increased it to five. The man that he gave one, buried it. When the master returned, he called his servants. *"To a day of judgment.* He asked the question, *"What did you do with what I gave you?"*

One servant said, *"You have given me five and I increased it to ten."* And the master said, *"Well done, thou good and faithful servant, because you have been faithful over a little, I will make you a ruler over much."* Then he called the man that he had given two talents. That man also increased his talent to four. The master was pleased with him because of the increase.

But the man that he had given one talent, buried it. He never put it to use. He wanted to give it back to the master the same way he received it. Needless to say, the master was greatly displeased with him and took from him his talent. He took that one talent and gave it to the man who brought about the biggest increase. The man with the one talent began accusing the master. *"Ah, you're a hard man. You reap where you have not even sown."* He is making excuses for his lack of the proper use of his talent.

The Honorable Elijah Muhammad said that the talent here represents faith. The greatest money a person has is their faith in Allah (God). But, faith counts for nothing except it is put to an exchange. As money should secure you some of the things that you need to make life more comfortable and the quality of life better for you and your family, it is *putting faith to an exchange that will improve the quality of your life.*

The man that buried his faith was in a *time warp.* He refused to grow. He was comfortable with the one talent that he had and did not see any need to improve on what the master had given him. He thought he would be accepted by giving back to the master what the master had given him.

He found himself cast into outer darkness and that which he had was taken from him.

What I see in that, is everyone whom the Honorable Elijah Muhammad taught, who claims belief in him, has to put their faith to an exchange. For as surely as the day follows the night, *he will return.* We will be called to account for our use of our faith; our use of our life; our use of our gifts, skills and talents. If we have not done properly, then we will suffer the judgment of our master, rather than the joy of having pleased him and being made governors and rulers over territory in his name.

So it would behoove all to come out of the comfortability of what you believed yesterday, because what you believed yesterday and the way you believed yesterday may not be acceptable in today's circumstances. However, you cannot come into today without a guide. So Allah (God) says, *I will not leave you comfortless. I am going* to *give you someone who will guide you in the absence of your master—as a comforter, but also as a guide* to *a higher level of comfort after the difficulty of change.*

Unfortunately, the rejection of that guide, as the continuation of the work of the master (the Honorable Elijah Muhammad), is absolutely confining us to a stage and a period of time that sentences us to death.

Brother Jabril: You just reminded me of something I said to some of us the other day. We oft-times refer to you as the reminder. We oft-times say this in our opening statements before an audience and sometimes in our prayers, thanking Allah for a "reminder" in yourself. But the *Holy Qur'an* also says, in more than one place, *"If you reject this reminder then chastisement* is *coming."* So, I want to bring up that point in this context.

Minister Farrakhan: Yes, they are not confident that he is guiding them aright, so they stay in that which they were sure of that was sanctioned by the Honorable Elijah Muhammad when he was among us. They do not realize that this new stage of their development was and is also sanctioned by the Honorable Elijah Muhammad.

When the Holy Qur'an teaches of Moses and Aaron it says,

"Go you both to Pharaoh, I *give you both a criteria and an authority."* This tells us that as Moses was given a certain criteria and an authority, Aaron was also given the same. Those who came up under the man like Moses did not have the same trust in the man like Aaron. They were more comfortable teaching that which they didn't have to struggle to grow to understand.

Brother Jabril: Then we have that warning in the Bible, which tells us, in symbolic form, that all 20-years old and older were divinely done away with. So those 19-years old and younger had the big chance to make it; (the youthful or the childlike eager state of mind) to learn and move ahead. These are all interconnected and the keys to our salvation today.

PART IX: REFLECTIONS FROM A MAN WITH A MISSION

September 1998

Brother Jabril: For those who didn't get a chance to see him, hear him or sit at his table, tell us about the sense of humor of the Honorable Elijah Muhammad.

Minister Farrakhan: The Honorable Elijah Muhammad lived the majority of his life with a very heavy weight on his head. His heart was with the *"weighty word"* and the Mission that Allah (God) had given him. Those were great blessings, at his dinner table, where we were involved in discussions and in hearing him expound on the Wisdom of Allah (God), as found in the *Bible* and *Holy Qur'an* and methods of going after our people, to bring them into the light of a knowledge that had been kept from them. Our discussion with him at his table were of a serious nature. So, it was most refreshing to sit at his table sometimes and hear him tell a humorous anecdote and laugh.

When he laughed his cheeks became *so* rosy. For me it was joy to see him laugh and sometimes he would laugh until tears welled up in his eyes. His sense of humor was unique because one would not think a man of his stature, of his tremendous wisdom, would even take the time to be humorous. But even in his humor he was always teaching lessons.

Brother Jabril: Now I am among the witnesses of the humor of both the Honorable Elijah Muhammad and of yourself; two men with the heaviest missions conceivable. I am among those who had the privilege of sitting at his table and now at your table there in Chicago. I have personally witnessed the *same* quality of humor in him as well as in you.

One of the fascinating experiences we have gone through was of course, the tremendous number and array of vicious attacks via the mass media of America; which often came through cartoons against yourself especially beginning in 1984. You have shared with some of us the use you would like to one day make of those cartoons. Would you repeat what that was, if you had the opportunity?

Minister Farrakhan: First, I am amazed at genius, no matter how genius is displayed. I marvel at genius. The way the cartoonists would depict me was literally hilarious. I saw the genius of these cartoonists used in a way to make light of me and the word. But I found them so funny that I wanted to devote a whole room in my house to gather all of these cartoons and make it into wall paper and just paper my wall with all of these cartoons. Then when I get in a depressed mood I could go and just look at these cartoons and laugh myself back into mental preparedness to do my job.

I can look at myself now, at my own sense of humor, and I realize that sometimes a funny story that makes a person laugh is something that makes a person comfortable in a situation where they might not be comfortable.

When people sat at the table of the Honorable Elijah Muhammad, believing he was a man who met with Allah (God); believing he was a man who could read your thinking; well, it was very frightening to be sitting in the presence of a man of whom you believe such. So he would always say something humorous, to relax the persons who were there at his table for the first time. That little joke, that little humorous word that he would say, would sort of take the edge off of those at the table, and set a friendly tone and open a person up for serious teaching and dialogue.

I have found in my own life that life is hard, but people love to laugh; especially when they are not the focus of the laughter. The Honorable Elijah Muhammad would make people laugh. Yet, there was wisdom in what he was saying and sometimes there was just folly; but it was hilarious even to hear the Honorable Elijah Muhammad say something that seemed like folly. However, he used folly for the foolish and he used folly to open the foolish up to wisdom.

So, I find myself, just naturally; not imitating our father, but naturally doing the same thing to make people to know that I am not a boogie man. I am their brother and I love them and I desire them to know the Honorable Elijah Muhammad. I desire them to know the truth and you cannot always jump on the person with heavy truths. You have to be skillful to open their hearts and their minds to truth and nothing does it better than a humorous anecdote or something that causes laughter.

Brother Jabril: Would you say that the ability to laugh at one's self is related to selflessness rather than self-centeredness?

Minister Farrakhan: Of course. You know a person who is humble of heart can see things of self that are funny and laugh at self and laugh at what people do and think of self, because they know that that is not the self. Just having a knowledge of yourself and who and what you really are; to be humble to recognize the Majesty of Allah (God), then what people write of you of evil, what people say of you of evil, what people plan against you of evil, never makes you evil.

It hurts you sometimes, to know it, to hear it, but, then you get over it. As far as my own self is concerned, I do not focus on those things at all. Sometimes I forget the evil that people say and the evil that people plan and do that I know of them. They could come in my presence and I will treat them just as well as I would treat a member of my own family or one of my helpers in this cause. I guess it takes people aback to know that I may know the evil that they have thought of me, that they have said of me, and yet, I am kind to them.

The Most Honorable Elijah Muhammad

An example of that is that I gave a four or five-hour interview to Dr. Henry Louis Gates of Harvard University earlier this year. The article he wrote in *The New Yorker* hardly represented much of what I gave him. He said what he wanted to say and left out what he wanted to leave out. The article did not represent the truth of what I said nor me as I naturally would like to have been represented.

When I was in Africa, in the wonderful, wonderful country of Ethiopia, he was in the same hotel as I. He was working on a piece on Christianity and Islam and their origins in Africa. When he learned that I was in the hotel, he wanted to interview me for his documentary. Of course, I obliged him. When he came up in the suite, with his camera crew, I am sure he was somewhat shocked that I never showed displeasure toward him. I may have mentioned my displeasure with the way that he characterized our interview, but, I was kind to him and went on with him as though he and I were long lost friends. Why? Because no matter what people write or say in their misrepresentations of me, I am always thinking that one day, Allah (God) willing, I will win them for the cause of Islam.

Brother Jabril: This is a two part question. Would you say that your wonderful sense of humor has been a factor in your ability to persevere under this most difficult set of circumstances? And what are some of the other factors that have enabled you to so persevere?

Minister Farrakhan: Yes, and I also think the greatest factor in my being able to persevere is being blessed to be humble enough to see the Greatness of Allah (God). I know that I am just an atom in the universe of billions and trillions and quadrillions of atoms. I know that I am so blessed to be able to serve Allah (God), in this time, and in this way.

In serving Allah (God), our people and humanity as best I can, and not taking myself seriously in terms of who I am and how people view me, I think, is the underpinning of my sense of humor. This is the underpinning of longevity and perseverance. This is the reason the evil that people do to me really does not affect me; it is because they never reach me. They cannot find me. I am so low to the ground that everything they shoot at me always goes above me; and they could only hit me if I began to think more of myself than I should.

Brother Jabril: The very source of the quality of your sense of humor, as I have had a chance to witness, is tremendously illustrated in the work of the cartoonist against you. The way you reacted and handled that entire episode is a perfect illustration of the truth of what you just said; the ability not to take oneself so seriously, which is related to not making oneself at the center of reality, but to be God-centered. This is what I was driving at. Your sense of humor comes from a quality of character, which the

Honorable Elijah Muhammad demonstrated among us.

Brother Minister, it is a fact that any of us who had the privilege of working with you up close well knows; anyone who has observed you from a distance, but has knowledge of you will bear witness to the same. I am referring to your stupendous and the strenuous nature of your travels; which you have kept up non-stop, going on twenty-two years, in fulfillment of your assignment. It is a fact that you have a schedule which is practically unbelievable, especially the traveling schedule, which is "unreal." To what degree do you feel love motivates and fuels you to do what you do in the way that you do it?

Minister Farrakhan: That is the answer. Love is the power. Love is the force. Love is the gasoline or the fuel that allows one, such as myself, to do what I do and appear indefatigable, untired, not worn by what one does, and it is precisely because I love so much of what I am doing.

I love to impart knowledge. I love to see the eyes of a human being come open to truths that mean something or can be a motivating factor to make their personal lives more meaningful. This is what gives meaning to my own life. As I give, I get; as I feed, I am fed; as I energize others, I too, am energized because I believe that is what I am born into this world to do.

Brother Jabril: Thank you, Minister Farrakhan.

Minister Farrakhan: You are welcome.

What comes below grew out of a lengthy discussion between Minister Farrakhan and one night last December, over the implications of points made in articles *[Farrakhan: The Traveler, Volume 18, Number 10 & Volume 18, Number 11]* about himself. In the course of that conversation, and in response to points respecting his identity, he attempted to describe how he saw himself. What he said was to me very interesting and highly significant. I was so moved by what he said that I could not sleep that night. That discussion was not record.

Two nights later, and again at dinner with a few others present, including his wife, Mother Khadijah, Minister Farrakhan made a statement that seemed to me that he was going to include what he said of himself two nights earlier. This was to me a valuable opportunity to capture something of great value to share with you, by means of this little book. He permitted me to record his statement.

Usually there is only very minor editing to be done in final drafts of interviews I have done with Minister Farrakhan. This is due to the magnificently clear manner he has of expressing himself. However, in this instance, he was expressing core of himself. This is never easy for anyone to truly do; it wasn't for him that night either.

I hope you are not offended by my near verbatim transcription of his words, but I want the reader to get a sense of that scene as we experienced it. Again, it was that valuable, in my eyes. So, for the purposes of this little book, and the one to come, here is the relevant part of that dinner discussion. I hope you will find it as valuable.

Minister Farrakhan: Any man who is made in haste is made of a fiery temperament. The creation of the universe and Allah's own Self-creation is not a hasty thing. He makes everything to go through stages and stages and it takes great time. He said He created the heavens and the earth in six periods of time. He does not say what those periods of time are, whether they are billions or trillions of years.

It takes time for a person to grow into the knowledge of self. And then the Honorable Elijah Muhammad said, "After you grow into the knowledge of self, then you have to learn how to hold yourself down, lest you get carried away with yourself."

I was telling Brother Jabril [two nights earlier] that no matter what people say of me and how people are saying things all over the world, I feel like a little boy inside of a mature man.

Now look at that picture: a little boy inside of a mature man. As the man is getting older and wiser, the people outside are relating to this mature man who is representing Allah (God), the Honorable Elijah Muhammad, Prophet Muhammad and the Truth, but, on the inside there is this little boy who is almost oblivious to the kudos and the praise and all that is being said to the mature man on the outside.

The little fellow on the inside may want to play. He may want to do some little silly thing. He is not even aware of the greatness that Allah (God) is making of him. He is just happy being a little boy on the inside of this mature man.

I keep thinking, as I look at myself, no matter what people say, *"how great he is,* yet I see myself just like I was when we (looking at his wife) were back in Roxbury, Massachusetts and I am this little fellow respectful of my elders and always willing to do little things to help this one and that one; never taking myself seriously. That is my protection. The little boy on the inside is protected from all of the praise and the kudos, fame, popularity, adulation, and acclamation, on the mature man growing on the outside.

The little fellow, if there is a cartoon that could be drawn of a man growing in stature and the lines in his face and the wisdom that he speaks and the audiences cheering, and on the inside there is this little boy playing hopscotch or playing with his marbles and he is oblivious to the people outside saying great and wonderful things about him. He is hitting that marble. He is just doing his "little boy" things.

So, no matter what people say; no matter how much they praise me; it does not affect me, because it only reaches the head of the old man, but the little fellow on the inside didn't hear it. He doesn't know it. You know? I don't know why I made that picture; but that's the way I feel inside.

Even though I know these words that you [Jabril] write are true and I know I am the representative of this Messianic dispensation; I know that I am that. I know that. I know that. But, then, I don't know it. Do you know what I mean? I know that I am becoming a very great man. But I am not aware to the point where I am carried away with myself, because the little boy on the inside does not allow it.

You know how old people can sit at a table and talk and the little boy is looking for a way to get away from table so he can do "little boy" things? Am I making sense? [We all laugh; for he is crystal clear and in a very touching and sensitive manner.] That's a heck of a picture, isn't it?

So I don't know what games people have on their minds, but little children do not [arrogantly] judge people. Little children have a way of looking at people, they may not go to everybody, but they are innocent. And because they are innocent, they have to be protected. That's that little fellow within. Now, the old guy might be wise enough to protect the little fellow within, but I think the little fellow within the old fellow outside just looks mature and sound mature and affects the world as a mature man; but on the inside, he's just a little boy, innocent, and will never be affected by the praise of the people.

And when death overtakes him, he won't know anything of his so—called greatness. He will only know he is grateful that he was blessed to live to serve a great God, Allah, and a great cause, Islam, and a great teacher, the Honorable Elijah Muhammad.

I was telling Brother Jabril how young people get fame and fortune quickly and lose it almost as quickly as they get it. It destroys them, because it really takes time to produce greatness. Real greatness; just takes time.

And so God, in allowing me to grow, I don't care if millions of people applaud me and cheer me, the little boy inside is oblivious to that. He hardly hears it and that is not his interest. His interest is in the game of marbles; not really marbles but, you know; I just don't know how to explain it.

Everyone there smiled and was moved by the beautiful and humble way Minister Farrakhan clearly expressed himself.

More next issue Allah willing.
Jabril Muhammad
February 14, 1999

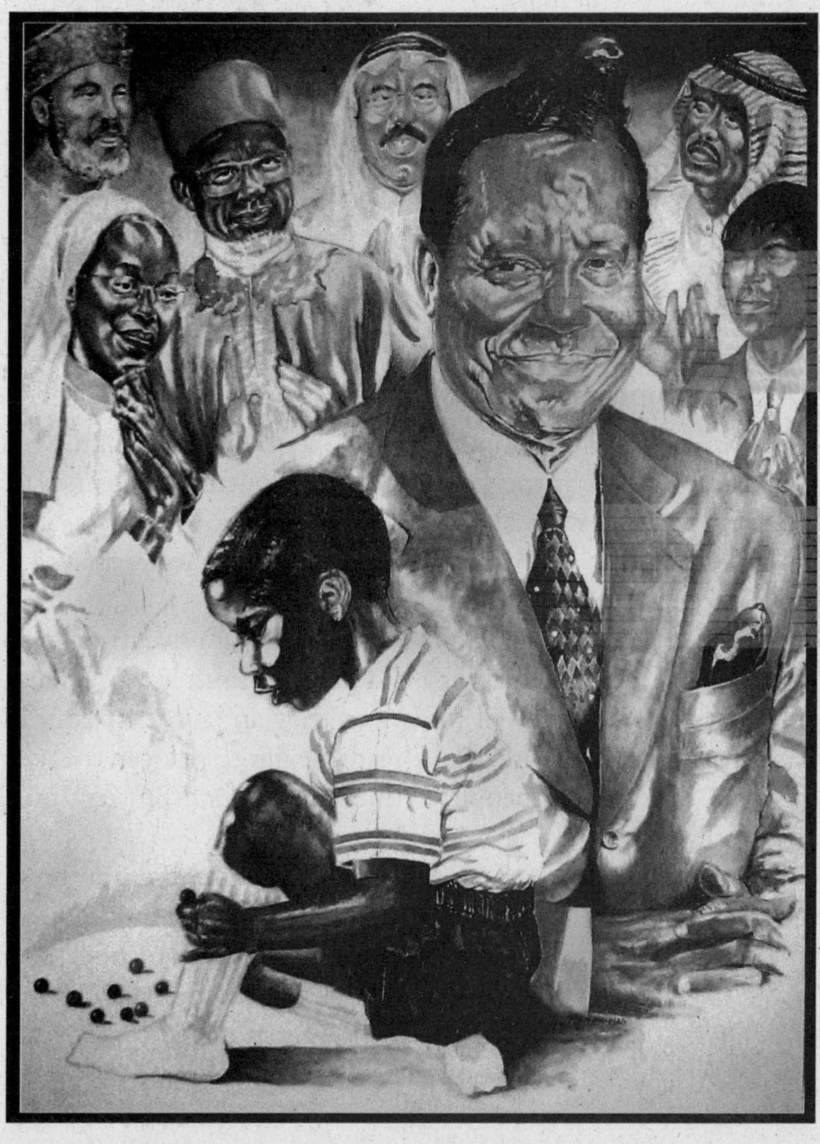

Portrait of the Honorable Minister Louis Farrakhan by Tracy Muhammad of Plainfield, NJ; presented to the Minister on the occasion of his 68th birth anniversary in 2001.

Section 3

Farrakhan: The Traveler
For The Final Call
Vol. 19; No. 23

Those critics of the Honorable Minister Louis Farrakhan, who are motivated by the spirit of Satan, are putting themselves in a terrible position with Allah. They are being shown up as people who wish to make and/or keep Black people as slaves, whom Allah is in the process of freeing.

There were reporters at our Saviours' Day Convention, who afterwards reported what they did about Minister Farrakhan's speech, from preconceived ideas that they and/or their editors had already planned. They had already begun to plant in the media what they wanted people to think about the Minister's motives and words before he made the speech.

They concocted lies and half-truths. They put this deadly brew in a language form that seemed plausible. They tied their poison to the legitimate desires of many Muslims—many of whom they know are new to what Minister Farrakhan teaches; the history and the rightness of his mission. These writers and editors are carrying out the desires of persons who are wiser and more powerful than they are.

What is their real and ultimate objective? Specifically, it is the ruin and murder of Minister Farrakhan and the destruction of what he represents, as well as his followers.

Such people are operating according to the planning of very wicked persons as part of a vast conspiracy that has been in force for a long time. Regardless to how this sounds, this is easy to prove.

Any of us who backbites, or in any way slanders another, has taken a step towards the destruction of that other, who then becomes a victim.

In the first verse of Surah 104 of the Holy Qur'an Allah says: "Woe to every slanderer, defamer."

What is "woe?" It is deep distress or misery, as from grief; wretchedness. Woe is intense, often a state of prolonged wretchedness or misery. This is what Allah has stored up for those who refuse to stop the evil use of their mouths and writing instruments against His servant(s).

Look in footnotes #6266 and 6267 of the Yusuf Ali translation of the Holy Qur'an of this same Surah.

Note #6266 reads: "Three vices are here condemned in the strongest terms: (1) scandal-mongering, talking or suggesting evil of men or women by word or innuendo, or behaviour, or mimicry, or sarcasm, or insult; (2) detracting from their character behind their backs, even if the things suggested are true, where the motive is evil; (3) piling up wealth, not for use and service to those who need it, but in miserly hoards, as if such hoards can prolong the miser's life or give him immortality: miserliness is itself a kind of scandal."

We ought to use our dictionaries and look up each word that tells us of the various forms of the wicked use of our mouths and pens, which the Almighty has declared war against and is now in the process of destroying.

Footnote #6267 reads: "Hutama: that which smashes or breaks to pieces: an apt description of the three anti-social vices condemned. For scandal-mongering and backbiting make any sort of cohesion or mutual confidence impossible; and the miser's hoards block up the channels of economic services and charity, and the circulation of good-will among men."

So you may call yourself "Black-minded." But if you are a slanderer you are yet an agent of Satan. You cannot deny that slander works against love and unity, without which Black people cannot ever rise from slavery and death.

Let us keep this in mind and never forget it: Minister Farrakhan has said that his teacher taught him that if we repeat a slander three times we become a part of it. At that point we are in the greatest need of Allah to help us get out of that kind of mess. We can get so deep in the grip of this evil that we cannot get ourselves out of it without help that is greater than its grip.

In connection with the words of God against slander in all forms, is this headline over an article in the March 19, 2000 of The Philadelphia Inquirer. It reads: "Farrakhan exhorts student leaders to fight oppression." It was written by Ms. Sudarsan Raghavan, with help from Annette John-Hall who, according to the bottom of the article, contributed to this article.

They (and their editors) opened with: "In an energetic and sometimes racially charged address yesterday, Nation of Islam leader Louis Farrakhan urged young black leaders gathered at Lincoln University to challenge the status quo and 'out-think' any whites who deprive them of opportunities."

No where in this article did these writers back up or show that his speech was "racially charged." I heard the entire speech. There is nothing Minister Farrakhan said that justified such mischaracterization of his words. So these writers deliberately misrepresented him to their readers who were not able to know better.

The next paragraph reads that Minister Farrakhan stated: " 'If you are a student or thinker, a critical thinker, and an analytical thinker, then you can out-think your former masters,' Farrakhan told a predominantly black audience of about 500 at the Chester County campus."

The fact is that there were between 3,200 to 3,500 persons in attendance to hear Minister Farrakhan teach.

They continued: "Farrakhan's remarks stood in contrast to those he made last month in Chicago, where he embraced a mainstream view of Islam that called for universal brotherhood among races."

What did he say in this speech that contradicted what he said last month? They never name it. Why not? Because he said *nothing* that contradicted what he said "in Chicago."

The article also contains the usual lies about statements that Minister Farrakhan has never made about Jews and others. This is another instance of the continuation of the technique known as "The Big Lie."

If you will contact Minister Don Muhammad of Boston, Massachusetts you can get the most detailed history of exactly how this controversy with the Jewish community began between them, Minister Farrakhan and the Nation of Islam. You may be surprised.

In deliberately misrepresenting Minister Farrakhan's clear words, even to lying about the numbers in attendance, these writers of *The Philadelphia Inquirer* revealed that they (and their backers) continue the will of our former slavemasters, who during physical slavery did all they could to prevent us from using our minds for our benefit.

It is traditional in America for the power establishment to work against any one who tries to uplift Black people.

It was the desire of our former slavemasters that the power of their Black slaves to think constructively for themselves be forever destroyed. They did everything that they could think of to eliminate the very root of the power of our enslaved ancestors to reason for themselves; to form rational judgments for their benefit and for their descendants; us.

One of the greatest proofs of the above, that even on a subconscious level, America is unwilling to grant her ex-slaves real justice is her current efforts in the repealing of affirmative actions programs throughout this land.

Dr. Martin Luther King, Jr. admitted that such programs were, in effect, the very least form of reparations to us for the evils America did to us.

In his book, *The Debt*, Mr. Randall Robinson quotes a friend of his as saying to him: "It's the strangest thing... We law professors talk about every imaginable subject, but when the issue of reparations is raised among white professors, many of whom are otherwise liberal, it is met with silence. Clearly, there is a case to be made for this as an unpaid debt. Our claim may not be enforceable in the courts because the federal government has to agree to allow itself to be sued. In fact, this will probably have to come out of the Congress as other American reparations have. Nonetheless, there is a strong case to be made. But, I tell you, the mere raising of the subject produces a deathly silence, not unlike the silence that greeted the book I'm sending you."

More about that book and even more important, more about the answers to the questions raised in my previous article and God's declaration of war on this country next issue, Allah willing.

JABRIL MUHAMMAD
MARCH 29, 2000

FARRAKHAN: THE TRAVELER
FOR THE FINAL CALL
VOL. 19; NO. 24

This article is being written on what is called "April Fool's Day." Why is this day called a "fool's" day?

Millions of children, in this country, over the last few hundred years, have engaged in tricking others on this day.

Were you one of those who first performed some act of deception that caused others into thinking as true that which you knew was false? Then after the other was under the power of the lie that we told, we exclaimed (with a measure of excitement and glee) "April Fool!" Were we calling the ones we deceived a fool, after we fooled them? Was not this also a form of mockery?

Further, why were we excited over the trick which deceived others? Most often the deceived child laughs too. Most would say, "Why make an issue over this? They were only having fun." Nevertheless, this is educating youth to love evil.

How did we come by this idea of tricking others and then using the words "April Fool!" Why should April 1st be called a fool's day?

Among the explanations of its origin are that it came from the change from the Roman calendar to the Gregorian calendar in 1582. The older calendar began each new year on April first.

Those who invented the new calendar changed New Year's Day to January 1st.

I'll skip the details and just state that one source states that the attitudes of the majority towards those who did not follow this new development, and the practices which developed from this change, were later introduced into America during colonial times.

Among the favorite jokes some played on others, included sending others on impossible errands and running so-called harmless lies in the media. When the others grew confused or realized they were being tricked, the trickster calls out to them: "April Fool!"

Was the change of the calendar a major factor in the loss of the knowledge of the time of the end of this world by its rulers when it came in 1914? Yes. In their changes they fooled themselves, even as they were deceiving our ancestors. This deception continued right through their false promises about giving us "40 acres and a mule," as reparations, on to their false promises of today.

If this is the time of the ending of this world, who and what should we have expected?

Let's go to the stage where the Honorable Minister Louis Farrakhan spoke this past Saviours' Day celebration. There were Jewish, Christian and (Orthodox) Muslim scholars on the stage too. Broadly speaking, Jews the world over are looking for the coming of the Messiah. Christians, the world over, are looking for the return of the Messiah. Muslims, the world over, are also looking for the return of the Messiah.

The Jews expect an Elijah like figure to be with the Messiah. Christians expect one to serve as a forerunner of the returning Messiah. The Muslims expect the Messiah to appear with another known as the Mahdi.

If you look into the beliefs of the Jews, the Christians and the Muslims (I'm generalizing)—you'll find that they expect these men to appear during the time period described in their scriptures under various names. Among these names for this time are: the end of the world; the end of time; the day of the Lord; the great and dreadful day of God Almighty; the day of the resurrection of the dead; the day of the establishment of the Kingdom of God or the Lord on earth; the day when God makes all things new; the days of Allah, and there are more.

These names describe those years when the rule of evil men is destroyed by the Divine Supreme Being, Who will, during those days, establish a brand new world under His permanent rule, right here on this earth.

The Honorable Minister Louis Farrakhan preaches that the Messiah that the Jews, Christians and Muslims are looking for has arrived. He also preaches that the Great Mahdi whom the Muslims, both Sunni and Shiite, have been looking for, has arrived.

Even if you think Minister Farrakhan is wrong you should still be certain that the Mahdi and the Messiah are present. Why? Everything that the prophets of God said would describe the end of this world is going on right now. This is the end. So they must be here.

Meanwhile, on the day before the Honorable Minister Louis Farrakhan delivered his Saviours' Day Address, a serious question was raised by one of the scholars, introduced by Imam Ahmad Tijhani as a very learned and widely respected professor, who said, in part:

"My beloved Sisters and Brothers, I greet you with the greeting words of peace and mercy, As-Salaam Alaikum. I just want to say a word or two and wholeheartedly congratulate the members of these unique Umma, the Nation of Islam I congratulate you. And I also congratulate all the Muslims all over the world to have a leader in the caliber of Brother, Minister, a leader, Imam, Louis Farrakhan. My dear Brothers and Sisters, do you really know who Louis Farrakhan is? If you don't know who Louis Farrakhan is, today in this new millennium, Louis Farrakhan stands in the place of our great leader, Muhammad, the son of Abdullah."

A few days ago I asked Minister Farrakhan a series of questions. The following are excerpts amounting to about 15% of that material.

Part of an answer Minister Farrakhan gave to a question was:

Minister Farrakhan: When my daughter told me what I said when I was on my deathbed crying out to Allah telling Him that whatever He brought into my life it was alright with me; and thanking him for allowing me to behold the majesty of His creation; and if it was time for me to leave this earth, I was pleased with God. When she told me the things that I said I broke down and cried because I then knew that I was a believer. So that He may know those who are truthful from those who are liars. He already knew but the He within me needed to know.

Brother Jabril: Are you also saying that after what your daughter [Sister Fatima] told you, you felt more of a sense of a oneness with Him; a greater degree of confidence?

Minister Farrakhan: Yes. I felt after hearing [her] words I was comforted to know that I love Him above all; and I'm grateful to Him above all; and that no matter what He brings or allows to be brought into my life I praise Him. I thank Him. I honor Him. I hope to magnify and glorify His name. That experience helped to prepare me for the great trial that I yet have to go through.

Brother Jabril: Do you believe that Allah allowed you to experience what you did to prepare you for aspects or for things yet to come; trials yet to come that are greater?"

Minister Farrakhan: Yes. He allowed me to go to death's door and He alone brought me back from it to show me [deeper] that He has power over all things; and that the greater trial is yet in front of me. But the same way He took me through this, if I maintain my faith in Him, He will take me through this next and the greatest of the trials.

Brother Jabril: Brother Minister, please comment. Some months ago when I learned...from you and your daughter that which was at the core of the 'change' people were just beginning to talk about and that they talk more about now – I wrote in The Final Call...what I saw as the core change. ...Naturally that person who is drawn ever closer to God, just naturally sees and feels more the way God does toward all of humanity. Please comment.

Minister Farrakhan: We are all on a journey. The journey or the goal of the journey is a meeting with Allah. On the road of this journey there are trials that are part of the process of purification so that when the servant reaches a certain level of purification; a certain point in his journey God can then use the servant greater than He used him in the past because of that servant's attitude, disposition and sense of knowing that he is with God and God is with him [as he passes through his trial.]

So the change that took place in me may not readily be seen necessarily on the outside. But that change is a large part of a process of purifying the heart of the man and giving him a certainty of knowledge that Allah is with him and it is Allah who is guiding his steps in this journey.

So there are subtle changes that no one, except one very close and observing can see. And there are changes that will be readily seen by the public in the manner in which the brother expresses the word of God.

Brother Jabril: Those subtle changes are more powerful than those 'changes' which are more readily seen. One is the basis of that which is the manifestation of the other.

Minister Farrakhan: That is correct. That is correct. Unfortunately, there are those who misread change. And there are those who purposely misrepresent change.

JABRIL MUHAMMAD
APRIL 1, 2000

FARRAKHAN: THE TRAVELER
FOR THE FINAL CALL
VOL. 19; NO. 25

How seriously ought we to view the report about Pope John Paul II's statement about this being the time of the end of this world, which appeared in *Weekly World News*, a tabloid, dated April 11, 2000?

The headline reads: "*Last Days Warning of Pope John Paul II,* The sub-titles read: Ailing Pontiff's final message predicts: *War in America! Nuclear Hell on Earth! Rise of the Anti-Christ! Death of Billions as World Ends!*

I won't go into the circumstances by which the Pope is alleged to have written what he supposedly wrote and how it supposedly became public. Time will tell if he actually said what he is alleged to have stated. I only want to narrowly focus on his alleged statements which, in effect, he allegedly stated that right now we are all living in the time described by the prophets of God as the end of this world and the establishment of His kingdom.

One of the statements attributed to him is that "The forces of Good and Evil will clash for a final time, as the Holy Scriptures have warned, in the Holy Land."

As a follower of the Honorable Elijah Muhammad under Minister Farrakhan's leadership, I agree with the above statements, whether the Pope really wrote them or not. The thing that I find very curious, however, is the way that so many leading scholars depict the United States of America and the Black man and woman in America in their overall description of what we may expect at the end of this world's time.

There are literally billions and billions of words spoken through the radio, television, articles, and books, every day, all over the earth, about the end of the world. But the words that are spoken and written, here in America about the end time, almost never show America to the Americans, as God showed America to His prophets. Likewise, almost no one shows Black people to Black people as God showed Black people to His prophets.

The exception to this, on both subjects, is the Honorable Minister Louis Farrakhan and those who are with him. There are a few others making an effort in this direction. However, at present, they are off the mark in significant areas.

The Holy Qur'an teaches that there is not a nation, or a people, whom Allah neglected, or failed to provide divine guidance for, by means of His prophets, messengers and warners. (Surahs 10:47; 16:36; 35:25)

So what people did Allah ultimately have in His mind as that people, or nation that never had one from Himself to guide them?

One of the most brilliant lectures I ever heard, which included this subject, was delivered in New York City by Imam Warith Deen Mohammed, in December 1957. His speech included such passages as I have just mentioned from the Holy Qur'an that there are no people who have been without divine guidance up until today.

Then with mathematical precision he preceded to show that Black people in America were made into an (altogether new people) by reason of the manner and method used to bring us to this country and then the impact of slavery on us. He proved, that day, that there were not another people who ever lived or who existed now, like the Black man and woman of America. He proved, that day, that a new people were produced through the furnace of the profoundest kind of affliction.

In the course of his speech he demonstrated to his audience that in Black people here in the Western Hemisphere, we have a new people who had never had the benefit of divine guidance until today. Before today, we only knew what we knew of God, His prophets, etc., by means of our evil slave-masters. These same slave-masters are the ones who robbed us of the very basis of self-respect. So it is natural, given these circumstances, that they would not teach their slaves the truth about, nor from, nor of God. And they didn't.

Of course, I'm not saying that the Imam's father had not already dealt extensively with that subject. He did. I'm only writing from the impact of that experience, which I had that day, sitting in Muhammad Mosque (called Temple at that time) No.7, as the Imam delivered a powerful speech.

I don't want to go too far away from my purpose in mentioning the alleged statements by the Pope. However, I do find it of great interest that at least three times in the Holy Qur'an we read that not only was there not a people to whom no divine warner was given, or raised, but that it (Holy Qur'an) was revealed among a people who had *never* received such divine warnings before.

For example, Surah 32 verse 3 reads in part: "...it is the Truth from thy Lord that thou mayest warn a people to whom no warner has come before thee that they may walk aright."

Muhammad Ali writes in footnote 1958a that "Makkah had not seen a prophet before the advent of the Holy Prophet Muhammad..."

Surah 36 verse 6 tells us that "a people" are being divinely warned "Whose fathers were not warned...."

And then in Surah 28 section 5, which is called "A Prophet like Moses," we read in verses 43 through 46, the following:

"And certainly We gave Moses the Book after We had destroyed the former generations—clear arguments for men and a guidance and a mercy, that they may be mindful."

"And thou wast not on the western side when We revealed to Moses the commandment, nor wast thou among those present; but We raised up generations, then life became prolonged to them. And thou wast not dwelling among the people of Midian, reciting to them Our messages, but We are the Sender (of messengers).

"And thou wast not at the side of the mountain when We called, but a mercy from thy Lord that thou mayest warn a people to whom no warner came before thee, that they may be mindful."

Muhammad Ali wrote in his footnote (#1883) these words: "This verse throws light on the significance of the foregoing verses: Thou wast not there, but it was Divine mercy that put a prophecy into the mouth of Moses regarding thee. This is made clear by the words a mercy from thy Lord that thou mayest warn.... The people to whom no warner had come before were the Arabs."

His words remind me of other words he wrote, right in his footnotes, which wherein he contradicts the text of the Holy Qur'an. For example, even though the text of the Holy Qur'an clearly states that Abraham and Ishmael taught and worked in Mecca, he writes that Mecca had never seen a divine prophet of Allah before the time of the revealing of the Qur'an to Muhammad.

Additionally, Muhammad Ali, as well as a whole hosts of translators of the Holy Qur'an, and other scholars quite freely point out that Allah raised several prophets among the Arabs in Arabia before the Qur'an was revealed to Muhammad.

It will take a few articles to complete what I am working on. I am not thinking that I can dispel the confusion, which has developed in the minds of many concerning the wisdom, the rightness, the timeliness of the moves Minister Farrakhan has and is making and will make. Allah has permitted this darkness. It probably will get darker, for some, while it gets brighter for others.

What I must do is to bear witness to what I know of the wisdom, the rightness and the timeliness of Minister Farrakhan's moves. If the job for some people is to be a devil, or worse, to be Satanic; to fool the weak-minded; to spread slander; to get others to move out on mere sick speculation; on wicked rumor; to get others to doubt and lie on Minister Farrakhan; to follow the lead of the wicked, with their evil track record of thousands of years, then so be it! Whatever we are, we are showing it now.

I heard the Honorable Elijah Muhammad say that one of the ways we know that we are in the judgment is that every one and thing will tell the truth on him/her/itself.

One of the major aspects of Minister Farrakhan's divine mission is not just to point out evil, where-ever it may be found (to the core of its core) but to show us how to get up out of its power forever!

The Honorable Elijah Muhammad spoke words, about Minister Farrakhan, which are backed up by the powers which uphold the universal order of things. And the wicked don't have the power to overcome that which Allah is bringing through Minister Farrakhan.

It can be shown that there is nothing you can do to stop Minister Farrakhan, from succeeding in the fulfillment of his assignment, unless, of course, you can blow out the light of the sun.

Be it the will of Allah, we will pick up in the next issue.

Jabril Muhammad
April 9, 2000

FARRAKHAN: THE TRAVELER
FOR THE FINAL CALL
VOL. 21; NO. 16

This is a dangerous time to make decisions based on assumptions. According to the truth of the 12th chapter of the book of Daniel, we've entered this most dangerous of all times, since time began.

A seemingly harmless example of the dangers of assumptions, (especially for us who are followers of the Honorable Minister Louis Farrakhan) is to assume, that the scientists of this world are correct when they claim that they've discovered solar systems beyond this one.

Another seemingly harmless example is to assume their calculations concerning Pluto, or Platoon, are correct, especially when we have the words of Minister Farrakhan's teacher's Teacher, in a lesson called The Problem Book.

Many claim that the 9th planet is probably not even a planet. One reason some of them make this claim is because their calculations are that Pluto is smaller than our moon. Wrong! Pluto is about 8.45 times larger than the planet earth, by Master Fard Muhammad's study. This one fact is bound to affect all of their other calculations about the 9th planet. Why assume that they are correct?

Furthermore, they don't have a clue to the spiritual side of Pluto or of any other object in space. The spirituality they attribute to the physical side of Allah's creation is down right demonic.

Minister Farrakhan has often warned us against acting like spiritual pigs swallowing everything that comes our way. He has warned us time and again against being judgmental and judging other than by what Allah has revealed.

Read Surah 5, section 7 of the Holy Qur'an, which repeatedly warns that, "Whoever judges not by what Allah has revealed, those are the disbelievers." Read the whole section for context and greater clarity.

If understood and obeyed, this alone would force us not to be judgmental. Wisdom does not give birth to a judgmental state of

mind, which is based on part knowledge, combined with a faulty use of our mental powers, all of which often leads to what's un-Islamic.

Please visit my website for Minister Farrakhan's comments on the word "judgmental" and the release of a brand new edition of *Is It Possible That The Honorable Elijah Muhammad Is Still Physically Alive?* It's: www.writtentestimony.com.

Some of us are so judgmental that we've decided the ultimate worth of others and then with supreme arrogance we've determined their place in Allah's mind. Then we influence others to treat them according to our judgment. Jesus warns us that with what judgment that we judge we shall be judged!

This state of mind opens us up to Satan's deceptions. One trick of the wicked is to get you to agree or to cooperate on something that they know you know they know. They start you out on something that appears harmless.

Consider this illustration from *This Is The One, Third Edition*, page 170, where the F.B.I. is speaking to Malcolm.

Agent: What we are interested in, basically, are the people who belong. The names of the members.

Malcolm: From what I understand, you have all that.

Agent: No comment. The teachings, plans, programs.

Malcolm: No teaching is more public than ours and I don't think you will find anybody more blunt in stating it publicly than we do. I don't think you can go anywhere on this earth and find anybody who expresses their views on matters more candidly than we do.

Agent: I can only agree with you. You are right.

This approach is one of the methods of wickedly intentioned and motivated people, white, black, or otherwise.

Now, how would you like to be jailed, found guilty, and sentenced to death on the basis of assumptions; misinformation; jealousy; envy; self-righteousness or outright lies?

If we are truly with Minister Farrakhan, we'll take his Study Guides much more seriously now than ever. He takes up those problems, that produce unjust divisions among us, and which stunts our spiritual development, without which God won't accept us! None of us are so good that we don't need to re-enter this study, in the way he ordained it, RIGHT NOW!

One of the signs that Minister Farrakhan is truly of God is that as he draws the hearts of human beings toward the Lord of the worlds and the Christ, he also draws human hearts one to another. There are others who claim that they are with Minister Farrakhan in this work. But if your work does not draw hearts toward God's definition of unity, you are drawing people into Satan's trap.

Satan asked to be respited "till the day when they are raised." After Allah granted that to him, Satan said, "I will certainly lie in wait for them in Thy straight path, Then I shall certainly come upon them from before them and from behind them, and from their right and from their left; and Thou wilt not find most of them thankful." Study Holy Qur'an 7:14-18.

Allah did not say that Satan would not succeed. He did say, "Whoever of them will follow thee, I will certainly fill hell with you all." Allah is Self-Independent.

Both demonic and divine works are occurring at great speed--simultaneously. Satan is working overtime to take all he can to that hell. The raising of the dead is also happening despite Satan and his helpers.

Several TV documentaries appeared this year about the American government's work against the Black Panthers years ago. The Nation of Islam, among others, suffered that evil then and now.

The wicked, both black and white, have sped up their evil work, externally and internally, to destroy the Nation right now. However, what ultimately guarantees that the Nation of Islam will not ever fall again is the limitless wisdom and power of Master Fard Muhammad. He and the Messiah are using your plans to serve Their Own.

The Backers of Minister Farrakhan are both the irresistible force, and the immovable object. This is not silly talk intended for laughter, or if spoken, to get a handclap.

This is not that silly talk that is written of in 2 Timothy 4:3-8, which speaks of the rise of hypocrites, especially at this time. This passage contains a second prophecy, of a man being rewarded by God despite them. Both prophecies are being worked out now.

It's written in Jeremiah 30:7, that this "day is great, so that none is like it. It is even the time of Jacob's trouble, but he shall be saved out of it."

We have, *through* Minister Farrakhan, and *from* his Backers, the realization of what is called, in 2 Peter 1:19, the "more sure word prophecy" which is a "light shining in a dark place." "Dark" here refers to spiritual squalidness. Read it in context, as we are living through this now. Minister Farrakhan's teachings of the Holy Qur'an, if understood, is "The Sure Truth."

This year is this world's New Years' Eve. Tomorrow many make New Years' resolutions. Consider this one: Reduce assumptions. Satan uses them against us. Read Holy Qur'an 17:53 and its footnote, before it's too late.

Read 2 Peter 2:9, 10. It's about you. The light of faith (Holy Qur'an 57:12) allows the Believers to see through trouble by Allah's permission.

Take Minister Farrakhan's faith and attitude as your guide through the trouble.

What is mercy?

JABRIL MUHAMMAD
DECEMBER 31, 2001

FARRAKHAN: THE TRAVELER
FOR THE FINAL CALL
VOL. 21; NO 17

There was a debate over reparations to Black people of America, held at Boston University, on November 11th, last year. They omitted God and whether or not He is an active part in the resolving of this explosive problem.

No subject is more controversial than God. So regardless to how controversial or explosive a subject may already be, it automatically reaches its extreme in controversy when God is introduced to the subject.

The majority of humanity claims belief in God, while also admitting that the world seems to be on the brink of annihilation. Certainly God is often superficially mentioned in relation to the serious problems in which humanity is entangled. But if God is really introduced in serious discussions of the world's affairs, the level of "controversial" goes through the roof.

How would the audience at Boston University have reacted if God were really introduced into that debate? If the Honorable Minister Louis Farrakhan introduced God at that meeting, it would have been 100% different and enlightening.

The Bible teaches, in John 7:24, "Judge not according to the appearance, but judge righteous judgment." (KJV) The Phillips Modern English Bible reads: "You must not judge by the appearance of things, but by the reality. The New English Bible reads: "Do not judge superficially, but be just in your judgments." The Amplified Bible reads: "Be honest in your judgment and do not decide at a glance—superficially and by appearances; but judge fairly and righteously."

Many make misjudgments respecting Minister Farrakhan's health; the intensity of his Godly love; his tremendous will power; and the fact that his Backers continuously empower him.

In *Is It Possible That The Honorable Elijah Muhammad Is Still Physically Alive???* I wrote:

"In the Holy Qur'an we read in Surah 10:36-39, part of which teaches us that the rejecters, who follow conjecture, reject Allah's revelations, which their state of mind won't permit them to grasp, even as they judge His wisdom, which is in the process of accomplishing that for which He revealed it.

"Such judgmental persons are casting unjust stones at the Honorable Minister Louis Farrakhan, and at we who follow him, even as others like them did to the Honorable Elijah Muhammad and his followers in the past.

"They don't realize that in their expressions of contempt for the Ambassador of Christ: the Honorable Louis Farrakhan, they are showing their contempt for the wisdom of the Honorable Elijah Muhammad, who chose Minister Farrakhan under divine guidance, to teach and do as he is."

English dictionaries are inadequate to define the state of mind in the word "judgmental." So, I asked my Brother and Minister. Ponder the wisdom of his answer.

Brother Jabril: Brother Minister, yesterday, in a limited way, we discussed the state of mind of one who is judgmental. You mentioned a tendency in human nature, which the word 'haste' defines. You mentioned history's judgment on the judgmental contemporaries of certain kinds of persons and why. Please comment.

Minister Farrakhan: Let's start with the word tendency. There is a natural tendency in the human being to look at a circumstance, an event, or a person and hastily make some form of judgment. Oft-times when that person comes closer to the subject, digs deeper into the event or the circumstance, they recognize that their first judgment was improper, incorrect.

This tendency that exists causes the human being great trouble because unfortunately, when we make a hasty judgment of an event, a circumstance, or a person, our ego can get involved in that judgment and therefore, that judgment could be a blinding factor in our properly relating to the event, the circumstance, or the person.

There is in human nature, as the Holy Qur'an teaches us, that the man is made in haste. This is why the Qur'an counsels us to gain the quality of patience. If we were by nature patient, we would not make hasty judgments. But because by nature, we are hasty, then we make hasty decisions based on hasty judgments.

I find, in my experience with our people and with human beings generally, that that tendency is real in everybody. It takes great discipline to withhold the tendency, or to control the tendency to make snap judgments without having not some of the facts, but as many of the facts that are possible to be known. This is why I believe that the Bible teaches, "Judge not lest you be in danger of judgment." Because no matter what we think we know, only God knows all of the factors in an event, in a circumstance and that which is in and surrounds a person.

Only God, the Best Knower, is qualified to really make a judgment. His judgment, then becomes a trial for the judgmental, because He sees so much when He judges, that it takes the hasty judgmental person time to catch up to the wisdom involved in a judgment, or a determination made by God, and they may do much harm to themselves and others until they catch up to His judgment.

This is why most great men are never properly seen by their contemporaries. The veiling of divinity, by the flesh and the drives of the flesh, causes people to be blinded by the flesh, making hasty judgments of that which is divine. So great men have to be judged by history, not by their contemporaries.

When our Beloved Brother, Martin Luther King was assassinated, and I looked at his funeral on television and began to weep, and I asked the Honorable Elijah Muhammad, why did I react like that, when we thought so differently from Dr. King? He said, "As long as the testator lives he is writing his testament."

The testator is the person, who every day of his life, is writing his testament. Life takes so many twists and turns that one can never fully know a person until death puts a period to the writing. He said, "Then the historians come and gather all of the bits and pieces of evidence of this person's life and work. Then the historians assign this person his or her place in history."

So in truth one can never receive ones' reward while one is alive. Your true reward comes after death has put a period to your testament and others can now view your life, its work, its impact, starting with the gathering of as many of the facts as can be known. Those facts give the person who reads them and digests them, maybe a totally different view of the person, or the event, or the circumstance, than [from] the contemporary, who lived when that person, was apart of that event and was a part, or an observer of that circumstance, whose judgmental state of mind miss-judged.

So in concluding my answer to that question, it would seem to me that none of us is truly capable of making a true judgment. And none of us is patient enough to wait for God to judge an event, a person and a circumstance. So history will always be correcting our judgments.

Brother Jabril: Would you say that in a limited circumstance, we can make true judgments, but not the truest judgments?

His answer, next issue, Allah willing.

JABRIL MUHAMMAD
JANUARY 10, 2002

FARRAKHAN: THE TRAVELER
FOR THE FINAL CALL
VOL. 21; NO 18

Brother Jabril: Would you say that in a limited circumstance, we can make true judgments, but not the truest judgments?

Minister Farrakhan: In a limited circumstance, we can make true judgments, but oft-times our egos are so wrapped up in the judgments that we make, we never leave room in our judgment for the possibility of mistake or error. That is the tragedy of judgment.

This is why, in my mind, to be made a judge of the human condition, is one of the greatest honors that can be bestowed on a person. But when you are made a judge, you are in the greatest position to come under the judgment of God.

So when I see a person robed in the garment of a judge, I often wonder how bias, how prejudice, how status symbols, how the nobility of a person, or the lack of it, enters into the judge's decision.

So when God says, "Judge not lest you be in danger of judgment," we ought to speak less, and think more, and desire to know as much as we can about the circumstance, the event, or the person, before we open our mouths to make a judgment.

That, unfortunately, is not always done. And unfortunately, this will always be the human condition, until we become so humble and righteous in character, that we desire to do no man or woman wrong.

So then we must speak less and we must counsel more, and do it with patience. This is what I find in the Qur'an that God is consistently counseling us to learn to be patient.

Brother Jabril: Brother Minister, since we will one day have a full blown judicial system, which will include judges, what are some of the qualities that immediately come to your mind that should characterize these kinds of persons?

Minister Farrakhan: I think the greatest quality must be first, a love of God; a love of truth and an insatiable desire to know more and more and more about the subject.

One must have the characteristic of humility. No judge should be arrogant because arrogance over your position makes you ineffective as a judge.

Humility always keeps your heart open for greater knowledge because you recognize the value, the importance of making a right judgment and you recognize the consequences of making an improper judgment.

It is the consequences of faulty judges and faulty decisions that bring down nations, societies and individuals.

So a judge must not just be one who has completed the course of study in law that is required, but the judge must have the quality of character that would make one a good judge of the affairs of human beings.

Brother Jabril: Brother Minister, yesterday we spoke a little bit about some of the factors involved in the advancement of human life, of society, of nations. You said that there was no advancement without sacrifice and that the advancement of humanity toward the ultimate objective of God, requires, on the part of some, or many, or all to one degree or another, pain, bloodshed and even the loss of life. Please comment."

Minister Farrakhan: There is no advancement without the sacrifice of life, bloodshed and pain. Those human beings whom God has chosen to advance us in whatever discipline that is, must first have the quality to endure suffering; to endure insult. Such persons must be able to endure criticism, made by judgmental persons, who are comfortable where they are and are challenged by where this human being is trying to lead us.

There is no advancement in any field without tremendous sacrifice and then life lost and bloodshed. Any advancement, in any field, has caused the one who leads us into that new field of knowledge and advancement, suffering or great suffering.

The Honorable Elijah Muhammad said, "Blessed is he who forges the way for others." There is a scripture that talks about

The Most Honorable Elijah Muhammad

the one whom God assigns the task of bringing in a world that is totally new. This would mean he brings in a new knowledge—a knowledge that challenges the scholarship of his day. So the scripture teaches, "No visage was more marred than his." This is because what he's doing is like cutting a path through a jungle.

The branches of the trees that you have to cut down hit your face and scar your face, but as you cut that branch down, the ones coming behind you feel little or no pain, because you have felt it for them.

So it says, "By his stripes we are healed." In the newness of the knowledge that he brings, and his intense love for the world that he sees in his mind, which is not yet in reality—this in what causes him to endure what he endures of the ignorance of his contemporaries. So, when his truth is established, he may, or may not be present, but he will be vindicated by history.

I can imagine the prophets of God, who saw beyond the range of vision of their contemporaries, who saw things yet to come. Such gifted persons, in certain areas, possessed gifts far beyond the gifts of the contemporaries, were subjected to thoughts that he is sick, or crazy.

So he is rejected of men and despised and evil spoken of and ill thought of, because he sees what others are unable to see. So there was no prophet that escaped the judgmental nature of his contemporaries.

I can imagine how lesser ones, such as Nostradamus suffered. I can imagine how Galileo, how Newton and Boyle and visionaries in every field, suffered.

Look at doctors who have discovered in the DNA, that which would allow them to clone a human being, to some extent, suffer the same.

Look at those who have discovered in stem cell research that they can now literally grow new organs, rather than implant organs of a different person into a different body. So they can literally take the DNA of that body and grow organs that would replace organs that are failing.

Well this kind of research has created controversy, debate, The doctors sometimes are considered demons rather than great doctors who are on the cutting edge of great new discovery.

I guess this is natural. I once read in a book, that when God sends a prophet, He ordains opposition for him, because it is only the severest opposition that tests the quality of the character of the bearer of the truth and tests the truth of the bearer of that truth.

So opposition is a necessity. So one must not necessarily be overcome by the judgmental. One whom God has given an assignment must understand in the nature of that assignment God has already ordered judgmental persons to attack him, to vilify him, to malign him, to say all manner of evil against him.

But he knows his Sender. He knows the value of the truth with which he has been sent. So he stays the course, knowing that his greatest vindicator and witness is God Himself.

Even if he does not live to see or witness his vindication, he knows, as the Honorable Elijah Muhammad knew, "I will be the winner living or dead."

Jabril Muhammad
January 10, 2002

Farrakhan: The Traveler
For The Final Call
Vol. 21; No 19

Brother Jabril: Brother Minister, to what extent does the judgmental state of mind opens us up to the wiles of Satan--and the Satan of self--especially the evil agents, the provocateurs, described in current TV documentaries about the government's infiltration of many groups to misdirect and hurt the members of these various organizations, but especially, of course, the Nation of Islam, in the 50s, 60s and the 70s.

An example was the COINTELPRO—the Counterintelligence program—that was designed to "disrupt" groups and "neutralize" individuals "deemed to be threats to domestic security." To what extent does the judgmental state of mind open us up to these wicked secret agents, who look like Believers, who we know are in the Nation to get Believers to unconsciously do their bidding? As I raise this question, I'm thinking about your Study Guide #17, wherein you raised the question, "Could we be unwittingly involved in a conspiracy against ourselves?"

Minister Farrakhan: When one makes hasty judgments on individuals, events, or circumstances that, in its initial interaction with us, causes us some degree of hurt or pain.

Once our egos get wrapped in our judgment, our ears close to words that might alter our judgment. Our eyes close to that which we might see that would alter our judgment. Our tongues become dumb to speaking a proper word concerning that event, circumstance, or person, and in that judgmental state, we can become guilty of slander, gossip, backbiting, which opens us up to the evil whispering of the sly slinking devil, who whispers into the hearts of men from among the jinn and the men.

The first devil we must confront is the devil of self. Once we have closed our hearts and minds on a particular view that we have concerning an event, a circumstance, or a person, those with whom we have friendship or kinship, we would have a tendency to share that view with others and because of our relationship with others and the amount of influence we have over others, our unfinished tainted view can become the view of others.

So unwittingly, we get involved in a conspiracy to put down and destroy members of our own tribe or family, church or Mosque, organization or community.

Satan, who is always listening as the righteous speak, can use our judgments, followed by our pronouncements, to make a chasm, and then widen it between individuals and then groups, depending upon who we are engaged in conversing about. In this instance, we become unwitting tools of Satan. This is why the Qur'an forbids backbiting and offers a "***Woe***" to the slanderer and the defamer who goes about exceeding the limits.

Allah says in the Qur'an that, "He can and does forgive hurtful speech." But we, who claim to be the righteous, would not desire others to form harsh judgments concerning us, if we forget or make a mistake or even an error. So we must refrain from being quick in doing these things to each other, which in the end damages the self; damages the person about whom we have made our judgment; then damages the community that we have some degree of influence in; and ultimately, we damage ourselves with Allah.

Brother Jabril: Brother Minister, from the time we enter the Nation of Islam, to become registered Believers, and even before that, we are told directly and indirectly to see ourselves as "students." We get Lessons, and we're referred to as "students." Even the Lesson, by which we are enrolled into the F.O.I. and the M.G.T. meeting classes, is referred to as the "Student Enrollment."

The concepts of *student* and *study* are put before us in various ways throughout our Islamic life. It was that way under the Honorable Elijah Muhammad. It is the same way under your leadership.

First, what are the fundamental or the primary characteristics of a good student?

Minister Farrakhan: The good student is seen practicing that of which he or she is studying. The more one studies, the more one must practice, for it is only the practice that refines our understanding of the principles.

Those who study oft-times become separated from those who do not study. Those who do not study, find themselves convicted of the truth that they have come to believe but not studious in that truth. Finding excuses for not studying more about that truth, they find themselves divided now within the group into different camps.

All of us who have come forth to follow the Honorable Elijah Muhammad must always see ourselves as students and be about the business of studying that which we have come to believe or to confess as our belief or our way of life.

Those who study will continue to grow. The more they practice and refine that practice, the more they will grow apart from those who do not study and do not practice. Then this leads again to judgments.

The studious person might (I don't say they always will) make a judgment against those who do not study. The one who does not study may find themselves judging the person or persons who do study. These judgments produce cliques. These behaviors produce groups within the group, which of course, gives Satan a field day to keep the house fully divided, fermenting strife and even belligerence and then even hatred and murder.

So one of the meanings of the word, "Taliban" is that they were students. They were students of a great universal message.

The problem, sometimes with students, who study, is that they begin to think that they are the equal of their teacher. Then these students want to implement practices that only demonstrate that they are students that are not even "half-learned." Sometimes when one thinks one knows, one develops arrogance. Once we become arrogant in what we think we know, we come out of the state of being a student. One of the characteristics of a student is that he or she is always humble, always open, ready and willing to learn something more about the subject matter in question.

So those who study must be careful of the heady wine that comes with thinking we know more than the other fellow who does not know, or is not advance in their studies, or more than we really know about the subject under study.

Advancement in our studies becomes a test of our character. How will we use our advancement? Will we use it to serve the non-studious to inspire them to study? Or will those who study make a judgment against those who are slow and slovenly in their studies? Will the studious refuse to serve them in the study? Or will they help them, by constantly reminding the non-studious, in a most humble way, that we all have come forth to study.

In our Lessons, the Honorable Elijah Muhammad says, "We can all accomplish the above said with very little study." He didn't say, we could accomplish the above said with no study.

Jabril Muhammad
January 13, 2002

Section 4

Farrakhan: The Traveler
For The Final Call
Vol. 21; No 20

Minister Louis Farrakhan: I often wonder why the Honorable Elijah Muhammad said to me, "Brother, you don't have to study." His words frighten me because I know the value of study. But he told me, 'Stand up and Allah will speak through you.'"

Some of us are favored by God in that way. This is what sets apart the prophet from the great historian who predicts and prophesied. The prophet does not need to study. It is the gift that God has given the prophet to see beyond what is presently seen. But the historian studies the cyclical nature of history and the cyclical nature of the struggle of the human being to achieve peace and security and fulfillment. As a consequence of that intense study, he can with fairly great exactitude prophesy. But those are rare cases and rare individuals. But for the most part, all of us have to study.

I close this point with the words of Prophet Muhammad (peace be upon him). He told his followers to seek knowledge from the cradle to the grave. Don't spare to go at any length to gain knowledge, even if you have to travel to far off places for knowledge, for that is what draws us closer to God. The more we know, the more we seek to know; the more we find God and love God and want to please God and be one with God.

May Allah bless all of the Muslims, whether followers of the

Honorable Elijah Muhammad or not, to be humble enough at heart, to become students. Even those who are considered scholars by the world, those who have gained degrees of scholarship, let not those degrees arrogate to ourselves 'that we know.' Let us be humble enough to continue to study what we think we know. And the more we study, our thoughts will change and grow from what we thought and believe and understood yesterday to that which is closer to the thinking of Allah."

Brother Jabril: Brother Minister, what is the value of the six written Lessons we were given? Why should we study them?

Minister Farrakhan: The value of those Lessons first, cannot be perceived, unless we properly understand who is giving the questions and who is giving the answers.

Once we have an appreciation of the value of Who the Author of the questions is, then we can begin to assign greater value to each and every question and by understanding the value of him who was being questioned and the state of mind that he was in at the time of his answers to that question.

Then we will learn that the questions are deeply profound, in that they stretch our minds from the past to the present into the future. If we start with the study of the answers given by one born to meet the Questioner, born to see and know the Questioner, then his answers have to be the basis of our beginning study of the course that would not just make us Muslims, in the common understanding of the meaning of Muslim, but make us into Gods, the very uncommon understanding of being a Muslim.

So one must approach the study with deep honor and respect and love for the One Who came; Who studied forty-two years to deliver us; for the One Who broke the circle of the Gods to bring us into equality with those men--these very great scientists. When we begin to look at it in this manner, we can begin to perceive the value of the six Lessons, that Master Fard Muhammad, to Whom praises are due forever, left with us for us.

Brother Jabril: Why were we given, as the first Lesson, these 20 statements, called the 'Actual Facts?' Why not real or true facts? Why "Actual Facts" and why should it begin like that? And how does this Lesson called the "Student Enrollment" enroll us?

Minister Farrakhan: I think that Master Fard Muhammad wanted us to always begin our process of study and growth with that which is actual, in the sense of that which is presently real, and that which is true at the time we are studying what we are studying of the subject.

The cells of the brain, as the Honorable Elijah Muhammad taught us, were/are created by God to think rightly. One cannot think rightly except that the basis of our thought is on the actual or that which is factual. So the student must always search for the real, the truth; the actual facts—the way things are at the moment he or she begins their study.

Some of those actual facts (in our Lessons) are not actual facts today. 'What is the population of the Original Nation in the wilderness of North America and all over the Planet Earth?' 'What is the population of the Colored People in the wilderness of North America and all over the Planet Earth?' Those were facts in those days (the early 1930s) but they are not actual facts today.

So how do you ascertain what is actual today from what was actual yesterday? But we start with those 'Actual Facts' to ground us in the time period of Master Fard Muhammad's manifestation to His servant and from that point our process of growth begins.

Now how do we enroll? Well, whenever you go to any course of study, you first must know what it is you want to study. Then you must know who the professor or the teacher is of that course. Then you must go and sign up for such course and gather the materials for such course and then be in attendance in that classroom, so that you can grow in that chosen course.

The moment we hear the teachings of the Honorable Elijah Muhammad two or three times, and we sign that form, we are acknowledging the headmaster of the school. We are acknowledging the teacher of the course. We are acknowledging what the course is and we do want to sign our names. Unfortunately, we were handicapped because we didn't know what our real name was so we signed our slave name.

Then to make sure that we were serious, we had to declare our intention and then we received what can be term as an entrance exam to complete the process of enrollment. Once we answered the ten questions and answers properly, we were accepted in the classroom as a student of a new Islam.

These ten questions and answers are the rules of Islam, meaning that, they teach us principles that will guide our study and the application of what we study until we come to the point of graduation.

May Allah bless us to be serious about our enrollment in this great class with such illustrious headmaster and magnificent teacher.

Before we go further, consider this. During all of the years I have interviewed Minister Farrakhan, only once did he have an idea of what I was about to ask him.

Look at the questions. Then think over the fact, that his answers have always been immediate, impromptu, or spontaneous, without hesitation! Heavy! Deep!

JABRIL MUHAMMAD
JANUARY 13, 2002

FARRAKHAN: THE TRAVELER
FOR THE FINAL CALL
VOL. 21; NO 21

This article is part of an ongoing series of interviews I conducted with the Honorable Minister Louis Farrakhan, before our Saviours' Day Convention held recently in Los Angeles, California. I expect to continue these interviews at least through Volume 21, Number 32. I intend to make brief comments, where I can fit them in upcoming articles.

Brother Jabril: How does the practice of prayer, the attitude of prayer and the spirit of prayer, help us in these studies?

Minister Farrakhan: Prayer is the preparation of the heart and mind for the course of our study; for prayer puts us in a right state of mind toward the Author of the study.

So the oft-repeated prayer of the Muslims sets the mind and

heart of the student for advancement. 'In the name of Allah, the Beneficent, the Merciful.'

Why are you enrolled in such a course? You are enrolled in this course of study because the Beneficent God had shown the utmost quality of mercy in coming to make you and me into Himself.

So it is right that we start, "Bismi-llah al-Rahman al-Rahim." Then we say the first verse of the seven oft-repeated verses, "Al-hamdu li-lla Rabbi-l-alamin"—praise belongs to God.

Why should this be the first verse of the oft-repeated prayer? It's because the God has found us groping and He is now showing us the way, the way from ignominy to eminence; the way from death into life; from weakness into power.When one is going to embark, on that kind of journey, one must know all along the path that the praise does not belong to the student. The praise belongs to God, Who is nurturing that student, from the time of his enrollment to the time of his graduation and perfection in the study. It will be God Himself, Who will be evolving that student, making that student to attain stage after stage on his way toward perfection.

"The Beneficent, the Merciful." At every stage, you will recognize the Supreme, Beneficence and Mercy of Him, Who came to involve us in such study.

Maliki yaumi-a-din "Master of the day or the law of requital." As students, as we practice this teaching, we are bound to make mistakes and errors, but the headmaster of our school and the professor is so loving toward the student, who sincerely wishes to succeed in the course, and is the Master of the law of consequences, so that master can withhold from the student the consequences of errors and mistakes, while pointing it out to the student.

"Thee alone do we serve and to Thee alone do we beseech for help." Every student needs help to get where the student desires to go. Who is the helper? The helper is God.

"Thee alone do we serve and to Thee alone do we beseech...." We constantly ask Allah to help us in our study, in our growth, in our development. Guide us on the straight or the right path.

Part of our progress in developing, as quickly as we can, is if we remain on a right course from the teacher. Sometimes the student will get off course and it's like getting off the main highway onto an access road that is very bumpy.

You want to get back on the main highway, so your constant prayer is "O Allah guide us on the right path;" the path that will keep us moving toward the completion of our study; the path that will keep us moving toward becoming what you enrolled us in class to become; "the path of those upon whom you have bestowed favor."

Doesn't the student want the favor of the teacher? No student would like to have the wrath of the Headmaster and the professor, poured on the student and have the student kicked out of the course. So we have to do that which pleases the Headmaster and the teacher by our constantly being willing, to be guided on the straight path; the path of those upon whom the teacher would show favors and not the path of those who anger the teacher and get punished or censored by the teacher or even expelled out of the class.

So prayer frames the mind. Prayer sets the tone. Prayer shapes the attitude of the student. And as one Civil Rights leader said, "It is your attitude that will determine your altitude."

So prayer, the constant remembrance of God, keeps you in the right attitude and therefore, there is no limit to your altitude.

Jabril Muhammad: Brother Minister, this question is really one question, but with two major sections to it. First, we ended the last session with the instructions of the Honorable Elijah Muhammad to you, at a certain point, in your ministry, "To just stand up and Allah will speak through you." I want to take that in stages and then go to the next part that has to do with music. Then we'll get to the third aspect of this.

First, please outline, your high school education that was so deep, so thorough, that when you got to college you didn't have to pick up a book.

Minister Farrakhan: My high school education was so superior that when I went to college, I never bought a book. I never was mentally challenged by anything that was being offered as a course of study. I went there because my mother desired that I have a fall back position, in case music failed.

The reason I went to prep school is because I graduated from high school so young. I was one month into my seventeenth year when I graduated from high school.

I, as a track man, who had equaled the state record in the 100 at 10 seconds flat, the coach in the South knew that the Brothers down there were running 9.7, 9.8. So in order for me to be worthy of a track scholarship, he wanted me to have one more year to grow and get stronger and then on the following year, after that one year of prep school, I would be allowed to have a scholarship to college. So prep school is free.

I went to school and I ran another year strengthening my ability to run the 100 yard dash, as well as the smaller dashes.

Brother Jabril: Brother Minister, what were the courses you took in high school?

Minister Farrakhan: Everything that is college preparatory. First, in foreign languages, I took Latin for three years; German; French; Spanish and of course, English.

My Latin gave me a more profound grasp of English because many of the prefixes and suffixes in English are from a Latin or a Greek root. So having Latin gave me insight into words and their meaning.

I had Ancient History, Medieval History, American History and some Modern History. I had Algebra, Plain Geometry, Solid Geometry, Trigonometry, and Calculus. I had Physics, Chemistry and Biology.

These kinds of subjects put me in a tremendous position of advantage going to a southern school that was preparing me to be a teacher. A Bachelor of Arts degree, would have allowed me to teach on the grammar school level, where once I learned methods, once I learn the history of education, a little psychology, I could have done that, teaching grammar school coming out of high school with the background that I had.

Brother Jabril: So you would say it's rather obvious then that the nature of the preparation you had in high school, is what made you to whiz through college the three plus years so fast?

Minister Farrakhan: That is correct.

Brother Jabril: Now you come into the Nation. You become registered in 1955. Did you study?

JABRIL MUHAMMAD
JANUARY 28, 2002

FARRAKHAN: THE TRAVELER
FOR THE FINAL CALL
VOL. 21; NO 22

Here are a few pointers about *Is It Possible That The Honorable Elijah Muhammad Is Still Physically Alive???*

Forty seven of the 98 pages of this book was *not* in its 1983 or its 1989 editions. Chapters 1, 4 and 6 contains some of the views (and positions) of the Honorable Minister Louis Farrakhan, of this book's subject. After looking at his words, consider reading chapters 7 and 8, both of which are excerpts from his larger unpublished works.

This is a new book.

A 144,000 were foreseen with a man symbolically styled as the "Lamb." Now, will one work to prepare ones self to meet a man one thinks is dead? This is doubtful. Then maybe such one will be as those virgins, of the 25th chapter of Matthew who were unprepared when the call came to go and meet with the "Bridegroom." However, the 144,000 were prepared. Think deeply.

Minister Farrakhan is not insane, nor is he a liar!

Now, let's get back to the interview.

Brother Jabril: You became a registered Muslim in 1955. Did you study?

Minister Farrakhan: Oh yes. This was a new field for me. I was so fascinated by the teachings of the most Honorable Elijah Muhammad, as taught by Malcolm X first; Minister Malcolm; Minister Lucius in Washington, D.C., Minister Karriem in Baltimore; the Minister in Detroit and other Ministers of the Honorable Elijah Muhammad and young Minister George, out of Philadelphia—these were men who were profoundly influential in my development.

Even though there were people over me in authority that may not have had a high school education, they were so well studied in the teachings of the Honorable Elijah Muhammad, it meant nothing to me that they did not have the amount of school time that I had, or the quality of preparation that I had. They had what I was trying to get. That was an understanding of the message of Islam, as taught by the Honorable Elijah Muhammad.

The discipline that I applied in the study of my music, once I gained the love of my violin, my mother no longer had to require me to practice. Every free moment I had I would practice my craft. Sometimes I would practice four hours, five hours, and six hours. Sometimes I would tell my wife, 'I'm going in this room. I won't be out for eight or nine hours.' I would go in and practice my craft.

So when I gave up music and became a follower of the Honorable Elijah Muhammad, my love for music, my love for my craft just was transferred to my love for Allah, my love for the Messenger, my love for Islam. I always had love for God and love for our people, but now I had a message, a vehicle to transfer—not a noun but a verb—in that I could actively demonstrate my love, by bringing Black people up out of the grave of ignorance, by sharing with them the profound message that Master Fard Muhammad had left with the Honorable Elijah Muhammad for our resurrection, restoration, reconciliation and civilizing us to be top human beings.

Brother Jabril: A few of us or some of us in those days are aware of the fact, that there were times when you would go to a hotel room and spend hours studying. Please elaborate.

Minister Farrakhan: I always desired to feed the Muslim community. They were feeding me. They were giving my family and I enough money to at least to afford bean soup. It was not the amount of money, because it was very meager, and we were very, very poor. But I felt obligated to study to serve this community. They came to follow the Honorable Elijah Muhammad. In order

Minister Farrakhan during a private performance at his home in December 1986.

to follow him they had to know him, they had to know what he taught and his aim and purpose. So if I loved him and loved them, then it was my duty to study to prepare these who love him and also to be strong helpers of him, in the cause of the rise of our people.

In those days I studied every thing I could get my hands on related to the message of the Honorable Elijah Muhammad. By immersing myself in his message, then everything that I learned in high school, prep school and college took on greater significance. Biology took on greater meaning. Chemistry, Solid Geometry, Algebra, Calculus, everything that I studied I could now use because Islam, as taught by the Honorable Elijah Muhammad was the key to use knowledge for the advancement of self, your family, your community and your people.

Brother Jabril: Now Brother Minister, talk to me for a moment about the time you received the order to put up your music.

Minister Farrakhan: Well, I was playing in a nightclub, in Greenwich Village, in New York, called The Village Barn. I could not come to the Mosque on that particular Sunday because I had to do a Matinee show at the time of the Mosque meeting. But after I completed my show and my responsibility to the night club, I came uptown to the Temple #7 luncheonette on 120th Street and Lenox Avenue to chat with the Muslims and get a bowl of bean soup.

When I got in the restaurant and sat down to order my soup, one of the Believers, I don't remember who he was, sat down and said to me "Man you know, the order came down today that all the musicians would have to get out of music or get out the Mosque or out of the Temple." This came as a shock to me. So I didn't drink the soup right then. I got up, I walked out of the restaurant, I walked East on 120 Street, maybe 20 to 30 paces, thinking as to what I was going do. In that 20 to 30 paces, the thought came to me, 'I can live without music. But I cannot live without the truth.'

I turned right around and went back in the restaurant and sat down and had my bowl of soup.

Our dear departed Brother Captain Yusuf Shah learned that somebody had said that to me. He was very angry because he wanted to be the one to break it to me in a gentle way and measure my reactions. When he came I told him, "I already made my decision Brother. I'm giving up show business."

I had until the end of December, this was around the first of December during Ramadan or something like that, I think it was, and I had to the end of December. I had 30 days to make that decision.

Brother Jabril: 1955?

Minister Farrakhan: Yes it was the end of 1955. That's correct.

Brother Jabril: And you just stopped?

Minister Farrakhan: Yes. In fact it was in November. It was not in December, but I had to the end of December to make the decision, but this order came down in November, one month after I had been a registered Muslim.

Brother Jabril: What then led to, and what were the circumstances, which were preparatory, under which the Honorable Elijah Muhammad said to you, "You don't have to study."

Jabril Muhammad
January 28, 2002

Farrakhan: The Traveler
For The Final Call
Vol. 21; No 23

Dictionaries define "story" to mean an account or a recital of an event or a series of events, or happenings, either true or fictitious. It's a narrative of incidents in their sequence. "Narrative," "story-line" or "plot," basically means the same. They all have beginnings and endings. So it is with the scriptures.

We are at the very end of the Bible's and Holy Qur'an's "story" or "narrative."

The interview, conducted by Jabril Muhammad, in January 2002, with the Honorable Minister Louis Farrakhan continues:

Brother Jabril: What then led to, and what were the circumstances, which were preparatory, under which the Honorable Elijah Muhammad said to you, "You don't have to study."

Minister Farrakhan: Well, as he made me his National Representative and allowed me to carry on his National Broadcast, he wrote me a letter and gave me the assignment. He gave some subject matter in a letter for four weeks that I would have to deliver these subjects. After the four weeks he was very pleased. He said "You can go on a little longer."

As I went on longer, he was pleased. So after six months or so, he said "You can go on for six years."

At that time, it would take me one week to do a half hour broadcast, because I would write down every word that I was going to say; every scripture that I was going to use. Then I would go back over the language and see if I could say it more succinctly and more effectively if I used this word as opposed to that word, this phrase as opposed to the other phrase. So then I would rehearse it; because I'm reading from a script. I did that for three years.

One day I went out to visit with him and he told me "Brother you don't have to do that." He said "You go and stand up and Allah will speak through you." I did that immediately. I just obeyed him. I never used notes. I started speaking on a subject and would allow God to feed me. This gave the Honorable Elijah Muhammad, I would imagine, a chance to see how God was using me.

At the end of the sixth year he called me. He said "Brother, I will be coming on next week. So you let the public know that Elijah Muhammad will be coming back on the radio next week." So it's like you give your baby a lolly pop and he's sucking on it. He gets use to it. But you gave it to him. It's your lolly pop. So then you ask him to give me back my lolly pop.

Well now he's looking at the baby to see what kind of attitude the baby had. Well how would he know that? He would know that by the way I introduce his return to the microphone. So my next broadcast was called, "Hearken unto the voice of God." So when I sent it out for him to play it in advance of his coming out, he then called me and said "Brother, you may continue."

I never gave it a thought that I would tell them hearken unto the voice of God. Then he allows me to continue after I'm supposedly introducing him, and he puts me back on. Well what was he saying?

Subsequent to that, it was getting now into the early 70s, and he is about getting ready to make his departure. He never would praise me in the public, as he did Malcolm. And he told me, when I became his National Representative that, "I'll never teach another Minister like I taught Malcolm until I have thoroughly tried him."

He was letting me know that I was going to be thoroughly tried before he would open up the wisdom of his wisdom to me. But what he began to see, I believe, in my extemporaneous teaching of his teaching, that God was already beginning to open up to me the inner or esoteric meanings of the teachings that it seemed like other ministers would only teach what he taught. They seem to be afraid to dig into his words to find all the jewels that were in the word. But I call that intellectual cowardice, wanting to be safe, but not wanting to explore the depth of what this man had gotten from God. So I decided I was not going to do that. I was going to dig into the teachings and expose that which God showed me.

One day I came out to Chicago. I had made a speech on the Mother Plane and I was showing its spiritual significance and not dealing so much with the physical. The Messenger was very angry, according to the way his assistant Minister, Yusuf Shah represented it to me. He said "There he goes, out there showing off; yelling out his wisdom." He was letting them know that I was right in what I was saying, but it wasn't the right time, you know. He was whipping me, but praising me at the same time. Somewhere along that time, I do not remember the circumstances, he told me "Brother, you don't have to study." I didn't ask him, "What, everybody has to study. Why are you saying I don't have to study?"

Then as I went on, as it's getting closer to the time of his departure, I began to see that as it was written, as I started standing up to deliver his message in his absence, that the scripture was being fulfilled.

As Joshua went forward, God said to him, "I will be with your mouth as I was with the mouth of Moses." Again, I saw this in the writings of Ezekiel and with the writings of the prophets. He's just with the mouth of those whom He authorizes. So I was gradually coming into the knowledge that I was authorized by God and the Messenger to deliver this message. So He was with my mouth. He also had told me some years before, "I want you to line your mind up with my mind so that there will be one mind." Well if that's what he wanted then Allah answers his desire. Well God, through the experiences that he was bringing me through, was lining my mind up with his mind, so that it was one mind.

When I opened my mouth, not only was God with my mouth, but I was speaking that which was from the mind and heart of the Honorable Elijah Muhammad himself. So the Honorable Elijah Muhammad was no longer absent. He was present, but he was present in that student that he had made.

I remember one night, at his table in Chicago, I had a tape recorder and I asked him if I could tape what he said at the table. He said "Yes." And during the time at the table he said these words, and unfortunately, I don't have the tape now as a witness, but God is sufficient as a witness. He said to me "Allah has made me to take His place among the people and I am making you to take mine."

I was shocked at the statement.

Jabril Muhammad
January 28, 2002

Farrakhan: The Traveler
For *The Final Call*
Vol. 21; No 24

Minister Louis Farrakhan: I was shocked at that statement. I knew that "am making" is the present progressive tense. So I was a work in progress and "am making," indicated that he (the Honorable Elijah Muhammad) was fixing me in a way that I could sit in his seat, in his absence, and represent him to the best of my ability to his people.

After 1985, and my experience with him [his more-than-a-vision experience] I even more clearly understood why I didn't have to study. Because this that I am going to (if it is the will of Allah) bring back from my next meeting with him, is that of which it is written, "no eye that has seen, no ear has heard," so no book contains it. So there's nothing for me to study. That's revelation.

When he reveals it to me, if I'm worthy, I'll reveal it to others; but there's nothing for me to study. It's just for me to get it in me and I believe a portion of it is already in me from my first visit with him. That's what I think the scroll was that came down that I saw--well something was being written in me, so that even right now, although I'm not a great student of Bible and Qur'an, but I stand and speak and the Bible comes up. The Qur'an comes up. Things come up. They come out of me in a very fantastic order.

Brother Jabril: It sure does.

Minister Farrakhan: So others may look at me and think that I'm standing up unprepared. But I've been prepared and am being prepared. So others should not imitate me. Others should not try to do what God has done to show the people, through me, that he is with my mouth, as He was with the mouth of our father, the most Honorable Elijah Muhammad.

I would not say to the students, that you don't have to study because in my own way, I'm always thinking, meditating, feeding my mind on words, on images, on circumstances, on events, on people. I look in my Qur'an. I look in my Bible. I look into things. I'm constantly feeding my mind.

Brother Jabril: What we've covered is directly related to what you shared with a few others the other night, concerning the public statement that you're writing for Saviours' Day; for the concert specifically. The essence of what you said to me the other night was that "I'm about to perform something that's beyond my ability. God would have to help me." I want you to correlate that statement with the broad experience you just outlined respecting your growth in the delivery of the word of Allah.

Minister Farrakhan: Yes. As you know, I have a passion and a love for classical music, which some of our people would define as European culture. I have a passion for the violin and this is a European made instrument. A dear friend said "It would have been better man, if you had played the saxophone rather than a violin." But all of the instruments that our people play have been fashioned or refashioned by the Europeans. The saxophone, the clarinet, the oboe, the flute, the base violin, the guitar, we have become masters of these European instruments, but not in the European idiom, but rather in that which came out of our culture of suffering and out of our creativity.

Well, Beethoven was one of these men that influenced the whole classical and romantic period of the development of music in Europe. They credit him with being the father of this period of music.

One of the Sisters that encouraged me, that is the promoter of this music festival called "Gateways," where I first performed the Mendelssohn with Maestro Michael Morgan and the tri-city members of the tri city symphony; (Armenta) said to me "I don't want to hear you play Mendelssohn or Bach or other European composers, I want to hear you do Beethoven." So she put me on Beethoven.

Later my teacher (Mrs. Foreman) suggested it to me. But she also told me "It's such a deep spiritual piece that your people may not like it. They would like the Bach or the Mendelssohn because of the bombast, the different dynamics of these things," but Beethoven came at it so different. I didn't realize the difficulty of playing the Beethoven violin concerto.

The difficulty is in its simplicity. It's like asking a person free hand, to draw a straight line perfectly. That's the difficulty. It appears that you should be able to do that. But try it, you know. Well that's Beethoven. So the more I got into the music I began to see that the playing of Beethoven was far beyond my years of training and study; far beyond the foundation that I had in music.

You have to be at a certain foundational level to attempt to play certain pieces in the classical genre. I guess that's the right word. But now I've jumped into Mr. Beethoven. The more I play him the more I see that something was lacking in my foundation that would not allow me to really express this man as wonderfully as I would like too.

I said I have accepted the challenge to do something far beyond my ability. When one does something far beyond the limitations of ones ability, if one is sincere and humble enough to recognize that, that person must seek the help of God, for the scholars say He "took ordinary people but with their reliance on God and following the discipline of Jesus, ordinary people were allowed to do extraordinary things."

Well that principle applies in everything. So I am an ordinary person with the violin. Maybe even less than ordinary, because I have not given myself to that study, with the diligence of a virtuoso, or the diligence of a professional, or a diligence of somebody who has made this their life's devotion. But I wanted to do it.

I knew that I had to do my part and my part was to practice; to give it the time that it would require; to learn as much as I could about that piece; about the state of mind of Beethoven when he wrote it, so that every nuance in the piece could mean something; so that I might be able to interpret his soul.

Well, the more I did this the more I realized that boy, do I need the help of God to do this. The more I struggled with my inefficiency, the more I relied and cried out to God, to please help me.

The Most Honorable Elijah Muhammad said to me "That when Allah created the heavens and the earth from nothing He destroyed the impossible."

JABRIL MUHAMMAD
JANUARY 28, 2002

FARRAKHAN: THE TRAVELER
FOR THE FINAL CALL
VOL. 21; NO. 25

Minister Farrakhan: And then from the writings of Paul, in this instance, I keep saying it over and over like a mantra, "I can do all things through Christ or through Allah which strengthens me." This keeps me focused on God because without Him I will not be able to do this, at all. Without God's intervention I would not represent Beethoven as well as I would like.

I'm begging Allah and believing that He's going to be with me and help me to take an ordinary talent and do something, maybe, a little more than ordinary, by His grace.

Brother Jabril: You told me of this conductor the other night.

Minister Farrakhan: You know, the fact that you ask me questions over the years, that you didn't prompt me on, so I never knew the question, but as you give me the question the answer is formulating in my head. So you, more than anybody, can attest to the truth that this is not regular; it's not necessarily ordinary, but that God is with Brother's mouth.

Brother Jabril: One of my purposes, in these interviews, is to show, through you what God has and is doing with you for us, to help us to have more confidence that He is with us. Brother Minister, I don't fully remember the man's name, it starts with a "V" and you said that he talked about what you are attempting to do, is a tight rope.

Minister Farrakhan: Charles Veal.

Brother Jabril: Please repeat what you told me that he said of the difficulty factor in what you are preparing to do.

Minister Farrakhan: He said that the difficulty factor in what I intend to do, is compared to a man walking a tight rope, a hundred feet in the air with no safety net. When he first heard me play he said, "You know, there were some moments of brilliance in what you did." He said, "You're close." But he came back then days later, after giving me some guidance he said, "Man what you've done in a week's time is amazing." He said, "You're there now."

Brother Jabril: All praises are due to Allah for blessing us with an example such as He has given us in you.

Now Brother Minister, be it the will of Allah, I intend to make of these interviews into a little "Gap Two" book, for in your words are many lessons for others—young Brothers and Sisters—who want to teach; who want to help advance the Nation of Islam. In a summary fashion, what would you want them to get out of your experiences that you just outlined, that would help them do what they are trying to do, or will try to do?

Minister Farrakhan: I wish that every Believer could see me in the role of a student. They always see me in the role as a teacher. But you can never be a good teacher unless you become a good student. And you can never be a good leader unless you become a good follower.

Now there are characteristics one must develop to become a good student. The reason I believe that I excel, as a student, is because my desire is so intense to know and to improve. So it doesn't make any difference how you critique me, my heart has been made by God so humble and my desire to be better is so great, that I suck up what you tell me like a sponge.

Brother Jabril: Of criticism or critique?

Minister Farrakhan: Yes, of both. So that when you leave me, I go to practice what you showed me that I was deficient in. I say this that most of us, as students, become knowledgeable too quick, and with that knowledge we become arrogant and we lose the desire to know. If we have the desire to know, our heart is so crippled by false pride, we don't humble ourselves enough to even accept critique.

When we meet again, I'm meeting the same person that I met the last time and that person is no better, after being critiqued, than he was before critique. But every time my teacher meets me, I'm better than the last time because my heart has accepted the critical analysis, because I want to be better at whatever I do.

Brother Jabril: The Bible says that Jesus was not a learned man and Paul was a highly learn man, according to that world's standard at that time. The Honorable Elijah Muhammad, as we know, had four grades of this world's education, which I heard him say one day, was just enough to teach him how to read and write. Although you did not graduate from college, you had, in comparison to him, quite a bit more of this world's education. Please comment.

Minister Farrakhan: The Honorable Elijah Muhammad is the most learned man that I ever met in my life. He may not have been learned in terms of what the world says is learning, but how could he be unlearned and teach those of us who had learning that which overwhelmed our knowledge, that we became his followers? Without a doctoral degree, he mastered those courses of study that we had spent years trying to study, trying to master, while the Honorable Elijah Muhammad could show us in our own choice of subject matter, that which we had never seen before.

He taught bankers, banking. He taught, architects, architecture. He taught scientists, science. He taught doctors, medicine. So then you have to ask yourself, since he did not have formal learning, who taught him? The student absolutely is a witness of his teacher. I bear witness that God taught the Honorable Elijah Muhammad.

Brother Jabril: Thank you. Now Brother Minister, that leads me to the second part of this question.

I am among those who have sat at your dinner table many times, when there had been a table full of Ministers; medical people, who not only are formerly trained, but had years of experience; in short, many in all of the major fields of learning and practice that represent the institutions that hold this society together. We've seen I have seen that all these people were profoundly impressed with your ability to educate them in their own disciplines, which you have not studied. They learned from you. You provided them with insights into their own field. How would you account for that?

Minister Farrakhan: Because I'm a student of the man I just described. If my teacher, having not letters, yet is learned, and I am his student having not letters either---because the only diploma that I can show you is a high school diploma, because I never finished college in order to have letters, although I was above average as a student---so then its my being his student, is what has caused me (and any of us who would diligently study the teachings of the Honorable Elijah Muhammad) to have the ability to help others in their chosen fields, even though, we may not necessarily have known much of their field.

Jabril Muhammad
January 28, 2002

Farrakhan: The Traveler
For *The Final Call*
Vol. 21; No 26

Brother Jabril: Brother Minister, about a week and a half ago I showed you the chapter, titled, *Minister Farrakhan's Magnificent Answer* out of the little book, *Is It Possible That The Honorable Elijah Muhammad Is Still Physically Alive???"*

You were somewhat amazed over your own words in it. There have been many instances where you looked back at words that you have spoken to me, in interviews, such as this interview, and in your speeches, etc., with utter and genuine surprise. Please comment.

Minister Farrakhan: I was with the Honorable Elijah Muhammad one day and they were playing a tape of him speaking. He made a point and he applauded. He was excited and he said "Boy, Allah really gave me something there.

Well I'm like that too. You give me a question I give you an answer, but the answer comes as inspiration. Then if I'm blessed to be able to read what I said, sometimes I ask the question, 'Did I say that?' Well I didn't say it. He said it through me, but now I'm fascinated and often overwhelmed by what came out of my mouth.

It just drops me almost to the floor in humility, to know that God would use me in this way to glorify Him and His servant, the Honorable Elijah Muhammad, and to help our people, and the people of the earth, out of the condition that 6,000 years of Satanic rule has put humanity under. I am awed and overwhelmed that Allah saw fit to use me in such a magnificent way. You are right.

To see the end of your faith, meaning to see the flourishing of what your faith has shown you. Although I may not live necessarily to see all of it because there's so much that the words of the Honorable Elijah Muhammad causes one to see, but at least, to get a glimpse into the Hereafter would be a tremendous blessing.

Brother Jabril: Well honestly I feel, you are going to get more than a glimpse. I earnestly believe that. Of course, many might say, "Well, that's just you talking, Jabril." But I believe that. I want that for you, my Brother—and all of us.

Minister Farrakhan: For all the Believers.

Brother Jabril: Right!

Read only The Living Bible, 2 Timothy 4: 3-5, especially 6-8, to more fully understand what's being discussed. Then read the same in any other translation you can.

Jabril Muhammad: What is the key in the interpretation of anything, especially in what you intend to do in the Beethoven violin concerto on February the 13th in Los Angeles?

Minister Farrakhan: In order to properly interpret anything that has been said or done by another, one has to be in harmony with the mind and the spirit of the one whom he or she desires to interpret.

People that wish to interpret the word of God cannot do so properly without His permission. That person must be in tune with the mind and the spirit of God, as He revealed His word, in order for one to properly interpret that word.

Every mind of greatness is from God. Every person of greatness in any field, who becomes a standard of measurement of proficiency in that field, must be studied, not from the mind of envy; not from the mind of jealousy; not even from the mind of self-aggrandizement.

For example, to study a prophet, whose heart was so humble that he could receive revelation from God, and in order for you to even approach the meaning of that revelation of that prophet, you would have to be in the same spirit of humility of the one who received God's word, for God to open that revelation up to you. **Based upon your capacity to grasp, God gives you.**

Minister Farrakhan's answer continues next article, Allah willing.

In upcoming articles, are such questions as, how he (Minister Farrakhan) uses adversity in his life to advance the cause of Allah. He also insightfully answered several other questions, including the divine purpose and place of chaos in the overall divine plan for our perfection and the fundamental spiritual scales, which must be removed from our eyes, if we are to make the progress we can to fulfill the purpose of Allah for our lives.

Meanwhile, study these words of Mother Tynnetta Muhammad's article, Volume 21 No. 21, part of which reads:

"The Honorable Minister Louis Farrakhan outlined 'Eight Steps of the Atonement Process' while delivering to us, and the world, the Redemptive Message that was intended to put us on the road to a high civilization as he addressed nearly two million men gathered for the Million Man March in Washington D.C., on October 16, 1995.

"It is due to this continual disrespect of the Principles of the Brotherhood to Practice Unconditional Love among us that is leading to distrust, immorality and a decline in our success as a people that is separating us into groups to be judged by God. This lack of discipline in our lives is also separating many from the bright light and example of the Honorable Minister Farrakhan while we are being grouped into ranks, some of whom are revealing themselves as uncongenial company.

"The Prophet was not made totally aware of the mischief-makers and their various machinations; only Allah and His Angels were given charge over them. Those who read these words may take note of their actions and better recognize who they are. Such uncongenial company will soon be removed from among the Believers by Allah, God, Himself, Who is sifting and testing us through trials and tribulation, as the Most Perfect Judge.

"Being guided by Allah's Spirit, I will only say, All Praise is due to Allah for His Presence and Saving Grace. Without His Abundant Mercy and Forgiveness, none would escape the Divine Chastisement of Allah. The Holy Qur'an reveals in the Surah 8 that the threatened punishment would not come while the Servant of God was still in our midst; but once he was removed, the executioners would come. This is a True Prophetic Picture of our present condition today."

The Honorable Elijah Muhammad has stated that, "disagreement is like a lighted fuse." He also said that "agreement is the basis of love."

Real Muslims are in agreement on the most relevant of truths. That's what makes their love so genuine. Consider this from the Holy Qur'an:

"O you who believe, should any one of you turn back from his religion, then Allah will bring a people, whom He loves and who love Him, humble towards believers, mighty against the disbelievers, striving hard in Allah's way and not fearing the censure of any censurer. This is Allah's grace He gives it to whom He pleases. And Allah is Ample-giving, Knowing. Only Allah is your Friend and His Messenger and those who believe, those who keep up prayer and pay the poor-rate, and they bow down. And whoever takes Allah and His Messenger and those who believe for friend—surely the party of Allah, they shall triumph." (5:54-56)

With this, read 1st John.

JABRIL MUHAMMAD
FEBRUARY 8, 2002

FARRAKHAN: THE TRAVELER
FOR *THE FINAL CALL*
VOL. 21; NO. 27

The Honorable Minister Louis Farrakhan continues his response to my question: What is key in the interpretation of anything, especially in what you intend to do in the Beethoven violin concerto on February the 13th in Los Angeles?

Minister Farrakhan: Now, Beethoven was inspired of God. His—I don't want to call it genius, because it's beyond genius—his divinity is seen in the magnificence of his ability to compose. Through adversity, his creativity was brought to a level of excellence, that has caused him to be an innovator and considered the father of a period in the development of classical music, called the romantic period.

He embellished the classical period and became the father of the romantic period. He was dark skinned, with a broad nose, born in Germany, a country that gave rise to Adolf Hitler and a people that found in his development of the Aryan supremacy theory, great resonance in the German people.

Beethoven was nicknamed, "the schwarzer," which translates into the "Black one." Black, in the language of white supremacy, is a very negative thing. Therefore, throughout his life he felt the sting of being "the schwarzer."

This was a large measure, a major factor in his creativity and the manifestation of his divinity in music because he wanted acceptance. He found women that he really loved. Some of them really loved him. But because of the social stratification in the German and Austrian society, the parents did not feel he was of the proper nobility of birth to be worthy of marrying their daughters.

It is something like Black persons, like Charlie Parker, Thelonious Monk, Dizzy Gillespie, Bud Powell, who were so innovative in the jazz idiom that many, many white people found a place for them in their homes, in their hearts, but this did not necessarily allow them to marry their daughters. So Black musicians have always found a level of acceptance in white supremacist societies simply because of what we provided for the white supremacist mentality, by the genius or the divinity of our expression.

Beethoven found a woman that he truly loved. But she was unable to marry him, although they would meet secretly. So after his death, they found a letter addressed to his eternal beloved with no name. They began to search: who could this be? Why could it not be known?

In my preparation for the playing of Beethoven, on my prayer rug, I asked Allah, if He would give me the spirit that He gave to Beethoven when He created this violin concerto. It is unlike any other violin concerto because it is a give and take. It is a conversation between the soloist and the orchestra and different segments of the orchestra. It starts with the timpani drum beating. This continues all the way through the piece and you will hear this beat, sometimes from the violins; sometimes from the base violin, sometimes from other instruments.

I liken this sound to the heart beat. His heart was affected by a woman that he could not fully have as his own.

I believe that this piece was his conversation with her; his deep love for her, hers for him; the highs and lows; the frustration that came about in his inability to make her his life long companion.

The more I studied the nuances of the music, the more I hear his crying; his pleading; her responses; the family; the anger, all of this incorporated in his music, which was an expression of all that he was going through.

It's like Quincy Jones saying, that when Michael Jackson composes, his life is intimately involved in the songs that he sings.

Jabril Muhammad: Adversity was the constant companion of this outstandingly great composer, Beethoven, yet he persevered. What accounted for his perseverance and success in spite of his adversities?

Minister Farrakhan: He suffered the adversity of being dark skinned in a culture or society that would one day accept an Aryan philosophy at the apex of white supremacy.

I read that he spent considerable amount of money trying to prove the nobility of his birth. I read that he was unfulfilled in terms of marriage and having a companion at his side, whom he truly loved and by whom he would have children.

Then the greatest adversity in his life was at the age of forty, when he began loosing the ability to hear. Yet the greatest of his compositions, according to those who study music in colleges, tell us that these compositions that he created on his going deaf and at his deafness were the greatest of all his compositions.

This meant that he had to rely on an inner strength and an inner connection to the God Who created sound and gave each creature a sound that is unique to that creature. So when he came to the point where he could no longer hear the sound, he had to remember; he had to dig deep in his capacity to remember the sounds of birds and he imitated that in his music.

He heard from the inner ear what God allows us at times, to hear, the unspoken as though he actually heard it spoken and to see the unseen, as if he were looking at it. He got in touch with the greater power of seeing and hearing, which afforded him the opportunity to make his greatest contribution to music, which meant he had to get in touch with God, on a more profound level.

His adversity, not only put him on a deep musical journey within, but it also took him on a deep spiritual journey, where he became more and more in tune with the God, Who created him and gave him this marvelous gift.

But as you raise this question, I thought of the teachings of the most Honorable Elijah Muhammad. Adversity accompanied God's Self-creation. So it's natural for adversity to accompany everything of value, and *it must be* accompanied by adversity. Adversity becomes the mother, out of which creativity and the genius or the spirit of God is made manifest.

Out of the darkness of space and the adversity of overcoming nothingness, came sun, moon, stars, life; all forms of life. So when one is created in the image of God, that means that adversity will accompany that life. This is why the Qur'an says "Allah has ordained struggle."

Struggle means that there is something that you must move against that is a natural impediment to prove yourself. You have to break through that impediment. What flows from that is a creation [one's self] that glorifies God.

Brother Jabril: Every one of us who really knows you, knows that you have had especially since the departure of the Honorable Elijah Muhammad, to deal with an unusual degree of adversity. Not just in the light of what you said, but in the light of all that you have learned from the Honorable Elijah Muhammad and from your life's experiences. Please explain, what has gotten you to this point, through the non-stop adversities in your life? How have you used adversity for your own growth and to advance the divine cause?

JABRIL MUHAMMAD
FEBRUARY 8, 2002

Farrakhan: The Traveler
For The Final Call
Vol. 21; No 28

Minister Farrakhan: One can never overcome the natural obstacles and impediments to ones growth without faith in God; that tells us that this that is in front of us is not an immovable object. So Jesus said "If you had faith the grain of a mustard seed, you could say to the mountain, be removed and it would be so. Or you could say to the sycamore tree, be uprooted and be planted in the depth of the sea.

Faith in God is the prerequisite to overcome adversity. With a Muslim, when we say, "Bismillah-Rahman-Rahim" it is a prayer seeking the help of Allah to help us in whatever we are engaged in.

Is there anything that we cannot do with the help of God and belief that you have His support? This is why the most Honorable Elijah Muhammad said to me, when David went after Goliath, he picked up five smooth stones from a brook, but he only used one. He said that that one was "Bismillah—In the name of Allah."

Every prophet of God, though one person, was able to do just magnificent things in the name and with the help of God. So all of us today are called to the apparent impossible—to raise a people from the dead; to overcome the adversity of a negative world; to plant and nurture the seed of a new world; and overcome all opposition to that truth until that truth is firmly established in the hearts and minds of the people. But it can only be done in the name and with the help of Almighty God Allah.

Brother Jabril: Brother Minister, from time to time, over the last near 25 years, we've discussed things that have come up in the Nation of Islam in America and events world-wide, that involve the reality of chaos. Adversity and chaos—of course these are relative terms because nothing is chaotic to the God. Nevertheless, there are times, as we move through our own lives, especially in this most critical of all times, so much seems absolutely upside down. Please explain the part that chaos has in the plan of God and how should we see it in our personal lives and utilized it.

Minister Farrakhan: It would seem to me that in order to understand what chaos really is and how it serves the purpose of God, in establishing order, one must go back to the origin of creation; to when the most Honorable Elijah Muhammad taught of God's Self-creation.

The first atom of life that sparkled in the universe contained positive and negative. Since the first atom that sparkled in the darkness, had positive and negative, then all of creation bears witness to that atom—that there is no positive without negative; there is no darkness where you cannot find light; there is no death where you can't find life. Death feeds life and life feeds death. They're companions of each other.

If light and darkness are companions and life and death are companions, then, in a certain sense, God and Satan are companions, good and evil are companions, chaos and order are companions, but one feeds the other and gives birth to the other.

So the scholars and scientists, who talk about the, "big bang" theory, talk about chaos as though it was first. Well, they don't really know the root of all of this. Out of what seemed to be chaos, came order. This produced motion.

The Honorable Elijah Muhammad, who taught us so much deeper than these scholars and scientists taught us that the first law is motion. How can you produce motion unless these opposites are present? With the positive and the negative charges, you produce motion. That motion may appear chaotic at first, but then the second law comes into existence, which is order.

Out of what seems to be only chaos comes order. Out of darkness came light. Out of nothingness came everything. Out of death comes life. So then, in another sense, out of evil comes good; out of demon, devil or Satan comes God. Well how is that?

Was God Satan at first and then becomes God? Not in that sense. But the Qur'an says that the jinn came before the man. In my humble opinion, it means that this fiery spirit and temperament is seen in the infancy of development, where one must learn to control the emotions in order for the rational mind of a man to come forth.

If you look at a baby, they want immediate gratification for the change of a diaper; for the bottle or for whatever they have a desire for. So they cry. If you don't attend to them right away, you will see in the baby their cry, demonstrating an emotion that makes their face to become red with the flame of anger. So in the development of the human being, we go through these stages.

Well, what about God? What about the making of a God? If we are created from God, then the adversity that He went through, to evolve into Himself, shows us the path of all things to come to that point or place in development that God intended.

So, what's called "chaos" serves order.

What we are experiencing now is the chaotic disorder of the breaking down of a world that will give birth to the order of a new world. So this chaos is absolutely and vitally necessary to create the motion toward order.

The evil that Allah has permitted to touch the earth, almost completely, has created such dissatisfaction with evil, that even the evildoer wants a way out of evil, because there is no peace in evil. There is no real productivity now in evil. There is diminishing return in the doing of evil. There is complete loss and frustration in the doing of evil.

The human being's nature is to be made secure. So now in this chaos, everybody is insecure. We're hungering for that security, which brings peace, for unrighteousness has had its sway.

Now the greatness of the evil, has determined the greatness of the good that has come out of the desire of the sufferer of evil and even the doer of evil, reaping the consequence of evil, to get out of that into peace and security.

Thus the evil, under the Satanic rule, demands the presence of God, to bring about order out of the chaos, as it is the presence of God in the world of evil that is producing the disorder and the chaos that is ending one world and bringing another.

The above explains why "we must through much tribulation enter into the kingdom of God." (Acts 14:22)

The worst kind of trouble arises from slander. Surah 114 urges us to seek refuge in Allah from the whispering of the slinking devil, who whispers, not into the ear, or the head, but into the very hearts of people. They do this so subtlety, that later the victims speak vicious slander about others with passion, from their very hearts, that of which they are either totally or partly ignorant (Also see Holy Qur'an 17:53; 88:8-11; 8: 13-17; 74: 74:42-47.)

Jabril Muhammad
February 10, 2002

Section 5

Farrakhan: The Traveler
For The Final Call
Vol. 21; No 29

The Honorable Minister Louis Farrakhan's answers, in these articles, are most critical to understanding the mind and acts of Allah and His Christ, especially now since we've entered *that* most dangerous of all hours, taught by the scriptures.

To misunderstand him is to misunderstand the current acts of God and His Christ, and in the immediate months to come, one may qualify for the worst possible of all human experiences.

The Holy Qur'an warns of a day when one will wish that he/she had responded better by this teaching. (See Surah 89 and pages 60, 61 and the top of 88 of *Is It Possible That The Honorable Elijah Muhammad Is Still Physically Alive???)* Such remembrance then will not help one out of the engulfing chastisement of Allah.

It will be inflicted by Him, Who, even though He created *everything* for His mercy, certain events (soon to come) will force *that* chastisement. But remember, that unlike lesser ones, God takes no pleasure in the death of the wicked.

Many will experience the most intense regret and the most agonizing grief imaginable. It's only a part of the consequences for the rejection of Minister Farrakhan and his Backers.

I've often said that you can tell time by watching Minister Farrakhan's mind. Many don't recognize Minister Farrakhan's divinity because they don't know God themselves nor the time. Therefore, many foolishly react to him as the scriptures teach;

whenever *motive* and *context* is omitted, mischief can always be made of another's words and acts.

So be it! Allah will annul their works! The FIRE awaits them for their evils said/done to him!

Brother Jabril: The next three questions are intimately interrelated.

It's recorded in the 9th chapter of Acts, that Jesus removed the scales from Paul's eyes. Then Jesus made it known that this man, Paul, is a chosen vessel of his, substantially to do two things. He is to bring a message to the Gentiles and their rulers and the kings and also to the children of Israel. How does this bear on your mission?

Minister Farrakhan: The scales are many. The first scale had to be the scale of hypocrisy, that the Minister had fallen asleep and went into darkness after having been exposed to the light.

The Qur'an says, "In the alternation of the day and the night there is a sign for those who would reflect." In another part it says, "The night is made for rest and sleep and the day to rise up again." Some scholars say, "Seeking the bounty of God."

In my losing sight of my father and Master Fard Muhammad, for a brief period of time, the scales that came over my eyes and my heart produced a period of darkness in my life, chaos and spiritual death, that later fed order, life and sight on my emergence from this condition.

When I read this wonderful book that you have written on the life of Jesus, which I read in three days, sometime between the first and second week in September of 1977, I experienced a resurrection. I experienced a new birth. When the understanding came to me, through the reading of certain passages, in that book, it energized me to then want to do the work of the Honorable Elijah Muhammad.

That was the first scale.

There were layers in the scales on Paul's eyes. The first scale was he had to see Jesus properly. Then he had to know that Jesus was in fact alive, so that he could declare that, "I know that my redeemer liveth and because he lives I too shall live and stand with him at the latter day."

In the removal of the second scale, a third scale would [also] be removed, which was to take Paul out of the limited vision of Peter and the disciples, who were more nationalistic in their focus on the Jews and not on the Gentiles.

Paul saw what Peter came to understand when he saw this cloth or sheet descend from heaven with all manner of meats on it. He said that he could not eat that which was unclean. Then he came to see that the vision was not talking about meat, but was talking about the different circumstances and condition of human beings beyond the children of Israel and that he could eat them. He could take the unclean and make them a part of the body of Christ.

Peter began his work with the Gentiles, but it was limited. But when Paul had the third scale removed from his eyes, then [came] the fulfillment of the Holy Qur'an, Surah 20, entitled *Ta Ha*, the prayer of Moses, that his breast would be expanded and that a knot would be removed in his tongue that they may understand his speech and that this helper would be made to bear his burden.

Paul then [in his] seeing the broad scope of the message of Jesus Christ, that Jesus was so important to all of humanity because he offered, in his person and in his wisdom a door to all of humanity, to access God's spirit; God's mind; God's wisdom, to become a little God; a reflection of the Almighty True and Living God—[another scale was removed.]

In Paul's having those scales removed from his mind and heart, he knew then that the mission of Jesus Christ, though starting narrowly, with a focus on the lost sheep of the house of Israel, now had to be taken to every nation, every kindred and every tongue, that every human being, demonic or otherwise, Jew or Gentile, Greek, male or female, would have access to God through this divine door that God had made for humanity in the person of Jesus Christ.

As these scales were removed from my mind, I came to see the Honorable Elijah Muhammad clearly again and believe in him clearly again and even see him beyond where I saw him before.

That happened when I read the manuscript of what you wrote.

The second scale and one of the most important of the scales, was to know that Elijah Muhammad was in fact alive. Without that knowledge I could not do what I am doing with the faith that I would be victorious and nothing of adversity would stop me from being successful in the mission of the Honorable Elijah Muhammad.

I had to have *that* scale removed.

My heart had to be expanded and God had to allow me to see how to loosen the knot in the language of the revelation of Master Fard Muhammad to the Honorable Elijah Muhammad that *that* word that *seemed* so nationalistic, in its first expression, could be made universal in this expression, that all of humanity could find refuge under the branches of this tree that started from the mustard seed of faith.

Now the Minister is at a point in his development, where he has the duty, before he can go, to receive what his father promised him. And by the way, a sister had an experience at Saviours' Day a few years ago, and she was here in Phoenix recently with her beloved mother, and she said, "Remember Brother that I was told to tell you, that everything that he promised you, he would fulfill."

Jabril Muhammad
February 10, 2002

Farrakhan: The Traveler
For The Final Call
Vol. 21; No 30

Minister Farrakhan: Here I am at the dawn of a universal assignment now that the scales are being removed from my eyes on a fourth level.

Not only do I see the universality of the message of the Honorable Elijah Muhammad, but in my growing understanding of the reason for evil, the reason for Satan, the reason for negativity, I can now with understanding approach the evil doer and say to them, "Well done. You have done what your father made you to do."

I can say in the language of Jesus, "You are of your father, the devil, the lust of your father you have done. He was a liar and a murderer. But Allah permitted that to serve the purpose of the birth of the Kingdom of God."

Now that you have served that purpose, I want to introduce you to a new Father; a loving Father—a Father of Whom the scripture says, "So loved the world that he would give his only begotten son" into this negative environment, "that whosoever believes in him should not perish", but be a part of a Kingdom that has no end.

To me, now, with this fourth scale being removed, do I see evil serving the purpose of good? I see Satan serving the purpose of God. I see hell and death serving the purpose of life and heaven. Therefore, I can now, not only invite the so-called righteous through that door, but I can call to the way of the Lord with goodly exhortation, in the best manner, in good voice and with justice, but with justice overpowered by the mercy of a loving Father, Who does not want to destroy humanity, but desires to save all who would hear and believe.

Brother Jabril: Such wisdom may help one look deeper in how weak believers, and even hypocrites serve strong believers, who may, in turn, be able to help them into belief and maybe even strong belief, before its too late.

Before going into the second part, of this question, please briefly comment on these words of Jesus: "I have other sheep not of this fold." Jesus didn't really teach beyond those people whom the scholars call Jews. That was for Paul to do. Jesus knew this before he departed.

Minister Farrakhan: Jesus was giving Paul a base in his teaching to argue with those recalcitrant Jews who wanted Jesus and the message of the kingdom to be confined to them. They wanted exclusivity of Jesus and the kingdom. Therefore, Paul had to fight against this spirit of recalcitrance, exclusivity and vanity in the people of the first phase of the mission of Jesus Christ. Therefore, Jesus had to leave for Peter/Paul words that they could use as a foundation for going after those sheep that were not of that original fold.

Minister Farrakhan delivered a speech in Phoenix, Arizona on September 21, 1986, about a year after he received *direct* communications from the Honorable Elijah Muhammad. Out of it came his Study Guides, about which he wrote that Allah ordered them through him, and that they were the launching pad of a world wide movement.

In the 1960s, the Honorable Elijah Muhammad told Minister Farrakhan that Allah had made friends for him all around the earth and at a certain time he would meet them. He was preparing Minister Farrakhan for his future world wide mission.

Were it not for the love of Allah, which as the scriptures says, "passes understanding," for millions of us, *beyond* 144,000, Minister Farrakhan would not have been produced. The *end* would have come in the mid 1960's. Many would not have been born, including those who are ungrateful for Minister Farrakhan. Problem Book No. 32 contains some of the proofs of what I just wrote.

. It's written that this number, which I heard the Honorable Elijah Muhammad say was "about 144,000" would be grateful to Allah and would make the effort to be qualified for the world wide mission written of them, to, as he once put it, "square the nations into righteousness."

All of us, as a people, were chosen for the greatest of divine purposes, but only a few choose Him Who chose us. Minister Farrakhan was divinely chosen to lead the way in this world wide assignment, with the backing of God and the Christ.

Jealousy and envy, is a great part of the "poison and rust" (see Problem number 32) which prevents many from seeing the fulfillment of significant prophecies by Minister Farrakhan right in our faces. Surah 39 of the Holy Qur'an states that Allah hates ingratitude in us.

"Negative" emotions unbalance the mind. Ingratitude does that. Ingratitude towards Allah's favors qualifies one for His chastisement—the deepest part of purgatory designed to remove the worst forms of "poison and rust."

Many of those ungrateful for divine favors are Minister Farrakhan's envious persecutors. These deceive the shallow minded to speak and write against him.

Envious people hate you for what you've worked for and earned. They hate you for that which you have, which they can't use or handle if they had it!

Those envious of Minister Farrakhan are becoming insane. Notice the progression of their evil talk of him. Eventually their words mark them as those of whom it's written of in such places as Jude 9 and 13.

Negative jealousy can be as deadly as envy. However, there is such a thing as positive jealousy, which is a sign of immaturity. But there is no such thing as positive envy. It has no redeeming features at all!

Now, we return to Minister Farrakhan's insightful words of February 8, 2002.

Brother Jabril: How was your breast expanded? I'm thinking specifically of Moses prayer, in Surah 20, which was fulfilled in Aaron, which was a sign of the Honorable Elijah Muhammad's prayer for you.

Minister Farrakhan: Let me say from the outset that my beloved mother, a beautiful Black woman, nurtured me on the love of our people and compassion for the suffering of our people. In the last month of my fifth year on this earth, she put a violin in my hand that she wanted me to learn to play and master.

I did not like the violin because to me, as a youngster, it had negative baggage in that Black children would look at you as a sissy if you played the violin and performed classical music.

As a youngster I was also very interested in boxing. My hero was Joe Louis because he gave so much to us at a time when we needed to feel better about ourselves.

Muhammad Ali was the super major of what Joe Louis did for us as a people. I shall always be grateful to God for Joe Louis and for Muhammad Ali. I pray that God will bless Ali and give him all the good of this life and grant him a life in the Hereafter, for what he has done for the universal scope of the teaching of his mentor, whom he did not fully understand, but his heart was big enough to love humanity and to feel the pain of human suffering.

Jabril Muhammad
February 8, 2002

Farrakhan: The Traveler
For The Final Call
Vol. 21; No 31

This continues the February 8, 2002 interview of the Honorable Minister Louis Farrakhan.

Minister Farrakhan: This violin and classical music caused me, at a young age, though fully conscious of my Blackness and hurting from the suffering of our people, to have a heart that also ached, but in a minor sense, for the suffering of humanity.

Black people had my greater focus. If you could see pictures of me in my youth, my face had a beauty that was almost feminine, because my heart was tender and full of love for humanity.

But I also liked to box, and would beat my friends through boxing, not fighting, so that they wouldn't think of me as a sissy for playing the violin. I made sure that all my friends knew that I could thump so they never looked at me as sissified because I played the violin.

When I was going to music school I would find a way to get there without notice, because I didn't want the stigma of playing the violin. At a certain point I use to carry my violin case, in the same manner that one would carry a saxophone. I would put a bee-bop tam on my head to let the community know I'm down. So don't vamp on me and "dis" me because of this violin.

When I became proficient at playing it, my friends and those who would criticize me, loved my playing it so well until many of them, outside of my immediate circle of friends, wanted to know how long it took me to play like that. When I would mention the years; that finished them. They didn't want to bother because they wanted to be able to play like that in one or two easy lessons. But that just isn't the case with the violin.

When I became a Muslim follower of the Honorable Elijah Muhammad my whole faith changed. My focus narrowed, totally and specifically on the Black man because that was the first phase of the mission of our father, the Honorable Elijah Muhammad.

One day the Imam, in 1958, visited my home in Boston and we were looking at old pictures of the Minister. He looked at one of my show business pictures and he said, "This man is alive. But this man is dead." I didn't quite understand what the Imam saw at that time. It hurt me. The Honorable Elijah Muhammad raised me from the dead. How could the man in this picture be dead and the man in the show business picture be alive?

It took years for me to understand that deep insight of Imam Warith Deen Muhammad, because the man in the picture of show business was free in his heart to love all of humanity. The man in the picture was focused and narrow and therefore that aspect of him died.

In 1974, the Honorable Elijah Muhammad had me to bring my violin out to play for him. After we had dinner, the table was full, I got my violin out and stayed by his side and played. He looked up at me and said at the end, "You really can play that thing." I smiled and thanked him and put my violin away.

Then sometime later in '74, he called me on the telephone and said, "Could you come out on Tuesday and bring your violin? There will be nobody for dinner, but Sister Tynnetta and her children and yourself."

After dinner, the living room chairs were all turned and Mother Tynnetta's children put on a show. Rasul got to the piano and he had a wig on and they just had a little fun, you know. The Honorable Elijah Muhammad just laughed and laughed.

Then I got up to play. After I finished playing he said, "Didn't you play that for me the last time you were here?" I said, "Yes Sir, dear Apostle." With a frown he said, "Well don't you know any thing new?" How could I know anything new? I hadn't been practicing. He was planting the seed then to raise me to a level, again, where my heart and my breast would be expanded through the playing of the violin that would now prepare me for the universality of the mission to take the message to the Gentles; to the kings; to the rulers; to the entire family of our planet.

For those who criticized me for even playing an instrument that is considered European, and criticized me because culturally they think I am extolling the value of European culture and as a Black man this is something that I should not do. I will say to my critics that I understand exactly what you are saying. I sympathize with your point of view. I will not be displeased or angry with you for your harsh criticism of me.

But you do not know *how* this instrument has prepared my heart to do a work for you and for others, that would lift you into the position that God created you for, and the rest of humanity for, who have oppressed us and inflicted pain on us, but who will, when you develop, not only tip their hats at you, but they will circumambulate around you, as all the races walk around the Kabah and fight to kiss the Black stone.

In an upcoming article we get into this "how."

I want to remind you that all the instruments that we play today are fashioned from the Europeans. But they are not the origin of these instruments. The Honorable Elijah Muhammad said a new God is forced to use the wisdom of His own Self to establish Himself as the God of His particular period of time. This world was to be ruled by white people for a certain period of time. But everything that they have developed, they developed it off an original creation that started with us.

We originated string instruments. We originated wood-wind instruments. We originated the use of the horn of a ram to make sounds to call people to worship. So out of that, the Europeans crafted a violin and put the stamp of their genius on what originally came from our fathers.

Before the white people ever developed strings, the Chinese had strings; the Indians from the subcontinent of India had strings. I recently saw a Chinese woman, with one string, make music that was so fantastic, that those who had the violin with four strings stood up and cheered. So the string instrument belongs to us and we should not feel threatened over this new evolution of instruments.

We are to master it and then create even new instruments to

make new and glorious sounds, even as we saw in Trinidad, where the Trinidadians took oil drums and heated them and created sound that we call the steel drum or the steel pan. Today they have symphonic orchestras playing the steel pan. This originated from the creativity forced by the adversity underwent by Black people.

This is only the beginning of new world instruments that will come from the unleashed creative genius of our people, when their spirit is no longer bound by falsehoods. You must be free to look at God's wisdom manifested in everything and respect it, use it and grow from it.

Jabril Muhammad
February 8, 2002

Farrakhan: The Traveler
For The Final Call
Vol. 21; No 32

What comes below ends the February 8, 2002 interview with the Honorable Minister Louis Farrakhan.

Brother Jabril: In the course of an interview of you, in 1994, which was on the morning of that year's Easter Sunday, you interrupted yourself and stated that you were experiencing a deeper realization of the relationship between the evolution of the Honorable Elijah Muhammad to your own; that what he was experiencing, where he is was making you a more effective instrument through which you could grow the clergy who were crying out for expansion.

We discussed the fact that the first phase of the mission of the Honorable Elijah Muhammad wasn't actually fulfilled by him before he went on to the next phase of his mission. You are completing that first phase of his mission, as you are on the way toward the second phase of your mission, which he has for you, while he is already in the second phase of his assignment.

This aspect of your mission included the loosening of "the knot" in the divine language and the growth that had to take place in you, to be able to loosen the knot in the teaching. This involved your realization of his higher self, which enables you to enter into the realization of your own higher self. These truths have the greatest implications for the growth of each of us here and throughout the earth. Please comment.

Minister Farrakhan: The thought that comes to mind is the words of Jesus, "It is expedient for you (or necessary for your development) that I go away. For if I go not away the comforter cannot come unto you. But if I go away I shall send him unto you, in my name and he will testify of me." In another scripture he says, "I go to prepare a place for you that where I am you may be also."

What this means to me is that we could not grow to the point or place that God intended for us as long as he was among us. Like children, we were so dependent on him that even the thought of his leaving us put us in a state of mental disrepair. But he knew that it was as necessary for him to go as it is for sun, light and water and earth to facilitate life. If he did not go to the place and position that God intended for him, then he could not affect that growth from where he is in us.

So he says, "I go to prepare a place for you that where I am, the plane on which I exist, you too can exist. But I'm going to send the holy ghost or the comforter unto you."

What is this holy ghost? He used the pronoun "he" not the pronoun "it." So it must have a bearing on a human being. "Ghost" means, in the darkness of the period of his absence and in the darkness, gross darkness of our misunderstanding of his "death" and the fall of what we all work so hard to build that produce a darkness, a most uncomfortable state of mind because we need answers, which would come through a person.

When the Honorable Elijah Muhammad said to his followers in the *Theology of Time* series, "Whenever you see him look at him." Because he wants the people to look upon a human being that is being worked on. "Whenever he speaks listen to him. For his teaching is a bearing of witness of me. He is one of the finest preachers within the bounds of North America. So continue to hear my Minister Farrakhan."

As I plum his words, with no vanity or egotism involved, to me, that "God has made me to take his place among the people" and "I am making you to take mine and I want your mind. I want you to line your mind up with my mind that there be one mind."

Then he was telling the people, just as Master Fard Muhammad, on His departure, told his followers, "to hear Karriem," he knew that he would be teaching them a greater elucidation, elaboration, and unfolding of what Master Fard Muhammad taught, which involved the identity of Master Fard Muhammad. That was the core that we had to get to see in order to appreciate the value of what we had.

Now he's leaving to go to his Teacher. And he tells his followers "Hear Farrakhan. Continue to hear my...." Possessive pronoun; he's mine. I have him. He is under my control. I'm still in the process of making him. He will come to you in the darkness, the gross darkness of your falling away, your misunderstanding and he will comfort you through the knowledge that he will impart to you of me and where I am and what has happen and is happening to me. I'm going to make him among you a sign of my exaltation in heaven with my Teacher, Master Fard Muhammad.

His going away was vitally necessary for me to recognize him in me; for me to recognize his being alive. Then from that removal of that scale, I could begin to be a comforter to the people and testify to the people of his exalted state.

Brother Jabril: This should greatly assist all those Brothers and Sisters, as we dealt with the *Closing The Gap Part One* material, who are stuck in a time warp.

A Sister, who wrote me about this series, which ends with this article, referred to them not so much as "interviews," but "innerviews" into the mind and heart of Minister Farrakhan. She nailed it! That was one of my major aims with this series.

Minister Farrakhan did not know what the questions were before he heard them. So, of course, his answers were unrehearsed. Look at the depth of the wisdom each answer contains. His answers are mini books!

Do you really know anyone else who could have given such spontaneous answers to these questions, the content he did not know before he heard them? (And wait until you read his answers to the other questions, in interviews that will appear, be it the will of Allah. Whew!)

Where do events originate? All events, originate in the hearts of human beings, without exception. To understand any event, in the best sense of that word, we must get as deep as we can into the heart of the one or ones, who spoke the word or performed the act, which constituted what we call an "event."

Seldom, if ever, do we read of the roots of the events, which is the heart(s) of the newsmaker(s). In the series of articles, which ends with this one, we have been provided with the opportunity of looking deep into the mind and heart of Minister Farrakhan, who is the most extraordinary "newsmaker" on earth.

What is the definition of "news?" How much of it is true? How much of it is "good." How much of it is the "gospel?" What is the relation between what is generally called "news" and the "gospel?"

JABRIL MUHAMMAD
FEBRUARY 8, 2002

FARRAKHAN: THE TRAVELER
FOR THE FINAL CALL
VOL. 21; NO. 33

One day, in May 1961, here in Phoenix, Arizona, the Honorable Elijah Muhammad told Minister Abdul Allah and I what would make *Muhammad Speaks* a great newspaper. He said these essentials were his articles of truth; witnesses to the truth he was teaching; the way we would report the news, both nationally and internationally; the way we would report the activities and progress of his followers around the country and elsewhere. Of course the content was also an essential.

The Honorable Elijah Muhammad wanted each page in *Muhammad Speaks* to impact the reader in such a way that would lead, directly or indirectly, by big or small steps towards an improved understanding of higher realities and the salvation of all.

Now, we have *The Final Call*, which was the title of the first newspaper the Honorable Elijah Muhammad published in the early 1930s. Its publisher, of course, is the Honorable Minister Louis Farrakhan.

It ought to be obvious to all that it's 100% appropriate that the articles of Minister Farrakhan appear in the centerfold of *The Final Call*, with the articles of the Honorable Elijah Muhammad appearing where it does, as the base and support of the Minister's teachings and work.

Both newspapers were/are the best newspapers on earth, in my view. The basis of my view is the fact that the core of both newspapers was/is the fact that each contains the "gospel." The "gospel" was and is being *published* by means of each newspaper and was/is contained *in* the articles by the Honorable Elijah Muhammad and Minister Farrakhan.

If you will use a Bible concordance and look up the word "publish" and closely related words, you'll find that prophets of Allah "published" the word He revealed to them, as a means of getting His truth to the people.

Each Believer is obligated to bear witness to the "gospel" in whatever way each one can and that witness must be appropriate. Furthermore, it's in the nature of a Believer in God's truths that they work hard to help the one who bears the weight of getting His truth to the people. That is the way it was with the Believers in the truth God revealed to His prophets. That is the way it is today with the Believers in the two men, the Moses and the Aaron of these times.

Prior to 1975 each one, who followed the Honorable Elijah Muhammad bore witness in various ways. Some did this of good and others did that of good to help. Chief among those who did good and bore witness, in a magnificent manner, to the rightness of the character and the truthfulness of the Honorable Elijah Muhammad was Minister Farrakhan.

Several years ago, prior to the fall of the Nation of Islam, Minister Farrakhan shared with me something the Honorable Elijah Muhammad told him that came up in the course of our February the 8th interview, which is relevant to the aim of this article.

Minister Farrakhan referred to the years when the Honorable Elijah Muhammad was working heavily with the business aspects of the building of the Nation. This included his buying farmland; setting up factories; and doing all of the things that would form the material aspects of the Nation, which naturally resulted from his spiritual teachings.

One day his teacher said to him, "Brother, when you're doing this kind of work, it takes away your spirit." He continued, "When I listen to your tapes, your tapes give me spirit. And that's why I have you teaching in the public, for as you give me spirit,

you give them the same."

Let's be very careful how we understand these words of the Honorable Elijah Muhammad to his prize student, Minister Farrakhan.

Let's look into what produces the spirit of our minds, whether its what we call "negative" or "positive." What produces the spirit of which the Honorable Elijah Muhammad spoke, which was/is definitely the spirit of Allah, which is always "positive?" Let's look into the Minister's study guides where he took up this subject of the production of "spirit."

All through out Minister Farrakhan's study guides he works

to guide us in our studies, to learn to think like God Himself, regardless to what confronts us; regardless to what the problem is, in our lives, that we are trying to solve.

In the interview of Minister Farrakhan that appears at the end of the 3rd Edition of *This Is The One* he stated: "I would conclude by saying this, that I heard the Honorable Elijah Muhammad say once, that two-thirds of the Qur'an were for him and one third was for some other man, and I would let that other man worry about his part. Well, he said the book that the Saviour gave him was the Qur'an, but two thirds of it which deals with faith would be established before he departed. But the other third would be established under his guidance from another place, in which he would be.

He said that he was like a guided missile that God was off in a secret place guiding him. He's a guided man. Well now, he has grown up into that kind of power where he can be where he is and guide his man in the fulfillment of his third. So this helper doesn't really have to worry about his part. All he needs to do is to reach up into his brain for the guidance that the Honorable Elijah Muhammad will continue to give him."

Now let's look at this principle, which Minister Farrakhan has been teaching especially since 1977, from another perspective. In *Farrakhan: The Traveler*, Vol. 16, No. 50 we read: "... whenever we are done an injustice and all appeals fail, and we finally take our case to Allah and seemingly receive no answer, what is going on? Whenever we pray to Allah for something with all of our hearts and have done all that we know to do to receive it and do not yet have what we earnestly seek, what is the purpose?

Do these problems have any relation to the concept of the "expanded breast" as mentioned by Minister Farrakhan...? Do the answers have anything to do with the concept of "heart?"

Let us go to the first chapter of 1st Samuel, which tells us that, "There was a certain man from Ramathaim, a Zuphite from the hill country of Ephraim, whose name was Elkanah son of Jeroham, the son of Elihu, the son of Tohu, the son of Zuph, an Ephraimite. He had two wives; one was called Hannah and the other Peninnah. Peninnah had children, but Hannah had none.

We read that Hannah was unable to bear children because "... the LORD had closed her womb."

Now, so we read, "because the LORD had closed her womb, the other wife, "kept provoking her in order to irritate her." And, "This went on year after year. Whenever Hannah went up to the house of the LORD, her rival provoked her till she wept and would not eat."

JABRIL MUHAMMAD
MAY 8, 2002

FARRAKHAN: THE TRAVELER
FOR THE FINAL CALL
VOL. 21; NO. 38

Although, I'm no expert on the history of sports, I don't recall a weekend so filled with major sporting events such as this one (June 7th through the 9th). As I write this article, upcoming is the Lewis-Tyson heavyweight championship fight; the finals of the National Basketball Association and the finals of the National Hockey League; a chance for a horse to become the first triple crown winner in 24 years; a tennis Grand Slam; and of course the World Cup games.

I read in one newspaper that about 600 reporters from all over the earth are to attend the Lewis-Tyson fight.

The most basic purpose in these sporting events is not so much to be competitive. That's almost never the real purpose in such events. It's to beat, defeat, win against, even to crush, blast, devastate, pound or smash the opponent, the adversary, or the other. It's about gaining or winning at the expense of the other. The winners will be glad. The losers will be sad.

This is not to say that there is no value in sports. But, how do these sporting events fit into the purpose of man's creation and the events constantly taking place throughout the vastness of the universe? Many would say who cares?

We all should care, for we now live in the time of the ultimate contest. It's called Armageddon. The winner rules throughout all of eternity. The loser will ultimately be extinguished. And right now, most of us are on the losing side.

The Holy Qur'an emphasizes that Allah created the heavens and the earth for a serious purpose, not for sport and play. What is that purpose? How does the answer relate to the place of the human being in the universe?

The Honorable Elijah Muhammad answered these and other such questions. However, the majority rejected his teachings. Now, by the power of Allah, these answers are being given again by the Honorable Minister Louis Farrakhan.

Minister Farrakhan's spiritual teachings, under the ongoing guidance and backing of Allah and The Messiah, continues to build on the base left by his teacher, for the understanding of how the physical universe works; for as his teacher taught, everything outside of us came from within us, including, of course, the forces which governs that which is outside of ourselves.

The smallest known objects known to the scientists of this world in the universe are called protons, neutrons, and electrons and there are others even smaller. Then there are the forces that hold them together or make them come apart. These scientists teach that there are four forces that "contain" all of the other forces, without which nothing happens. The understanding of these forces accounts for or "explains" the actions of everything.

These particles and these forces are inseparable and make up these tiny particles that make up this newspaper, as well as yourself, all of the people who have ever lived, who are alive now, or ever will live; all of the plant, insect, and animal life; all of the rocks and, in short, everything that makes up the earth, other planets, everything in the solar system and everything beyond it, the stars, etc.

The scientists teach that four forces govern everything and are called: 1) gravity; 2) the strong force; 3) the electromagnetic force and 4) the weak force. It is not a waste of time to look into this. For example, the strong force holds the nucleus of every atom together. The scientist states that it's the strongest force in the universe. Is it?

The scientists have and are now striving to get to the ultimate source of these forces. Many of them believe that if they go to this source, they would be in the position to understand and therefore, control and rule the universe.

The Honorable Elijah Muhammad and now, Minister Farrakhan have humbly, but with total conviction, presented the truth of this ultimate source, which is what the scientists of this world seek to understand. Everyone will come to see that this is true.

The Author of the Holy Qur'an clearly states that it contains the explanation of all things. Millions and even billions of people have studied that beautiful book. But how many have the explanation of all things from studying it?

Nevertheless, I quoted the Honorable Elijah Muhammad words to me for *This Is The One*, page 127, wherein he stated: "The Holy Qur'an is filled with roots of our testimony." He proved it.

Hopefully, we'll see in Minister Farrakhan's wisdom that which can enable us to do better than we have by Allah's truths.

College catalogues provide very brief sketches of the courses that these schools offer. They also contain the name of the instructor and the times when the classes are to be attended. With this in mind, consider these words of Minister Farrakhan's teacher.

"Master Fard Muhammad aims to raise the Lost-Found (so-called Negro) into the knowledge and wisdom, the very ideas, of the Gods of the past."

(We've been introduced to and are being raised by the intelligent use of His wisdom, by His guidance of the two men, through whom His wisdom has and is being taught—the Honorable Elijah Muhammad and Minister Farrakhan.)

"He also aims presently, to raise His people into His own ideas, in Himself, that the scriptures may be fulfilled: that those to whom He reveals Himself become the sons (and the daughters) of God... sons and daughters in the wisdom of God."

(As was his teacher before him, Minister Farrakhan was introduced to this; and so are those *who follow* Minister Farrakhan.)

"He aims not only to reveal His ideas for the present creation of the universe, but also to give to man the nature and the creative wisdom to produce creative ideas as The Father of Civilization."

This is what was prophesied: that God would make man like Himself. He aims to make The Nation of Righteousness, who will rule in the Hereafter, with the potential knowledge of producing and bringing into action or existence that which He has been able to produce. We call this "ideas." He aims to make each one into a God.

This wisdom is soon to come, although the Honorable Elijah Muhammad once told me that in this present teaching one could all but become a god/goddess. In fact, his exact words to me were, "In fact about it Brother, you can all but become a god yourself in this teaching." Of course, he was speaking of those who would seriously study and practice his teachings, under divine guidance.

Hopefully, it will become clearer, as we study Minister Farrakhan's upcoming words, the deeper reasons *why* he works so hard to clear us from toxic, poisonous, disease producing thinking and emotions. He does this 24/7 that we may graduate from the kindergarten of Allah's wisdom and get into the next stage, if we are to fulfill our destiny.

Furthermore, I believe we'll better appreciate the above quoted words, of the Honorable Elijah Muhammad, which appears on page 128 of *This Is The One, Third Edition*, *after* we conclude the May 1st interview of Minister Farrakhan, which begins next article, Allah willing.

Jabril Muhammad
June 7, 2002

Farrakhan: The Traveler
For The Final Call
Vol. 21; No. 39

Brother Jabril: Brother Minister, as you know, the scriptures teach that the evil move that was made against Joseph, by his brothers, was out of envy. Jesus, of course, suffered envy. A great deal of what happens today, in America and elsewhere, is motivated by jealousy and envy. What gives rise to jealousy and especially envy?

Minister Farrakhan: All of us, as human beings are creatures of desire. God, in order to move us toward any goal, first, must create in us a desire.

Every human being who is blessed with a bit of the divine, it creates within us desire for greatness; desire for recognition; desire to be known; desire to leave behind us a great witness of our presence.

All of these desires are found in God. He was not known. He desired to make Himself known. He wanted those who sought Him to come closer in finding Him. It was not out of a spirit of vanity, but it was out the timeliness of man's knowledge that man could grow closer, and to move faster, toward the goal of perfection.

Having said that, each of us has to cope with our desires and the possible disappointment and frustration of our desires. Sometimes we may desire more than what we're capable of achieving. Sometime we, in recognition of our own greatness, think more of ourselves than we should. So these emotions that accompany desire, its fulfillment or frustration, leads to other dangerous emotions.

If I desire something, but someone else has what it is that I desire, then this persons' having it and my not having it, but desiring it, becomes a test for me. I can reason with myself and say, "Oh Allah, maybe this was not for me. But I thank you for giving it to A, B or C. At least someone has what I had desired. Let me help them to accomplish the desire." That then, disallows envy, jealousy or enmity. Then it allows the person who has the desire, but someone is fulfilling desire, to grow even greater in the manifestation of his own gifts, but in service to the one whom God has chosen to fulfill such a desire.

It is when we cannot cope with someone else having what we desire and therefore, feeling a frustration and disappointment and not being able to handle that, then the ugly disposition of envy manifests.

At first it's passive, "I just dislike this person." But as God raises that person more and more into that which I desired for myself, which I feel that person is really unworthy of, then the envy turns to hatred. The hatred then becomes active. Then my mind, as it was with Cane, turns toward murder.

Understanding what God has for us and praying the prayer that the Honorable Elijah Muhammad asked us to say seven times a day, becomes so important in fulfilling the answer to this question.

"O Allah, I seek Thy refuge from anxiety and grief." Because when someone has what you desire and you're not handling it properly, then when you see that person there's anxiety. Then, it is accompanied by grief because he has what you think belongs to yourself. "O Allah, I seek your refuge from anxiety and grief, from the lack of strength and laziness."

You know, it takes great strength, inner-strength to recognize one's own limitations and to rejoice in what God has given to me, and to rejoice in what God has given to my Brother or Sister. The same God that gave to me gave to them. If I can rejoice in what God has given me, then I can rejoice in what God has given to others. So my thanks and gratitude for His gift to me makes me grateful for the gifts that He gives to others. That sense of gratitude, which takes inner strength to realize, undermines the wicked emotion of envy.

"O Allah I seek your refuge from cowardice and niggardliness." It is an act of cowardice that disallows us to face the reality of our own incapacities; inabilities; shortcomings. "I don't want to face myself." So in not facing myself I can never summon the strength to deal with myself. Therefore, that increases my hatred for the other person who has what I desire.

"Niggardliness" gives you an uncharitable spirit. "I cannot help you with your gift that may be good for all of us. I'm niggardly. I not only won't help you but I'll work to hinder you in what it is that God has gifted you with an assignment to do."

"O Allah, I seek your refuge from being overpowered by debt and the oppression of men." We are all debtors. But when you know that your debt is to God, that debt cannot over power you if you are working in His cause as a re-payment for your debt. But you can get over-powered by debt if you're not doing what it is that you owe God. That, of course, puts you in a position to be oppressed, either in the way you think or in reality.

Lastly, "Suffice thou me with what is lawful." I only want what is lawful to me. "Suffice Thou me with what is lawful and keep me away from what is prohibited. And with thy grace make me free from want, or desire, of that which is beside God."

If I can keep my desires in harmony with what God wants and if God did not want this for me, then there is something that God wants for me. So let me keep my desire in that framework and I will never be envious of my Brother or Sister.

In answering that question, there are sometimes things that may look like envy, but it is [really] a great misunderstanding. The person that is evilly motivated and hateful, because of envy, that's one thing. But when a person misunderstands the motivation of what his Brother says or does, and attacks his Brother out of that misunderstanding, this doesn't necessarily have to be envy.

It could be the impact of an action, or the lack thereof, and it effects the heart and mind of one whose desire is now frustrated by what you've said or did not say; what you've done or did not do, which brings up anger out of the frustration. That anger is then what causes a person to act out of uncontrolled anger because of disappointment and frustration of desire.

So these are twins too—envy the worse of all. A misunderstanding can be cleared. When one misunderstands, then that one can repent of what he did in anger, due to misunderstanding. But once we have entered that field of envy, then hatred, then murder—it will take the intervention of God to change our heart. Sometimes He does. Sometimes He uses your envy as a means of manifesting even more greatness of the one whom you envy.

Brother Jabril: As, in the case with Joseph and his Brothers.

Minister Farrakhan: Yes.

Jabril Muhammad
June 4, 2002

Farrakhan: The Traveler
For The Final Call
Vol. 21; No. 40

Brother Jabril: Brother Minister, you have just summed up, Allah willing, how to uproot envy and jealousy. What are the roots of gratitude and of ingratitude?

Minister Farrakhan: I would say that the root of gratitude is the humbleness of heart; to be able to appreciate every little thing that is done to advance you in your growth and development or move you toward your goal or suffice for you a need.

The root of ingratitude, it would seem to me, is an arrogance that makes you think you deserved what you got. So you never quite see things as you should. So you act by what you've received, to advance you toward your goal, as if you only got what you deserve. So the opposite of humility is what produces ingratitude.

We come into this world naked, as the Bible teaches, meaning we have nothing. But out of this world everything that we desire can come to us either through God's intervention, directly or indirectly, but it always comes by the hand of another human being.

When one goes through life humble enough to be grateful for *everything* that God gives us, when you begin to feel down, if you start counting your blessings, you begin to see you've been blessed with so much abundance that this little disappointment, or unfulfilled desire, should never alter your attitude of gratefulness.

Brother Jabril: How is gratitude related to love?

Minister Farrakhan: I would say the first commandment that Jesus gave, and the greatest of all, "to love God with all your heart, soul, mind and strength" is the beginning of recognition of all the *wonderful* things He has done, and continues to do, to enhance our lives.

When I love God purely, I'm grateful. When I rise up in the morning to see by His grace another day, I'm grateful. To look at His sun, I'm grateful. I'm grateful for the water that I use to refresh myself after a night of sleep. I'm grateful for the advancement in science that allows me these different tools that I use to make myself presentable. I'm grateful for every insect, creature and flower and fruit and tree. I'm grateful to be able to witness and marvel over His creation.

Gratefulness is love of God. So, when a teacher comes to give me what I didn't have, or share with me knowledge, that I didn't have—that's from God. So it is the love of God and the purity of heart that allows me to see Him everywhere I look and to be grateful for even a smile or a kind word.

Brother Jabril: Allah used Joseph in the redemption of his brothers. What were the roots of this redemptive effort, which included freeing them from envy?

Minister Louis Farrakhan: Sometimes you envy a person, as I said earlier, because they have what you desire and you feel more worthy of this than this person. This was the case with Joseph's brethren. From Joseph's heart came great good to his Brothers that deeply affected them and ultimately caused a change in their hearts.

Only Allah can intervene and bring about a tremendous good from the heart of one who is envied that has a supreme benefit to the envier. God has to allow the envier to see the purity of the heart of the one from which this great good comes, that's so beneficial to the envier.

In some cases good increases the hatred of the envier. In this case the great good from Joseph's heart touched the divine in them. The divine in them was touched and watered by the good from Joseph's heart. So it undermined and uprooted the envy in them, which changed the hearts of his Brethren. That change was manifested in their bowing to their Brother, which is something he did not desire, but it was what God had promised.

Now I say that to say this: My love for our father, the Honorable Elijah Muhammad, naturally extends to his wife, Mother Clara, his wives and all his children. My love for him has caused me to continue to do good for them. At some point in time the great benefit of good for them, from one who was envied by some of them, undermines the envy and causes them to see God using their Brother to benefit them. Out of their love for God their hearts are changed.

Those of us, who suffer from the envy of the envier, must realize that if we allow hatred and bitterness to set up in us, we cannot do the good that ultimately overcomes this evil. Even those who don't understand me and why I do what I do, they may become blind even to a change of heart that may be manifested in those that once envied. They keep seeing the person as what they were, rather than recognizing them for what they are and are becoming, by the good of the heart that God is using for their redemption.

This is the position that we're in today. I heard the Honorable Elijah Muhammad say that all of us would leave him. One of his ministers said, "All of us dear Apostle?" And he said, "Well, the few that are left that would be with me would be so weak that it would look as though all have left me." Then after what seemed to be eternity, he said, "But you all will return."

I was too dumb ask him, by what means, by what method shall we who leave you return. Never knowing that it was in my person that God and He would use my heart and my love for Him, and my love for them, to take abuse and never respond in kind, but continue to do good. As a result, He would turn the hearts of the children back toward their father and the fathers heart would turn back toward the children, and the curse that was on us by our division would be lifted.

Brother Jabril: Are you saying that love is *that* instrument by which this tremendous evil, called envy is to be uprooted under those circumstances that Allah brings about?

Minister Farrakhan: There's a saying, "That love conquers all." I don't know where that came from. But it was the ability of

Joseph to love; the ability of Jesus to love; the ability of Muhammad to love; that ultimately overcame much, not all, of the envy of the envier.

Jesus, in the scriptures, and his awesome willingness love to suffer to redeem others becomes ultimately able to uproot envy and produce in the human being the kingdom of God. When he said that the Kingdom is within you, but it's buried under all of these negative emotions; with envy the worse of all.

But his love was so strong and the benefit from his love was so great that they have a song that they sing about him "He looked beyond my faults and saw my need." In sufficing that need and over looking the fault, the great benefit that came from the sufficing of the need, under cut the heart of envy and turned it into that which would bring about the Kingdom of God.

JABRIL MUHAMMAD
JUNE 8, 2002

FARRAKHAN: THE TRAVELER
FOR *THE FINAL CALL*
VOL. 21 NO. 41

> *"Go your way, Daniel, for these words are concealed and sealed up until the end time. Many will be purged, purified and refined...none of the wicked will understand, those who have insight will understand."*
>
> *— Daniel 12:9, 10*

> *"Seal up what the seven thunders have said; do not write it down."*
>
> *— Revelation 10:4*

As we study the magnificent words, of the May 1st interview of the Honorable Minister Louis Farrakhan, let's not forget for one second the context of the time in which we live when he is fulfilling his awesome mission.

Today, July 4th, ought to be a great reminder of the true nature of these times, if we understand that this was the day, 72 years ago, when Master Fard Muhammad chose to declare our freedom. Let's now deeply reflect.

Today, The Declaration of Independence and Mr. Thomas Jefferson will be mentioned over and over again.

A great national temple was built to honor Thomas Jefferson's memory. It's named *The Jefferson Memorial.* It's located in Washington, D.C. President Franklin Delano Roosevelt dedicated it on the 200th anniversary of Jefferson's birth, which was on April 13, 1743.

According to an official brochure, "Inscriptions at the memorial were selected by *The Thomas Jefferson Memorial Commission* and were taken from a wide variety of his writings on freedom, slavery, education and government."

The section of the inscriptions that deals with freedom and slavery runs as follows, in part: "God who gave us life gave us liberty. Can the liberties of a nation be secure when we have removed a conviction that these liberties are the gift of God? Indeed I tremble for my country when I reflect that God is just, that his justice cannot sleep forever."

Did Mr. Jefferson write what he foresaw that caused him to tremble? Yes! The commissioners omitted it from the inscriptions on the monument. Why?

Secretary of State Colin Powell was asked this question, when he was the head of The Joint Chiefs of Staff: "The Declaration of Independence is unprecedented, a watershed moment in the nation. How did it apply to black people?"

His answer was: "The Declaration of Independence is one of the most remarkable documents in the world, and certainly in the English language or in Christendom. And in just a few words, it captures the essence. You know, 'inalienable rights,' rights not given to you by the state, but given to you by God, so they can't be taken away. And the purpose of the state is to secure these rights, not to give them to you or to tell you what you're supposed to do with them, but to secure those rights for you.

What are those rights? Life, liberty, and the pursuit of happiness. "We hold these truths to be self-evident." In other words, you don't have to prove them. It's self-evident. Why is it self-evident? Came from God. They're inalienable. Government secures them. Remarkable document. It didn't apply to black folks.

It still doesn't.

Israel's recent rejection of Minister Farrakhan reminds me of a statement quoted from Einstein, in a book titled: "*The Einstein's Files,*" by Fred Jerome. On page 110, of this book, he is quoted in a letter he wrote to the Zionist leader, Chaim Weizmann: "If we do not succeed in finding the path of honest cooperation and coming to terms with the Arabs, we will not have learned anything from our 2,000 year old ordeal and will deserve the fate which will beset us."

Mr. Jerome continues: "Cooperation with the Arab population, in Einstein's view, was both the only 'practical possibility' and 'moral justification' for Zionism."

He pointed out Einstein's effort to be even handed by citing that he "was also critical of Arab nationalism."

The above, of course, is but a thin slice of Einstein's thinking and efforts, on behalf of what he deemed to be a better world.

Regardless to how Minister Farrakhan's peace mission turns out; it will not be a failure, any more than any of the men of God, who were turned down by those whose hearts refused to know.

By the way, the sub-title of this book is: *"J. Edgar Hoover's Secret War Against The World's Most Famous Scientist."*

Now, back to the interview I conducted with the Honorable Minister Louis Farrakhan, on May 1st of this year.

Brother Jabril: John 19:30 records Jesus' last words, at the moment of his death as: "It is finished." Some translations put it: "It is accomplished." Still others: "It is done." What was finished, accomplished or done? Why was it accompanied by such excruciating suffering? Why was this a necessary factor in the planning of God?

Be it the will of Allah, the first part of his answer will be fully stated at the end of this interview, with the reason given.

Minister Farrakhan: He first went to the root of suffering. He continued: Even though He said "Be" and it is, that which accompanied His will was great suffering to bring into existence what He desired.

He stated that what Allah now desired, "to bring in was even greater than His bringing in the sun or the moon or the stars." Minister Farrakhan explained, in part, that His bringing into being, at present, "the perfection of human beings through whom would come a perfect world" is greater than that which He brought in prior to this day.

He said that Allah is now bringing in "a new heaven and a new earth." So if an imperfect world is accompanied by great suffering to bring it in; an imperfect universe was accompanied by great suffering to bring it in, how much more should the suffering be to perfect the man through whom would come a new heaven and a new earth.

So the words, "It is finished" means to me, that what I was to endure to produce that which would glorify God, the suffering that was endured to accomplish the will of God it was done. "It is finished" and in it is being finished, it has been accomplished and the result of this is the exaltation of man; the reconnection of man to God and the fulfillment in man for the purpose of His creations.

(For more on *"It Is Finished,"* see chapter seven, which starts on page 75, in "*Is It Possible That The Honorable Elijah Muhammad Is Still Physically Alive???*")

"So the Saviour said to his Servant, Elijah Muhammad, "Take plenty Brother. Take plenty." How could he take plenty, if he didn't have plenty of love for that which he was going to take plenty from? How could he take plenty, if he did not have faith in the results of that which he would take plenty from or what it would produce?

It was love. It was faith .... that love produced faith; love produced long suffering. That's why Paul (1st Corinthians chapter 13) described, in this way, what love was. It suffers all. It hopeth all. It endureth all. Why? Because in order to bring about what was to be brought about, that redemptive agent had to be able, through that love, to suffer all that was necessary to accomplish the task it [he] had.

Notice Minister Farrakhan's pure humility.

JABRIL MUHAMMAD
JULY 4, 2002

FARRAKHAN: THE TRAVELER
FOR THE FINAL CALL
VOL. 21; NO. 42

Brother Jabril: The word "endure" comes up in this redemptive task, in the scriptures. In one place it reads: "In your patience possess ye your souls." We've entered the dark hour the scriptures teach of and it's going to get darker before it gets brighter.

Patience is a primary key the Believer must have to get through to the other side. We have spoken of patience many times, especially in these last 25 years. You have patiently and often answered questions about patience and have brought out different aspects of the need for, as well as the roots of patience. How does patience fit into what you've just covered about suffering and it's roots?

Minister Farrakhan: One cannot have patience, where one does not have knowledge. One cannot have patience, where one does not have faith. One cannot have patience, where one does not have love.

The Holy Qur'an teaches us that man is created in haste and we are like spiritual children who want the gratification of our desires as quickly as possible. Therefore, patience is something that has to be acquired. What God demands of us is patience because without patience, we cannot see the out-working of His will.

Without patience, *The "Word"* looses its value in your own heart and mind. Without patience you cannot endure the pain that accompanies the process of growing us into manifestations of God. So the Qur'an as well as the Bible encourages us to be patience.

Well in my own humble opinion, we will never have enough

knowledge, comprehensively, to see the out-working of God's will through knowledge alone. Without faith, under-girded by love, we'll never be able to endure what is to be endured in order to become what God desires for us to become.

The race, He says, "Is not to the swift, nor even to the strong." Even strength will not allow you and me to endure. But the love of God, which passes all understanding; the love of God that gives you faith in Him, that His word is as real in your heart and mind as though it is actually manifested, then you will wait on God and suffer as you wait to see the fulfillment of His word. So Allah commands us to have patience. Paul said, "Of faith, of hope and of charity or love, the greatest of these is love." So without love we will not be able to endure to the end of this process.

Jesus endured. Because he endured, he was able to say, in the darkness of his hour, "Father forgive them for they know not what they do." If they understood, they would never have said, "crucify him." They would never have chosen a thief over the servant of God, if they but understood.

Yes, I'm nailed. Yes, I'm in great pain. Yes, I'm being mocked; ridiculed. Yes, there's a crown of thorns on my head. I'm left here to hang and suffer, with agonizing pain, while people walk by and spit on me and throw stones and I cannot defend myself. But when I open my mouth to speak, I curse no one. I curse not God. I say, Father forgive them, for they know not what they do. Into Thy hands do I command my spirit. It is finished. It is accomplished.

Brother Jabril: This, of course, takes us right back to Moses and the wise man that we touched on in our earlier conversation that was not taped. Now, we're back to that subject.

There were three specific tests that Moses failed. What are the lessons we must focus on ***now*** that we've entered the first stages of the darkest of all hours, called in one place, "The time of Jacob's trouble... " But, it adds, that: "he shall be delivered out of it."

Minister Farrakhan: First we must understand that this is not Moses following God. The Honorable Elijah Muhammad said, "This is the way my followers follow me in doubt and suspicion." Since I am seated in his seat by his permission with authority to continue to do his work, then those who continue to follow me do so with the same doubt and suspicion.

We'll never have a comprehensive knowledge unless God gives it to us. The wise man did not show his comprehensive knowledge of things until it was time for the parting of the ways. If the person characterized by Moses loved the wise man and had faith in him, he would not need a comprehensive knowledge to understand that even in that which appears negative, there is great good. The faithful one says, "I can't see it all and I don't understand it all, but I believe that this man that I'm following and what he does, is good."

Unfortunately, doubt and suspicion were there from the beginning because when the Saviour left, the Honorable Elijah Muhammad began to say who the man [Master Fard Muhammad] was. They did not hear the man say that. So immediately, there were those who said, "He's trying to make more of the man than the man made of Himself, so he could make something more of himself." There's the doubt. There's the suspicion. So some went on with him, but in doubt and suspicion. Then as he did other things there was doubt and suspicion.

Every time the wise man called him to the promise that he made he said, "Yes, yes, yes, I'm sorry. Please allow me to go on." But by his not explaining he didn't erase the doubt. And by the doubter making a judgment, and going on with the wise man, his doubt was not erased and so his judgment of the wise-man produced a gap in the following. So at every point the wise man went further ahead and the doubter went further behind.

When they came to the parting of the ways they had already [spiritually] parted, but now I'm going to tell you why you and I are separated. Since you could not have patience with me, because you didn't love me; you didn't believe in me from the very beginning. So you doubted and had suspicion of me in whatever I did, according to your [limited] understanding of, or lack of understanding of, the modern Moses, Elijah Muhammad. So you used his law and his teachings to [mis]judged me as the Jews used the law of Moses to judge Jesus, and as many [mis]judged the Honorable Elijah Muhammad.

Gaps continued to develop and broaden. So it's written, "That day shall not come except there be a falling away first and the man of sin be revealed."

Falling away is a gap. They will not any longer endure sound doctrine, a gap. Who are these teachers that you are now heaping to yourselves that tickle your ears. See to tickle your ear means they say the thing that is congruent to the [mis]judgment that you've made of the wise, thus increasing the gap, which confirms you in your madness.

To get through the dark hour now one has to look deep into one's self.

The completion of his answer, next issue Allah willing.

JABRIL MUHAMMAD
JULY 5, 2002

FARRAKHAN: THE TRAVELER
FOR THE FINAL CALL
VOL. 21; NO. 43

As in the interview, published some months ago, in *The Final Call*, the Honorable Minister Louis Farrakhan continues to explain how we may get through this dark period into the light of the better day; the Hereafter. The scriptures verify his efforts.

The scriptures are very valuable. Use a concordance, take a little time and look up such words, as "dark" and "darkness." This yields great benefits, but only in the light of the teachings of the Honorable Elijah Muhammad, to which the Honorable Minister Louis Farrakhan bears illuminating witness.

Our ignorance of the scriptures has (and is) being challenged since the arrival of Master Fard Muhammad and His resurrection of the Honorable Elijah Muhammad, with the true meaning of the scriptures, which tally with the events of our day.

If we try to understand why, the Honorable Elijah Muhammad's Teacher made the understanding of the scriptures an essential part of his/our new (and supremely better) education, we would have a healthier attitude towards the scriptures than many do. We would also be thankful for the exquisite wisdom of the use of the scriptures by Minister Farrakhan (and his teacher) to advance us. False pride, jealousy and envy are among the hindrances to such gratitude.

Understanding reduces stressful surprises.

Now, we just can't intelligently deny Isaiah's words, for instance, that refer primarily to Black people here in America, with the rise and work of the Honorable Elijah Muhammad, in 1931, and with the rise and work of Minister Farrakhan, from 1977 onwards.

"The people who walk in darkness have seen a great light; those who live in the land of intense darkness and the shadow of death, upon them has the light shined."

" ... on that day shall the deaf hear the words of the book, and the eyes of the blind shall see out of gloom and darkness. The humble would rejoice in the Lord and the needy or the poor among men shall rejoice in the Holy One of Israel. For the ruthless, the terrible one shall vanish; the mockers and the scorners will be cut off. Those who lay traps with meaningless arguments, against those who uphold the right, will come to an end. (9:2; 29:18-21)"

We're warned in 1st Thessalonians 5:20, (and throughout the Qur'an, as Mother Tynnetta Muhammad continually preaches), "... do not treat prophecies with contempt." But many still do. So in the words of Minister Farrakhan, "... gaps continued to develop and broaden. So it's written, "That day shall not come except there be a falling away first and the man of sin be revealed."

Falling away is a gap. It's written that "... they will not any longer endure sound doctrine ... " a gap. Who are these teachers that you are now heaping to your ears that tickle your ears? See to tickle your ear means they say the thing that is congruent to the judgment that you've made of the wise, thus increasing the gap, which confirms you in your madness.

To get through the dark hour now one has to look deep into one's self.

Now the wise man is gone, but he has shown us a comprehensive knowledge of why he did what he did. That which he shows you, what did it produce in the follower? Did it produce love? Did it produce faith? If it did then you will go back and remember all the things that he taught that you had doubt in and you will make it through the dark hour until his return.

But if his comprehensive knowledge makes you say, "Awe this is more falsehoods. He's trying to justify the garbage that he did."

Then you will stick to your judgment of him and in the dark hour you will be the loser.

The fuller part of what Minister Farrakhan quoted of 2Timothy 4:3 reads: "For the time will come when they will not any longer endure [tolerate] sound doctrine... " This *is* that time. This passage goes on, in part: "... and they shall turn away their ears from the truth, and shall be turned to misguided ideas."

"... whoever acts hostilely to the Messenger after guidance has become manifest to him and follows other than the way of the believers, We turn him to that to which he (himself) turns and make him enter hell... ."(Holy Qur'an 4:115)

The good ones are advised (in several translations), in verse five, to try to be: "calm, cool, steady, sober, keep your head in all situations, keep control, be careful and sane" as they "endure afflictions, sufferings, face hardships, accept and suffer unflinchingly every hardship, stand steady." How long? Until HE comes, Whose right it is to rule. (There are levels here). *Meanwhile, let's take example after Minister Farrakhan.*

Brother Jabril: In the gospel (good news) of Luke, 18:8, we read: "When the son of man returns shall he find faith on the earth?"

In the 12th verse of Surah 57, of the Holy Qur'an we read: "On that day you will see the faithful men and the faithful women, their light gleaming before them ... Good news for you this day! ... That is the grand achievement."

Verse 13 (of Surah 57) is directly related to the parable of Jesus of the ten virgins, in the 25th chapter of the gospel of Matthew. In these verses the Holy Qur'an emphasizes "faith." Why the emphasis on faith?

Minister Farrakhan: It would appear that the wicked have triumphed over God and the righteous, in this lull before the storm. So like the five foolish virgins who used up all of their oil, they were unprepared when the bridegroom came. He would come when it was dark, and they had no oil left.

If he came in the day they wouldn't need oil. But he comes at the darkest hour, which is just before the dawn of a new day. They can't go out to meet him because there's insufficient oil, or light in them, to light their way to him. But there would be some wise virgins who had some oil left.

There will always be a faithful few that will come out to meet him.

Brother Jabril: Your words remind me of what Elijah was told, in the book of 1st Kings. He thought he was by himself. But God made him to know that there were 7,000 that had not bowed their knees to Baal.

What is the primary quality that must be developed in those of us who would correspond to this 7,000, who will not bow their knees to Baal and who will qualify to be the five wise virgins?

Minister Farrakhan: The greatest of the qualities is humility. Because humbleness would allow us to be clearer in sight of what the Master has taught. You can tell the righteous, they walked the earth full of knowledge? No! They walked the earth full of money? No! They walked the earth heavy with power. No? They walked the earth in humility and in humbleness. If we're humble, messages can come to us from sources whence we think not, to keep us going through the dark hour until the dawn of the light of a brand new day.

Jabril Muhammad
July 8, 2002

Section 6

Farrakhan: The Traveler
For The Final Call
Vol. 21; No. 44

According to current media reports the Bush Administration plans to officially start the forming of millions of Americans into civilian spy teams in August. Reportedly, this plan is to make spies of millions of American workers, who, in the daily course of their work, are in positions to serve as extra eyes and ears for the government. This adds to America's great number of spies.

Might whatever you read, discuss, or do in the privacy of your home, or in public, make you look suspicious, in the eyes of these new government agents? They already have access to your home, such as workers for the phone companies, the cable installers, the deliverers of your mail and others whose work takes them into your homes, *etc.*

What happens if these people merely *think* they have noticed something about you that they *think* makes you look like a potential terrorist? Might your name be placed in a computer database for individuals engaging in possible terrorist activity; despite your complete innocence? Does this mean that any American citizen, through *any* means, is now subject to becoming a suspect, involved in conspiracies against America?

This government has laws allowing its agents to conduct searches in our homes, in our absence, which the police would not have had the lawful authority to conduct without a warrant, a short while ago.

There is a huge number of ignorant; nosey; judgmental; vain; vindictive; biased; spiteful; vicious; jealous; envious; extremely insecure; insane, or otherwise just plain evil people in America, excluding those who make honest mistakes. Who are going to screen these would be spies? Who qualifies the qualifiers?

Will this increase neighbors being turned against neighbors; friends against former friends; parents against children and children against parents; employees against their employers and vice versa, *ETC*?

Have we come full circle *(but far greater)* to the turbulence and the paranoia of the 60s and 70s? That was a time when it seemed to many that America was on the brink of civil and international war. Later, governmental agencies and other powerful entities of America, supposedly working for the citizens, were exposed as their enemies. However, deceit continues, from all quarters, to the hilt in America.

For thousands of years, wicked leaders have used wicked means to gain and to hold on to their positions over others. But such wicked wisdom is now exhausted, and thus, America is stumbling headlong to the very edge of the cliff, after which is the abyss—the lowest place in hell—a nothingness, from which she can never return.

Objects falling to the earth reach their greatest speed just before they hit. It takes something or someone of great *strength* and *dexterity* to halt such a falling object, just before it hits.

America is falling, with great speed. However, she has one in her midst who is authorized and backed by God and the Christ, who has what it takes to halt her fall, *IF* she will take his advice. *That man is the Honorable Minister Louis Farrakhan.*

This is hard for many to see or take. But, just think it over.

The Honorable Elijah Muhammad spoke several times of the value of his followers, in the eyes of Allah. But the value of Minister Farrakhan, said his teacher, was greater to him than all of the wealth that is in the earth, for through him he will get all of his people. *Again, Minister Farrakhan can halt America's fall.*

By now, any claim of ignorance, by Caucasian Shriners and

wise Jews is unjustified.

Suppose you were living in the days of any of God's prophets? How would you have looked on them, if, for example, you saw them in the market places, shopping for food? They did ordinary things. But they were *extraordinary* persons, because God chose them for *extraordinary* service for the people among whom they were raised. Although not a prophet, Minister Farrakhan is such a man, and then some.

We read that Isaiah said, in the book that bears his name, that "... the Lord spoke thus to me with His strong hand upon me, and warned *and* instructed me not to walk in the way of this people, saying, do not call conspiracy ... all that this people will call conspiracy ... neither be in fear of what they fear ... ."

"The Lord of hosts, regard Him as holy *and* honor His holy name by regarding Him as your only hope of safety, and let Him be your fear and let Him be your dread lest you offend Him by your fear of man and distrust of Him.

"... He shall be a sanctuary a sacred and indestructible asylum to those who reverently fear and trust in Him; but He shall be a Stone of stumbling and a Rock of offense to both the houses of Israel, a trap and a snare to the inhabitants of Jerusalem." (Isaiah 8: 12-14)

Look at and hear Minister Farrakhan, for he exemplifies these guiding divine principles, during these increasingly dark and dangerous times, when betrayal among former friends and the misjudgment and mistreatment of the righteous is on the rise. These are days of betrayal and the abuse of power, which are just moments from reaching their apex.

All of this was foreseen and written of long ago. So was that which would bring these days to a close, or no flesh would be saved, and that which comes after.

Isaiah continues: "Behold, I and the children whom the Lord has given me are signs and wonders that are to take place in Israel from the Lord of hosts, Who dwells on Mount Zion."

The Honorable Minister Louis Farrakhan, his teacher, and we who follow them are the fulfillment of Isaiah's words of himself and his followers.

" ... when the people, instead of putting their trust in God, shall say to you, consult for direction mediums and wizards who chirp and mutter, should not a people seek *and* consult their God? Should they consult the dead on behalf of the living?"

"Direct such people to the teaching and to the testimony! If their teachings are not in accord with this word, it is surely because there is no dawn *and* no morning for them."

"And they who consult mediums and wizards shall pass through the land sorely distressed and hungry; and when they are hungry, they will fret, and will curse by their king and their God; and whether they look upward, or look to the earth, they will behold only distress and darkness, the gloom of anguish, and into thick darkness *and* widespread, obscure night they shall be driven away."(Is: 8: 18-22)

"But in the midst of judgment there is the promise and the certainty of the Lord's deliverance and there shall be no gloom for her who was in anguish." He continues: "in the latter time He will make it glorious ... ." (Is 9:1)

Why? *Because*:

"The people who walked in darkness have seen a great Light; those who dwelt in the land of intense darkness and the shadow of death, *upon them has the Light shined*." (Is 9:2)

More next issue—from Minister Farrakhan's words, on what makes strong Believers—Allah willing.

JABRIL MUHAMMAD
JULY 25, 2002

FARRAKHAN: THE TRAVELER
FOR *THE FINAL CALL*
VOL. 21; NO. 45

Brother Jabril: Some misunderstand aspects of these interviews. I love my Big Brother. I love what and how he teaches. Moreover, I want everyone to understand you in the light of God's truths.

I was real happy when a Sister wrote me saying: "Thank you

for these interviews, which are really ***inner-views*** of the Minister." I love what she wrote. She got to the core of what I'm doing this for.

And, there are so many valuable lessons in your life, from which we all can benefit, as it was with the Honorable Elijah Muhammad, due to the special positions in which Allah has placed you both.

Minister Farrakhan: There are those who failed to grasp the lessons that are manifested in their Brother. So those who would strike that [the spiritual roots] from the record would do so because the gap in them has become so great they cannot see the value in such questions and in such answers.

Brother Jabril: An understanding of the words of Allah depends a great deal on the quality of our understanding of the bearer of that word.

Then Minister Farrakhan went into the fact that many of us follow him, as he stated, in this May 1st interview: "out of a superficial understanding of him, [while] the scriptures says, 'Take my yoke upon you and *learn of me* for I am meek and lowly of heart and ye shall find rest unto your souls.'

Minister Farrakhan: Learning *of* a man is learning the inner workings of his mind, which then gives you the spirit out of which he does what he does and this is why God is using him. If you want God to use you, don't be an imitation of his word, or his dress, or his [external] manner. But get in tune with his spirit, for then you will become magnetic, as you will draw people unto you, that you may bring them to him, that he may bring them to the Messenger, and that the Messenger may bring them to Allah.

To blind yourself to aspects of him that made him chosen of God and to relegate this aspect [the spiritual] to unimportance does not show the unimportance of the articles that you write. It is showing what has happened to those hearts and those minds that are blinded to the value of profound answers to simple questions.

Brother Jabril: Right.

Minister Farrakhan: Every incident or circumstance or event that comes up in my personal and national life will give the Believers and historians a view of the heart of the man that has been so thoroughly condemned by those who misunderstand.

Brother Jabril: That's right. Then of course, it's written that you are to become even more successful despite, and in some ways, because of their opposition. And, it says that many will come to see and believe.

Minister Farrakhan: That fuels the intensity of the effort of those who condemned and worked against me. Now in their having a change of heart, by their coming to understand, by the permission of Allah, then they work even harder for the cause for which this person suffered so much, but did not respond in kind to those who caused him pain.

Brother Jabril: There is a general truth, written in the second chapter of 1st Corinthians, that if the princes of this world really understood, "they would not have crucified the Lord of Glory."

Minister Farrakhan: That only bears witness that for some, who rejected it, at first, it was not envy. It was gross misunderstanding.

I saw in the history of Prophet Muhammad (PBUH) that when the emissaries from Mecca met him three miles out from Mecca, out of which came the Hudiabiya treaty, when in the writing it said, "Muhammad, Messenger of God," they said, according to the historians, "If we had believed that he was the Messenger of God, we never would have opposed him." So that let me know that it definitely was a misunderstanding because they did not believe in him as his followers believed in him. Out of their disbelief in him they opposed him. But it was not envy.

Brother Jabril: In August 1961, we attended a Minister's Conference, during which the Honorable Elijah Muhammad said: "Some come to believe only but for a short time." You've covered many times how we can become un-stunted and really make real progress, after our misunderstanding, which is implied in your great assignment from God and the Honorable Elijah Muhammad to you.

This leads right back again to this, from another angle: in the light of what he said, what is the root of Moses' doubt and suspicion?

Minister Farrakhan: I think the words that are given to Jesus in the scriptures reads, "All that came before me were thieves and robbers." So when a people have had thieves and robbers in front of them posing as leaders, and in another sense, hirelings who lead because it's profitable, taking advantage of the misery of the people, to profit from their misery and then when you get a true leader, he suffers the weight of those who were before him that mislead.

It's like a woman having married a man, or two men, and having suffered great hurt; injustice; evil from the man or men that she married, by the time the third marriage comes, she is filled with doubt and suspicion, because of her experience.

I think at the root of that doubt and suspicion of our people, is the history of thieves and robbers who came before God raised our father to lead us. So he had to bear the pain of their doubt and suspicion and the wickedness of the enemy, whose job it was to cast doubt and make the people suspicious of him through their propaganda. So it was a double whammy that he had, because he had the history to overcome and the wicked misinterpretations of his good by the wicked while he worked.

Our Brother, Minister Farrakhan suffers the same and for the same reasons. But, as it is written, he will overcome, by the power of the backing of Allah and the Christ.

Every day the media contains news that constantly bears witness to the truth of Minister Farrakhan's teachings and work. Furthermore scientific studies are being released almost every day that does the same.

Relevant to the above are these verses from the Holy Qur'an. Consider them with a broad mind.

"And if good befalls them, they say: 'This is from Allah'; and if a misfortune befalls them, they say: 'This is from thee.' Say: 'All is from Allah. But what is the matter with these people that they make no effort to understand anything?' " (4:78)

"What is the matter with you that you help not one another?" (37:25)

"What is the matter with you that you hope not for greatness from Allah?" (71:13)

Question: Can we enter Minister Farrakhan's spirit, which is his teacher's spirit, which is the spirit of God Himself, without an understanding of the scriptures and without *that* particular kind of love *of* which he, Minister Farrakhan, speaks and acts?

JABRIL MUHAMMAD
JULY 10, 2002

FARRAKHAN: THE TRAVELER
FOR THE FINAL CALL
VOL. 21; NO. 46

In chapter 27, page 148, of *Our Savior Has Arrived*, the Honorable Elijah Muhammad wrote:

"Concerning faith in Allah (God), the Bible teaches you and me that Allah (God) met Abraham and upon submission he was able to get the honor of being the friend of God because Abraham submitted to the Will of Allah (God). The history of Abraham is the history of all of the righteous who submit to do the Will of Allah (God)-they are successful."

On page 77 of volume 11, which introduces Surah 37, of *The Meaning of the Qur'an*, Mr. S. Abdul A'la Maudidi wrote:

"The most instructive of the historical narratives presented in this Surah is the important event of the pious life of the Prophet Abraham, who became ready to sacrifice his only son as soon as he received an inspiration from Allah. In this there was a lesson not only for the disbelieving Quraish, who waxed proud of their blood relationship with him, but also for the Muslims who had believed in Allah and His Messenger. By narrating this event, they were told what is the essence and the real spirit of Islam, and how a true believer should be ready to sacrifice his all for the pleasure and approval of Allah after he has adopted it as his Faith and Creed."

"The last verses of the Surah were not only a warning for the disbelievers but also a good news for the believers who were passing through highly unfavorable and discouraging conditions on account of their supporting and following the Holy Prophet. In these verses they were given the good news that they should not be disheartened at the hardships and difficulties they had to encounter in the beginning, for in the end they alone would attain dominance, and the standard-bearers of falsehood, who appeared to be dominant at the time would be overwhelmed and vanquished at their hands. A few years later, the turn the events took, proved that it was not an empty consolation, but an inevitable reality of which they had been foretold in order to strengthen their hearts."

Starting in Volume 20; No. 6, of this newspaper, I reported the deathbed confession of the Honorable Minister Louis Farrakhan. Witnessed by others, it was a powerful testimony of the quality of his heart; his faith; his love.

I wrote of a meeting with Minister Farrakhan, in September 1999, when he told me what his daughter, Sister Fatima, told him that he said, while he was unconscious and literally dying in a hospital room a few months earlier.

He asked his daughter to come into the room where we were, that I might hear her testimony. She told me that while Dr. Alim, her and others worked feverishly to save his life, her father slipped into unconsciousness. He was about three minutes from death. In that state, she said, he thanked Allah for *everything* that He had either put or allowed into his life. She told me that he said to Allah, that if it was His will that He take him in death, at that time, then he, Minister Farrakhan, was ready. She said that he thanked Allah over and over again.

I was, and am, very privileged to have heard what I did. I wrote that it was significant to me that a lawyer, Lewis Meyers, was present, when she later told her father what he had said. Brother Lewis and later Ministers Ava and Arif Muhammad (both also attorneys) explained to me the value of deathbed confessions, which I put in those articles. New subscribers may obtain the series on Minister Farrakhan's deathbed confession (and a series on "PAIN" any day on or before August 26th at: www.writtentestimony.com.

Minister Farrakhan is a man of great compassion, from which springs his empathetic sensitivity, which Allah used for his peace mission. There was danger from aspects of the American government. There was danger from overseas powers. There was danger from those who love him, but misunderstood him. There was danger from the shallow-minded and also from the weak of mind. Then there were the hypocrites. Danger yet persists.

He was prepared to die, if necessary, for the principles embodied in the purpose of his peace mission. Even though he did not feel it would happen, he did those things one does in preparation for the possibility of imminent death. Minister Farrakhan is a strong believer in the complete righteousness and the absolute authority of Allah to do as He wills.

Remember, his teacher promised him they would meet again and, in short, he was divinely promised *much* that he would attain *before* death.

He has been a most extraordinary worker for the Nation of Islam, since 1955 when he entered it. Can we really say he has been rewarded for his hard work and sacrifice from then until now? Sure, he has a few creature comforts as they are called. But can we call those things his reward, while he has and is catching *hell* from every quarter; from every segment of the population in this country. No and yes, as doing good brings its own reward. But has his name been fully cleared?

Many, whites and otherwise, know he is a righteous and a truthful man. Their voices are not heard, however, above the noise of the wicked and the ignorant. There are also those who wait to see which way the wind is blowing. They won't speak truth to those whose power is both tiny and limited. They don't have the courage of their convictions.

Can we say that he has lived to see the fruition of his life's work for which he has sacrificed all? Not materially!

Yet he was willing to die for the cause, for which he has proven his love and to which he has dedicated his life, if that was Allah's will, in spite of all that he was promised.

I'm saying straight up that Minister Farrakhan is motivated by the highest kind of intelligence and the deepest kind of love. He did not do what he did for personal gain, nor vanity, nor reward. He acted straight out of divine guidance which utilized his intelligent love of the truth, of and from Master Fard Muhammad; the Honorable Elijah Muhammad; our people in particular; humanity in general.

Some years ago he wrote that his Study Guides came on the order of Allah. He said the same of The Million Man March. He said the same of every significant thing he has done, especially since his more-than-a-vision-experience, on September 17, 1985 when the Honorable Elijah Muhammad spoke to him from the Wheel.

Did you see, hear, or feel, what he did that moved him to say and do what he has, especially since 1977? What do we really think of him? Allah knows. We Muslims mention Abraham's name in our prayers every day. We accept Allah's words about his worthiness. Now, suppose you lived about 5,000 years ago. One day you see Abraham, taking his son up a mountain. You learn from him, or others, that he was taking his son to a place to sacrifice him. You hear that God told him to do this. What did you really think of Abraham when you first heard this?

JABRIL MUHAMMAD
AUGUST 1, 2002

FARRAKHAN: THE TRAVELER
FOR THE FINAL CALL
VOL. 21; NO. 47

"... Moses said, I will provoke you to jealousy by them that there are no people and by a foolish nation I will anger you."

— Romans 10:19

"... you are a chosen ... people; that you should show forth the praises of Him Who has called you out of darkness into His marvelous light ... ."

— 1 Peter 2:9, 10

What would we have thought of this great Prophet of Allah, if we were there when Abraham was about to kill his son? How could we know that this that *appeared* so unjustified—even outright evil—was of God Himself? What would have convinced us that Abraham's act involved the highest kind of righteousness and that his acts had a bearing on this, our day?

Suppose Abraham told you that God stopped him just when he was about to plunge the knife into his son. Would his acts have produced a gap between you and him? What would close it?

This may remind us of lessons in the Holy Qur'an's narrative of Moses and the Wise man. (Surah 18, section 9 and 10).

Some have written that at a certain point Abraham's son knew that he was to be sacrificed by his father. According to the 22nd chapter of Genesis, Abraham tied up his son and placed him on an alter, which he built. It would seem that his son had to know what was up by that time, even though at one point he asked his father what was going to be used for the sacrifice.

Some have written that Satan appeared to the boy and tried to get him to rebel on his father. He turned Satan down. It's beyond this article's purpose to get into that. Nor will I get into whether this son was Ishmael or Isaac. One day, I hope to take up these issues, as they are related to the current world situation.

History teaches that whenever Allah raised a man to elevate the people, the devil always sought to destroy that work through all forms of deception, evil suggestions, intimidation, inquisitions, threats and the like.

The Holy Qur'an states: "... We never sent a messenger or a prophet before thee but when he desired, the devil made a suggestion respecting his desire; but Allah annuls that which the devil casts, then does Allah establish His messages.

"... He [makes] what the devil casts a trial for those in whose hearts is a disease and the hard hearted. And surely the wrong doers are in severe opposition.

"And that those who have been given knowledge may know that it is the Truth from thy Lord, so they should believe in it that their hearts may be lowly before Him. And surely Allah is the

Guide of those who believe, into a right path.

"... those who disbelieve will not cease to be in doubt concerning it, until the Hour overtakes them suddenly, or there comes to them the chastisement of a destructive day. The kingdom on that day is Allah's." (22:52-56)

God and Satan *must* do what each *must* do. It's incumbent on Allah to establish His truth and create His new world. Likewise, Satan must do his best to oppose Him by keeping his science of tricks and lies in force as long as he can. However, Allah will thoroughly defeat Satan.

Now, the Holy Qur'an teaches that one day, when Abraham's son was old enough to work with him, he told his son that he had received a divine order that he must sacrifice him. His son told his father to do as he was commanded. He told his father that with Allah's help he would be found patient and constant under trial.

The next day, as Abraham was about to slay his son, Allah stopped him and told him, at the last moment, saying that he had fulfilled the vision. Their lives were prophetic.

What vision? In several places in the scriptures we read of a vision that will be fulfilled at the end of time. It involves the establishment of a nation, by God Himself, right here in America, called the Kingdom of God. It's happening now.

The 11th chapter of the book of Daniel describes those who will exalt themselves to seek to fulfill this vision. They will fail, but will yet serve the divine cause.

This next section of the May 1st interview with the Honorable Minister Louis Farrakhan is short but very powerful, as it takes us closer to the root of what explains all things.

Brother Jabril: The wise man did things that were guided by God that looked evil despite how righteous these acts were.

Now, it looked like wicked leaders, these hirelings, you spoke about the woman with two husbands and they were bad to her and now comes along a good man, and in words, she sees him in the light of this bad experience. Since so many of us, even in the Nation, are engulfed with that problem, what are some of the keys to overcoming that kind of hasty judgment?

Minister Farrakhan: Evidently there is not too much you can do about it, because the people are naturally inclined this way because of circumstances and events in their lives as a result of which they have become this way. So it is only in being what they've become and acting out their doubt and suspicion that allows them to overcome it when greater knowledge and understanding is given, other than that they remain as they are. They can't help themselves. And that's why he could say, "Father forgive them for they know not what they do."

Brother Jabril: He had to have a profound understanding of their condition to tolerate, not just love, but to love in—

Minister Farrakhan: In a profound love, which gave him the profound understanding of their condition. Other than that there's no way.

Brother Jabril: No way.

Minister Farrakhan: No. And you know I can't say that I understood. But it was my love of our people and my suffering with them that God allowed me to come to understand why we are like we are.

Ponder his words with great care.

As things darken up let's heed the Qur'an's warnings .

"And surely this your community is one community, and I am your Lord, so keep your duty to Me. But they became divided into sects, each party rejoicing in that which was with them." (23:52, 53)

"And say to My servants that they speak what is best. Surely the devil sows dissensions among them." (17:53)

"... and dispute not one with another, lest you get weak-hearted and your power depart ..." (8:46)

"In the name of Allah, the Beneficent, the Merciful. Say: I seek refuge in the Lord of the dawn, from the evil of that which he has created, and from the evil of intense darkness, when it comes, and from the evil of those who cast (evil suggestions) in firm resolutions, and from the evil of the envier when he envies." (Surah 113)

Subscribe *before* August 26th at www.writtentestimony.com to get my articles on Minister Farrakhan's deathbed confession and a series on "**PAIN**."

JABRIL MUHAMMAD
AUGUST 15, 2002

FARRAKHAN: THE TRAVELER
FOR THE FINAL CALL
VOL. 21; NO. 48

Two days ago, on Saturday, August 17, 2002, the Honorable Minister Louis Farrakhan, in about 10 minutes, put in perfect perspective the whole matter of reparations, primarily for Black people in America, and for the oppressed in general.

Today, August 19, I watched via C-SPAN, an event titled, *"Congressional Forum on Police Misconduc.."* It was held in Inglewood, California. It was chaired by Democratic Representative Maxine Waters and about nine Black legislators worked with her.

The testimonies, by professionals and the public, were effective and revealing. It's heavy supplementary material to update *The National Agenda*, which is still before America (and the world) by Minister Farrakhan and the Nation of Islam, the subtitle of which is *Public Policy Issues, Analysis, and Programmatic Plan of Action.*

This televised event unintentionally served to justify the efforts of the rally for reparations two days before.

As I watched many memories came back to me. Among them was a statement made by the Honorable Elijah Muhammad during a 1956 meeting at his home, when I was being confirmed as a captain, under my then Minister, Brother Philbert. I suppose a major reason I vividly recall that experience is because that was the first time I met him in a personal way.

He said, "Until people do unto others as they would like to be done unto themselves, we will always have a need for a police force."

Later I saw in his words, a part of which I'll now state: a

good police force enforces what good teachers teach; the law of love. This generates more love that becomes mutual wherever it wasn't.

According to news reports, and our experiences, the planet earth is a dangerous place to live--especially true here in the U.S.A.

On page 207 of *Our Savior Has Arrived*, the Honorable Elijah Muhammad wrote:

"The population of the earth is the greatest that it has been for the past 6,000 years under the rule of the white race.

"On our planet earth, every race in every country, city, and town is now so full of people that they have to look for room for expansion."

Later, he stated:

"Allah Himself threatens to reduce the seemingly over population of the earth by removing all of the people of the planet earth who are unwilling to submit in obedience of Allah (God), His Messenger, and the Message that he has sent.

A great vacancy would be left, for there is only a small percentage of the population of the earth who want to do righteousness.

The prophecy in Genesis 15:13-15 is relevant to all of the above. It contains a very brief, but comprehensive description of Abraham's experience during which Allah transported him to the horrible years of our physical servitude in America. We've done the 400 years mentioned in this prophecy. The extra 30 years, mentioned elsewhere, brought us to 1985 during which the Honorable Elijah Muhammad—who is very much alive—contacted Minister Farrakhan, on the Wheel."

We are coming up on the 17th anniversary of that communication, which was September 17, 1985. It involved great science.

This 400-year period of time began in 1555; not 1619. Certainly, we are not as physically abused as we use to be. But that can be misleading. We are in a great many ways more abused than ever by what many call by the phony term "the system," when they really mean people. To get into this properly requires another article.

One of the main forms of this abuse, however, is the advantage they take of our disunity, which they produced during physical servitude. In very cunning ways they have now made it worse, through deception, now that our Savior has arrived.

Disunity produces stress. Disunity is contrary to our nature. Disunity kills in countless ways. Disunity is Satanic.

Now we are at the last section of the May 1st interview of Minister Farrakhan. He answered questions on sciences leading to the explanation of all things.

How often have we discussed Abraham during the last week, or month, or year? He is more important, for instance, than Michael Jordan, whom we don't mention in our prayers as we mention Abraham. How often have we discussed any of the Prophets, since their experiences, their followers and what went on in their days has a direct bearing on our lives?

Do you recall reading in the scriptures where the prophets did things you considered hard to understand? Did you read that they did things that seemed to you to be crazy, if not evil? If what was strange, or hard to grasp, is now familiar and easy to see; if there are things they said or did that seemed crazy or even evil, but make so much sense now, what caused the change in our thinking and feelings about them?

It's helpful to know that a paradox "is a statement, proposition, or situation that seems to be absurd or contradictory, but in fact may be true; a statement or proposition that contradicts itself; somebody who has qualities that seem to contradict each other; something that is contrary to or conflicts with conventional or common opinion."

There is a principle in higher mathematics that involves paradoxes and can be stated: the more improbable an event the more information it yields.

Whether or not an event is improbable to us depends on the state of our minds, the extent, the quality, the depth of our wisdom. What is impossible for one is easy for another. What is possible or improbable for some is impossible or probable for others.

A simple expression of what we are getting into is that according to a law of nature (a law of aerodynamics), that I read several years ago, that the bumble bee's wing span is too short for his body's weight. So, it is not supposed to be able to fly. Yet, it flies.

The simple reality is that this insect flies by an aspect of that law of which those who say it is not suppose to fly, are ignorant. The truth is this insect flies in violation of their understanding of this law. It's flying in accord with aspects of this law that is beyond or higher than what they knew, or of which they are even aware.

As these scientists come to learn the higher aspects of this same natural law, the less improbable this insect's ability to fly will seem to them. In other words the bee's activities make sense to them as they gain more sense. Increased knowledge and understanding reduces the sense, the idea and feeling of the improbable.

Meanwhile, Allah never doubted that the bumble bee could fly, since He created it.

The "Jews" condemned "Jesus" for violating certain laws of the Sabbath, even though they could not deny the good effect of his work. Their attitude was like those who said that the *flying* bumble bee can't fly. But, if their information was greater and their hearts were cleaner to receive truth, they would have seen Jesus as fulfilling, not violating, the law.

It's said that Jesus performed "miracles," Were they that? Or was he manifesting higher aspects of wisdom, law and power that his critics did not understand?

Jabril Muhammad
August 19, 2002

Farrakhan: The Traveler
For The Final Call
Vol. 21; No. 49

Today, August 21st, Congresswoman Cynthia McKinney was defeated in her effort to be re-elected for another term in the Congress of the United States of America. But I believe her defeat at the polls may prove to *really* be a victory of greater value. Sounds silly? Strange? Paradoxical? Not really, for Allah is at work.

It's written in more than one book of the Bible, that God's work would often seem strange to the people at the end of the world.

The principles in the deepest of paradoxes, as defined in this series of articles, applies with far greater significance in the life, mission, teachings and work of the Honorable Elijah Muhammad and the Honorable Minister Louis Farrakhan and in the lives of the Black people of America, than what most--historians and other scholars--would dare to even consider.

After the indigenous people of America were brutalized and forced into slavery by the Spaniards, Black people were enslaved by the millions on millions and tens of millions to work by the white race in what was then called the new world. Blacks helped America to become the most powerful nation this world has ever seen, in the last 6,000 years. What was really at work?

"Really" means, "in fact or in reality, especially as distinct from what has been believed until now."

Is it really true that God permitted Black people to be enslaved in America that we might help her become the fulfillment of that which ancient Egypt was a sign of today (God's greatest opponent) even though most Americans don't yet see this?

Could it really be that we were under extreme pressure, to be made to be the people through whom the Messiah would come, as it's written in America's best selling book, the Bible?

Could it really be that America's only way to live beyond this the most critical of all times, is to heed the words of two of her ex-slaves: the modern Moses and Aaron of today—the Honorable Elijah Muhammad and Minister Louis Farrakhan? Could it *really be* that Jesus and Paul are also two powerful signs of these same two men?

If this is really so then everyone has to thoroughly re-assess everyone, everything and all that we ever knew and do it right away!

There is much that should have already compelled everyone

to re-examine whatever we've thought of these two men, their teachings and work, if we've thought unfavorably of them. However, if you are one who sees them with any degree of accuracy, don't stop there.

In the sixth chapter of, *Is It Possible That The Honorable Elijah Muhammad Is Still Physically Alive???* Minister Farrakhan stated: "In education there is a thing that is called a 'plateau of learning'. When one reaches a plateau of learning, and stops there, the process of learning stops and the process of intellectual death begins."

Ponder this statement from a book titled, "Life and Death In The New Testament" the subtitle of which is, "The Teachings of Jesus and Paul," by Xavier Leon-Dufour. It reads:

"In his account of the ministry of Paul, Father Leon Dufour describes a paradox often found in the life of Jesus' disciples: that new life and possibilities arise, as God's gift, from amidst misfortunes and setbacks."

To better understand these particular paradoxes, we must grasp science and then enter certain sciences brought by God, which are beyond that which this world's scientists know and teach. We must come to understand that we have entered the time the scriptures predicted, when God, The Greatest of all scientists, would come. He has arrived, so teaches Minister Farrakhan, as his teacher before him, as Moses and Aaron announced the presence of Jehovah in Egypt.

Despite the mighty efforts to hide the reality of God's presence and work by America's scientists of propaganda, people from every area of this country are coming into the knowledge of His truth.

Minister Farrakhan represents that man, the Messiah, who was taught and trained by Almighty God, Who is bringing about the tremendous changes now taking place throughout America and the earth.

This is that time that the Bible and Holy Qur'an plainly tells the reader that an entire new world of thought and action would be introduced to the inhabitants of this world through the most wretched of humanity, the original people living in this country.

Many would deny that we are the most wretched. Among the things I heard one scholar state was that 75% of Blacks in America are in the "middle-income" bracket. That's deceptive!

Wicked scientists, in Harvard and in other universities, are working to reduce the number of Blacks who were forced into slavery. They are with others who, in many *slick* ways, are trivializing what happened to Black people during physical servitude, and up to today, when the deception of Black people is going on big time, day and night.

We, as a people, just don't understand where we've come from, nor the real truth of the complex set of factors that has brought us to this point, nor the Master Mind Who started, fosters and is directing the course of our development.

The three Hebrew children, according to the Book of Daniel, were thrown into the fiery furnace, which became cool only on the appearance of "one like the son of man."

We need a deeper understanding of science, scriptural and otherwise, lest we be like those who claim the bumble bee can't fly, even as they watch it do so.

It is science, in the best sense of this word that explains everyone and everything to us. And, without explanations, we cannot live our lives as we should or could. Today, from the wisdom of God coming through the modern Moses and Aaron, we are learning for the first time, the sciences of life.

Life often seems unfair, confusing and puzzling. However, what we may call paradoxes, puzzles, and the like, is never that to Allah. The wiser we become the less confusing things get.

Good advances and evil retards our spiritual and moral development. Good brings us closer to Allah. Evil separates us from Him. Now, there are acts that are of God's active will. Then there are acts that are of His permissive will.

Most aspects of His will are relatively easy to understand, although there is an ascending scale of knowledge and practice involved for their realization in our inward being. Then comes those aspects of His will that primarily involves those whom He uses for the benefit of humanity and whose impact is felt long after these very noble beings have passed. Allah's prophets are in this special category of beings.

There are acts that God wills, which may seem different from the other acts He actively wills. These acts occur in exceptional instances, and are rare, in terms of the number of human beings in whose lives they occur.

We'll conclude this set of points next issue, Allah willing, and show its relevance to the pregnant scientific truths, Minister Farrakhan made in his May 1st interview.

I intend to make chapter seven of *Alive, Well and in Power*, available to subscribers to my website (www.writtentestimony.com) starting September 17th. It's titled: "More-Than-A-Vision."

JABRIL MUHAMMAD
AUGUST 21, 2002

FARRAKHAN: THE TRAVELER
FOR THE FINAL CALL
VOL. 21; NO. 50

I awoke today (August 26) remembering that this is the 56th anniversary of the release of the Honorable Elijah Muhammad, from a Federal prison in Milan, Michigan in 1946. He was arrested in Washington, D.C. May, 1942, on the orders of President Roosevelt in violation of America's own selective service laws. He was over the age the law stated men could legally be drafted for America's war effort.

A few days after his release, one in authority informed him that Roosevelt had him arrested to get him out of the public, as America prosecuted the war.

Thirteen years later, in 1959, he triumphantly entered Washington, D. C., with a police escort, to meet and teach 10,000.

Tonight I saw and heard the Honorable Minister Louis Farrakhan interviewed by Mr. Phil Donahue, on his televised program. *Minister Farrakhan was divinely brilliant!*

Mr. Donahue tried, but failed to bait Minister Farrakhan with his immature efforts to degrade the Minister. He said he understood Minister Farrakhan. If he does, he hid it in his immature effort to marginalize him. He's wrong to say people come out to hear him because he speaks to their anger.

In this confused and dangerous state of affairs, people want understanding. Minister Farrakhan fearlessly serves that need with truth, which clears away the confusion of deceivers. He brings sanity where insanity resides. He casts truth where lies prevail. He rises above the evil planning of the wicked, regardless to their power; their wealth and so-called wisdom.

How? It's by the wisdom, power, wealth and strength of Him, Who is infinitely superior to Minister Farrakhan's opposers.

Think over Minister Farrakhan's words respecting reparations for Black people, that it must include *a transfer of knowledge, along with the knowledge of how to use that knowledge for the benefit of self, kind, and land.*

God Himself has placed Minister Farrakhan, after his teacher (the Honorable Elijah Muhammad) in the forefront of the transfer of *that* knowledge, which is the foundation of all knowledge.

This fact was obvious at the reparations march. It was obvious on Donahue's program, which in my view was orchestrated by others, of which Mr. Donohue was the visible part. Their plan backfired. Donahue looked embarrassed.

In my last article, I closed a set of points with, "There are acts that God wills, which may seem different from the other acts He actively wills. These acts occur in exceptional instances and are rare, in terms of the number of human beings in whose lives they occur."

What were called miracles and wonders occurred every so often in the lives of the general mass of the people. Such terms were also used with reference to events in the lives of the prophets. However, such events occurred with greater frequency in their lives.

The rise of science in the Western world has now provided explanations for that which until then was mysterious.

That wonderful book, the Holy Qur'an, contains variations of the following statement. Allah states in (Surah Yusuf Ali) 12:111, in part, that it is, "a distinct explanation of all things..."

True explanations generate truth and are always scientific.

God has come. So there is nothing now that cannot be explained. There is now nothing that cannot be understood. God's supreme wisdom is being taught. But we are slow to comprehend it. Is it because it has come through a Black man and is being proved again by a Black man—both born in America?

Jesus taught how little children can show us how to relate towards God and His wisdom. America's leaders need this lesson too.

Recall Minister Farrakhan's words on patience. The Qur'an repeatedly teaches patience. The Honorable Elijah Muhammad said, "To teach truth in a land where falsehood has reigned supreme, takes patience on the part of the teacher as well as the ones being taught." Without patience we can't grow.

Now, there are acts that God wills, which may at first have the appearance of evil, but are good. Again, the history of the prophets of Allah contain such incidents, which to many (then and now) seem paradoxical; contradictory; inconsistent; irrational; illogical; absurd; confused; incompatible and irreconcilable to their ideas of how things ought to be done.

Some acts that He permits, may at first have the appearance and feel of good, but are evil. Of course, this has occurred often during the past 6,000 years of Satan's rule.

According to history, the Almighty has permitted, what seems, by the ordinary standards of this world, that which is evil, to facilitate His good purposes.

Whenever He initiates or permits the above kinds of acts it is due to exceptional circumstances and serves His purposes to effect exceptional and profoundly widespread good and value for that time period and far afterwards. His supreme wisdom and unique foresight is always called for and involved, in these very special situations. Furthermore, He uses His wisdom and power in ways that predetermines the outcome or consequences of such acts to serve His righteous purposes, without doing injustice to anyone.

The enslavement of Black people in America is a huge example of these truths. This in no way is saying that to produce good, evil must be done. To think this is to manifest the Satan of self. To think this is to say that Satan preceded God; that evil preceded good and that lie preceded truth. And yet, there is a huge truth here. The greater the evil God permits—not initiates--the greater the good that will come afterwards. Minister Farrakhan covered this in an earlier article, even to the value of chaos.

The Holy Qur'an teaches this principle in several ways. One is: "After difficulty comes ease." Yusuf Ali puts it that right in the difficulty is the ease, or the way out of the difficulty.

Allah always provides the way to Him and success. But, will we take that way out to Allah? It's also stated that in every difficulty or seemingly impossible hardship, or situation, is the seed of a superior benefit or condition, but only comes after the bad condition the person(s) was/were in.

We must make Allah's will our will and continue to become like Him to achieve such blessing. This is key towards getting out of the bad and into the better.

If one rejects, when shown the way out, the person's retardation intensifies. This refusal, if not halted, drives the person towards the meeting with a horrible, disgraceful and miserable state. Take the seed, or the way that Allah has provided, in our condition, regardless to what it may be, and make it to grow by obedience, and we come out of it into that which is far superior.

This and more is right in Minister Farrakhan's study guides. As our attitude towards God's man matures, we grow spiritually, which under-girds all other growth.

On May 1st, Minister Farrakhan responded to questions about six sciences, of which this world has some information. They were the sciences of music, medicine, color, business, mating and warfare; then came the seventh the "mother of all" sciences.

Subscribers to www.writtentestimony.com can get the link to my 25,000 plus word-testimony to Minister Farrakhan's *More-Than-A-Vision* experience this September 17th.

JABRIL MUHAMMAD
AUGUST 26, 2002

FARRAKHAN: THE TRAVELER
FOR THE FINAL CALL
VOL. 21; NO. 51

The Honorable Elijah Muhammad's teachings clarify what humanity already knew, by providing a deeper understanding of that knowledge. Next, he presented truths on subjects, which this world's best brains have only been able to give vague hints. Furthermore, he taught knowledge that the best brains of this world could not obtain. Then, he introduced wisdom that none ever knew, except his Teacher.

In the best meaning of the word, the Honorable Minister Louis Farrakhan has best *amplified* the body of knowledge his teacher left behind.

This wisdom is sufficient proof (which is beyond evidence) that this is the time of which the scriptures teach when the Supreme Being and the Messiah would be present, in every sense of that word. Minister Farrakhan represents and is backed by both.

This is not some spooky, irrelevant, so-called "metaphysical," unconnected to the real world, and it's problems type teaching. Some may say, "Can it be verified?" Yes. It's been often verified. Currently, Minister Farrakhan's work should be sufficient verification. Then, there's coming the ultimate verification. We'll examine this, and its relevance to the "science of everything in life," after the May 1st interview of Minister Farrakhan.

Before we resume it, consider these excerpts.

In *Closing The Gap, Part One*: Minister Farrakhan spoke of two kinds of helpers who come to help "leaders of consequence, particularly divine leaders... ."

Minister Farrakhan: His help has to evolve with him. All of his help may not necessarily have been formed under the unique circumstances that led to his evolutionary development from before he was actually in physical form, even while that which produced him was being formed."

A little later he stated:

"Now, therefore, God, in helping His servants (the prophets) gives them help from Himself, which is the best help. That help is the best help because they grow along the same long lines that he grew under. They're formed in the same way that he is formed and their heart is formed in the same way his heart is formed. Therefore, these helpers see into this man what other helpers don't, or may not see, because the latter were not made from God to be his helpers, in the same way or degree, as the former helpers.

"However, they (the latter) accepted the role of a helper. Nevertheless, if they don't stay in constant submission; in constant obedience; in constant study; and in constant growth; then gaps will develop between the teacher and the student that will lead the student (sometimes) to be critical of the teacher when the teacher grows beyond the particular need of that helper that motivated that helper to first want to help."

In a 1936 letter to some of his ministers, the Honorable Elijah Muhammad wrote, "The wise man is he who has made a careful study of the past events, of ancient and modern history. The knowledge of the future is judged by the knowledge of the past.

"There are some men who are born with the gift of prophecy, while others are trained into it through an intense study of history."

Pete Rose lacked the natural talent of Ty Cobb, who was a baseball player of extraordinary gifts, who became one of the greatest baseball players of all time. Pete Rose was nicknamed "Charlie Hustle" because of how hard he worked at his chosen profession. He made himself into one of the best who ever played that game. He ended his career with more hits than Mr. Cobb and everyone else.

The Honorable Elijah Muhammad didn't always state the same truth in the same way. Here is an example of that, which brought rich fruit from the mouth of Minister Farrakhan, for this interview.

Brother Jabril: Brother Minister, the Jesus said, "Those who are well need not a physician." We're obviously a very sick people. You spoke earlier (off tape) of the centuries of depression we've suffered, when we were discussing the question of why suffering is really an integral part of the redemption of our people. I want us to go back over the subject of suffering and healing from another angle.

You know, the Honorable Elijah Muhammad once told me, that although they didn't have to be musicians, doctors or photographers, he wanted his ministers to have some knowledge of medicine, music and color. Why do you think he said this and how does that kind of skill and knowledge help in the redemptive process of our people?

Minister Farrakhan: I never heard him say it like that. What I heard him say was that music, those who understood or knew music, medicine and the science of color, would make his best ministers.

I don't think everybody who wants to be a minister has to necessarily go and take a course in the study of music or medicine or color. But those who came to him with this kind of understanding would see deeply into the aspect of his word that would produce healing.

First, music is a force that is universally recognized and accepted. The basis of music, great music, is harmony. So those who understand what it takes to produce harmony, to cause different instruments with different ranges, different sounds, to utilize those differences in a magnificent way to produce symphony, or the same sound or harmony; to take different colors and learn how to put this color with that to produce something different from both colors to feed the human spirit; to learn the science of medicine, which is the use of chemistry, to induce or to produce the feeding of the natural function of systems and organs, can make the best helpers.

Once one is blessed with that kind of knowledge, then we should be able to pass on the word of God better; putting this with that, to produce a message that would produce the same effect on the soul of man that beautiful music produces; that the right diagnosis and the right prescription of medicine produces in the human anatomy; and the effect that the proper use of color produces, in demonstrating what you wish to paint, to get over to your audience.

This, to me, is why he said this because learning how to use the word of God to heal is the job of any disciple of the master. For the master in his person, in his heart, in his character is born to offer healing, not only to his people who are sick but the whole of humanity is sick--if we look at what God's intention was in creating Adam and what man is as a result of his disobedience to divine instructions. So the whole planet is groaning under illness.

This to me is why this Messianic figure is taught the word, the Gospel, the Torah, the Book and the Wisdom, and is sent with the guidance and the true religion; not only that he may make it overcome other religions, but he may make it overcome the illnesses that religion has not been able to heal.

Visit www.writtentestimony.com and get my testimony to Minister Farrakhan's *More-Than-A-Vision Experience* of 9/17/85 and how to become a wholesaler of *Is It Possible That The Honorable Elijah Muhammad Is Still Physically Alive???*

Jabril Muhammad
September 11, 2002

Farrakhan: The Traveler
For The Final Call
Vol. 22; No.1

Today, Friday the 13th, I was blessed to be part of the MSNBC-TV audience who saw and heard the Honorable Minister Louis Farrakhan fulfilling what was written of him, thousands of years ago, as he appeared on the "Buchanan And Press" program. He was questioned on President Bush's plans to make war on Iraq—a very critical issue. Minister Farrakhan came across simultaneously, as he is; principled, knowledgeable, passionate and fearless. Get the tape—preferably the video version.

We're continuing the concluding parts of the May 1st interview of Minister Farrakhan, which includes the Messianic work with science to accomplish the resurrection of the dead.

Minister Farrakhan: He [the Messianic figure] is to harmonize the Torah, the Gospel and the Qur'an; taking the universal principles they contain and marry them even to the contemporary teachings of the Prophet and use it all in a way to produce medicine for the sin sick condition of humanity. That is the work of a true minister of the Honorable Elijah Muhammad today.

I think that is why he [the Honorable Elijah Muhammad] wanted his ministers to pattern after the Minister. I think this is why he said of me, "Brother I did not make you." And I said, "Oh yes you did make me dear Apostle." He said, "No I didn't." And I insisted that he made me. He insisted that he didn't. Finally his insistence wore my insistence down by his saying "No Brother, I gave you the same that I gave everybody else. But only Allah could show you how to put the teachings together as you do. No Brother, Allah made you for me."

A pattern, in this context, means "a plan or model used as a guide for making something; a model that is considered to be worthy of imitation." Of course, imitation is not what Minister Farrakhan desires of his helpers. He explained this in article (Vol. 21-No. 45) when, in part, he stated:

"Learning ***of*** a man is learning the inner workings of his mind, which then gives you the spirit out of which he does what he does and this is why God is using him."

For his whole answer, please read the article.

Brother Jabril: Brother Minister, the Honorable Elijah Muhammad said that there were three scientific fields of knowledge that the slave master did not want the slave to ever learn. What are those areas of knowledge and what has that ignorance produced in us as a people? How does knowledge of music, medicine, and color, help in overcoming that ignorance?

Minister Farrakhan: The three sciences, as I recall, were: number 1) the science of business, 2) science of warfare, 3) the science of mating.

In the word business is: b-u-s-i, and the "i" is interchangeable with "y," "busy."

When a person is busy, they're active. So the science of business is the science of the life activity. The life activity, that is dictated by the nature in which we're created, is that we must utilize what God has given to us; develop it through knowledge and use that with what God has already put here to become productive; to be producers.

The science of business is the knowledge of how to satisfy the natural needs of a human being in the manner that pleases God. Business, which takes, of course, into consideration the acquisition of wealth; the proper use of wealth or the creation of wealth; the making of a product; the sale and distribution of what one makes; the creation of a means of satisfying necessities—food, clothing, shelter, trade, and commerce—all of this is really a science.

When one does not know it, then we are subjected to the one who does know it. We become their servant, and, at worse, their slave. So if the enemy wanted to keep us as perpetual slaves, this then is a science that we were not to become familiar with because that would free us from the state of dependence that a slave existence determines.

Second is the science of warfare. One must know how to protect what one develops from an enemy. So the science of warfare is a science that can free you from an enemy as well as protect you from an enemy. Since the enemy did not want us ever to be freed from them, nor able to protect ourselves from their wickedness, they never wanted us to learn the science of warfare.

The third science is the science of mating: to know how to properly marry this or that in order to produce a better future. They learned how to produce great horses, pedigreed dogs and how to do this with other life in the animal kingdom. This same science is applicable in the human sphere.

(He touched an example where Caucasians used this knowledge among themselves in Europe.)

They did not wish for us to learn that science because that would mean that through proper mating we might produce those that would free us from their grip, ultimately and challenge their ruler-ship over us and over the planet. So these three basic sciences were not to be taught to us.

Now we were taught the science of music. But we were never taught how to marry the science of music to the science of life. We were taught the science of medicine, but we were taught it in a way that we could never relate it *spiritually* to the overall sick condition of even the doctor who learned it and to the sick condition of our people and to the sick condition of our world. We were in art courses that taught us the science of color, but we never learned how to apply it as a force for healing.

It is only after learning the wisdom of the Honorable Elijah Muhammad that we could utilize these various sciences and turn these sciences into instruments of healing. It is only after coming into the light of what the Honorable Elijah Muhammad taught us of the knowledge of God, and self, and of the enemy of God and self, and the true religion of God, that we could then go after the science of business, the science of warfare, and the science of mating, that we would never again be a slave to any man, dependent on other human beings for our food, clothing, and shelter and the necessities of life and that we would become producers of this for ourselves.

We thank Allah for His coming and giving to us such a masterful teacher, as the Honorable Elijah Muhammad.

The next question opened with: "Now we come to all of these sciences from another angle or I should say from the ultimate perspective."

Here is where we get into—not just the explanation of all things—but the roots of this explanation. The fact that this has been explained is enough to tell us that God is present.

Visit www.writtentestimony.com and get my testimony to Minister Farrakhan's *More-Than-A-Vision* experience of 9/17/85, and information on becoming a wholesaler of *Is It Possible That The Honorable Elijah Muhammad Is Still Physically Alive???*

JABRIL MUHAMMAD
SEPTEMBER 13, 2002

Farrakhan: The Traveler
For The Final Call
Vol. 22; No. 2

Here are the Honorable Minister Louis Farrakhan's concluding answers to the May 1st interview.

Brother Jabril: Now we come to all of these sciences from another angle or I should say from the ultimate perspective.

One day you told us that the subject of love came up between you and the Honorable Elijah Muhammad. You said he was deepening you (and the others there) on this subject. You said he raised that question to you: "What is love?" You gave an answer and he then went on to teach that it was freedom, justice, and equality.

Now, of course, you know he taught us that freedom, justice, and equality was related to the sun, stars, and the moon, in that the sun, the stars, and the moon were symbols or signs of freedom, justice, and equality.

Brother Minister, since freedom, justice, and equality undergirds our successes, in the use of the other six sciences on which you've just commented, how then, is freedom, justice, and equality, love?

Minister Farrakhan: It would seem to me that freedom, as the Honorable Elijah Muhammad taught us, is essential to life. So is justice. So is equality. These are basic essentials to life.

Since God is the Author of life, He is the Source of these basic essentials of life—freedom. Everything He created always starts from a seed, or something small and insignificant. But in order for us to see what it is, that it may glorify the God Who gave it to us, it must be free to develop. Once it develops, it justifies its existence and is equal to all things in creation.

He created everything out of this awesome power of love, then He created all things to be free, to be justified, and to be equal. It is only when we help people to develop the best that is in themselves—so that they may justify their existence and thus become equal to everything else that justifies its existence—that we demonstrate that we love.

Naturally, parents love their children. But freedom is not license. Freedom has to be within the sphere of a law that regulates the behavior of the creature so that it does not destroy the life that it has been given. So there is no love without freedom and there is no freedom without love that restricts us from that which is destructive of our being and that would disallow us to justify our existence thus making us equal to all things in creation.

Love is life and life is love. There is no life without freedom, justice, and equality. And there is no love without the same.

Brother Jabril: How—not only are human beings—but how is anything that He created justified? In what way is it justified?

Minister Farrakhan: From my understanding, a thing is justified by being itself. Being itself means developing in accord with the nature of its creation. When it develops along the natural lines for which it was created, it fulfills its purpose for creation, thereby, justifying itself.

Brother Jabril: How, in this great diversity of life forms and things, throughout creation, is anything equal?

Minister Farrakhan: It is equal in that, from the tiniest atom, to the hugest planet, they all function in accord with a law. It is by means of that law that they are in existence and perpetuate their existence. So the atom is equal to the far planet even though the atom is microscopic and cannot be seen with the naked eye and the planet is so huge that it cannot be mistaken, you know. (Both laugh.) But they both are equal by means of law.

Brother Jabril: Freedom, justice, and equality—Islam. What is Islam's relation to these other sciences that we were *not* taught, but now we have to learn in order to benefit self and others? What is Islam's relation to the other sciences that we *have been* taught, but have not yet learned how to properly apply?

Would you say again that—and you've said it different ways—this that is called Islam, which is freedom, justice, and equality, which are essentials of life—is that which we must master, in order to make proper use of all these other sciences? Please comment on these relationships, especially now, that we are right on the threshold of the birth of a brand new world.

Minister Farrakhan: This day have I completed my favor on you and perfected for you your religion and chosen for you Islam as a religion.

To me, Islam, as taught by the Honorable Elijah Muhammad, is the completion of God's favor and it offers to us the greatest degree of freedom because it gives us the greatest knowledge of the offer of freedom and the greatest knowledge of our connection to Him that we now are made free to grow into Him.

This Islam that the Honorable Elijah Muhammad gives us represents a new sun, a new moon, a new star; a greater freedom, a greater justice, a greater equality, which will supplant the old freedom. The old freedom is the old freedom because it was not sufficient in the knowledge that it gave and the understanding that accompanies that knowledge and the guidance that came with that knowledge to perfect the human being and grow the human into God.

He was not yet fully free to justify himself. And I believe that's why one writer said he (the Jesus figure) thought it not robbery to equal himself up to God, in the sense that now he was given the knowledge to be what God had created him to be and the freedom to be that.

That is why none of these sciences can be made as useful as they will be made except through that wisdom that was brought to us by Master Fard Muhammad and taught to us by the most Honorable Elijah Muhammad.

This ends the May 1st interview. It began in Volume 21; Number 35. If you've not read the whole, please get back issues of *The Final Call* or visit www.writtentestimony.com.

My interview of Minister Farrakhan, *which preceded this one*, started in Volume 21; Number 17, and ended in Volume 21; Number 32. Again, please get the back issues of *The Final Call* or visit the same website *for the wisdom in them of Minister Farrakhan.*

I also intend to give Minister Farrakhan's answer to the "why" of the six women and one man, who were at the foot of the cross, when Jesus was being crucified.

In a very humble manner, Minister Farrakhan asked me, why I asked him such questions. I gave him a short, respectful, and loving answer. He nodded his head and smiled. I'd like to share that answer. It has everything to do with "the explanation of all things."

Many may ask, are Minister Farrakhan's brief and simple answers, in this interview, the explanation of all things?

The Holy Qur'an says it contains, "the explanation of all things." Christians claim this for the New Testament. In certain places, it reads that way.

I began this series by noting the physicists' (scientists') efforts to gain "the explanation of all things."

Jabril Muhammad
September 14, 2002

Farrakhan: The Traveler
For The Final Call
Vol. 22; No. 3

> *"And those who disbelieve say: Why has not the Qur'an been revealed to him all at once? ... they cannot bring thee a question, but We have brought thee the truth and the best explanation."*
>
> *— Holy Qur'an 25:32; 33*

> *This "is ... a verification of what is before it, and a distinct explanation of all things ...."*
>
> *— Holy Qur'an 12:112*

In my last article, I wrote these words: "This ends the May 1st interview." I meant that the Honorable Minister Louis Farrakhan's answer to my last question (as it appeared last week) ended the interview, in the sense that he satisfied my purpose for the interview.

I then went on to ask him a different set of questions about his music, to complete my purpose, for another interview that I conducted last year, with Minister Farrakhan and one of his teachers,

Mrs. Ayke Agus. My primary purpose for that interview was to bring out how his music "expanded his breast" and brought him closer to Allah. By the help of Allah that will be put together and sent to *The Final Call* soon.

The Honorable Elijah Muhammad taught not the coming of God but the presence of God. *If* God is present, then everything can be known. *If* God is present, then everything can now be explained. *If* God is present, then everything can now be understood.

That knowledge, that explanation, and that understanding has been available since the arrival of Master Fard Muhammad and His meeting with the Honorable Elijah Muhammad in 1931.

In his work, which includes the amplification of the body of knowledge left by his teacher—the Honorable Elijah Muhammad—Minister Farrakhan has verified the steps or approach to, and the solution of the most difficult and the most explosive problem that has ever existed on our planet.

It's a problem that is so difficult to really understand; so intricate or complicated; and so dangerous; that only a superior degree of the wisdom that was used in the beginning of the creation of life and the universe will suffice to solve this problem. This is no exaggeration. It's now here.

The scripture verifies the above written in bold. So do today's actual facts.

Now, how well have we understood it? By "we" I am including *everyone*, here in America. How well have those called the wise or learned or educated, understood the wisdom Master Fard Muhammad taught the Honorable Elijah Muhammad, of which Minister Farrakhan is the chief exponent?

To most Christians, the coming of God is inseparable from the coming of a man 2,000 years ago, named Jesus, to whom they attribute the title, "the Christ" or "the Messiah."

To most Muslims, the coming of God involves this same Jesus, who will accompany a greater man, who is to bear the title "the Mahdi."

Most Jews expect the appearance of a man, under the title "Messiah," at a time variously called "the last days" or "the end of the world" and by other more descriptive names. However, they disbelieve that he was here 2,000 years ago.

There are differences among Jews, Christians and Muslims respecting the Messiah. However, there are major points of agreement. One such agreement is that the Messiah would bring wisdom that would be supreme in every sense of the word and it would produce a brand new world. It would explain everything.

The Honorable Elijah Muhammad, Minister Farrakhan and other helpers (witnesses) have presented this teaching in depth throughout America in an open manner. Among those who have deeply studied this teaching, are scholars, on the payroll of the government of America. The Honorable Elijah Muhammad stated that they have studied prophecy in relation to his work and know the scripture verifies it.

Why haven't the officials of the government of the United States of America openly announced that the Messiah has arrived? Well, answer this: why hasn't the government informed the American public of the truth concerning the flying objects popularly called U.F.O.'s?

What is their explanation? Does their explanation provide an adequate defense of their position? Why is it "top-secret?" What will happen when it all comes out to the public? Does the truth explain why they call Minister Farrakhan dangerous?

If certain government officials, and other powerful persons, privately agree that the wisdom presented by Minister Farrakhan (from his teacher) is true, and if they have kept it from the public, does this qualify as a conspiracy of the highest order or the mother of all cover-ups?

If such a cover-up has been and is still in effect, how does it relate to the massive campaign of deception that is in full force against Black people in America, that the Honorable Elijah Muhammad described years ago?

In yesterday's *The Arizona Republic*, dated October 7th, it was reported in the press that the well known entertainer Ms. Alicia

Keys stated "the pressure she is under to be sexy makes her sick." The article continued: "she is constantly fighting with her stylists over the clothes they try and make her wear."

Are these "stylists" part of a vast conspiracy, even if they don't know it, hatched by evil demons, several decades ago, and continued by their descendants, to fog-up the minds of the public from realizing the presence of God?

Mr. Denzel Washington is a great actor. He won the Best Actor award for his role as a corrupt policeman. Many Blacks wonder why he did not win it for another movie, which brought out something sinister in the medical profession? What's the explanation?

There are Black newsmen sitting beside white women (or vice-versa) reporting the news on TV, even in little cities where Blacks are few. Is this just a matter of the best qualified person for the job, or is it something else? It's an increasing phenomenon that forms a pattern. What's the explanation?

What is the explanation for the increase of romantic roles involving White women and Black men in movies, and to a lesser extent, the same kind of roles involving Black women and White men? There are an increasing number of "Black and White" together movies, while most Blacks live in hell. What's up?

How clear are the minds of Black people to the reality of the times in which we live? Are we "living it up" like the people of Noah and Lot were moments before the rains and the hot stones fell?

What is ***the*** root explanation of disunity among Black people in America? What explains good; evil; laughter; foolishness; insects; planets; the universe?

What does it mean to explain? What is an explanation? How does an explanation generate understanding? Can we defend anything we cannot first explain? What must we first have in order to explain anything to ourselves and to others?

It is better not to assume that we know what these words mean if we've never really examined them in a thesaurus, a dictionary and a synonym book. A thesaurus provides us with words for ideas we have that are hazy to us. Dictionaries define words. Synonym books refine our understanding of the meanings of words by providing us with the differences between words that are similar in meaning.

Now is the time when everything—the science of everything in life—can be understood. Why? God and the Messiah are present!

Jabril Muhammad
October 9, 2002

Farrakhan: The Traveler
For *The Final Call*
Vol. 22; No. 4

The Holy Qur'an teaches much on the subject of "ignorance" and those it calls "the ignorant."

This subject is relevant to the work of the Honorable Minister Louis Farrakhan, in his effort to help President Bush, his primary supporters, and millions to see what The Almighty God, Allah has blessed him to see. Minister Farrakhan is inspired to speak from what God revealed to the Honorable Elijah Muhammad, which the scriptures predicted and prophesied would take place in these days.

I am fully aware that many others—prominent and not—have raised their voices against the President's policy towards Iraq. However, none of them have the mandate from God Himself and His Christ—insane as this may sound to many, to say what Minister Farrakhan says on this subject.

"Ignorance" is defined in the sixth edition of *Black's Law Dictionary* on page 746, as "The want or absence of knowledge, unaware or uninformed."

Further down it continues: "Ignorance is not a state of the mind in the sense in which sanity and insanity are. When the mind is ignorant of a fact, its condition still remains sound; the power of thinking, of judging, of willing, is just as complete before communication of the fact as after. The essence or texture, so to speak, of the mind, is not, as in the case of insanity, affected or impaired. Ignorance of a particular fact consists in this: that the mind, although sound and capable of healthy action, has never acted upon the fact in question, because the subject has never been brought to the notice of the perceptive faculties."

That's the general definition. Then it goes into details under "General Types" among which are: "Culpable" "Involuntary" and "Voluntary" ignorance. When we fail "to exercise ordinary care to acquire knowledge" culpable ignorance is the result. In other words, we can be held responsible.

"Involuntary ignorance" is ignorance that "does not proceed from choice, and which cannot be overcome by the use of any means of knowledge known to a person and within his power.

"Voluntary ignorance" exists when a party might, by taking reasonable efforts, have acquired the necessary knowledge."

The Holy Qur'an covers all aspects of ignorance covered in the law books of this world. It also covers what such dictionaries do not cover; the most important of which is ignorance of God Almighty.

As The Almighty formed Aaron to share the burden or mission of Moses, in his service to the slaves, and to Pharaoh and those with him, so did The Almighty form Minister Farrakhan to share the mission of the Honorable Elijah Muhammad.

God did not destroy Pharaoh and his hosts until they were thoroughly educated and not before the extreme of mercy was extended to them, through Moses and Aaron. So it is today.

Excluding God, we are very ignorant. Certainly we "see" what we "see" of our profession, work etc., though it's not to the root. But how many of us know how to fly an airplane; perform brain surgery; design a bridge, or do the countless things that serve billions of people throughout the earth?

Let's be real. How much do we know of all that the rest of humanity knows, not to think of all that there is to know that humanity does not know?

Look up at the sky at night? How much of what we see, do we know, excluding how to explain what we see? Of course, when we look up at the stars we see but a tiny bit of what there is to see.

But even if we knew a million times what we now know, but did not know God, we would be ignorant of the most important and the most valuable of all knowledge.

To be "ignorant" of God when He is present is the worst kind of ignorance. To refuse to accept His truth after it's been presented to us is worse yet.

To seek to deceive others about that truth and its bearer and to seek to destroy that truth and its bearer exceeds all other forms of ignorance. This earns such persons the worst of God's chastisements.

Our collective "Involuntary ignorance" that did not proceed from our choice, and which could not be overcome by any of us, has been overcome by the power of God through His revelations of truth through the modern Moses and Aaron.

What they (and other helpers/witnesses) have delivered to all in America is that truth that would come that would be so plain that even fools would understand.

Why do the deniers reject this truth? False pride? Jealousy and/or envy? Did they fail "to exercise ordinary care to acquire knowledge" that resulted in "culpable ignorance?" Culpable means we are held responsible and deserve blame and punishment.

But those whose ignorance is "Voluntary ignorance" means you have taken "reasonable efforts" and you "have acquired the necessary knowledge" but what did you do with it? Some simply sit on it, while others seek to destroy it and its bearer.

There are government officials and others (Shriners included) who know that Minister Farrakhan is teaching God's truth. It's written that some of you will make public your witness of this truth.

According to the Holy Qur'an, a believer from among Pharaoh's people finally stood up. Others stood up with him against Pharaoh's policies against God, Moses and Aaron.

Question: is this prophecy conditional or unconditional? See Qur'an Surah (chapter) 40, section 3-5.

Muhammad Ali wrote this in his introduction to Surah 40, of

the believer from among Pharaoh's people: "This man pleaded for Moses, when Pharaoh wanted to kill him, and drew attention to the fact that, if Moses preached the truth, no opposition to him could prosper."

There's a situation much like what I've just cited from the Holy Qur'an and from Muhammad Ali, in the third through the fifth chapters in the book of Acts.

A prominent member of the Council stood against their fury, in which they "decided to kill them." (5:33) But "... Gamaliel (an expert on religious law and very popular with the people), "addressed his colleagues as follows: 'Men of Israel, take care what you are planning to do to these men!' " (5:35)

He drew from history to make his case. He concluded with: "And so my advice is, leave these men alone. If what they teach and do is merely on their own, it will soon be overthrown. But if it is of God, you will not be able to stop them, lest you find yourselves fighting even against God."

I suggest we study or restudy these passages in both books, in context. Compare these histories to the history of America and Blacks in this country. Then look at the history of the Nation of Islam.

On page 182 of *This Is The One* we read:

"Don't look only into outerspace... Some of those stars, the light of which we see, no longer exist. It is *in* this—the wisdom that fuels the Nation of Islam in the West—that the scientists can find the understanding of the origin of life and the key of the governance of the universe."

Look carefully into the government's small-pox vaccination program.

JABRIL MUHAMMAD
OCTOBER 11, 2002

Farrakhan: The Traveler
For *The Final Call*
Vol. 22; No. 5

This short introduction to the interview that follows is being written on the eve (October 15th) of one of the most pivotal speeches the Honorable Minister Louis Farrakhan has ever given. This interview was conducted on May 2, 2002, in Phoenix, Arizona. It answers some of the questions at the end of the interview of May 1st, for which see Vol. 22, No. 2.

For better than two and a half decades, I've often stated, to whoever would listen or read my words, that if you watch the movement of the mind of Minister Farrakhan, you can tell time—of which the scriptures foretold.

His words provide crucial study material for we who follow him and for everyone else. His words contain invaluable insights into the core of what is taking place here in America and elsewhere. His words are essential for us to gain a better than average understanding of what we must do to survive the madness of this falling world.

Brother Jabril: Brother Minister, after the experience of Jesus in the garden of Gethsemane, where God had an angel (Luke 22:43) to help him get through that moment, he was made to appear before Pilate and the other officials. Then came the trial, after which they put him on the cross. Now, his last words, (in John 19) while on the cross were: "It is accomplish." or "It is finished." It's put in different ways in different English translations.

There were six women and one man, who were his followers, who stood by him as he hung on the cross.

There were Roman soldiers there too but their mind-set was different. One of them, however, was finally affected by the way Jesus handled himself in that horrible moment, and bore witness to his identity.

What are your views on this? Why were the six believers there? What were their motives? What could they offer him? What did he get from them, if anything? Why do you think we're even told this in the first place? What bearing does all of this have on *our getting through,* so that when *that* time comes, in fulfillment of the scriptures, we can answer in the affirmative to the question in Luke 18:8: "… when the Son of Man comes, will he find faith on the earth?"

Minister Farrakhan: That very dark hour of Jesus, when he was in that certain and delightful spot that he loved so well, called the Garden of Gethsemane, in the Mount of Olives, there they say he prayed until sweat was dropping from his brow. In that same hour when he was praying, (for he was conscious of the hour) his disciples were in a state of sleep or suspended consciousness. They were not aware of the hour.

It appears that there were aspects of what he said and taught that they didn't agree with and did not necessarily believe; not because they were disbelievers, but they could not bear the pain of the thought of his leaving them. Nor could they bear the pain of the thought that they might not see him again for awhile. Some may have even had the thought that they would never see him again.

In that dark hour of their suspended consciousness, when they awaken to the reality of that hour, the soldiers were already upon him and them and took him.

Then, of course, there was the trial, where he fulfilled what the scripture teaches, that he would not even speak in his own defense because it was not his trial. It was the trial of all of those whom he had taught, among whom he had worked, and among whom he had done so many wonderful and miraculous things.

Now they were called upon to be a witness for him. In that hour of the cry of "crucify him" it appeared that there were no witnesses for him. The people, in their sickness, could accept a thief more easily than they could accept a man of God. So at his crucifixion, none of them, according to scriptures, none of them were present, except for John and these women.

The six women and the one man represented an untold number that were growing into belief in him *but were not present.* The events of the hour were making a whole new cadre of believers.

Regardless to their lapse the disciples could have been raised *in the next instance,* or they could have been replaced by those who bore resemblance to them, in terms of faith. But under a new reality, they became renewed in the knowledge that he was in fact alive.

Some of the old can be made new but most of the old will be gone; unworthy, unfit to be with him in that next dispensation.

I feel that in my going overseas, that my mission is to do everything in my power to stop a war, which the present administration of the United States of America is bent upon. It is in my heart to announce my purpose even before I go, that the world will know that the Brother is a peace maker, who does not wish to see one American soldier; Black, Brown or poor White lose their lives to fulfill the vendetta of several presidents against Saddam Hussein, who has been and is a thorn in their side.

It is my desire to visit some of these countries that are referred to as the "axis of evil." But in the root of my thinking is that, if the Muslim world could unite in a significant way, they could stop this war from taking place.

It will hurt the Bush administration. It may hurt his chance for re-election and, therefore, the Minister will be seen as one that has to be destroyed.

They are trying to build a case, falsely, against Saddam Hussein to justify their destruction of what is a thorn in their side. They are those Zionists, in and outside of the government, whose desire is to use the power of America to destroy, not one who is any potential threat to the United States of America, but one that Israel feels, if it develops any weapons of mass destruction, it will be a threat to Israel's power to dominate and destroy the whole Arab world.

As a result of my effort, which will be seen on both sides and interpreted by many, I may be charged with sedition or treason and whatnot. Under these charges they might want to freeze bank accounts and do harm to the Nation. It will cause many to feel that I deliberately did something to harm the Nation and I had no business thinking about Iraq or Muslims over there; that I should have concerned myself with the Nation here and as a result of my predisposition to help the Muslims outside of America, I put the

Muslims inside of America into a position to be threatened and persecuted by the United States government.

"But what they don't realize is that what I'm doing is directed by God and the Christ, which will give God the justification for His attack on this world."

JABRIL MUHAMMAD
OCTOBER 15, 2002

FARRAKHAN: THE TRAVELER
FOR THE FINAL CALL
VOL. 22; NO. 6

This is being written on the day after the Honorable Minister Louis Farrakhan delivered a momentous speech to America and to the nations of the earth, on October 16th. His May 2nd statement provides insights into his speech as well as context.

Here's the conclusion of that interview started in last week's article.

Minister Farrakhan: So then at my trial and in this time of trial, I will lose many. Some of the females that truly love the Minister will be present and the one male disciple, who will be present, will represent thousands who are absent, but who in the darkness are growing in faith because they are unhindered by the hypocrisy that will have been manifested inside the house, for they have grown up on the outside with a more pure sight on the man than many whose sight has been dulled by their lack of faith; their doubt; their suspicion, which now manifests into absolute hypocrisy.

All of this is as it was written. It leads to the glorification of God and His Christ. It also leads to the exaltation of the servant of God. In that darkness, I believe he will be taken. And there are those who will see him as he is taken, to bear witness to the others, that the stone that appeared to keep him where they thought they had him, has been removed and he is gone.

So that is my answer to that question of deep significance that maybe the answer should not be given until a certain time.

Brother Jabril: Yes sir.

This ends the May 2nd interview.

This is *that* certain time. However, as it is his right, Minister Farrakhan has shared this with his staff across the country.

There are many ways to start the explanation that shows that Minister Farrakhan's answers, which appeared (in Vol. 22, No. 2) constitute, "the explanation of all things."

I'm starting in the way that I am, due to the increasing gravity of these times, which fulfills the scriptures.

Let's begin with a series of points. Why doubt the fact that high in the Bush administration, plans have been made for the imprisonment and death of Minister Farrakhan? Has this government ever sought to harm individuals and groups based on lies and wicked motivations?

If they really understood who Minister Farrakhan actually is, they would not even think evil of him, let alone plan his death?

The 19th chapter of the gospel of John describes Jesus' death on the cross. Does this chapter teach of the one more or the last thing he was to do, before being taken alive to his father? Was it, "dying?"

God has allowed Christians to hand down, throughout the centuries, the image of a nearly nude Jesus, hanging on a cross, between two others, who were deemed criminals. The authorities counted Jesus as a criminal. This has meaning for today.

President Bush and his cabinet swore on the Bible as the major part of their induction into the offices that they hold over the people of America. Are President Bush and his cabinet scholars of the scriptures? If not, then on whom do they depend for their views and insights into the thinking of God Almighty, who is the ultimate Author of the scriptures? How much does this influence their actions?

Do they believe that Jesus is up in the sky, from which he is to return to judge this world? Does "this world" include America? Do they believe that we are in the time described in the book of Revelation, especially in chapters 12, 13, 17 and 18?

The 12th and the 13th chapters contain predictions of their persecution of the Honorable Elijah Muhammad and his followers, especially Minister Farrakhan. The 17th and the 18th chapters teach of the consequences of this persecution of their ex-slaves.

Certain officials of this government have been studying that huge half-mile by a half-mile plane, in the skies over America. Do they see this plane as the fulfillment of the 19th chapter of Revelation that teaches of the awesome return of Jesus the Christ from the sky? Is this plane the reality of Ezekiel's vision of the wheel in a wheel?

Is there a relation between the above and this from the book, *JFK* by L. Fletcher Prouty, who was the "Mr. X" in the movie titled "JFK" directed by Oliver Stone?

Mr. Prouty wrote on page 287-288: "During the Kennedy years, people within the government and their close associates in academia and industry discussed frequently and quite seriously many of the major questions phrased by Leonard Lewin in Report From Iron Mountain. I had been assigned to the Office of the Secretary of Defense before the Kennedy election and was there when the McNamara team of 'Whiz Kids' arrived. Never before had so many brilliant young civilians with so many Ph.D.s worked in that office. It was out of the mouths of this group that I heard so frequently and precisely the ideas that Lewin recounts in his 'novel.' A brief sampling will show these words' power on the thinking of that era:

'Lasting peace, while not theoretically impossible, is probably unattainable; even if it could be achieved it would most certainly not be in the best interests of a stable society to achieve it.

'War fills certain functions essential to the stability of our society; until other ways of filling them are developed, the war system must be maintained---and improved in effectiveness.

'War is virtually synonymous with nationhood. The elimination of war implies the inevitable elimination of national sovereignty and the traditional nation-state.

'The organization of a society for the possibility of war is its principle political stabilizer... . The basic authority of a modern state over its people resides in its war powers.

'There is no hard evidence that this political philosophy was that of President Kennedy or of senior members of his administration. Indeed, the Kennedy administration had already undertaken several courses of action that showed a clear intention to slow the forward thrust of the Cold War. One of these, of course, was spelled out in NSAM #263, which announced plans for the Vietnamization of the war in Indochina and the scheduled, early withdrawal of all American personnel.' "

Several paragraphs later and on page 289 Mr. Prouty wrote: "Kennedy's plans would mean an end to the warfare in Indochina, which the United States had been supporting for nearly two decades. This would mean the end to some very big business plans, as the following anecdote will illustrate." (Visit www.writtentestimony.com for details.)

So the rich continue to become richer, at the expense of the poor. For example, a major hospital, especially needed by Blacks, Mexicans and the poor here in Phoenix, has been purchased by a company that plans to replace its emergency and obstetric services with a money-making surgical unit.

Blacks, Mexicans, a few politicians and others are publicly speaking up for the community, who generally are calling this a case of "economic racism." What's happening to hospitals serving the poor in your cities?

The rich generally deem the poor as "no-bodies." Example: They refuse reparations, let alone apologize for enslaving us—neither of which is justice.

JABRIL MUHAMMAD
OCTOBER 17, 2002

Section 7

Farrakhan: The Traveler
For The Final Call
Vol. 23; No. 14

On December 14th a four-hour long documentary aired on The History Channel titled "In The Footsteps of Jesus." It was introduced with these words: "Two thousand years ago an extraordinary man made a journey that changed the world forever.

It's a commemoration from his birth in Bethlehem to his death in Jerusalem. Now researchers are tracking down the very path he traveled.

Generations of archeologists continue to comb that area of the world for evidence that might link various sites to the gospel stories. Their findings appear continuously in journals, TV, radio, and books. Cover articles in national news magazines, such as *Time*, *Newsweek* and *U.S. News and World Report* are on Jesus, the so-called lost Gospels, Women of the Bible, and that America is rethinking Jesus.

This documentary, like so many, especially during the Christmas and Easter holidays, has its "experts," who disagree on almost everything pertaining to Jesus.

As an example, Shamon Gibson, an archeologist who appeared on this program, is among those who think he can pinpoint the exact location where Pontius Pilate interrogated Jesus.

He stated: "We're here on the Western side of the old city of Jerusalem and as you can see, specifically here, on the North, behind the wall here was the palace of Herod the Great and I like to imagine that this is a spot that perhaps Jesus was bought up in order to be at this trial in front of Pontius Pilate.

"... there was another flight of steps over here leading up to the place where I think the tribunal would have been where Pontius Pilate would have climbed in order to think about what he was going to do with this rascal or problematic person, named Jesus." (Note: "imagine," "perhaps" and "think.")

This program's narrator continues: "Every Friday afternoon Christian pilgrims gather to take part in the way of the cross or Via Dolorosa, which commemorates Jesus' final journey from the tradition site of the Praetorian to Golgotha where he was crucified.

"In light of recent archeological discoveries, some are beginning to question the accuracy of this route. The present Via Dolorosa has absolutely no claim to be historical. It starts from the wrong point and, of course, a number of the episodes on the Via Dolorosa had no basis in the New Testament, like Veronica wiping his face, for example.

'These were the development of popular piety in which historical certitude has no place at all.' "

The narrator: "Despite the scientific evidence against it, however, thousands of pilgrims continue to take part in the way of the cross every week."

Father Jerome Murphy-O'Conner: "But the end results of scholarship have no impact at all on the traditions of piety in Jerusalem. I mean the Via Dolorosa is established by faith, not by history.

"But what I think would be wrong would be for academics to say, 'This is the wrong place, therefore, you can't go there.' Because places, however tawdry, however fake, they have been venerated by people of great courage and great faith. They have a claim on our human sensitivity even though they may be historically wrong. So I would never discourage people from going to such places."

Thus ended the third hour of this documentary.

Does God agree with this? If not, how ought such believers to be helped? With intelligence, empathy, skill and truth.

The narrator starts the fourth hour with:

"The final footsteps of Jesus are commemorated every Friday in Jerusalem in a medieval processional route known as the Via Dolorosa. Fourteen stations marked the events surrounding Jesus' agonizing march to the cross, ending with the traditional sites of his crucifixion, burial and resurrection, which are housed inside the present day church of the Holy Sepulcher."

Gabriel Barkay, Ph.D: "We're now in the Chapel of Golgotha. And underneath the glass here, one can see the exposed bedrock very well. The exact spot of the cross is underneath the altar."

Narrator: "Beneath the rotunda of an adjacent chapel stands perhaps the holiest of all Christians' sites, the tomb of Jesus. The rotunda has in the middle of it an edifice which marks the burial place and place of resurrection."

There is a little more of Dr. Barkay's statement, then the narrator continues: "Pilgrims have been venerating the traditional sites of Jesus' death and burial for nearly 1,700 years. How do they know they are authentic?"

This question is followed with the conflicting views of the "experts." They, as do many Christian scholars, theologians, differ on the exact location of Jesus' tomb.

Near the end of the program the narrator concludes: "In the end most experts admit that we may never conclusively prove where Jesus died and was buried but perhaps that is how it should remain." I intend to provide the final words of this program next article.

But what of the position of most Jews, that Jesus was not the Messiah; that the Messiah was yet to come?

The New Testament teaches that Jesus was yet to be revealed. It's further written in 1John 3:8 that the "Son of God" was made manifest that he may destroy the works of Satan. The world is much more wicked now than it was 2,000 years ago when Jesus walked the earth.

The real truth of Jesus has been revealed. He has returned, but not in the spooky way we've been taught. The Honorable Elijah Muhammad taught the irrefutable truth of Jesus and the Honorable Minister Louis Farrakhan has borne irrefutable testimony to this truth on "Jesus."

In 1957 the Honorable Elijah Muhammad wrote: "There certainly is a surprise in store for both worlds (Islam and Christianity) in the revealing of this last one. Many of the religious scientists are already wise to it."

The revealing of Jesus raises the dead to life and brings on the judgment of this world. Remember this when we get to the core of Minister Farrakhan's assignment.

Thoroughly relevant to the subject of Jesus, is the Honorable Minister Louis Farrakhan's answer to this question:

More of his answer next issue, and its relevance to Jesus, Allah willing.

Jabril Muhammad
December 22, 2003

Farrakhan: The Traveler
For The Final Call
Vol. 23; No. 15

Brother Jabril: Brother Minister, the Honorable Elijah Muhammad stated that he was given a list of 104 books by Master Fard Muhammad, as part of his studies. After his Teacher's departure, when he was in Washington, D.C., he said it occurred to him to call his wife to send the list to him. He then began that part of his study. What did you hear him say concerning those books and their contents and what were they for?

Minister Farrakhan: I heard the Honorable Elijah Muhammad say that Master Fard Muhammad gave him 104 books to study. He said the best of those books was the Holy Qur'an. The other books contained certain aspects of and incidents in the life of Prophet Muhammad. Those are his words to me.

As I reflected on those words I asked the question, why would Master Fard Muhammad give him the Holy Qur'an, which was the book that details the revelation that Allah gave to Muhammad, and 103 books (making the 104) dealing with specific aspects of the life of Prophet Muhammad, that gives the context or circumstances that surrounded that revelation and the instructions that Allah gave to him concerning his mission and this revelation?

When I reflected on that, I thought that the path that the Honorable Elijah Muhammad was to travel was to use the footsteps of the Prophet to guide him in establishing the faith of Islam in the United States of America. So as Prophet Muhammad walked and worked in Arabia, so Elijah Muhammad, his companions, his followers would work for the establishment of Islam in America.

Before Prophet Muhammad departed this life he said to his followers, "If you follow this Qur'an and my Sunnah you will never deviate from the straight path of God."

From what I understand the Sunnah represents his actions in accord with the directions that he received from Allah in the establishment of the Qur'an and Islam.

By Master Fard Muhammad giving the Honorable Elijah Muhammad the Qur'an and giving him the footsteps of the Prophet, it seems to me that He was saying to His Messenger that the path that you will follow, if you follow this book—Qur'an—and the steps that the Prophet was guided to make in establishing the faith, plus the wisdom that I'm giving you of these books, you will never deviate and those who follow you will never deviate from the straight path of God.

Of all of the men whom Jews, Christians and Muslims today refer to as prophets of God, or Allah, the lives of none of them have come down to us in greater detail than that of Muhammad ibn Abdullah, through whom the Holy Qur'an was revealed, around 1,400 years ago.

What are the titles of these books? Was the Honorable Elijah Muhammad given the whole of each book to study? Or was it certain sections of each he was to study, whether or not he read the whole of them later? What impact did this study have on him and why? How did he relate these studies to his knowledge of the Bible and to his meeting and experiences with his Teacher—Who was born in Arabia? How did these studies inform his understanding of people whom he already knew and those he would meet later?

What he did with what was important to him, has profound relevance, not just to those who knew and know him, but also to countless numbers everywhere, even though this is yet to be really known.

Naturally, when we first learn of his study of "the 104 books" an interest arises in us to know more. However, everyone who seeks such knowledge does not do so from the same motives. Some use what they know, or think they know, to look important in the eyes of others. For instance, some claim that they have read some of the books on this list. Some say that Master Fard Muhammad used this or that book during the time He was in Detroit or Chicago. But the Honorable Elijah Muhammad said that he asked Him if these books were in Detroit. He said His answer was a simple, "No." They were in D.C.

But many more are interested in this subject because they are sincerely interested in him. But how many have thought of this subject, as has Minister Farrakhan? More of his mind on this critical subject to come, be it the will of Allah.

The Honorable Elijah Muhammad's Teacher first gave him a copy of the Qur'an in Arabic. He couldn't read it. Then He gave him the Muhammad Ali translation of the Qur'an. A little later, He gave him a copy of the Yusuf Ali translation. And He taught him how to understand it.

Now, consider the implications of Minister Farrakhan's words above. The Qur'an teaches that you will find no change in the ways of Allah. He is consistent. This is evident in His ways with His prophets.

If we knew His mind, or words, that He gave the people, through the prophets, in this or that circumstance, would not this benefit us, if we found ourselves in similar circumstances?

We have a lot to cover from Minister Farrakhan's wise observation, that could be of the greatest benefit to us, NOW, if we would but hurry and open our minds and hearts *wider* to his message and overall mission, *before* "all hell breaks loose!"

Now, here are the concluding words of the documentary, entitled: "In The Footsteps of Jesus," which aired this month (December) via The History Channel.

"Devout Christians believe that on that first Easter morning Jesus rose from the dead to bring salvation to the whole world. It is the bedrock of the Christian faith, even if there is no empirical evidence to prove it.

"While archeology enables pilgrims to walk in the footstep of Jesus, ultimately it is a journey that could only be completed by faith.

"Archaeology and history—all these different sciences, are marvelous helps to us, if they can help us to be sure of what we believe. But we need to remember that belief is faith. We're basing our faith on what is unseen.

"In the past archeology and faith were more or less antagonistic. Faith tried to use archaeology to prove that it was true. Archeology, at times, would be guided by faith, or misguided by faith, to look for particular things. I think in recent years they have a much more beneficial relationship. That is to say if the Christian faith, or any faith, wants to have depth to it; it needs to understand its traditions in their historical contexts.

"What archeology does for us is to contextualize the Gospel story. We simply understand better where the Gospel said Jesus went here, or he said this, now we understand it, because archeology lays bare what it looked like, the kinds of things people were doing, the customs, the tools, that's the real value of archeology. It doesn't really prove anything. It clarifies much."

JABRIL MUHAMMAD
DECEMBER 28, 2003

FARRAKHAN: THE TRAVELER
FOR *THE FINAL CALL*
VOL. 23; NO.16

The New Testament writers' teach that Jesus is to be fully revealed at the end of time. Generally, it's the end of the time of the wicked and their evil rule over the people of the earth. It's when God Himself takes full control of everything and establishes His own perfect infinite rule.

The 66th book of the Protestant Bible is titled, "The Revelation." Theologians teach that this book is about the times, people and the events involved in the full revelation of a man, who is of such great importance that the world of Christendom divides time, from times' beginning, and then throughout eternity by him.

Jews, Christians and Muslims have differences in their respective beliefs. Jews, Christians or Muslims have their sects, parties, or schools of thought, which contain varying degrees of conflicts with each other.

Nevertheless, the theologians, scholars, or the wise men of the Jews, Christians and Muslims all teach of the physical appearance of this man—the Messiah, Christ Jesus—at the time of the end of this world. They base their expectations of his coming on their understanding of the books they hold as sacred or divine. These books are called the Torah, the New Testament and the Holy Qur'an.

The wise men of these religions have spoken and written much about Jesus. Their expectations of his arrival, person and what he is to do, are contained in many volumes, most all of which are publicly available.

This man, under God's guidance, is to establish the kingdom of God on earth, permanently, and bring into existence a holy nation, through which humanity is to be summoned to dwell under Allah's sovereignty forever. Catholics see this man as God, or as God incarnate, or God in the flesh, or God in the person of Jesus.

It might take you quite a while to read through the sacred books of the Jews, the Christians and the Muslims and the many volumes of the writings of the learned of each group as they gave their understanding of God's word. This includes not just what each group of theologians has spoken and written of their own beliefs on the Messiah, but also the differences among themselves, as well as their respective differences with the other religious groups.

Suppose you knew all of their learning? Would your learning of their view of him match the reality of the Messiah's self-concept? No. If you put the wisdom of the most learned of these three religious groups together, the totality of their wisdom would not prove to be as true as the Messiah's self-concept, which comes from God Himself. The Messiah's arrival ends all disputes about himself, as he is the truth of himself. When the wise know he has arrived, they improve their knowledge and understanding of him from him.

The sacred books of each body of believers declares that the Messiah's arrival marks the time when God Himself ends all disputes on every matter. The process of the ending of all disputes and false arguments is proceeding now, as this is the Day of God's Judgment of everyone and everything.

It's through God's own self-disclosure and His revelation of the identity of the Messiah, that every one (and all values, etc.) is revealed. This paves the way for the new world to come into being.

The world was in spiritual darkness until the Messiah's recent arrival. Total darkness? Mostly, yes, and especially for the masses, and, even those who have and yet rule this dying world have really been in the darkness by which they have ruled.

Does the fact that the world was in darkness until this day affect the understanding of the theologians whether Jew, Christian or Muslim? Of course it does. Now, they either grow into greater understanding or they oppose God and become fuel for the fire. Either way they become witnesses to His presence.

By now the theologians should publicly bear witness that the Messiah has arrived.

The Holy Qur'an teaches of the controversies surrounding Jesus' name. Why did not Muhammad, through whom the Qur'an was revealed, able to thoroughly dissolve all of the confusion around Jesus' name? This work involves the resurrection of the dead and that was not to occur until the end of Satan's time—NOW. His people were not those who are described as the dead to be raised at the end of the world.

What difference does knowing or not knowing the truth of Jesus really make to you, your loved ones, to America, to the whole of humanity? If you knew the answers to these and every other worthwhile question concerning Jesus, how would you teach or share it with others? Why would you teach this? Again, how careful must you be with this subject? How powerful is the truth of Jesus?

Have you noticed that when you type (with word processing software) you are "told" to spell the word "Satan" with a capital "S" rather than a small "s?" Why did the programmers also make the software so that when you type, a small "d," is in front of "devil," the software indicates that you have spelled the word correctly? Hear Minister Farrakhan's Saviours' Day speech next month for the answer.

What is the "difficulty factor" (to use a scientific term of the Honorable Minister Louis Farrakhan) in convincing the world, in general, and Black people in America, in particular, of the real and full truth of Jesus? Can it be done by only presenting this truth, in plain language, taking into consideration the mind sets/beliefs of everyone?

The scribes of America's press and her media, resembles the scribes who participated in and urged the assassination of Jesus. Why do I state this, at this juncture, of this article and of this series? What is the difference between a murder and an assassination? Was Jesus murdered or assassinated? Why was Jesus, according to The New Testament, crucified between two thieves?

Why do the members of the press, refer to an aspect of its own behavior such as the way they are handling Minister Farrakhan and Brother Michael Jackson, which is what they call "a feeding frenzy?"

Webster's defines, "feeding frenzy" as: "An intense violent period of eating that occurs when a large number of animals of the same or related species, for example, sharks or piranhas, converge on a food source.

"An instance of frantic activity centered on a person or organization that occurs when other people, especially journalists, sense an opportunity they can exploit."

What are we being told, by Allah, as we observe these scribes? What are we to learn from them, as we battle them, with wisdom, following Minister Farrakhan's lead? Are they fulfilling the prophetic picture of the mind-set of the scribes who did the bidding of their high-ups and who intensified the atmosphere, to crucify Minister Farrakhan between thieves? Read of the scribes and their bosses in the Bible and compare them to these modern scribes.

The Bible teaches that they crucified Jesus out of ENVY. We'll look into envy, as it's directed against Jesus, next article, Allah willing.

I'll close with this article with this question. What would happen to the state of mind of America's press if Allah orders the Blacks on Mars to show themselves? Yes, Blacks!

Jabril Muhammad
January 9, 2004

Farrakhan: The Traveler
For The Final Call
Vol. 24; No.9

"Repel (evil) with what is best ..." (Holy Qur'an 41:34; 28:55); "... repel evil with good ...." (Holy Qur'an 13: 23; 23:96)

"As the preaching of truth inevitably brings in its wake hardships for the preacher, the verse enjoins upon him to bear them patiently and with fortitude, and even to return good for the evil he receives at the hands of his persecutors."

"The believers follow the course best suited for the eradication of evil." After a detail the commentator continued: "In short, they cut at the very root of evil by whatever method is appropriate in the circumstances." (The Holy Qur'an edited by M.G. Farid, footnotes 2636, 1435.)

The above cannot be accomplished without the right motivation and the right understanding of certain knowledge, which when coupled with the right set of experiences and the right understanding of these experiences, occurring over time—*and if Allah wills it*—then, real wisdom is generated in a person.

The Honorable Minister Louis Farrakhan has real wisdom.

"I am for the acquiring of knowledge or the accumulating of knowledge--as we now call it; education. First, my people must be taught the knowledge of self. Then and only then will they be able to understand others and that which surrounds them."

"No followers nor any other people are more zealous about the acquiring of knowledge than my followers. Throughout the Holy Qur'an, the duty of a Muslim to acquire knowledge is spelled out." (From *Message To The Blackman* by the Honorable Elijah Muhammad.)

This article continues the interview I conducted with the Honorable Minister Louis Farrakhan, of which the following was published in *The Final Call* Vol. 21; No. 22.

For the sake of others, I asked him what year he became a registered Muslim, which he answered was 1955. Then I asked him: "Did you study?"

His answer was: "Oh yes. This was a new field for me."

He continued that he ... "was so fascinated by the teachings of the most Honorable Elijah Muhammad, as taught by ..." and he went on to list the Brothers who, to use his words, "were profoundly influential in my development."

He continued: "Even though there were people over me in authority who may not have had a high school education, they were so well studied in the teachings of the Honorable Elijah Muhammad, it meant nothing to me that they did not have the amount of school time that I had, or the quality of preparation that I had. They had what I was trying to get. That was an understanding of the message of Islam, as taught by the Honorable Elijah Muhammad.

"... once I gained the love of my violin, my mother no longer had to require me to practice. Every free moment I had I would practice my craft. Sometimes I would practice four hours, five hours, and six hours. Sometimes I would tell my wife, 'I'm going in this room. I won't be out for eight or nine hours.' I would go in and practice my craft."

In those days I studied everything I could get my hands on related to the message of the Honorable Elijah Muhammad. By immersing myself in his message, then everything that I learned in high school, prep school and college took on greater significance. Biology took on greater meaning. Chemistry, Solid Geometry, Algebra, Calculus, everything that I studied I could now use because Islam, as taught by the Honorable Elijah Muhammad was a key to use knowledge for the advancement of self, your family, your community and your people.

Brother Jabril: Now Brother Minister, talk to me for a moment about the time you received the order to put up your music.

We've covered how this occurred. That part of the interview ended with:

Brother Jabril: And you just stopped?

Minister Farrakhan: Yes. In fact it was in November. It was not in December, but I had to the end of December to make the decision, but this order came down in November, one month after I had been a registered Muslim.

Now, why was he able to obey so quickly and under those circumstances?

The interview continued with my asking him: What then led to, and what were the circumstances, which were preparatory, under which the Honorable Elijah Muhammad said to you, "You don't have to study. "

Let's look again into the above, but not with a glance. Let's piece some of his words apart. Let's get deeper into the spirit of his mind. This process will help us to understand his answer to the words of the Honorable Elijah Muhammad to him: "You don't have to study."

This will also help us better understand the words of his teacher for his and our own future, especially as 2005—a momentous year—comes in.

The Holy Qur'an 23:45-49 reads: "Then We sent Moses and his brother Aaron with Our messages and a clear authority to Pharaoh and his chiefs, but they behaved haughtily and they were an insolent people. So they said: 'Shall We believe in two mortals like ourselves while their people serve us?' So they rejected them and became of those who were destroyed. And certainly We gave Moses the Book that they might go aright."

Have the Caucasian Muslim sons fully warned the Caucasian leadership of America of the above, whose arrogance blinds them of the truth of Minister Farrakhan and his **teacher, of that which they have learned is the truth?**

His answer, next issue, Allah willing.

JABRIL MUHAMMAD
DECEMBER 1, 2004

FARRAKHAN: THE TRAVELER
FOR THE FINAL CALL
VOL. 24; NO. 10

"If you know teach. If you don't know, learn. If you think you know, STUDY HARDER!"
— Dr. Mwalimu I. Mwadilifu, Author of ELIJAH MUHAMMAD on African American Education

My last article ended with this question (from *The Fi-*

nal Call, Vol. 21; No. 22): "What, then, led to and what were the circumstances (which were preparatory) under which the Honorable Elijah Muhammad said to you, 'You don't have to study.' "

Minister Farrakhan: Well as he made me his National Representative and allowed me to carry on his National Broadcast, he wrote me a letter and gave me the assignment. He gave some subject matter in a letter for four weeks that I would have to deliver these subjects. After the four weeks he was very please. He said "You can go on a little longer."

As I went on longer, he was pleased. So after six months or so, he said "You can go on for six years."

There was and is the profoundest kind of mathematics involved in Minister Farrakhan's development. Yours too!

One of the lessons that followers of the Honorable Elijah Muhammad, under Minister Farrakhan's leadership receive is called The Problem book. It teaches us of our condition in a mathematical way and provides like answers. In it we are addressed as "students." In fact the words "student," "students", and "student's" are mentioned about 24 times in the lessons and the introductory material to them.

Before we continue the interview of 2002, let's fast forward to December 4, 2004, when I asked Minister Farrakhan this question.

Brother Jabril: Brother Minister it's my conviction that a major factor in you're having been divinely chosen, to say and do, what you say and do was that you were to serve as an example throughout your life for us. One aspect of that, early, on in your life was that you were an exemplary student. So my question is two fold.

The first part is; what are the characteristics of a good student or an excellent student? The second part is; what made you an excellent student, both past and present, of the teachings of the Honorable Elijah Muhammad?

Minister Farrakhan: I don't like the characterization of "excellent" because that is for someone else to say, and especially the teacher. If the teacher says that I'm an excellent student, then it must be so.

But there must always be in the student a desire to learn, a desire to know. If one grows to love what it is desired to know more of and loves the person who is imparting to you that which you desire to know more of, then the student humbles himself completely to the teacher. This allows the teacher to impart to the student. One of the things that a teacher loves is a student that is anxious and willing to learn. Then when the teacher is absent from the student, the love that the student has for what he has learned makes the student work very hard to practice what he has learned in order to prove to the teacher, when he meets the teacher again, that "I am learning or have learned what you have shared with me."

I have never seen myself as a great student. But when I began to pick my violin up again, I learned all over again what it means to strive to be a good student. I humbled myself completely to my teachers. And they will admit, if you ask all who have shared with me their knowledge of the violin, how humble and beautiful I was in taking instruction *and* loving the critique—"Don't do it like this. Do it like this."

No matter how good I thought I was doing it, if my teacher was displeased with it, immediately I wanted to know how to do it in a manner that the teacher would be pleased. I guess that is what makes one a good student.

I close this by saying, Jesus, knowing that he was the door to God and to the Kingdom of God, and knowing that he was dealing with the people who had been shaped in iniquity and born in the sin of the transgression of God's law, he said, "Except you become as a little child you cannot enter the kingdom of God."

One of the things about little children is their nature of curiosity and wanting to know. "What is this? Why does this do that when I do this?" So to become as a little child, means you become humble to instructions and you're open to be shaped by the teacher who is giving instructions. That's the way it was when I came to the Honorable Elijah Muhammad. He had what I wanted to learn. Not only did he have it, but also those whom he taught had it. So I became humble, not just to the master teacher, but I was humble to all of his students who had been in the classroom long before I got there and knew more of what I wanted to learn. So that humility, and that desire to learn, was seen in every teacher that helped to shaped me to where I am today.

Jesus, at some point said, "Physician, heal thyself." When one studies and learns and teaches and through teaching guides and through teaching heals, when does the one who teaches get taught? When does the one who heals, get healed? When does the one who gives counsel, get counseled?

I called Bishop Brazier, in Chicago the other day asking him to come to the meeting, it was two days before the meeting, it was terribly short notice. He said, "Minister I would love to come but the notice is too short and I had something else that I was to do." I told him how much I admired his preaching and that I would like one day just to come and sit in his church and be nurtured by his preaching. I don't know what he thought of me when I said that. But I wasn't just saying that, because every good preacher needs a preacher. Every bad preacher needs one too.

I sometimes lay in my bed and I'm looking for something to look at on the T.V. and I get to where Bishop T.D Jakes is on, or Bishop Patterson, of "The Church of God in Christ," or Dr. Fredrick Price and sometimes its somebody that is not known—just a little old church service with terrible sounding choir. But I would listen because I'm always listening for God to give me instruction on something that I'm seeking and you never know where it is going to come from.

These great preachers, they water my spirit and my soul. If you're humble enough and love the word of God enough you really don't care who speaks it. You are anxious to hear more of what you love. That is all part of being a good student because no teacher can be a good teacher except he is a good student. If he has a reputation of being a good teacher, or a great teacher, he or she will lose the edge of his greatness once he or she begins to think he knows it all and stops learning his craft.

Now, can a Muslim really learn from Christian ministers, whether Black or otherwise, without becoming confused or compromising the principles of Islam? Yes. Minister Farrakhan's answer, next issue, Allah willing.

Jabril Muhammad
December 5, 2004

Farrakhan: The Traveler
For The Final Call
Vol. 24; No. 11

The Honorable Minister Louis Farrakhan ended our December 4th interview which appeared last week, in this column with: "So these great preachers, they water my spirit and my soul. If you're humble enough and love the word of God enough you really don't care who speaks it. You are anxious to hear more of what you love.

"That is all part of being a good student because no teacher can be a good teacher except he is a good student. If he has a reputation of being a good teacher, or a great teacher, he or she will lose the edge of his greatness once he or she begins to think he knows it all and stops learning his craft."

The article ended with: "Now, can a Muslim really learn from Christian ministers, whether Black or otherwise, without becoming confused or compromising the principles of Islam?" Yes. Minister Farrakhan's answer, next issue, Allah willing.

On December 8th Minister Farrakhan answered: Could Prophet Muhammad listen to Jesus speak on what God revealed to him and get confused and compromise the revelation that God had given to him, when truth bears witness to truth? There is a saying in the 85th Psalms that "Mercy and truth are met together; righteousness and peace have kissed each other." Well, truth loves more truth.

When a people say that they are Muslims, and they believe in the Qur'an and the Qur'an bears witness to the scriptures revealed to the former prophets, and then you hear Believers in one of the great prophetic voices of God talking on that revelation from

God, if you love God and love the word, that word, preached by somebody who's not yet where you are, will nurture you.

So no. I can't be compromised on what I know and believe, because what my Christian Brothers believes bears witness to what I have been taught. I look at the cosmopolitan nature of what was revealed to Prophet Muhammad. I look at how the Prophet understood the Torah and understood the Gospel, (aspects of it) and judged people out of their own book. If he heard a Rabbi teaching from the Torah, how would that confuse him with what God had revealed to him that has its root in that which the Torah and the Gospel are rooted?

No, I'm strengthened in what I've been taught when I hear the Gospel preached, and when I hear the Torah preached or when I hear the preaching of any sage or wise man who I can recognize came from God. I am strengthened by that preacher. It's only a fool who would close his ear to a Christian pastor or a Jewish rabbi or a Zoroastrian teacher, or anyone who's preaching truth. For Prophet Muhammad says, "Seek truth even if you have to go to far off China, seek it." The Honorable Elijah Muhammad told us "To respect truth and honor truth, no matter who is speaking it."

The truth of the Bible bears witness to the truth of the Qur'an. The truth of the Torah bears witness to the truth of the Gospel and the Qur'an. So when any pastor preaches the truth of the Bible I am edified by such preaching.

I would encourage people to stop being so narrow-minded when it comes to the word of God. This was the failing of those who received former revelations. They were so fixed on what God revealed to them that they weren't open for a new revelation that bore witness to that which was in their very hands. They often lost what they had by rejecting that which came from God that bore witness to what they believed.

Their own arrogance and feelings of insecurity about what was new, since they didn't see where their honored place would be in the new, they blindly rejected the new. They then lost a grip on what they themselves had been given by God.

If we accept what God brings that verifies that which is with us, we grow into a new growth. When we reject what God sends that verifies that which is with us, we can't even hold on to that which is with us, we begin to deteriorate like a body that fails to take on new oxygen and dies.

That's why Prophet Muhammad said, "He who goes out in search of knowledge is in the path of God until he returns." Because if you go out in search of knowledge, you should never return, because once you say you found it, you lost it."

Minister Farrakhan's words remind me of the Holy Qur'an 31:27: "... if all the trees in the earth were pens, and the sea with seven more seas added to it (were ink), the words of Allah would not be exhausted."

In his *Theology of Time* lecture of August 6, 1972 the Honorable Elijah Muhammad stated: "Lots of us take it for granted that the Holy Qur'an is something inferior to the Bible. The only inferior part is that, it came after the Bible and the Bible went before the Holy Qur'an. The Holy Qur'an is not as old as the Bible, but it verifies what is written in the Bible and the Bible verifies what is written in the Qur'an. They are not two enemy Books, they are two Books which verify each other."

That which Master Fard Muhammad revealed to the Honorable Elijah Muhammad, which Minister Farrakhan has spread throughout the earth, verifies the Bible's truths and the Holy Qur'an. These books verify that which Master Fard Muhammad revealed.

It is sheer foolishness to reject Allah's words.

It's written: "... it behooves not a believing man or a believing woman, when Allah and His Messenger have decided an affair, to exercise a choice in their matter. And whoever disobeys Allah and His Messenger, he surely strays off to manifest error." (Holy Qur'an 33:36)

The word "behoove" is used three times in the Muhammad Ali translation of the Qur'an in very interesting ways. First, in 26:211, we read that "And the devils have not brought it. And it behooves them not, nor have they the power to do (it)."

Secondly, it's used in Surah 33, as mentioned above, where

this verse introduces a significant subject. Thirdly, it appears in verse 53, which reads, in part: "And it behooves you not to give trouble to the Messenger of Allah ... ."

Note its use: " ... it behooves them *not;*" "it behooves *not* a" and "it behooves you *not* ... ." [Emphasis mine]

Behooves means: "to be necessary, proper, or advantageous for; to be necessary, fit, or proper, *appropriate*."

It behooves us all to study the articles written by Minister Farrakhan and Mother Tynnetta Muhammad in the last issue of The Final Call, as the 70 weeks of Daniel are all but finished to accomplish six things.

That time period was "determined concerning your people and your holy city to put an end to rebellion, to bring sin to completion, to atone for iniquity, to bring in perpetual righteousness, to seal up the prophetic vision, and to anoint a most holy place. (Daniel 9:24)

If you have time read this verse in other translations.

Jabril Muhammad
December 11, 2004

Section 8

Farrakhan: The Traveler
For The Final Call
Vol. 24; No. 12

"And when thou seest them, their persons please thee; and if they speak, thou listenest to their speech. They are like pieces of wood, clad with garments. They think every cry to be against them. They are the enemy, so beware of them. May Allah destroy them! How they are turned back! (Holy Qur'an 63:4) "And whoever keeps his duty to Allah, He ordains a way out for him, and gives him sustenance from whence he imagines not.

— Holy Qur'an 65:3

During a recent segment of the weekly-televised program named "Book TV" I watched a brilliant Native woman, Mrs. Wilma Mankiller, answer questions as she is on a book tour promoting her book. titled: "Every Day Is A Good Day."

She was sharing her wisdom with the students at Haskell Indian Nations University in Lawrence, Kansas, from her book and her experiences.

At one point she was asked: "What do you think is behind the oral traditions? Is there a meaning behind oral tradition of [the] tribes? If so, what do you think that that meaning is?"

Her answer began with: "Most of our history has been, recorded orally. And among Cherokee people—I don't know about other people, but among Cherokee people, there was a time way back in history when there was a person who was designated to listen at meetings. That was his job. It was to listen to what went on and then pass it on."

After sharing more with the students on this subject she ended her answer with:

"In the state of Oregon, one group filmed a very sacred ceremony and ... you have to be a tribal member in order to view it. So people are looking at innovative and new ways of using technology to capture information that has been passed down orally.

"We would not still have a strong sense of inter-dependence, I don't think, and strong sense of responsibility for one another, if that value hadn't been passed down. And again ... I think that in most tribal communities, traditional and tribal communities, value, like the value, for example, of respect--the most respected people in our communities—traditional communities, Cherokee communities and probably other traditional communities, are not people who have acquired great individual wealth, or who are people of great personal accomplishments."

The people who are mostly respected are people who help one another and people who remember that they were born into a set of reciprocal relationships and are responsible for one another. So I think that the values have been passed down orally. So it's very, very valuable.

A few days ago the Honorable Minister Louis Farrakhan shared with me an interesting experience of his that he recently had in Los Angeles. It was during the ninth anniversary of an event hosted by Stevie Wonder called "Toys for Tots." Stevie has been inviting top entertainers and musicians to this annual event, over the last nine years and this was the biggest, with about 10,000 or so in attendance, for this year's event, which was held at the L.A. Forum.

The purpose of this annual charitable event is to raise monies to buy toys for children, who might not otherwise have them, especially during the Christmas Holiday season.

Minister Farrakhan was seated in a place where he could hardly be seen. However, at a point near the beginning of the event

Mr. Jamie Foxx announced to the audience that Minister Farrakhan was present.

A roar of welcome and approval went up from the gathering, which became thunderous, when the Minister's image was projected up on three large screens.

With this in mind, here was the aspect of Minister Farrakhan's experience there that resonated with me and that's relevant to what Mrs. Mankiller shared (as mentioned above) and more.

Some of the stars wanted to meet him backstage: Minister Farrakhan said to me: So when I went back stage and there was this singer, Rachelle Farrell, she's great, in terms of her art and how other sisters of the arts relate to her. As we're shaking hands and I'm telling her how much I enjoyed her presentation, she asked me the question: "Do you know how much you have affected people?" I said, "No. I'm not really aware of that." She said, "You're not?' I said, "No, I'm not." She said, "Well, maybe that's good that you're not."

She responded, "Then you'll never change the way you are." Then she told me of the effect that I have on people.

I then told her that, "Each of us have come into this world from God. Since He created nothing without an aim and purpose, there is no human being that He sends into this world that does not have a significant purpose to fulfill with a gift that each can do excellently."

Whoever of us does what God intends for us to do, we are rendered equal to all others who likewise have gifts and who use their gifts to fulfill the purpose for which they've been sent into the world.

She just kind of marveled when she told me, "I am so honored to meet you" and I told her "I am so very honored to meet you." Her reaction was like wow, how could you be honored to meet me, I'm just a singer of songs and I've done well, but you are so far above me, in so many words. She didn't use those exact words, but that's what she was signifying. That's when I said to her what I did that renders us equal when we use the gifts God has given each of us, etc.

Twenty-two years ago, in November, 1982, I wrote these words for The Final Call, which now appears as part seven, in the book, "Farrakhan: The Traveler," Volume One:

One of the major points of this series of articles was to show that even as Minister Farrakhan traveled the length and breadth of modern Babylon, issuing The Final Call, he was traveling inwardly towards his Lord. This inward, forward motion is what was going on in this unusual Brother as he outwardly made his near 300,000-mile journey during a six-month period in 1981.

Of course, this was and still is the case (externally and internally) during the whole of the 60-plus months since he rose up for, took his stand with, and invited 30 or more million Black people to the Honorable Elijah Muhammad. Let us take a very brief but intense look at this inward journey and then take the same kind of look at Who backs Minister Farrakhan and with what.

In Volume 20, No. 14 of *The Final Call* I mentioned that: *Farrakhan The Traveler, Volume One* is composed of articles that I wrote for *The Final Call* from the summer of 1981 through the end of October 1984.

My aim in those years, and ever since, in all that I've written and spoken about the Honorable Minister Louis Farrakhan was and is to help others see this magnificent Black man more like Allah and His Christ saw and see him.

How many physical miles has Minister Farrakhan traveled doing good to and for other people? God only knows. In his inward travel Minister Farrakhan has been blessed to draw very close to oneness to his Lord.

More of his inward travel, next issue, in relation to all of the above, Allah willing.

Jabril Muhammad
December 25, 2004

FARRAKHAN: THE TRAVELER
FOR THE FINAL CALL
VOL. 24; VOL. 13

In December 2000, I wrote an article that appeared in Volume 20 No.13 of *The Final Call*. Here it is with the rest to follow next issue, Allah willing.

In the A. Maududi translation of the Holy Qur'an, 3:54, we read that, "(It was to carry out His secret plan that) He said, 'O Jesus, now I will recall you and raise you up to Myself and cleanse you of (the uncongenial company and the filthy environment of) those who have rejected you... .' "

Reflect over this as you look at what comes below from the book titled, *Farrakhan: The Traveler, Volume One*. On page iii in the introduction is this:

The aim, purpose and objective [of the articles that went *before* those which appear in this book as well as those which appeared *in* it, is to] help the readers think about the Honorable Minister Louis Farrakhan in a manner that is pleasing to the Divine Supreme Being and His Christ, the Honorable Elijah Muhammad.

When anyone disrespects another, they will, to some extent disregard the words of the disrespected one; even when such disrespect is unjustified. Such disrespect leads to the underestimation and even (in its later stages) hostility and then hatred for the one who is the object of such disrespect. In these cases, it starts out as disrespect and develops into contempt. In some cases, it becomes worse.

To disrespect Minister Farrakhan means that one will misunderstand the message he has from God for our guidance, welfare and the future both of our families and ourselves, regardless to your color, sex, age, profession, etc.

It is my aim, in presenting these articles, to stimulate deep enough thought about Minister Farrakhan, which will increase our insight into this extraordinary man of God.

One of the underlying purposes of these articles is to aid those who are joining Minister Farrakhan to help lift the name and works of the Honorable Elijah Muhammad. How? By stimulating their minds to see the Minister more as Allah, His Christ and the original Writers of the scriptures, sees him. Why? Because it is only by divine sight that we can properly relate to him.

Of course, this principle holds true in all of our relationships. The more accurately we see the better we can relate to others; even to improving self that we might relate even better to others.

The Authors (Wise original Scientists) of the Holy Qur'an 3:85, raised this question as they pondered our condition, 15,000 plus years ago: "How shall Allah guide a people who disbelieved after their believing, and after they had borne witness that the Messenger was true, and clear arguments had come to them? And Allah guides not the unjust people."

Then after a paragraph I wrote:

Only 144,000 were prophesied to escape the doom of this world, by some of the Wise Scientists. One "slim" last chance, or way was outlined in the scriptures, however, to save the millions of our people; even to providing others of this world a way out. It's there in the scriptures. It involved the production of Minister Farrakhan, by the Lord of the worlds, and special preparation by and the prayers of the Honorable Elijah Muhammad for him, before his departure in 1975. All of this, and more, ultimately depended upon the exquisite execution of the Divine plan by Master Fard Muhammad, which is recorded in the scriptures. He brought the Honorable Elijah Muhammad into the understanding and into the power of working with Him to bring aspects of it into reality.

The position Minister Louis Farrakhan is growing into "...in this world's life..." reflects the position of the Honorable Elijah Muhammad in the "heavens." Furthermore, it is only from the exalted position, the pinnacle of this world's life that Minister Louis Farrakhan can meet with and receive from the Honorable Elijah Muhammad, the new teachings that will eventually bring our nation to infinitely higher grades. He must go up and be up to meet again with his teacher.

Finally, as we consider Holy Qur'an 3:85, remember Allah resolved the apparent contradiction involved in the question of how shall we be guided after having rejected the Honorable Elijah

Muhammad, after bearing witness that he was true, in the presence of clear arguments. We've been greatly unjust to God and ourselves. However, as it is written of Allah, His mercy encompasses all things. From His grace He has made special provisions.

Muhammad of Arabia reportedly said, Allah had given to the world one part of His mercy and had reserved the other 99, in effect, for His people in the Day of Judgment. This is that day.

This act of Divine grace does not come from a contradiction in the character in the Divine Supreme Being. It comes from His infinite understanding and immeasurable love for us.

Let us show gratitude; and help our Brother, Minister Farrakhan, our people, each other, and ourselves from unselfish motives. Let our acceptance of our Brother, the Honorable Louis Farrakhan, be whole and not partial.

May these articles help in that process. Thank you for reading this.

Jabril Muhammad
June 17, 1983

Then from an article, written in May 1982, on page three of this same book, I wrote:

Generally speaking, an analogy involves showing the similarity in some respects between things, otherwise unlike, that partially resembles one another. More specifically (in the science of logic), it is the inference that certain admitted resemblances imply probable further similarities.

Analogies are properly used to help one see what you are trying to get them to see about someone, something or some event. Up to a point, analogies may provide some evidence that may lead to proof. However, analogies by themselves do not have the power to produce proof. No one can prove the truth of any argument or case solely through the use of analogies. Anyone who tries to do so is either lacking in understanding of the nature of analogies, evidence and proof; or is a double-minded deceiver.

Analogies are properly used, to put it very simply, to help others see what you see. Naturally, helping another see what we see does not mean that what we see is true. Nor do we prove as true (in the ultimate sense of the word) a fact, to be a fact, by merely stating that what we say is a fact.

Generally speaking, it takes less time to state something to be a fact, than to prove that what is stated is true.

After stating blunt, but clear truths about Minister Farrakhan and his teacher, in terms of what was written in the scriptures, which is misunderstood to have happened 2,000 years ago, I wrote on page five:

Envy is the main evil quality that blocks, any otherwise good mind, from seeing the divine significance in the mission and message of Minister Louis Farrakhan. Minister Farrakhan has crisscrossed America, delivering the knowledge of the meaning and message of the Honorable Elijah Muhammad in an astounding manner. He has done this accurately and consistently. The reaction of the overwhelming majority to his presentation makes it clear that not only is his preaching of *The Final Call* welcome, but it is on time.

Now, this is being written on the last day of 2004. Is 2005 the 70th year mentioned in Daniel? What's written that's coming up?

JABRIL MUHAMMAD
DECEMBER 31, 2000

FARRAKHAN: THE TRAVELER
FOR THE FINAL CALL
VOL. 24; VOL. 14

My last article ended with: Now, this is being written on the last day of 2004. Is 2005 the 70th year mentioned in Daniel? What's written that's coming up? Why? Because of current events, both small and large, within the Nation of Islam and otherwise, that corresponds to what is written in the scriptures to occur during these days.

The last article was on the evil of envy and continues: If this is so, and it is, what is it about envy that blocks, impedes, or blinds a person from seeing that which is not only good and timely, but good and timely in the ultimate sense, in that it is divine?

What is envy? What are its roots? Why is it so destructive? Dictionaries are of little or no help in defining the state of mind and feelings that the word envy represents. If you ever probe the study of morality, you will find that the extent to which envy influences vital issues are generally avoided by most writers, teachers, politicians, and scholars in all fields. Envy wears many faces or disguises.

Have you ever considered that it is all but impossible to depict a person who is posing by his or herself, in a picture, in a way that tells the viewer that the person is envious? If you were to draw an envious person, how would that person look? It is very hard to do, if not outright impossible, due to the fact that envy in a person cannot be detected apart from that person's relation to the other that he or she envies. This is not always easy to see.

Envy is an emotion that is directed towards another. Without the other (a target, a victim) envy cannot happen. As in paintings or sculpture, you can show fear, happiness, anger or grief with far greater ease, than you can show envy. It is no easy thing to portray the mind of a person who despises another for having a reputation, or some skill, which the person who envies may or may not lack, to some degree, but who rejoices at the other's loss of such assets, even though that loss would not mean a gain for the person who envies.

The article continued that, envy in no way can be a characteristic on which one can build brotherhood.

The above are excerpts from materials written in 1968. But these subjects yet need to be re-studied by us all, especially since we've all now come to the "end."

The word "uncongenial" means: "not sympathetic or compatible; not fitted; unsuitable; not to one's taste; disagreeable." It also means "offensive and unfriendly." Due to the time, look further into this, in other translations, to deepen your grasp of what is in Allah's words.

This is indeed God's day of separation of which the Bible, the Holy Qur'an, the Honorable Elijah Muhammad and the Honorable Minister Louis Farrakhan have been teaching and warning.

In the article that followed (Vol. 20, No. 14-written December 29, 2000) I wrote: "*Farrakhan The Traveler, Volume One* is composed of articles that I wrote for *The Final Call* from the summer of 1981 through the end of October 1984.

My aim in those years, and ever since, in all that I've written and spoken about the Honorable Minister Louis Farrakhan, was and is to help others see this magnificent Black man more like Allah and His Christ saw and see him.

In the course of this effort, I've had to take up the subject of jealousy and envy. There has never been a Black leader in America who has not suffered from those whose hearts are diseased with jealousy and/or envy.

Given both the depth to which we have fallen, and the depth of the depravity of our former slave-masters, opposition to any Black leader, working to lift us from hell, will intensify in proportion to that leader's nearness to the Almighty God.

Given the condition of the people of America, the maximum degree of opposition is to be directed to those directly chosen by the Divine Supreme Being to re-educate, reform, and free Black people of America.

A major factor in this opposition is the exploitation of jealousy and envy, which already exists in Black people. We must know the history of Black people in America, to understand that deadly form of jealousy and envy, which has plagued us as a people during our stay in America. Think into this.

Human beings always make comparisons between human beings and between things. Without the ability to make comparisons we would have no science; humans could never become civilized; progress would be impossible.

It is not the comparisons that are evil, in and of themselves. It's why and how we make comparisons that determines whether or not jealousy and or envy, arises in our hearts. Jealousy and envy are among the worst spiritual diseases, which we must be absolutely freed from if we are to see the best part of the hereafter. These diseases are love killers! The Holy Qur'an gives terrible warnings to those of us who "blow" our salvation due to these diseases.

It's impossible to grow into one's own divinity, which also means growing ever closer to Allah, except to the extent that we remove envy and jealousy from our hearts. After we have heard and read about these spiritual diseases, it is still up to each person to do this service for ourselves.

We've heard that God helps those who help themselves. Does God ever help those before they help themselves? In the case of the Black man and woman of America, God had to help us before we could even begin to help ourselves.

Recently, Minister Farrakhan shared insights with me that I desire to share with you. So I want to continue this subject on "envy" after we read his words. I also intend to include a commentary on these words of the Messiah, at his home in 1972, in working out a serious problem, which were: "Whenever you accuse an innocent man of that which he did not do, the heavens and the earth cries out for justice for the innocent man. And the punishment he would have received, if he was guilty, falls on the head of the accuser."

Minister Farrakhan respectfully raised the question of forgiveness. I desire to share his teacher's response, including the conditions for forgiveness, Allah willing. Many have slandered and libeled Minister Farrakhan.

On December 20, 2004 I asked: Brother Minister, one day, be it the will of Allah, we will have ambassadors through all the nations of the earth. What are the characteristics of a good ambassador?

Minister Farrakhan: Every good ambassador is well versed in the policies of his government. If he's an ambassador for Christ, he must not only know the laws and principles that govern the Kingdom of God but he must also have some knowledge of the people and their culture and their ways to whom he's being sent as an ambassador. Out of respect for the people and love for the people, and respect for their culture and their ways, then he uses the key of his knowledge to raise those people as a part of his ambassadorial assignment.

Minister Farrakhan continues next issue Allah willing.

Jabril Muhammad
January 6, 2005

Farrakhan: The Traveler
For The Final Call
Vol. 24; Vol. 15

"... my brother, Aaron, he is more eloquent in speech than I, so send him with me as a helper to confirm me. He said: ... We will give you both an authority, so that they shall not reach you. With Our signs, you two and those who follow you will triumph."

— Holy Qur'an 28:34, 35

On December 4, 2004 I asked the Honorable Minister Louis Farrakhan: "By the time you came into the Nation of Islam in 1955, you were already acquainted with the importance, the value and the use of such tools as dictionaries, thesauruses, synonym and antonym books. How did you first use them, even up to the present time?"

Minister Farrakhan: Being a student of Latin, you become knowledgeable of suffixes and prefixes. And you become knowledgeable of the root of a word; how the word evolves; what is the origin of that word in terms of its origin? Where did it come from? You learn that most English words evolved from either Latin or Greek. The romance languages are French, Italian, Spanish, Portuguese and they come out of Latin.

Latin is considered a dead language, but as the Qur'an says "He brings the living from the dead and the dead from the living." So if you don't know something of the dead language, you are missing the understanding of the living languages that are being used today by a great number of people on the planet.

Naturally, the meanings of words, and their shades of meaning are very, very important in developing our communicative skills.

The Honorable Elijah Muhammad one day told me of Clarence Darrow and President Woodrow Wilson, and he said, "The degree of knowledge that they had of the English language was profound." He said, "...that's why Clarence Darrow never lost a case." When he told me that, even though I was a baby in English to him in terms of his depth of understanding of the language, he was telling me that when you master words and the various shades of meaning of words, you can take one word and use it as a weapon of offense and you can take the same word with another shade of meaning and use it as a weapon of defense.

That is why I believe the Saviour, Master Fard Muhammad said in The Problem Book, "You will not be successful unless you learn to speak the language well." The entanglement of the people is an entanglement of words, and how they perceive the meaning of those words. So the freedom of people is the untangling of their understanding or perception of meaning and giving them a new and better meaning of a word that they think they know or understand. That goes back to the Qur'an in Surah 20 when he said, "Loosen the knot from my tongue that they may understand my speech"

The word of God that came to the Honorable Elijah Muhammad was a word that was designed to fit the condition of our minds at that time but a deeper study of that same word, would disentangle us from a limited understanding of what we thought we understood when we first heard that word.

Through the plain language *and* the metaphorical language, which is the language that uses nature and the creatures of God to describe characteristics of human beings and nations; the forces of nature; the wind; the weather; aspects of zoology; aspects of botany; aspect of anthropology; aspects of meteorology; aspects of physics and chemistry and science, all of this language is used in scripture to couch and hide even truth, as well as to give a mind that is not yet ready for deeper aspects of truth enough to free that mind; to start a movement toward the deeper understanding of what God had in mind when He revealed what He revealed.

Brother Jabril: He said to me one day that Master Fard Muhammad told him the number of dialects that both Clarence Darrow and President Woodrow knew of English. The number was around 23 and 22 respectively or close to that. I just don't remember the exact number right now. Did he ever mention to you anything like that?

If any one reading this ever heard the Honorable Elijah Muhammad speak on this please write me at www.writtentestimony.com

Minister Farrakhan: No. He mentioned to me the degrees of understanding of the language that they both had mastered, which set them apart from their contemporaries in their ability to master language.

Sometimes, Brother Jabril, I didn't use the dictionary. I would just use what I understood of the prefix, the suffix and the main word if it had a Latin root then I would compare what I saw in the definition, even to what *Webster* said. Then sometimes my definitions were deeper and more profound than what was in the dictionary.

Brother Jabril: Now, Brother Minister, that's getting really deep into the very origin of the word—its very spirit!

Next, Big Brother, there is an obvious and profound relationship between the "We" who wrote what they wrote in the original scriptures and its power so deep into the nature of things that it's as good as done, long before it takes place! It passes down through the generations and it has everything to do with the very genetic makeup and the DNA of that human being. Please comment.

Minister Farrakhan: Those who write the future of events and circumstances and write the future of persons who create these events and circumstances, know that there are circumstances that surround the womb of an individual of consequence that helps to manifest what is already in the DNA.

No matter what's in a seed, if it does not have the right environment in which to manifest what is within, the seed never comes to fruition. So many of us die as seeds that do not fulfill the aim and purpose for which we are sent into the world because sometimes we are placed in an environment that literally stifles the expression of what God has put within.

Every circumstance has to be made right for what God has put within to manifest. When I was listening to the T.V. early this morning, and they talked about the nature of Jesus' birth—the circumstances, the hiding from a circumstance that was felt to be destructive to that one's life; the lowly manger or ox stall in which he had to come to birth and all of those circumstances plus the star that pointed out to the wise men where the baby would be, these are circumstances that allowed what he was programmed, before birth, to bring about—those circumstances and conditions allowed what was in him to come forward.

None of us are separated from the environment that produces us if God intends for us to do great things, He supplies the environment, the circumstances that others may see as negative, but He knows that those circumstances are absolutely positive to bring forth this person to fulfill his purpose and thus glorify God.

To correct my article Vol. 24; No. 12, the number in attendance at Stevie Wonder's "Toys for Tots" event, held at the L.A. Forum, was approximately 13,000, which Minister Farrakhan attended.

For it's written: "And say not of anything: 'I shall do that tomorrow, unless Allah should will." (Holy Qur'an 18:23, 24) And, let's not add foolishness to this.

JABRIL MUHAMMAD
JANUARY 6, 2005

FARRAKHAN: THE TRAVELER
FOR THE FINAL CALL
VOL. 24; NO. 16

On December 4, 2004, I asked the Honorable Minister Louis Farrakhan: Brother Minister, in a recent web cast you informed us, in a very brief manner, what led to you're inviting Dr. Alim to your bed side, when you were convalescing, to put on his mind that to which he later responded to, in a letter, that led to the formation of The Commission and the start of their work.

You wanted to pattern the next stage of the Nation's development more along the lines of the structure and function of the human body. When were you first conscious of this idea and what was the progression of that guidance Allah put you on?

Minister Farrakhan: I don't exactly know when, but I'm sure it's been happening over a long period of time. First, starting with the learning of the nine systems of the human body and the 10th, they never talk about the tenth, they say nine, but when I looked at the Student Enrollment and the ten questions, and the Honorable Elijah Muhammad talking about "the big 10" the nine planets and the sun as the tenth—I related that to the human body.

As I, over years, read the writings of Paul and he says, "What if the body were all eye, where would the hearing be, and if it were all ear, where would the seeing be?" He started relating things of the human body to teach the early Christians about the difference of organs and their different purpose but they're working for the common good of this thing called the human body. He was trying to get the early Christians to respect differences but these differences were absolutely necessary to promote the work of the Kingdom of God.

Then I remembered, in my limited study of Biology and from the Holy Qur'an, that we start from a single essence of sperm, as the Qur'an calls it "worthless water," that mixed with ovum in the right environment at the right time produces the first cell of life and how that cell divides, then multiplies, the organism grows from a very simple organism, with one function, to a very complex organism with many functions serving one great purpose.

I looked at the Honorable Elijah Muhammad's writings, talking about the forms that we filled out and it goes through nine laborers. Then I looked at the mathematical language; one through nine then zero. I know that all of this is related. I looked at how the Saviour, to Whom praises due, (really forever) organized the Nation, where the Minister, the Captain, Secretary, Sister Captain and you have lieutenant, inspector, investigator, the teaching instructor.

I looked at how he set this up and I said, 'Well this is the simple structure that can be evolved into the complex structure when you start thinking Nation.' There's nothing that the Saviour did that doesn't have far teaching implications, so nothing that the Saviour said or did can be thrown away, but must be looked into because in it is the germ of where you want to go.

Laying in the hospital, which brings you to the realization of your mortality, and then looking at our Nation and seeing it revolving around a charismatic personality and knowing that personality will one day be gone from us, then if you love your Nation and you love the people, you don't want the people to revolve around your person or your personality, but to revolve around the principles that under-gird your person and your personality that makes you magnetic or attractive to the people.

I was in the hospital on the last day of October or the first of November. The operation was the first of November, so this had to be the later part of November or very early December. I'm in a home, on the banks of the Potomac River, which one of the Sisters Protocol Sister Brenda her cousin has a home there and he allowed me the use of that home. So next I'm laying there, thinking, from the middle of November to around the second or third week in December.

Now, as I laid there, not able to walk well, I mean I was in a very, very difficult condition. My mind, of course, is on the Believers, on the Nation and on the future of this when I am no longer in the world.

I called Minister Alim to my bedside to share with him my anguish. My anguish was over my knowing that the Nation would not survive in its present form. It had to evolve beyond where it was in order to make room for the talented people that are in the Nation, but more, the talented people that are outside of the Nation. But if we could not make use of the talent that has come to faith, then God would never send us the talent that is yet in their mental grave.

I told him my concern, my anguish. Then I mentioned structure. I mentioned organization, that there must be a minister. The minister carries the word and the guidance for the mosque. So if you have nine ministries then you must have someone who is the prime minister serving that particular function. But he needs a captain, not necessarily called captain, but somebody who executes on the instructions of the head.

You need a secretary to take the minutes of the meetings and the records of the function of that ministry. You need lieutenants who teach and train the functionaries of your ministry when your ministry becomes statewide; when it becomes national; when it becomes international.

All these are your lieutenants though that's not the actual titles, but they function as that because they are under the orders of an executive and they are in the field teaching and training the private soldiers.

Then you have an investigator, somebody who looks to see if something is going wrong in the ministry. Or you're sending something out, it's not coming back as you would like. Then this person, whatever their title is, would compare to the Saviour's naming of an investigator.

He investigates. Then he charges he brings his facts, or his findings, to the executive officer. Then they make a charge or they make a correction.

You have an inspector, who knows how things should go. He travels to inspect, to see that things are being carried out in the manner.

I said to myself, "Everything that Master Fard Muhammad gave to the Honorable Elijah Muhammad was a seed that when watered in the right environment, over time, would produce the fulfillment of what He gave us in seed form in 1930 to 1934 when He departed."

I am a witness of the fact that Minister Farrakhan has been pondering the future of the Nation, the problems of its future and more, for many years now. Some things he said were put on tape and other points were not.

The point here is that it all came together, just as you read above, and under the circumstances that it did. Allah's timing is perfect.

Jabril Muhammad
January 9, 2005

Farrakhan: The Traveler
For The Final Call
Vol. 24; No. 17

Minister Farrakhan: Dr. Alim went away with my words and he thought critically on the Nation. Then he wrote me a letter. He thought that I might be upset because of his critique of the Nation. But when I read his letter, I got him on the phone and told him that is the exact thing that I wanted to hear. So, let's come on. Let's get busy.

Then he came up with the thought of the caterpillar and the forming of a chrysalis out of which comes the butterfly. Nothing of the caterpillar phase is lost in the chrysalis. Nothing in the chrysalis is lost in the caterpillar. It's an evolutionary process that brings us to this beautiful thing.

I mentioned the nine ministries and the 10th being the light of it [them] all must be the spiritual.

Then we tried to figure out what should these nine ministries be? Well, you know, if you look at the systems of the body, now you're coming back to look at this, you know. What is the endocrine system? What is the circulatory system? What is the digestive system? What is the muscular system? What is the structure, the bone? So when you look at the systems and how they function then you make a corresponding ministry to serve the same function as that system.

I started looking at God. I say "OK." Well how did He form Himself? The Honorable Elijah Muhammad gave us clues. Christians say "stepped out on space." Ah, come on. The Honorable Elijah Muhammad call that 'his fancy.' But in the darkness he said, "The first atom of life sparkled. He made Himself up out of the material of the darkness."

There's matter in the darkness. It is considered nothing because it has neither form nor function, but it's matter. So, now He's forming. As He forms Himself, He studies Himself. Then He makes a reality that corresponds to Himself. Well, later He said let there be light. There was already light in Him. The Honorable Elijah Muhammad says, "He was a light of Himself." So what He did was to bring out of Himself a reality and put it in a beautiful form and gave it purpose to manifest who He is.

I thought, well, since He was before the universe, then we would have to be before the Nation is formed. It has to form out of us. So when Jesus said, "The Kingdom of heaven is within you." How did he mean it? So the thing that we have to do is study us, and then see how is the Kingdom in us, and then bring it out of us and make it real.

Then I looked at governments and their various ministries, the Ministry of Culture, the Ministry of Trade; the Ministry of Foreign Affairs; the Ministry of Defense, you know.

Well all of these things began to feed my mind and then I said well, if the Minister is tax exempted, then ministries that do this kind of service should also be tax exempt. So when you have a Ministry of Information, then how does that ministry function?

How does the Ministry of Culture function? How does the Ministry of Health function? How does the Ministry of Education function? How does the Ministry of Defense function? What are the sub-organs coming out of these various ministries that make it relevant to a structure that now represents the Kingdom of God?

Now that's where I am.

Now, where are we?

All of these things took place, in my mind, over years. But it was brought to fruition when I became painfully aware of my mortality and the reality of the Nation and not wanting to see a repeat of what happened when the Honorable Elijah Muhammad departed. All of those things were motivating factors in my coming up with the thought of the nine ministries."

Brother Jabril: Dr. Alim came back to you with a letter within about two months of the conversation between you two, during the first part of 2001. When did the commission actually begin forming? When in 2001 did this occur?

Minister Farrakhan: He had begun meeting with friends that he knew in the mosque in Washington, D.C. who shared similar dissatisfactions and a similar desire to see the Nation progress. So over many weeks, and months, they met. Then out of that meeting he came to me with – I think he was the one who came or I called it "The Commission"—and the title was "The Commission For The Reorganization and Restructuring of a Nation."

Brother Jabril: When did the Commission become formalized?

Minister Farrakhan: In the latter part of 2001. They had their first big meeting in the fall 2001.

Brother Jabril: Umm. The timing of all of this is divine. Allah determined it.

Minister Farrakhan: Yes and I felt comfortable with the ministers that were in the commission; with the Believers that were in the Commission; with the youth that were a part of the Commission; with an element of dissatisfaction that was a part of the Commission.

As I went back to think about how the Saviour structured the

Nation and the laws that He set up, I realize that He set up laws to protect us against ignorance; in other words, slack-talk.

Here you got an unqualified person trying to be a laborer. We would tear him down before God could build him up. Since that's the way the slave-masters made us, slack-talkers, He had to set up a law that would protect us in the days of our ignorance so that we could evolve, and unity could evolve so that the idea could make progress through the darkness until we could mature.

We see everybody that criticizes us as an enemy, you know, because we are so ego deprived, if I could use that term that any criticism of us is taken as an attack on our hurting egos. Most of us who were the helpers of the Honorable Elijah Muhammad could not handle severe criticism because we never had authority. We never were involved, as such, in something like this. It was a very brand new experience and we needed to be protected and shielded from that which would destroy us before he could build us up to take criticism.

When Dr. Alim came up with the idea of lawful dialogue, which is brilliant, in that it's lawful now to critique, not you as a person, but an idea to flush out its weaknesses.

The enemy's government has built-in opposition in it, to help with balance, because they have moved away from dictators.

Now, you may remember in the web cast, I mentioned that the Honorable Elijah Muhammad, asked me in 1972, to bring the intellectuals and the professionals to Chicago because he wanted them to help him save and build the Nation. He gave a picture that he already has a tree; it's already grown; there's fruit on it. He said, "Why don't you come and help me fertilize the ground where the tree is growing and then we all can have something to eat from that tree."

Jabril Muhammad
January 10, 2005

Farrakhan: The Traveler
For The Final Call
Vol. 24; No. 18

Minister Farrakhan: Well, the more I thought on why he did what he did, since he knew the Nation was going to fall, and had told me that it would, then there's nothing that those professionals or intellectuals could do to save it anyway. So he was priming me for the future, when I would one day make a call to the intellectuals and they would respond positively to help me build and save a Nation.

The other night, knowing that I'm coming here [to Phoenix] and not wanting to leave the city of Chicago without calling the movers and shakers of that city to sit down with me, so that I could share with them why I felt the time was right for the remobilizing of the Million Man March; and although I knew it was short notice; I made a call. Within forty-eight hours those men and women stopped what they were doing to answer that call. When I looked out at that Salaam and at the type of people who were there, I mean these were powerful men and women, I was moved that they all responded. That meant and bore witness to me that if I made the call that the intellectual community would respond to help save a Nation and to help build a Nation. The talent is here. Now God, through the Honorable Elijah Muhammad has put me in a position to make that call and scholars will answer from all over the world. This is wonderful.

Somebody even mentioned the word "pinnacle," this third one, like the first, *The Million Man March*, *The Million Family March,* and this third one, they felt that this would be the one that triggers whatever it's going to trigger.

You remember *The New Testament* says that when Lazarus responded, it triggered something among those of the Sanhedrin. The first time, in '95, they didn't think it would happen. They were caught by surprise, in a sense.

I was brought some polling information, put out by CNN, USA Today and the Gallop Poll, around October 6, or 7, 1995. They said, "Reverend Farrakhan may very well get his million men from the polls that we have taken. But they didn't publish that at that time. But they had gone out when the men had gathered and they had figured at least a two million. Isn't that something?

Minister Farrakhan and I had to stop, but agreed to return to this subject, be it the will of Allah.

Then on December 20, 2004 I asked Minister Farrakhan: "A few days ago, we touched the talks that you made, in the last few weeks, on the East Coast, your increased or deeper study of the Word [of God] combined with your being alert to the news of developments and your recognition of the increased subtlety of the enemy's tricks, these things combined, with Allah's guidance, enabled you to speak to these audiences, and caused the Brothers and Sisters who are studied, to see more of that which they didn't see just before you made this or that point. Please, let's go back to that."

Minister Farrakhan: Yes. In New York City, I took time with a friend, Gil Noble, with whom I spoke privately and later with the leaders, to show them how language is used to change perceptions of our people and the realities of what we're looking at.

I talked about how the word "Negro" was used and how limited that term was and how the Honorable Elijah Muhammad used the term "Black" in such a way that it developed in us a body and the nervous system that connected us to our people all over the world.

That is when something was done in the Congo, years ago, in the killing of Patrice Lamumba, there was a demonstration by Black people at the U.N. When Martin Luther King was murdered a hundred cities were set on fire because we had developed a nervous system that allowed us to feel the pain of one another through the language that the Honorable Elijah Muhammad used.

So the enemy stepped up his studies of us. He wanted to know what was it and who was the leader that ignited us to burn up a hundred cities, when all of the people that were burning the cities were not followers of Martin Luther King, Jr.

They concluded that it wasn't a specific person that was causing this as much as it was the way the media was used. It had given us as a people one shared attitude toward white people and toward what we called "the establishment."

These attitudes harden into a system of belief that all of us shared, no matter where we were in America, a belief about police; a belief about government; a belief about white people, that was very real. That attitude and belief grew into ideology—a common idea—that all of us shared and we had become a national community, even though we were in different groups; different churches and mosques, etc, there was something that bound us all together.

When the enemy saw that television had served that purpose and the name Black, Brother and Sister, had caused us to see ourselves as kin to people of color all over the world, they decided after the assassinations of Malcolm and Martin and the departure of the Honorable Elijah Muhammad, they had to change language.

They started that by again using the term "minority." Once we accepted the terminology, "minority," a certain frame of mind came with accepting that language.

The fact that we are the "majority" was destroyed and then we became the "disadvantaged." Then we became "the largest minority in America." Then we became "African Americans" and there we've stayed minority, disadvantaged, African Americans.

But what happened to us as a result of accepting that language? It killed the nervous system that the language of Blackness created. Then, every television show with Black as an adjective describing it, such as "Black News" in New York; "Black Journal," "Black Star" program in Baltimore, every city had something "Black" as a description of the main noun, and so "Black Journal" became "Tony's Journal;" and "Black News" was eventually taken off the air. "Black Star" was gone. Now you have no program anywhere on television with the name "Black" in front of it.

The subtlety of the enemy, in deceiving us was that he knew the value of language and that if you shift the language you shift perceptions. What he did was to create the death of our nervous system that connected us as a family.

Then we could become tribes and kill one another and not feel the pain of our Brothers in the Caribbean, our Brothers in Brazil, or our Brothers in Africa.

We began to be less and less global, and more and more narrow, in our focus, to be narrower right down to gangs and tribes in terms of denomination and organization, and kill each other throughout America and not really feel the pain."

More, next issue Allah willing on how Minister Farrakhan works to help the original people of America becomes *sufficiently united to be saved.*

JABRIL MUHAMMAD
JANUARY 10, 2005

FARRAKHAN: THE TRAVELER
FOR THE FINAL CALL
VOL. 24; NO. 19

> *"And what will make thee realize what hell is?—Over it are nineteen.—Thus Allah leaves in error whom He pleases, and guides whom He pleases."*
> *— Read Holy Qur'an 74: 26 thru 30.*

The Honorable Minister Louis Farrakhan is a very precious and valuable human being. The enemy sees this too, but differently. So they work against him night and day to break his influence and finally to murder him. But, to use the words of the scriptures in this situation: "They feared the people."

Of Jesus, soon after the start of his mission, we read in several places, "the people became divided because of him." With time, Jesus' influence grew to the point that the chief concern of those who secretly plotted became: "If we don't stop him now, all people will follow his lead." So it is today.

This brings me back to Volume 24; Number 14, of *The Final Call*, wherein I mentioned that I desired to share Minister Farrakhan's words with the reader from interviews. I stated that I wanted to continue this subject of "envy," *after* we read his words. I also stated that I wanted to include a commentary on these words of the Messiah, at his home in 1972, in working out a serious problem. His words were: "Whenever you accuse an innocent man of that which he did not do, the heavens and the earth cries out for justice for the innocent man. And the punishment he would have received, if he were guilty, falls upon the head of the accuser. "

At that moment, you could have heard a pin fall on cotton. Then, as I wrote: "Minister Farrakhan respectfully raised the question of forgiveness." I continued that: "I desire to share his teacher's response."

Let me be clear on why I'm taking "ENVY" up at this time, *with* the words the Honorable Elijah Muhammad spoke back in February 1972, as the base.

I don't know what will happen between today, when this article, Allah willing, appears in print, as all of the articles, from Volume 24; No. 16 to this one were prepared on today, January 10th. However, I fully expect that Minister Farrakhan, and those of us who are with him, will have made progress towards the realization of the 10th Anniversary of *The Million Man March*.

Likewise, the wicked expect to make progress against him and us. To think that there are not those, who are working openly, *and especially covertly*, to hinder, derail or otherwise destroy the aim and purpose of this "March" would be foolish and even ridiculous.

The ultimate aim of such people will continue to be to destroy Minister Farrakhan in the eyes of the public, with the method they have always used ever since this world was born: **SLANDER—THE WORST FORM OF LYING.**

Let's go back to the words of the Honorable Elijah Muhammad, which are the basis of what I am trying to now convey. That was 1972. A brother was accused of horrible crimes, anyone of which would show that he was a very wicked hater of the Honorable Elijah Muhammad.

The Honorable Elijah Muhammad's handling of this matter was so filled with wisdom that much of it could not be seen at that time. But it bears directly on us today.

I know that what I'm touching of that incident, 33 years ago, hardly provides even the barest kind of outline or context of it.

The context of an event, in which significant words were spoken (or written), always helps us understand the people, the event, etc., better than otherwise. However, there are many truths we can and do learn, even in depth, without the original context, if the lessons to be learned are given in a way that impacts us as if we fully knew the original context of the event; when the significant words were produced.

Let's now focus on the Messiah's words and piece them apart. He said: "Whenever you accuse an innocent man of that which he did not do the heavens and the earth cry out for justice for the innocent man." STOP.

Have you ever been accused of what you did not do? How do you know? Did the heavens and the earth cry out for justice *for you*? Did you hear the heavens and the earth make any sounds *for your* benefit? Have you ever heard such sounds in behalf *of others* who were falsely accused?

Do you think the Honorable Elijah Muhammad was exaggerating to drive home his point? Or do you think he was speaking from the highest kind of wisdom?

Hyperbole, according to the *Encarta World English Dictionary*, is the "deliberate and obvious exaggeration used for effect, for example, "I could eat a million of these." *The American Heritage Dictionary* states that it's a figure of speech in which exaggeration is used for emphasis or effect, as in "I could sleep for a year" or "this book weighs a ton." *Webster's Dictionary* defines hyperbole as "an extravagant statement or figure of speech not intended to be taken literally.

Did the Honorable Elijah Muhammad intend for his words to be taken exactly as he stated them? There were about 90 of his laborers there. How did they see his words? More importantly, how did the Lord of the Worlds see his words that night? It's one matter if his words were intended merely for effect. But if he was speaking of a law of the nature of the heavens and the earth, that's another thing entirely.

The Holy Qur'an (104:1) declares: "Woe to every slanderer,

defamer!" Do these words express a law of the nature in which the universe was created?

Two weeks ago an event of huge proportions disrupted the lives of millions, while killing over 160,000. As a consequence, it seems that more than ever people are talking about "GOD." I watched the "Larry King Live" TV program a few nights ago (January 7th) wherein a law of nature was cited, which bears on ***all*** of the above.

Mr. King opened the program with: "How do we find God after losing so much in a historic tragedy? How much is our faith in a higher power tested by the tsunami killing of more than 150,000 people in a matter of moments? We'll ask spiritual and religious leaders of faiths from around the world."

Later in the program, a part of Deepak Chopra's answer to a question was: "And you know, there's lots of evidence, even scientific, that the earth is a living organism... ." Is it possible that our consciousness and the turbulence in our consciousness has anything to do with the turbulence in nature?

Michael Lerner just referred to that. One of the very interesting things that happened with the tsunami was, no animal died. The elephants, the hares, the rabbits, the birds--they were so tuned in to the forces of nature that they escaped. They ran. Some of the elephants broke their chains and ran to the high level mountainous area where the tidal waves could not reach. We have lost that connection.

Is there a way that we can collectively transcend to a level of consciousness where we see that the turbulence in our collective mind, possibly, is inseparable from the turbulence in nature, because we are part of nature?

Yes. Minister Farrakhan represents that way. How he does this, next issue, Allah willing.

JABRIL MUHAMMAD
JANUARY 10, 2005

FARRAKHAN: THE TRAVELER
FOR THE FINAL CALL
VOL. 25; NO.1

"For he must reign until he has put all his enemies under his feet..." Now when it says that "everything" has been put under him, it is clear that this does not include God himself, who put everything under Christ. (1 Corinthians 15:25-27)

"In your patience possess ye your souls." (Luke 21:19) "So be patient with a goodly patience. Surely they see it far off, and We see it nigh." (Holy Qur'an 70: 5-7)

There is a straight line between the **stand** the Honorable Minister Louis Farrakhan took, 28 years ago to rebuild the Nation of Islam, on the foundation laid by his teacher, the Honorable Elijah Muhammad, and the stand he took earlier this year, that launched the Millions More Movement, which culminates and re-launched on October 14-16 when he will again, stand tall in the capital of a land that has spelled hell for original people for centuries.

It was like the arousal of a powerful lion, when Minister Farrakhan arose and took his stand in the most western part of America, in September 1977, to do as the Holy Qur'an reads "arise and warn ... ."

From that first day of his rise onwards he began informing others of his intentions and in November he publicly announced in Chicago and then at Rutgers University his intentions to rebuild the Nation of Islam.

There was an uproar, but his stand was firm. And in the month of December Minister Farrakhan wrote what we called "the stand," which Minister Akbar spread in the Black press throughout America.

I hasten to add, however, that his stand has always been a compassionate stance that everyone of good will could find his or her place in it.

I was thinking of what he (and the microscopic number of us who were with him) did in those days, as I recently sought a deeper understanding of Michael's stand, according to the first verse of the 2nd chapter of the book of Daniel.

At that time I was looking at the definition of Michael's name in order to see deeper into his stand. I first went to *Strong's Concordance* where the name "Michael" means: "Who is God?" I thought: "Is this all?" and "Who else's name is defined with a question?" and "How does this meaning relate to the stand Michael took?"

I suggest that we study the whole of the 12th chapter of the book of Daniel, since, as the Honorable Elijah taught it's of this time in which we now live.

It begins: "At that time Michael, the great prince who protects your people, will arise." (New International version)

"And at that time shall Michael stand up, the great prince which standeth for the children of thy people ... ." (Daniel 12:1.

It was something the Honorable Elijah Muhammad once told me that now made me look deeper. So I decided to go to the works of some Jewish scholars to see what else I might learn. But before I could get to their reference books, I received a call from Minister Farrakhan, who was then in Atlanta, GA.

He was exhausted, but still pushing on to the full realization of the salvation of our poor people and the oppressed everywhere. He had taken his stand, when he first accepted to follow and help the Honorable Elijah Muhammad back in 1955. He renewed that stand in 1977 and was now more openly than ever working to get millions to take their stand with his.

Part of the meaning of stand is: "to be or to put something in an upright position; to get into an upright position; to have and maintain a position or stand on an issue; to hold one's ground; to fight resolutely or to give battle; a view someone has or an attitude someone takes on a particular subject.

We first must have the basic definition of whatever we seek to understand, as that is a prerequisite to gaining the significance of your subject, issue, matter or subject matter, area under discussion. So later in our discussion I raised the question of the definition of Michael's name.

I told him what *Strong's Concordance* had for the basic meaning for Michael's name, which was: "Who is God?"

Minister Farrakhan responded, "Let me see what I can do with it." Now, for reasons I hope to make clear to the reader, I wish to divide his answer into two parts. He started with: "It seems to me that it was the stand of the angel, Michael that answered the question put before the people in his person or name: "Who is God?" The rest of his answer next issue, Allah willing.

His answer is related to something the Honorable Elijah Muhammad told me of two Jewish scholars, in Washington, D.C. who told him that they knew his identity. That conversation, he told me, was in the 1930s—while he was on the run!!!!

Then he cited these verses from the Holy Qur'an, which read:

"Those whom We have given the Book recognize him as they recognize their sons. And a party of them surely conceal the truth while they know."

"Those whom We have given the Book recognize him as they recognize their sons. Those who have lost their souls -- they will not believe." (Holy Qur'an 2:146; 6:20)

They and or their descendants likewise recognize his student, Minister Farrakhan.

A brother loaned me a VHS tape titled: *CORRECTIONS*. The cover reads:

"Private prisons are back."

Then here is what follows:

"... a brilliant and searing essay...a glaring cry for justice, for the befallen, for the poor, for all who believe in justice." — Rod Hewitt, Roughcut

"With over 2 million in prison, 7 times the number in 1970, the U.S. finds itself in crisis. *CORRECTIONS* explores one response to this crisis, a revival of 'prison privatization,' where people invest in prison growth and profit off more & more prisoners; where punishment is tough on crime' politics meet the end of welfare, and the legacies of racism and poverty...

"CORRECTIONS TAKES YOU TO:

"A prison trade show and the corporate headquarters of leading prison firms;

"A poverty stricken community enticed to house a new prison for 'economic development';

"A timeline of the 'Tough on Crime' movement, following its beginnings in the Civil Rights Movement;

"An African American community alive with the memory of prisons for profit, still battling for social and economic justice;

"A juvenile prison where violent defiance of human rights law is perpetrated upon children as young as thirteen.

"PRAISE FOR CORRECTIONS:

"CORRECTIONS is a groundbreaking critique of the role politics and profit play in the denial of children's liberty. It is a must see for anyone trying to understand the forces that have allowed more young people to be incarcerated while crime continues to drop..."

Vincent Sheraldi, *Justice Policy Institute*

"... powerful & persuasive... Hunt's well-rounded film defangs such ubiquitous slogans as 'getting tough on crime."

Merele Bertand, *Film Threat*

"A compelling indictment of U.S. corrections policy, prison privatization, and the growing prison industrial complex."

David Faithi, *ACLU Nat'l Prison Project*

"This is about prisons in America."

This tape demonstrates one of the many justified reasons for The Millions More Movement! So does Mr. Bennett's, President Reagan's former Secretary of Education, genocidal comments, which reveals our enemies' hearts, when on his satellite radio show (9/29/05) he said that "you could abort every black baby in this country, and your crime rate would go down."

The full context of Bennett's words reveal worse than what I quoted.

Jabril Muhammad
September 30, 2005

Section 9

Farrakhan: The Traveler
For The Final Call
Vol. 25; No.3

The interview of the Honorable Minister Louis Farrakhan by Managing Editor Sister Dora Muhammad of *The Final Call*, Volume 24; Number 50, was splendid.

All that was written has been recently or is being fulfilled!

> *"Allah has written down: 'I shall certainly prevail, I and My messengers.' "*
>
> — *Holy Qur'an 58:21*

> *"I will live in them and move among them, and I will be their God, and they shall be my people. Therefore come out from them ... and I will be a father to you, and you shall be my sons and daughters ... ."*
>
> — *2 Cor. 6:17, 18*

> *"I will give ... a name better than sons and daughters; I will give them an everlasting name which shall not be cut off."*
>
> — *Isaiah 56:5*

> *"Thus says the Lord God, who gathers the outcasts of Israel, I will gather yet others to him besides those already gathered."*
>
> *— Isaiah 56:8*

> *"And other sheep I have, which are not of this fold: them also must I bring, and they shall hear my voice; and there shall be one fold, and one shepherd."*
>
> *— John 10:16*

When Minister Farrakhan launched the *Millions More Movement* I thought to interview him to contribute to the public's understanding of the ultimate origin of this idea and why opposition against it will be fruitless. The following is that interview, conducted on October 9, 2005, in Phoenix, Arizona.

Brother Jabril: Brother Minister, I have two questions that bear on what sits up under the *Millions More Movement*. The Honorable Elijah Muhammad referred to you as his lead Minister. First, what do you think he meant by "lead."

Minister Farrakhan: Well I can't say what was in his mind when he said that. I would have to ask him, but he did call me like a lead wire. I looked that up.

A "lead wire" is, I think, a wire that's connected to a generator. The lead wire breaks the current down so that other things will not be overwhelmed by surges of energy that they cannot handle.

I would assume that a lead minister is one who would forge the way for others. As the Minister is under the direct control of Master Fard Muhammad and His Messiah (the Honorable Elijah Muhammad), as They feed me, then the energy is transmitted broken down in such a way that other ministers can get the energy from that generating source broken down through the lead minister or the lead wire.

Again, he said, "Blessed are those who forge the way for others." The Bible talks about no man's visage was more scarred or marred than that particular prophet, because he opened the way for others. When God calls upon you to introduce a revolutionary concept, or idea, that takes the struggle to a new level, then you have to bear the burden of the opposition. You have to bear the burden of those who malign the new idea thinking it is this or it is that.

On radio this morning, I spoke to the people of the beautiful island of Jamaica. I mentioned three things that come up when you come up with an idea. Number one; *the timeliness* of the idea. Number two; *the persons* who would embody the idea. Number three; *the opposition* to the idea (and to the persons) who embody or promote or promulgate or espouse the idea.

The idea is thoroughly tested by the person who advances it. He is thoroughly tested by the opposition to the idea and those with him are thoroughly tested. When the opposition finds that they cannot uproot the idea, it's because it's an idea whose time has come.

The right person is the embodiment of idea. The right persons are the believers and practitioners of the idea and therefore they overcome all opposition to the idea and then the idea is established.

I think that that's maybe what he means by referring to the Minister as his "lead" Minister.

Brother Jabril: Could it also have to do with the Minister's constitution, his heart and his physical ability to handle the message itself?

Minister Farrakhan: Well the Qur'an answers that in these words: "Allah knows best where to place His message." So *since* He is the Originator of the message, and the Originator of the person who bears the message, and He knows the weight of the message, and what constitution that person must have to carry the weight of that message, and the weight of the mission that is to be imposed by the message, and the degree of opposition that would come because of the nature of the message, *then* He knows best the constitution of the person, the heart of the person, the spirit, mind and soul of the person. That's why He does not leave the choosing to others. He makes the choice Himself.

Brother Jabril: Your answers lay the basis for what I'm driving towards. You've told us, on the web cast, what caused you to make the decision that generated *The Millions More Movement*. Please retrace it.

Minister Farrakhan: Questions were asked, "Minister what are you going to do for the 10th Anniversary of *The Million Man March*?" And I said, "Nothing." I wasn't planning to do anything.

The Million Man March is what it is, was what it was. It's foolish to try to duplicate something that God gave us, at that moment in time that did what it did. Only unwise people try to duplicate what was, but persons who understand what was can build on what was to create what is needed for the new moment.

So, after saying that I had nothing in mind, but I thought again about the suffering of our people. I thought about the valley of the shadow of death that our people have entered and the devastation in all of the systems, that make up this world and the life that we have adopted, which the Bible says, "There's a way that seemeth right unto a man, but the ends thereof are the ways of death."

Then Isaiah the prophet, as taught by the Honorable Elijah Muhammad said that, "Your covenant, your agreement with hell will not stand and your covenant with death will be annulled."

Well, when a covenant has been made it takes a great power to break it. To annul something means that there is an actor, or actors, who have the power to break a bond that has been covenanted or agreed to by both parties.

Now having said that I began to think on something that the Honorable Elijah Muhammad had me to do 32, now 33 years ago. He sent me to New York to bring back the learned of our people to help him save the Nation. He said he had invested the poor people's money and we were in danger of losing everything that he had invested of the poor people's money, in the various business ventures that we have started because of poor management.

He offered me $10,000 if I would go and bring the learned to help him save the Nation. Well, I told him that, "Dear Holy

Apostle, I don't want the money to do it. I'll be honored to go and do that."

JABRIL MUHAMMAD
OCTOBER 9, 2005

FARRAKHAN: THE TRAVELER
FOR THE FINAL CALL
VOL. 25; NO.4

This is the second installment of the interview I conducted with the Honorable Minister Louis Farrakhan on October 9, 2005, in Phoenix, Arizona.

Minister Farrakhan: I went back to New York and with the help of Brother Akbar, (who was then Brother Larry 4X) and others, we called together the learned Black people of New York. We hired six Eastern Airline jets and they paid their own way to come to Chicago to help the Honorable Elijah Muhammad save the Nation.

The Honorable Elijah Muhammad gave them a speech and let them go. Needless to say I was somewhat disappointed. I thought he was going to take them into a room, talk to them about the problems of the Nation and organize their talents in the areas where the Nation was in need, or insufficient, so that he could save what he had invested of the poor people's money.

But I didn't have the courage to ask him, "Why did you ask me to do that and then you didn't let them do that?" Because I didn't have the courage to ask him, and he had asked me to do something that he deliberately didn't act on, he knew that, *that* would stay in my mind. And it did. It stayed in my mind as an unresolved question.

So while thinking, I don't know what triggered it, I said, "Oh my goodness." This is what he was doing. He was giving me a dry run of something that I would be asked to do many years later, but not to save a Nation that he had already told us was going to fall and it would rise and never fall again. He couldn't have brought those people out there to say that. But what he brought them out there to see, and what he dealt with in that lecture on

The Theology of Time, is what God had blessed him to do with the poor people's money and with those on the bottom of the socio-economic latter.

"He gave us a model of what the unity of our dollars, behind his guidance and program, would allow us to do when we were properly united on the proper vehicle.

So then I remembered something that he said to me. He said, "Brother when the learned of my people understand my program they will take it and put it over over-night."

Well then I called the learned in New York because I was very popular as a young Minister in New York. Now God has blessed me to be popular throughout America and in many parts of the world. So what is popularity? Is it a vanity badge? What is it? It is to be used to make change. It is to be used to make advancement for the people.

Then the idea crystallized: 'You are to call the learned of our people together and present them with the program of the Honorable Elijah Muhammad; then get them to agree with this program; then mobilize the people to accept their leadership with regard to that program. As that program solves the problems for a few of us it can be used to solve the problem of all of us.

That's the time that we're living in now. That's the underlying motivation of *The Millions More Movement*. That is the underlying motivation for the call to the learned scholars. This is what makes it necessary for us to clearly present to them the program of the Honorable Elijah Muhammad.

Once the learned understand that program and agree to work that program then the repair, the making whole and wholesome the healing of our people can and will begin.

Brother Jabril: Might this lead to the presentation of the program to Congress?

Minister Farrakhan: Yes it could. It could. What has to happen now is of course the implementation of such a program that will bring the best out of us and the worst out of our enemies. Of course, *if* the enemy is angered by our sincere commitment to ease the horror of what 300 years of chattel slavery; 100 years of Jim

Crow and lynching and 50 years of governmental abuse of our organizations and leaders has done; *then* this would clearly show that they are our open enemy.

Only when the open enemy is completely manifested and exposed, then the idea of separation from them becomes clearer, more palpable, and more realistic *if* our sincere efforts to do for self are opposed. This will lead to clashes. It will have too, because if you would oppose us to do something for self then we have to fight. We have no other alternative. You are strangling us with the economic situation that we're under. When we try to relieve ourselves of that burden, you further want to strangle us.

Then we are in a life or death struggle. We're already dead. So you will die too and we will die. Then out of the bloodletting (blood shedding?) the idea would come up: What can we do, to end the bloodletting (blood shedding)?

Then Congress can be brought in and the program put before Congress. But that's going to take what I just said to bring it about.

Brother Jabril: Thank you sir.

I turned off the tape recorder. But, there is more to this interview, as we'll see.

In response to a question in *The Final Call* interview (Volume 24; No. 50) Minister Farrakhan said: A Sister called me and told me of a dream where she saw the Honorable Elijah Muhammad. He was holding small meetings with select people. He said to her, "Tell the Minister that there is much that he sees and there is much that he does not see, but I see what he sees and I see all that he does not see. Tell him about this Millions More Movement, on that day, I will be completely in charge. Then, he said, I want to see him and my son Wallace, because I want my family to know that I am alive."

Consider the following.

Eighty-nine percent of blacks believe the federal government should offer a combination of cash payments, debt forgiveness and social welfare programs to compensate for the devastating effects of slavery and racial segregation, according to a new survey released Tuesday.

Kevin Herrera wrote this of the Reparations Research and Advocacy Group's ongoing poll, which was started by David Horne, Ph.D., in April 2002 while teaching Pan African Studies at California State University at Northridge. Barnar Muhammad said: "During Minister Farrakhan's October 15th speech, he made a reference that we should have a poll on the question of 'How many believe that Black people should be compensated for 400 years of free labor?' "

He continued: "... fifteen minutes after the Minister raised the question, I was able to put together a quick online poll that ran on the MillionsMoreMovement.com website that asked viewers to respond."

The immediate result was that 3,040 of 4,201 (or 72%) voted "Yes" to: "Do you believe that Black people should receive reparations for 400 years of free labor?"

The percentage has gone up since then.

JABRIL MUHAMMAD
OCTOBER 9, 2000

FARRAKHAN: THE TRAVELER
FOR THE FINAL CALL
VOL. 25; NO.5

On the marquee of a Church here in Phoenix, are these words: **"Two people cannot both love God and hate each other."**

This is the third installment of the interview I conducted with the Honorable Minister Louis Farrakhan on October 9, 2005, in Phoenix, Arizona.

When I asked the Honorable Minister Louis Farrakhan: "Might this lead to the presentation of the program to Congress?" This ended what I had in my mind for the interview. I had even received an extra answer to an extra question—the last one. So I turned off the tape.

At this point I thought to share the primary thoughts that occurred to me, over the months, as I watched and listened to him, especially when he went into the homestretch of his effort to generate *The Millions More Movement* on the Mall, last month. I did not intend to put them on the tape.

When I mentioned the first one, Minister Farrakhan immediately responded and I quickly turned the tape back on, not knowing what he was going to say.

I realized that this was going to force me to go deeper than I originally intended in my commentary to come after the interview ended.

Here is what I said to Minister Farrakhan that was not on the tape, and his response that was taped.

The Honorable Elijah Muhammad had a way, at certain times, of first saying something to you and then interrupting it with something else; then returning to the first thing he was saying. He did it smoothly, not brusquely, harshly or abruptly but in a natural manner, as if he wasn't doing what he was doing.

However, it would not fully dawn on you until much later. You would get and think on or act according to the part that was interrupted. Then you would forget it. But the part that he used to interrupt, the first part, is the part you would not forget. But it would not come up in your mind until later; often quite a while later. It would also be as clear in your head as when he first told it to you.

The Honorable Elijah Muhammad's words to me in May 1966 that were one of the factors that led to this interview, that I shared with Minister Farrakhan when the tape was off were: **"Master Fard Muhammad took me into the mind of Yakub and showed me how the idea of devil arose in his mind. And then, of recent, Brother, He took me into the mind of the first God and showed me how the idea of universe arose in His mind."**

Minister Farrakhan responded: It seems to me that what he said to you, that you could not remember anything else, but that was to stay in your mind for a reason. It's because we are at the time when those two Gods, and the way the ideas arose in their minds--is necessary to understand, because we're now at the time of *the* God Who is going to make all things new.

He wanted his chief helper, upon whose shoulders He's going

to put all powers, to know how that idea arose in the mind of the Originator of the heavens and the earth and how the idea of devil arose in the mind of Yakub, because now we are the *new* Yakub and the Yakub's history is for us to study how to make a god, but it's the reverse of how you make a devil.

You begin making devil by going among the dissatisfied. You begin by telling lies. You begin by making your laborers liars and then murderers. Over time the lie and the murder can be birth into the nature of the people that you are making. So that's what a devil is. He's a liar and a murderer and an opponent of the God of truth and life.

Now you're going to make a god. So you reverse the process. But you start with the same group, the dissatisfied. So you find among them those most willing to suffer for the sake of change. Then you start by telling them the truth; which gives them life, spiritual and physical. Then the more they love the truth and love the life that truth dictates they become the willing participants in the making of a people that will ... bring into existence the new heaven, the new earth, that whole new civilization.

JABRIL MUHAMMAD
OCTOBER 9, 2005

FARRAKHAN: THE TRAVELER
FOR THE FINAL CALL
VOL. 25; NO.6

This is the final part of my interview with the Honorable Minister Louis Farrakhan on October 9, 2005, in Phoenix, Arizona.

This interview grew out of my desire to share with others his (and my) response to this question: Who, and with what power, motivated Minister Farrakhan in his call for *The Millions More Movement*?

There is the most intimate and profound relationship between the love, wisdom and the power in the experiences that the Honorable Elijah Muhammad shared with his teacher, Master Fard Muhammad, prior to 1975, and Minister Farrakhan's call for *The Millions More Movement*.

The power in the Minister's call is due to the fact that the Honorable Elijah Muhammad has been raised to the position of the greatest eminence and influence to which a servant of God could be raised.

Again, there is the deepest connection between the authority of the Honorable Elijah Muhammad and the rise of Minister Farrakhan.

The public will soon come to see Allah's reasons for Minister Farrakhan's rise to ever greater degrees of eminence, right in the midst of the enemies of freedom, justice and equality. They will come to see his rise as a manifest sign of the eminence (or glory) to which God desires to raise His people.

Here is the conclusion of the short (and I hope interesting) interview I conducted with Minister Farrakhan for the purpose of showing what sits under and energized Minister Farrakhan's call for *The Millions More Movement* and which will continue to energize and invigorate this movement until it accomplishes it's objectives—and beyond.

Minister Farrakhan: So the God wisely chose a people that were empty vessels. He didn't have to empty us. We didn't have anything [wisdom] in us. Then He begins pouring into us that truth that's embodied in the idea of the new; the idea of the new heaven and the new earth that is embodied in our lessons.

Overtime, the dissatisfied would come to the truth, put in a form that appeals to their child like minds, but as they mature and grow, the idea would grow in them ... it's in their DNA ... in every generation getting them closer and closer to what the God envisioned; a Nation of Gods."

Brother Jabril: So we are in that—what's the word—

Minister Farrakhan: We're in like the door. That's the best way I can describe it. 'I am the door,' Jesus said. Well the door means you exit out of one thing and you enter into another.

We're at the time of the end of one thing and in the beginning of another and that's a very dangerous point, because you can go either way. You could fall backward into the old of in the difficulty of perusing the new. Or if your heart is the right material, you'll be strong enough to enter the door, close the door on the old and remain fascinated by and fastened to the new.

Brother Jabril: So Michael comes right in the start of the new beginning. He is called a protector of his people; a great prince; a champion. He is divinely placed in the position that he occupies. He's put in this position, right in the—I'm trying to think of the word—

Minister Farrakhan: "Nexus."

Brother Jabril: "That's it! The nexus! This makes his stand produce what the books says it would produce.

According to the work of scholars, in *Strong's Concordance*, a major part of his name means: 'Who is God?'

We talked a little bit about this on the phone, when you were in Atlanta, a few weeks ago, when I raised the question: Why would a man be given a name that's defined by a question?

Minister Farrakhan: "Because what he does, answers the question. Because everybody believes that there is a God—most everybody. Most everybody believes that the One, Who created the heavens and the earth and all therein, is the God.

Most everybody in the world understands and has felt and been manipulated or moved or destroyed by the power of the ruling powers of the present world.

As they see the present world in trouble and they see that they too are in trouble and in a time of trouble everyone starts calling on their God. This is as it was with Jonah when he was in the ship and the waves started battering the ship, everybody started praying. But their prayers were of none effect until they found Jonah in the ship. Then they asked him to pray. Then when he prayed (because he knew the God was after him) it was effective. So it was his prayer that brought peace to the troubled waters.

It was Jesus' prayer when he was in the boat with his disciples and the waves and the winds came up and they were so afraid, they awoke him, he stood, looked at them and said, 'Peace be still.' And the waves calmed and the winds calmed and then he looked at them and said, 'Oh ye of little faith.'

Well they were with Jesus, but they still did not know the

power that he had and the potential power, that they had.

His stand should then answer the question: 'Who is God?' So today Michael's stand ends the confusion, because no one is willing to go, where he's willing to go because in a time of trouble, people want to hide from the attacks of the enemies of their rise.

But here's a man who stands up in the midst of all of it. He stands for a people who are cowardly in fear, not knowing what to do. He answers the question for them, 'Who is God?'

The scriptures, the 37th chapter of Ezekiel, when the winds begin to blow it was then that the bones stood up and the scriptures says, "When I have raised you out of your graves, then shall you know that I, the Lord, am God, and beside me there is no Savior."

It was an act of prophesying unto the winds that put life in the bones that caused the bones to come up to see who is God.

Here, the interview ended. It's a witness of the fulfillment of Exodus 4:10-16, (from a bible translation titled: *The Message*) which reads: "Moses raised another objection to GOD: 'Master, please, I don't talk well. ... .'

"GOD said, ' ... who do you think made the human mouth? .... I'll be right there with you; with your mouth! I'll be right there to teach you what to say.'

"He said, 'Oh, Master, please! Send somebody else!'

"Don't you have a brother, Aaron the Levite? He's good with words. I know he is. ... In fact, at this very moment he's on his way to meet you. When he sees you he's going to be glad. ... I will be teaching you step by step. He will speak to the people for you. He'll act as your mouth, but you'll decide what comes out of it.' "

Jabril Muhammad
November 5, 2005

Farrakhan: The Traveler
For The Final Call
Vol. 25; No.7

"And because iniquity shall abound, the love of many shall wax cold. But he that shall endure unto the end, the same

shall be saved."

— Matthew 24:12,13

In *The Living Bible, Paraphrased*, in the book of *Exodus*, chapter 4:1, 10–16 we read: "But Moses said, 'They won't believe me! They won't do what I tell them to. They'll say, 'Jehovah never appeared to you!...'

"Moses pleaded, 'O Lord, I'm just not a good speaker. I never have been, and I'm not now, even after you have spoken to me, for I have a speech impediment.'

" 'Who makes mouths?' Jehovah asked him. 'Isn't it I, the Lord? Who makes a man so that he can speak or not speak, see or not see, hear or not hear? Now go ahead and do as I tell you, for I will help you to speak well, and I will tell you what to say.'

"But Moses said, 'Lord, please! Send someone else.' Then the Lord became angry. 'All right,' he said, 'your brother Aaron is a good speaker. And he is coming here to look for you, and will be very happy when he finds you. So I will tell you what to tell him, and I will help both of you to speak well, and I will tell you what to do. He will be your spokesman to the people. And you will be as God to him, telling him what to say.'"

The implications, of the above passage, for this time was a factor causing me to interview the Honorable Minister Louis Farrakhan, *as* I did on October 9th. As Minister Farrakhan drove himself to get as many as he could of the leadership of the Originals and poor people, generally, to join him in what became the *Millions More Movement,* I thought of the problem of envy.

If you lived during the time of Moses and Aaron could you imagine anyone from among the slaves *whom God came to free* becoming jealous or envious of Moses or Aaron, if they really understood God chose them for the benefit of the people as a whole?

Each man was chosen by the Supreme Being, Who *best* knows how to get done whatever He wants done. He wisely made His choices for the benefit of everyone, including the slave-masters.

The Honorable Elijah Muhammad explained that the God Who raised him informed him that He was allowing adequate time for the slave-masters to repent of their evils done to Black people. At the same time He was allowing adequate time for us to make the decision to agree with His plan for our salvation and future.

Every thing tells us that *that* time is all but up.

I'm prefacing my statements about envy with a brief mention of some questions I intend to take up later. Why have there been so many revisions and new translations of the many previous revisions of the Bible into English? Has their number increased? Why did the Honorable Elijah Muhammad state that only God Himself, or one taught by Him, could accurately or truthfully interpret the Bible? How does this relate to the resurrection of the dead? How did Moses and Aaron finally convince the slaves that they should follow them and let Pharaoh go?

The subject of envy was a critical problem for Joseph to overcome in his *successful* effort to unify his family. Saul's intention to murder David was envy. Pontius Pilate is represented in the Bible as saying that the prime motivation of those who delivered Jesus to him to be *murdered* was envy. The Bible informs us that envy was the motive of those who repeatedly sought Paul's life.

Envy produces tragedies, which occur *every minute* in this country. Envy governs a great deal of the behavior between Caucasians and Black people in America. There is jealousy and envy on the part of Blacks towards Caucasians and of Caucasians towards Blacks. The root causes are different, however. There is also jealousy and envy by Caucasians of Caucasians and by Blacks of Blacks. The atmosphere is filled with the emotion of jealousy and envy.

Unity among us is impossible unless we confront the problem of jealousy and envy *head-on* and thoroughly destroy it.

Minister Farrakhan taught that unity would solve 95% of our problems. Minister Farrakhan confirmed his teacher's teachings while exposing and condemning these evils.

The Honorable Elijah Muhammad once put me on a study of envy. One fact that stood out for me, in this study, was that envious people *always* slander others when this spiritual illness develops to a certain stage. Always? Yes, always!

Slander does not always come from jealousy and envy, but slander will always come out of people who are infected by jealousy and envy when the infection reaches a certain stage.

Slander was *in* the root of the idea of the formation of this world. It's in its fullest bloom now. For example, there are many people who earn their living by including in what they do the slandering of others. And they are widely respected and imitated for it too.

If you are in a position of leadership, you have *the* obligation to help rid our people of jealousy and envy--*immediately*. You must study its spiritual roots; the course it takes; the forms and disguises it takes on; the way it twists and distorts our perceptions; and the fact that this spiritual disease "attacks" or cuts across all (so-called) class distinctions.

We must understand *why* envy always leads to murder, if allowed to run its natural course, and finally, how to rid ourselves of it, if we are likewise infected.

The Honorable Elijah Muhammad knew how to get up under envy. That's essential to permanently uprooting and destroying it. Minister Farrakhan has demonstrated how to do this.

I was unable to travel, but I saw and heard and wrote some of it, as I watched my Brother, Minister Farrakhan, marching, like a general, throughout America, urging others to take a stand for the complete liberation of the original people in this land and for the poor and oppressed. I thought to interview him and then make the kind of comments that would further stimulate and foster the idea of our looking more deeply than ever, into the roots of Minister Farrakhan's words and then to determine to be of greater help than ever to the cause which he represents, especially now, that the meeting on the Mall, in D.C. on October 15th has passed.

Again, it ought to be obvious to us all that basic to generating the power we need to truly overcome the obstacles we face in our rise toward becoming a unified and productive people, is our need to overcome and destroy jealousy and envy from among us forever--*with love. Why "with love?"*

Numbers 14: 26, 27 reads: "the Lord said to Moses and Aaron, how long will this evil congregation murmur against Me?"

God threatened to destroy His people. How did Moses and Aaron react?

Jabril Muhammad
November 8, 2005

Farrakhan: The Traveler
For The Final Call
Vol. 25; No. 22

> *"If you are ungrateful, then surely Allah is above need of you. And He likes not ungratefulness in His servants. And if you are grateful, He likes it for you."*
> *— Holy Qur'an 39:7*

In Volume 25; No 12 and repeated, in part, in No.14 of *The Final Call* I wrote: "What is the best way to comprehend this whole 'thing' that has happened in America, from the appearance of God, to this moment, and what's in the immediate future? Moreover, why ought we to understand this anyway?

"The best way to start, or begin, is by studying Minister Farrakhan. I intend, by the help of Allah and His Christ, to show and prove this to be true—be it the will of Allah—until it is 'concluded.'"

In *Farrakhan: The Traveler* volume numbers 16-20 I wrote some of what I wrote in 1988 about Moses and the Wise man, as recorded in the Holy Qur'an, Surah 18: verses 60-82. I did this to cover what *our attitude ought not to be,* through the example of the symbolic "Moses," towards the two Messiahs, namely, the Honorable Elijah Muhammad and the Honorable Minister Louis Farrakhan.

By the word, "our" I am referring to us who have accepted to become students of the teachings of the Honorable Elijah Muhammad, under the direction of Minister Farrakhan.

I cited the references above, to make it easier for my fellow students to locate the words that plainly tell the specific purpose and aim of this specific series of articles.

After I finish taking up what our attitude towards Minister Farrakhan *must be,* for us to become successful students of God's word, I intend to cover Minister Farrakhan's example as a model student, of the Honorable Elijah Muhammad, of the word of God. Then we'll get to the proofs, Allah willing.

Although many wonderful significant events occurred, during this past Saviours' Day Convention, the addresses made by Minister Farrakhan were especially significant, because they were marked by certain finality.

The reality of this "finality" was emphasized in what he told me (while he was in Phoenix, Arizona) of his intention for the talks he was preparing *and* in what he told me on the phone *after* he delivered his Saviours' Day address. Still deeper a week later when he called me after he delivered his address in Mosque Maryam.

His said to me after he delivered part one, "It is done!" His words after the second part were, "It's now really done!"

These words of his deserves as much attention as his addresses.

I went to the Bible, because I knew the phrase "It is done," was used in it. But I was not sure of the context. I was almost sure this phrase was not in the Holy Qur'an though the idea is there, but put in different words.

"It is done," is mentioned two times in the Old Testament and three times in the New Testament; twice in the last book, Revelations.

In Revelations 16:17 reads: "The seventh angel poured out his bowl into the air, and out of the temple came a loud voice from the throne, saying, 'It is done!'"

Revelations 21:6,7 reads: "He said to me: 'It is done. I am the Alpha and the Omega, the Beginning and the End. To him who is thirsty I will give to drink without cost from the spring of the water of life.' He who overcomes will inherit all this, and I will be his God and he will be my son."

Paul wrote near to the end of his work with the early Christians, in 2 Timothy 4:7: "I have fought the good fight, I have finished the race, I have kept the faith."

Is there a connection between these acts? Do they bear on our lives and the lives of our loved ones right now? Yes.

Please, let's not say we don't have time to study God's word, yet we breathe His air, and benefit from His mercy and grace, every fraction, of second of every minute we live. That is gross ingratitude! Moreover, we are severely hurt by our stupidity; not Him.

To go deeper in God's reason for the narrative of Moses and the Wise man let's remember that the two Messiahs now, for a bit over 70 years, have taught that our history is written under the histories of other people in the Torah, the Gospels and the Holy Qur'an. It must be read and understood in that light.

This narrative is composed of the relative few verses of the Holy Qur'an, which is a witness of the Bible's truths, which is made of histories, ceremonial laws, other kinds of writings and, of course, prophecies. Both books were written ultimately for this day. There is not a page of these books that are not written about *you*.

Now, on the subject of Moses and the Wise man more questions could be raised to deepen our thinking and feelings into the words and ways of Allah. For instance, why did the Wise man tell Moses that he would not tell him the "whys" of his actions until a certain time? Was it a matter of timing? If so, what did timing have to do with informing him of the reasons of his actions, which would bring him into the regions of higher wisdom? Why could he not tell him before, or at least, at the same time he did what he did?

How was/is this "wisdom" of a higher order? Was patience involved? If so, how major a factor, which would have enabled the Moses, here, to walk *all the way* with the Wise man?

Remember, Moses was in a school of special training and education. It involved more than trust. Faith *and more* was also involved.

Minister Farrakhan's life demonstrates the behavior of the

model student, which we ought to study and emulate.

All of this bears on the path produced by Master Fard Muhammad, through the Honorable Elijah Muhammad, on which the Honorable Minister Louis Farrakhan is traveling and onto which he is inviting others to travel. Again, Master Fard Muhammad created the right path, and set the Honorable Elijah Muhammad on it. Both back Minister Farrakhan to show us all who would come, how to get God, peace, power and plenty; the prophesied Kingdom of God or Heaven on earth!

This path is described in all of the scriptures. Here is an example in these excerpts from Isaiah 35:4-6 and 8,10.

"Say to them that are of a fearful heart, Be strong, fear not: behold, your God will come with vengeance, even God with a recompence; he will come and save you. Then the eyes of the blind shall be opened, and the ears of the deaf shall be unstopped and the tongue of the dumb sing: for in the wilderness shall waters break out, and streams in the desert.

"And an highway shall be there, and a way, and it shall be called The way of holiness; the unclean shall not pass over it; but it shall be for those: the wayfaring men, though fools, shall not err therein. And the ransomed of the LORD shall return, and come to Zion with songs and everlasting joy upon their heads: they shall obtain joy and gladness, and sorrow and sighing shall flee away."

Really study Minister Farrakhan's words to survive the "Flood."

Jabril Muhammad
March 10, 2006

Farrakhan: The Traveler
For The Final Call
Vol. 25; No. 23

Revelations 16:17 reads: "The seventh angel poured out his bowl into the air, and out of the temple came a loud voice from the throne, saying, 'It is done!' "

Revelations 21:6,7 reads: "He said to me: 'It is done. I am the Alpha and the Omega, the Beginning and the End. To him who is thirsty I will give to drink without cost from the spring of the water of life.' He who overcomes will inherit all this, and I will be his God and he will be my son."

Near to the end of his work with the early Christians Paul wrote, in 2 Timothy 4:7: "I have fought the good fight, I have finished the race, I have kept the faith."

Is there a connection between these prophetic words and acts? Do they bear on our lives and the lives of our loved ones right now? Yes. Yes.

The Honorable Elijah Muhammad taught that the white race has mixed up what the prophets of God brought so much that they lost the knowledge of its truths. They entangled the scriptures so thoroughly that only God Himself could untangle them and He gave their secrets to the Honorable Elijah Muhammad, the Messiah, as a major part of his divine education.

Minister Farrakhan, the best in the class of the Messiah's students, was divinely anointed and backed to present the scriptures' truths clearly to us today.

It's written in the scriptures that Aaron was divinely anointed with the oil of divine wisdom. Aaron was a sign of Minister Farrakhan, who has further lit up this world with divine understanding. Take it or leave it!

The above scriptures were written long, long ago of the events of today.

The work of the seventh angel is among the most serious phases of the overall judgment of this evil world by Almighty God, Allah, about which the Honorable Elijah Muhammad warned us and then continued to warn us through the Honorable Minister Louis Farrakhan for decades.

These seven angels or men, are mentioned in Revelations 15:1, which reads: "And I saw another sign in heaven, great and marvelous, seven angels having the seven last plagues; for in them is filled up the wrath of God."

Under the authority of Master Fard Muhammad they have already conferred *in person* with the Honorable Elijah Muhammad. There is vast power behind Minister Farrakhan.

Revelations 16:1 reads: "And I heard a great voice out of the temple saying to the seven angels, 'Go your ways, and pour out the vials of the wrath of God upon the earth.' "

As Minister Farrakhan has clearly stated, continue watching the weather; the insects, the sun, the droughts, huge hail stones and other weapons that one of the prophets called the "arrows" of God.

Circumstances force me here to make a change in what may appear for the next few articles. By Allah's help I'll return to what I am working on later. For now, let's start by going back nearly six years to the following interview I conducted of Minister Farrakhan. It's helpful to note that the book you have in your hands is what was Closing The Gap, book one and two—now one book.

Brother Jabril: This is Memorial Day, May 30, 2000. It's a Monday. This is the start of *Closing the Gap, Part Two.*

Minister Farrakhan, I came by your home, a couple of nights ago and when I came into the living room, you were there with Sister Ayke Agus, Sister Saffiyyah and your daughter, Sister Fatimah. You all didn't see me slip in and I just sat quietly. I watched with rapt attention. I witnessed a learning experience, with you as the student and her as the teacher.

I don't recall all the things that were said. Much of the musical language went over my head. But I was profoundly impressed. I couldn't stop smiling at what I saw.

When there was a break and you stood up and saw me, you smiled. I was already smiling because of what I saw. An article, or a series of articles, were forming in my mind: "Farrakhan," in this case, "The Student," or "Farrakhan: The Model Student."

At one point, Sister Ayke Agus, spoke of you as a "fast learner." So, Brother Minister, what makes for an effective student?

Minister Farrakhan: I would say that the first thing is the desire to know what one does not know. Then the humbleness of heart and mind to accept instruction and more importantly, to accept critical analysis of whatever the person (student) is doing and desires to improve in, that he or she (student) may move a step closer to perfection.

The student must also have the ability to focus; to concentrate on what the teacher or the lesson that the teacher is giving. Next, the student must be willing to practice in order to perfect what he or she desires to do. And lastly, there must be a willingness, on the part of the student, to sacrifice time, in order to give to the endeavor the requisite time and effort, to improve and grow or develop the technical skill necessary to become proficient in that endeavor.

Brother Jabril: How important are the qualities of humility and patience in relation to the quality and the speed of a student's learning?

Minister Farrakhan: Humility is the greatest of the characteristics of any student. One may have the desire but the desire will soon dissipate, if the student is not humble enough to recognize his or her need for more and more instruction, in that of which the student intends to perfect or prosper in.

Jesus said, "Except you become as a little child, you cannot enter the kingdom of heaven." Children are born with a nature of curiosity and it is this curious nature of the child that makes it humble toward instruction.

So this is a principle that is seen in everything, pertaining to being an effective student.

The hardest person to teach, as I heard the Honorable Elijah Muhammad say, is the one who thinks he or she already knows. That person uses what they think they know to argue against what they're being taught. As a result, they don't accept instruction. Their desire to improve begins to dissipate and weaken, then the will to become what they thought they wanted to become is broken, and the person looses out and does not wish to continue in that pursuit any longer.

I'll close this by saying, so many people that I have met, in my short life on this planet, want to become great, but they lack the will to sacrifice and to be patient with themselves as they practice that which would give them skill in their chosen endeavor.

A lack of humility also makes you impatient. Impatience means you want to get there and you don't wish to take the necessary steps to get there. You want to rush and so you end up breaking your neck.

Brother Jabril: We've all heard the old expression that to be a good leader you must first become a good follower. But some have stated this expression this way, that to be a good teacher you must first become a good student.

How important is the relationship between being a good student first and an effective teacher later on?

JABRIL MUHAMMAD
MARCH 10, 2006

FARRAKHAN: THE TRAVELER
FOR THE FINAL CALL
VOL. 25; NO. 24

This article continues an interview I conducted with the Honorable Minister Louis Farrakhan for *Closing The Gap, Part Two* on May 30, 2000.

Brother Jabril: We've all heard the old expression that to be a good leader you must first become a good follower. But some have stated this expression this way, that to be a good teacher you must first become a good student.

So, how important is the relationship between being a good student first and an effective teacher later on?

Minister Farrakhan: A good student learns from the good teacher, the method, the psychology of how to deal with the mind of the person in whom you hope to place a certain type of knowledge. You may not understand motive. You may not understand method, but as you mature in the practice of what your teacher is giving to you and you become one in spirit with the teacher, you then grow into the understanding of the method, the motivation and then you are of the same mind, the same spirit, the same accord of the teacher. Now the student can become a teacher.

Brother Jabril: Prominent in our conversation, last night over dinner, was the factor of love in the learning process. Sister Ayke Agus, shared her views and experience with us in her relation to her teacher, Jascha Heifetz. You commented on that.

Now, we know that there are some subjects or areas of knowledge, where the love factor does not seem to be a major factor in the learning of those subjects, even though it *must* be there to some degree for successful learning experience to occur.

One may be in a computer school and your learning may be of a technical knowledge or nature. One's study may be in some other field, again, where that love factor does not seem to be as key as in other areas of learning. However, in the higher fields of learning, especially in *the* highest area of knowledge, where the subject matter involves the study of God, the love factor becomes more obvious and predominant.

How important is the quality of love in the study of any subject, but especially in the higher areas of learning? What position does love occupy in a student learning from a teacher, these higher aspects of knowledge, and, in your case, your learning from the Honorable Elijah Muhammad?

Minister Farrakhan: Love is never absent from a student who desires greatness in his or her chosen field of endeavor. First of all, we study ourselves. All of us have been given a gift from our Creator. The greatest joy and peace of mind is when a person finds the purpose for their being, for their existence, for their life, on this planet and the peace of mind comes, not just when you dream about the purpose, but when you actually are working toward the fulfillment of your purpose.

Once you discover your gift, you must love the gift and love the Giver of the gift, in order to become great with that gift. Now, if it's basketball, if it's baseball, if it's boxing, if it's computer science, if it's medicine, if it's law, whatever field of endeavor you chose to become great in, *you* have chosen that field. The worst motivation is to choose to be something for the sake of money or for vanity, rather than for the sake of service and the glorification of God, Who is the Giver of the gift.

In loving the gift, you automatically will fall in love with the one who teaches you how to become proficient in your gift. I don't know of any basketball player that has become great, a baseball player, tennis, boxing, music—whatever your endeavor is—that does not remember with great fondness the teacher, who made them excel in their chosen field of endeavor. *So love is all the way through.*

Now the degree of love, that is required to become great in anything, must be a high degree. But the greatest degree of love is required, when one is to interpret the word of God. One has to be so in love with God, that he or she knows God in a hint or a sign and can look at the word of God and is so in tuned with God, because of the profound love of the student for God, the Master Teacher, that the student can look at the word and know God's intention in revealing such a truth.

That's the highest level of love. Prophets and messengers don't reach that *highest* level. They reach, or I would say, they come close to that level. But the Messiah *reaches* that level, because his love for God is *so, so* magnificent, and so great, until he subordinates himself, *so,* totally to God that he becomes *one with* God.

God lives *in* him and dwells *in* him and manifests Himself *through* him. That cannot happen, except with the profoundest degree, the superlative degree of love.

If you put it in the cheap vernacular, when you love a person to the "mostest and the bestest." I say this with a smile behind it.

Brother Jabril: This reminds me of the scripture where the Jesus says, "I'm in my father and my father is in me."

Minister Farrakhan: *Yes.* Only love allows the person who is traveling to travel *in* you. Love is the vehicle that allows the teacher to ride inside the student. And even when the teacher is absent, the teacher is present, because love has allowed the student to drink the teacher in, to the degree that the student and the teacher become one.

Brother Jabril: The presence of your present violin teacher, Ayke Agus, over the last few days, during the course of your conversations, has given rise to expressions of great truths. One of them involves a vital aspect of the teacher-student relationship. We looked at those things about teachers, or certain kinds of teachers, that many students find difficult to grasp.

She [Ayke Agus] is an example of a student of a master, who

saw through certain difficulties of her teacher. Because of her love for her teacher, she was by him as others were not, who later walked away from him, but who later on regretted their behavior towards him. She was of those who stuck by him, despite the difficulties involved.

In part of your comments, yesterday, on what she said on this subject, in your own personal case, who, regardless to what the Honorable Elijah Muhammad laid on you—and he laid some heavy trials and tests on you—you would not let him go. Of course, there were a few others like this. But I am not referring to them here. None of them were being prepared to sit in his seat but you.

What he put on you, of tests and trials, only brought you closer to him, rather than drove you away from him. Others might have considered your reaction to him as silly, or ridiculous, as they would not have gone through what you experienced, because they didn't look at such experiences as you (and a few others) did. Please comment.

Jabril Muhammad
March 10, 2006

Farrakhan: The Traveler
For The Final Call
Vol. 25; No. 25

This continues the interview I conducted with the Honorable Minister Louis Farrakhan on May 30, 2000.

Minister Farrakhan: It is difficult for a student to comprehend the ways of a master—the methodology of the master, the psychology of the master, the spiritual sensitivity of the master. A good teacher prepares the student, not only in the art or science of the profession, but the teacher, if he or she is a good one, recognizes that your gift becomes the means of your trial.

The gifted person, who has the gift but has not the character to go along with the gift, must be careful, because the gift can become the means of the student's destruction. So a good teacher will carry the gifted one to the threshold of pain and then take them over that threshold and continues to give the student painful experiences. Why is this? Because to become great in any field, you will inspire the evil emotion of envy in others, who want to be great in that field but cannot equal the one who is supremely gifted of God.

The envy of the envier causes the envier to criticize you harshly, to throw stumbling blocks in your path. If you lack the character to persevere past or through your pain, from someone who is in your field, but hates you because you are doing well or better than he or she is doing, if that embitters you, if that becomes an impediment in your spirit, then you cease to become as great an artist or a professional as you could have become, if you did not allow the surrounding emotions to become a stumbling block in the pathway of your progress.

In the case of the Honorable Elijah Muhammad, he was looking for a student who would be able to carry or share the burden of his mission in his absence. Which meant that the student, must not only be proficient in the teaching of the message, but that the student must be able to bear the pain that goes along with success.

In the case of the Honorable Elijah Muhammad, whom God has raised at the end of the world of Satan, to be with him, you would have to endure the wiles of Satan; the schemes of Satan and how he uses people whom you love to overturn you and destroy you. Well if you only know the teachings and know it well, but you lack the character, to bear the burden, then you're not the one that the teacher was looking for.

Any great master has an idiosyncrasy, if you will, or ways that the student may not understand. If you love the teacher and the instruction, then you will absolutely look pass the things that you don't understand and one day you will come to understand, that what the teacher appeared to be doing *to* you, he or she was actually doing *for* you.

You know, Brother Jabril, one of the hardest things for a student to take is a severe rebuke by the teacher. There's a proverb that says, "The fool despises correction. The wise man changes often but the fool will not." Well what would make the fool change? It will be when he/she comes into a greater knowledge or understanding.

(Note: Minister Farrakhan did not use the word, "fool" in the common derogatory sense of the word. He used it as the scriptures uses this word, as it's defined in *Vines's Expository Dictionary of Old and New Testament Words*.

(According to Vine's the word for fool is from a Greek word that signifies "without reason; want of mental sanity and sobriety, a reckless and inconsiderate habit of mind or the lack of common sense perception of the reality of things [both] natural and spiritual.")

(There are two other Greek adjectives, which also define this word, which I intend to get to, be it the will of Allah.)

Well how did you come into a greater knowledge? You had to be humble enough to recognize it when it came. So, the scriptures says, "Whom the Lord loveth he chastens much." Why? Because it is only through the chastening, that the process of learning and growing is being refined in the student. So if you cannot accept chastening, you cannot become refined in the field, which you chose to become great.

Now some of us are so gifted, that we seem to do with ease, what it takes others real hard work to manifest. The supremely gifted one finds things so easily, that oft-times the supremely gifted one is careless with the gift and never works as hard as he or she should, because they accomplish so much with so little ease. So the gift then becomes the supreme trial for the supremely gifted one. Sometimes you think you know so much, till you don't wish to be taught any more. You want to teach the teacher. As a result, you really become a fool.

The Holy Qur'an teaches that, "He who rejects the religion of Abraham is he who makes a fool of himself." What is the religion of Abraham? It is found in these words: "Surely I have turned myself to Thee Oh Allah, to Him Who originated the heavens and the earth and I am not of the polytheist." I ultimately have no other Teacher to focus on but you.

"Oh Allah, Thou art the King [Thou art the Master Teacher] there is no God but Thee. Thou art my Lord, [my Nourisher, my Evolver, my Sustainer, my Grower into perfection. You're the only one] and I am of those who submit."

That is the heart, mind and soul of Abraham. That's what made him the *friend* of God. And that's what will make any good student the *friend* of the Master.

"I submit. I surrender. I yield myself over to your mastery of that which I hope to become. Now put yourself in me. I tell you, *that* is love to the 19th power!" [We laughed.]

The Honorable Elijah Muhammad taught: "The Bible is full of prophecy. The Holy Qur'an is not. The Holy Qur'an is a message directed to Muhammad, the Messenger. This is why it reads, 'Say so and so and so. And when they say so and so and so, you say so and so.'

"This is a direct message to a *student* under the teachings and guidance of Allah. I want you to understand these things." ("Theology of Time," August 20, 1972.)

How *blessed* we are today that the Honorable Elijah Muhammad, under the guidance of Master Fard Muhammad, prepared his best *student*, Minister Farrakhan, to say and do as he has for 28 (going on 29) years throughout America and the world.

One of the best ways that we can show our *gratitude* to Minister Farrakhan's Backers, and our *understanding* of his significance and his presence and work; and the times in which we live; and the needs of the original people of this land; is to spread the Saviours' Day addresses Minister Farrakhan delivered on February 26 and the two he delivered on March 5, 2006—*three* altogether.

JABRIL MUHAMMAD
MARCH 10, 2006

FARRAKHAN: THE TRAVELER
FOR THE FINAL CALL
VOL. 25; NO. 26

This concludes the interview I conducted with the Honorable

Minister Louis Farrakhan on May 30, 2000.

Brother Jabril: Brother Minister, you have been "ill" for the last few years. What are just some of the immediate lessons you would like to share with others about going through such an experience? What comes immediately to your mind about how to help them get through such an experience as "illness?"

Minister Farrakhan: Allah says in the Holy Qur'an, "He created man and woman to face difficulty." In another place it says, "Allah has ordained struggle." I've never read it in the Qur'an, but it's there in other words, that Allah has ordained pain as the mother of new realities. So we cannot go through life without pain. We cannot go through life without difficulty. We cannot go through life without struggle. God has ordained this because these are the circumstances of life that manifest the quality of our character, our heart, the core of our being. If the heart is diseased, the person is indeed ill.

When a misfortune befalls the Believer, the Holy Qur'an says, "Allah is my patron and to Him is my eventual return." What beautiful words. He's my patron. He's my backer. He's my support. He's my friend.

Well if my eventual return is to Him, what are the events that come up in my life that might bring me to the point of return? If I am ugly over an event in my life that suggests return, then I'm not really a true Believer in God. If I go through that difficulty with an improper attitude, then this makes manifest a core sickness in myself, as an individual.

Whatever your lot is in life, the attitude that you take toward the thing that God has permitted in our life, that you may have brought about, or that God brought about or permitted to be brought about, however you look at it, the Holy Qur'an says, "Good is from Allah, misfortune is from Allah. It is all from Allah."

Even though sometimes we have a hand in producing our misfortune, yet, it could not happen unless Allah permits it. So He takes full responsibility. So now, what is your attitude? How do you like *that*? OK, I'm going to let your own foolishness bring something on you. How do you like *that*?

"God, why me? I always knew you didn't love me. I always knew you didn't care about me. I hate you God. I love my daughter. I love my son. Why did you take my son? Why did you take my daughter? Oh, my God I served you well. I prayed. I did all of this. Now, I find I got cancer. I got multiple sclerosis. I got this disease or that disease."

Hush. Hush. Hush. Yes. But the worse disease you could have is a disease of the heart, which the manifestation of physical illness has brought about or made manifest in you.

So I thanked Allah, that when I was at the doorway of death I never asked Him to spare my life. I thanked Him for my life. I thanked Him for allowing me the privilege of living in the majesty of His universe and beholding His greatness. I thanked Him for allowing me to serve and I thanked Him for the pain that I was suffering and it was excruciating. It was my *attitude* that even further purified my heart for greater service for God.

Because of my *attitude*, though I'm not completely healed yet, I'm not worried about it, because my eventual return is to Allah. And if this is the means by which I return, well that's the highway that I'm on.

My return is to Allah. Maybe you'll take one highway. It's called tuberculosis. Another one is called AIDS. Another one is just called old age. Another one is called an accident that just happened. Well this is life. Welcome to the planet.

If you did not want to struggle, you should never have come. If you did not want misfortune, this is the wrong place for you. I don't say suicide is a good way out, but if that's what you wish to do, that's up to you because you're not willing to face difficulty, "Well let me kill myself. Let me destroy my life." Oh that's so foolish!

Your *attitude* toward the problem will help you to solve it, if you have the correct *attitude*. For instance, if darkness has overcome you, you say, "In the beginning there were total darkness. Yet there was a light sparkling in the darkness. Surely in this darkness, there is a light. Let me seek it and I shall find it."

Attitude.

I heard a Christian preacher say, "It is your *attitude* that will determine your *altitude*." And if you have an improper *attitude* toward misfortune, you won't get too high in the sight of God.

To all who may read this, study this, take the *attitude* of love for God. Love for Allah.

Regardless to what He brings or allows into your life, "I love you Allah and I thank you, for surely, in my trial, there is good for me because I know you mean good for me. I'll find good in it."

The good student will always find some good in what the master teacher is doing to them. And in the end, they will understand, that every thing that he did to them, he was their best friend and patron because he did it all for them, willingly or unwillingly.

Brother Jabril: Your words remind me of what I use to say to those who were catching hell unjustly from others. I said, "I'd rather be the wood than the sandpaper."

Minister Farrakhan: Right. Some people are your teacher and they don't even know it. They're like sandpaper and you're like the piece of wood that God wants to smooth out. So He sends some rough riders into our life.

Well, it's rough going through it now, if you were a piece of wood and the sand paper was rubbing on you. Well, you wouldn't like that too well. But, the more the sand paper rubs, the more sand comes off the sand paper and it can't do you any further harm. 'Grin and bear it,' the old saying goes and thank God for it and you will come out the winner.

FARRAKHAN: THE TRAVELER
FOR THE FINAL CALL
VOL. 25; NO. 27

Farrakhan: The Traveler, Volume 25; Number 12 contains this: "I conclude this part of this article with a question. What is the best way to comprehend this whole 'thing' that has happened in America, from the appearance of God, to this moment, and what's in the immediate future? Moreover, why ought we to understand this anyway? The best way to start, or begin, is by studying Minister Farrakhan.

"I intend, by the help of Allah and His Christ, to show and prove this to be true, be it the will of Allah, until it is 'concluded.'"

I proceeded with the use of the insightful narrative from the Holy Qur'an often called Moses and the Wise man, in Surah 18, sections 9 and 10, or verses 60-82. My primary purpose was to show the attitude, and disposition of a "bad" student.

Then we went into the mind and attitude, the very spirit, of the best student of the Honorable Elijah Muhammad, the Honorable Minister Louis Farrakhan.

Now we enter the area of "the proof" that I mentioned earlier.

Where would we be as a group, or nation, if we had done better by the study guides of the Honorable Minister Louis Farrakhan based on the September 1986 speech he made, titled: *Self Improvement: the Basis For Community Development*?

In the letter that introduced the study guides, he wrote: "This speech, in my judgment, formally ushers in that which is the launching pad of a world wide movement."

His words compel the question: What is "that which"? It's a group of people—dedicated students of the word of God—who under Minister Farrakhan's ministry study his study guide material. Then they meet on Friday nights, in their respective Mosques, prisons or wherever study sessions are conducted as per his instructions. In essence, that constitutes the "launching pad of a world wide movement."

The wicked have worked hard to kill this movement in various ways. But they will be overcome.

Many have under-estimated and misunderstood the profound significance of what he asked us to do revolving around his study guides. However, it must be understood that we are exactly where we should be, at this very moment in history. The proper reading of the scriptures shows us the external and internal evidence that bears witness to this truth. Ultimately, Allah is the Sole Source of this understanding.

It's also written that Allah would provide the needed course corrections and the various stimulants, to keep us moving in the direction of His will. He has, and will continue to do this, as He is The Loving Supreme Guide, Whose Identity the Honorable Elijah Muhammad has explained *and which Minister Farrakhan continues to explain.*

Minister Farrakhan continued in that letter that: "Resurrection is that process that begins with the self-accusing spirit and does not end until we become one in perfect harmony or peace with Allah and His Creation."

"That which" is also the process that began *in us* with our use of Minister Farrakhan's study guides. This that was/is repeated each week is the external part of this process, as Minister Farrakhan wrote, that "Leads to our resurrection" on the highest possible level. This essential key is the core of the process that, of course, includes other activities that collectively constitutes factors that are a significant part of our daily live.

In that letter he referred to each of us as helpers "in the Cause of Allah."

Those of us who have made the proper study that Minister Farrakhan has exhorted us to make, and who have studied a little deeper and more consistently since 1986, into his aims and purposes in producing these study guides, are those helpers who have entered more deeply than otherwise would be the case, into the wisdom of Allah or the life of a Muslim.

The following quotes are words of the Honorable Elijah Muhammad in *Theology of Time*, June 11, 1972.

"If the religion of Islam takes for its base, the root meaning of the universe for its religion, then I say you have an awful job trying to tangle with that type of people. They'll have you running round looking for something to prove what you say."

In *This Is The One*, I quoted the Honorable Elijah Muhammad:

"A religion whose origin or roots cannot be found in the universal order of God's creation cannot be said to be the religion of God.

"… if your religion's roots are not found in the universal order of things, it is not from Allah (God).

"Almighty Allah has taught me that if we study the universe and the nature of the earth: its plants, animals and insect life; if we study this part of Allah's creation and the natural laws working among them, we will have the key to the understanding of the way of life intended by God for you and me.

"This is the language of a scientist."

Let's focus, for a moment on a few of his words. He said: "… Islam takes for its base the root meaning of the universe for its religion …" Exactly, what did he say? He said that we are, or will grow, to be living our lives *everyday*, based on an understanding of Allah's root meaning of the universal order of His creation. This implies that we will have studied, learned and practiced the principles of Islam to the point that we will understand how to live (with ourselves and with others) in accord with Allah's understanding of His root meaning of and purpose for why He has created what He has created.

Minister Farrakhan's study guides and sessions are critical to this growth.

Obviously people are presently living their lives throughout America, and in every part of the earth, according to how they choose. But how many of them are living their lives according to the Supreme Being's perfect understanding of the root meaning of the universal order of Allah's creation, in which they were born and are living their lives? How much longer will He allow this? Not long!

We have now enrolled in a new school of the most exquisite wisdom imaginable, which was established here in America, to prepare us for a new world, God's kingdom, which is growing to include all of the peoples of the earth.

The Honorable Elijah Muhammad has said that we are in the kindergarten of Master Fard Muhammad's wisdom. We are moving upwards, in our learning, in this classroom or kindergarten, which has stages, that we as a people have gone through from the 1930s to where we are in the present.

My aim, with this series of articles, is to go beyond the fact of the unusually brilliant mind possessed by Minister Farrakhan. It's to witness the fact that he was divinely produced for the Honorable Elijah Muhammad's use for our benefit and to show us the way to grow into our divinity.

We must learn to use our study time better. Satan continues to publicize useless knowledge that they admit is based on gossip, conjecture, guesses, slander, half-truths and outright lies. Let's be careful of his diversions, distractions, tricks and lies.

JABRIL MUHAMMAD
APRIL 5, 2006

Section 10

Now we are at the conclusion, or final set of interviews, for this book. I must again say that I have been honored and privileged to conduct these interviews with the Honorable Minister Louis Farrakhan. Off and on, over the last few years, I have been thinking about when might be the most appropriate place to end this book. I knew and know that my Brother, Minister Farrakhan was and is so filled with the spirit and wisdom of God Almighty that we could go on, literally for thousands of pages easily.

When he was here in Phoenix, preparing for his Saviours' Day address, for February 2006, he shared with me what he had in mind to say to Black people, to America, and to the world, with the help of Allah. What he said to me made me to think and feel that the next time I got the chance to interview him that set of interviews would represent the concluding sections of this book.

So when he arrived in Phoenix on June 2nd and I was blessed to have dinner with him that night, I looked at and listened to my Brother for signs or hints that this was it! The next morning when he came to my home it was clear to me from the jewels that began to drop from his mouth that this was it!

A few days later, on June the 5th I asked him a question concerning a letter the Honorable Elijah Muhammad wrote me back in 1966. I was considering whether or not to place it in the next and final edition of *Is It Possible That The Honorable Elijah Muhammad is Still Physical Alive???*

I interviewed the Honorable Minister Louis Farrakhan on a few topics. One of them was what he thought about my idea of placing the letter that the Honorable Elijah Muhammad sent to me back in November 1966, in this book. Here was his response.

"There is no witness stronger than his own witness of what he knew would come to him, except Allah. He told you in the letter that he would escape a death plot. He gave several instances of scripture that confirmed that.

"So our saying he's alive is strengthened by his words and he confirms what we've been saying that he is alive in the face of those who say: 'Well the Honorable Elijah Muhammad never said nothing like that' or 'I never heard nothing like that' or 'I don't believe the Honorable Elijah Muhammad is alive.'

"Well here's a letter that he wrote at such and such a time in a certain context. And he bears witness that he would be taken on the heels of a death plot. Then, in connection with this death plot, the Honorable Elijah Muhammad told you that, 'If Allah had not shown me how I was going to escape, I would have no hope.'"

In other books to be reprinted, and in others to be published soon, be it the will of Allah, I intend to cite testimonies from Minister Farrakhan and others on this subject of the veracity of the Honorable Elijah Muhammad's statement in his letter, and that he is, indeed, alive, well and in power.

In *The Fall of America,* chapter 58, he wrote: "The disbeliever believes that which he sees present and not that which is prophesied to come."

JABRIL MUHAMMAD

What I've just covered is vital, although this was not the material I really wanted to get into. I wanted to ask Minister Farrakhan questions that would bring from him answers directly intended to help the Believers get more of the light that is mentioned in Surah 57 verses 12-19.

This passage begins with verse 12 and says: "On that day thou wilt see the faithful men and the faithful women, their light gleaming before them and on their right hand."

One does not have to be a scholar of the scriptures to see that there is a direct relationship between this passage in the Holy Qur'an—especially verse 13—and the parable made by Jesus of the five wise and the five foolish virgins. I am among those who heard certain words from the Honorable Elijah Muhammad and Minister Farrakhan that illuminates these two sets of scriptures.

I strongly feel that his departure is nigh. Therefore, I wanted to ask him questions that would produce from him answers from his Backers which would cast increased light on the path on which that the Believers are moving on as this hour grows darker.

As I wrote earlier in this book, my questions are the outgrowth of specific things which both the Honorable Elijah Muhammad and the Honorable Minister Louis Farrakhan asked of me, which Allah guided me to ask. I'm grateful to Allah for guiding my heart to raise the questions that I did to my Beloved Brother.

This book represents a major aspect of the help I have tried to be, and provide, to the Ministers of Minister Farrakhan, specifically since February 1991 and that I had in mind when I was privileged to speak for about a minute at some point before Minister Farrakhan delivered his Saviours' Day address in 2004.

Let us begin. And, let us begin with the mention of the condition Minister Farrakhan was in. I think it's important for the reader to again reflect on the fact that Minister Farrakhan was not well and oftimes was in pain; sometime terrific pain that also affected me. Then he would slowly sit down and look to me for my question or questions.

He did not know what I was going to ask him during this time period, during June and July 2006 as was with all of the questions I had asked him in all of the interviews over the years, except possibly one. In that one, I inadvertently may have given him the barest kind of hint of what was in my mind.

Every morning and every afternoon, when he came to see the doctor and myself, I would be standing outside of my door, to greet him. I also studied him. Some mornings or afternoons he would walk up to my door in obvious discomfort. There were other times when he would be stepping quite lively.

Although I did not keep track of when he looked pretty good

and when he didn't—in terms of a count—certain scenes stand out in my mind as I'm writing this now in September 2006. So I'll make comments on this at the head of various interviews, which follows.

INTERVIEW OF THE HONORABLE MINISTER LOUIS FARRAKHAN
BY JABRIL MUHAMMAD
PHOENIX, ARIZONA
JUNE 8, 2006

By the help of Allah, I had determined that when I knew for sure that Minister Farrakhan was up for doing the interviews, that my first question to him would be intended to elicit his answer to speak on the purpose and value of excellent conversation that we must now quickly get into and get ourselves into, as fast as possible. I knew that we also must quickly get into the habit of quality conversation. Of course I did not know how my Brother would answer questions intended to elicit responses from him that would serve this critical need of us who follow him and our people and other in general. But I said a short prayer and began on a day he wasn't feeling too bad.

Jabril Muhammad: My question is two or three questions in one. How would you define the art of conversation and then how would you define the best kind of conversation Muslims should be engaging in, especially in this critical hour, as it's getting darker?

Minster Louis Farrakhan: Allah gives to every creature the ability to communicate with its own to be able to share with other members of its species, what its aim is, what its desire is and the fulfillment of the natural inclination of the species.

The highest manifestation of communication is language that He gives to the human to express its desires, its concerns, its needs, its disappointments, its frustrations. But all of it is manifested through language.

The art of communication is a lost art among human beings. I guess the Tower of Babel and the confusion of languages is demonstrative of the chastisement of God in disallowing human beings to be able to communicate at the highest level.

With us as a people that were taken from our original language and culture we have developed skill in communicating through various means; sometimes other than language. But the highest form of communication is language that is used to communicate the wisdom of God.

The Honorable Elijah Muhammad told me once that, "It takes five hundred seconds, eight minutes and twenty seconds for the light, traveling at a hundred and eighty-six thousand miles per second, to travel from the sun to the earth." Likewise, he said, "It takes five hundred seconds, eight minutes and twenty seconds for the blood to make a complete circulation between the heel and the brain and back." He said "When you go to visit a person that is sick, if you put the right word in their ear, within eight minutes and twenty seconds you will see a change in the spirit of such person."

What that told me was, that the level of energy, light, spiritual power that is contained in right words, communicated from the right motivation, energizes the brain of the recipient of such word. That energy is delivered to every part of the body, thereby, increasing the energy level of that person.

As I looked at what the Honorable Elijah Muhammad was saying to me, I recognized that there were levels of conversation that carried varying degrees of electrical energy. The lowest form of conversation, which takes away from the energy of the human being and causes that person's shoulders to droop, their face to drop, their countenance to change; the body to react, is conversation that is negative, dealing with slander, backbiting, gossip. This type of conversation which is so disruptive to unity, to brotherhood, to social relationships that reflect the highest quality of civilization.

Allah says in the Qur'an that the slanderer, the defamer, the gossiper, He likens that kind of person to the worst and most hateful of all His creatures, which is the swine or khanzir. The Honorable Elijah Muhammad said khanzir means "I see it foul and very foul." The Qur'an says, "I will brand him [the human being] on his snout," which says that this type of person is like the pig groveling in filth looking for dirt to spread about another human being. I see it foul and very foul.

When you communicate, with this foul discourse, it can never lead to the type of activity that a higher level of discourse would bring about. So, slander, gossip, defamation, secret counsels that engage in this foul, despicable means of communication, leads to a person falling down, mentally, spiritually and humanly to then act on the lowest level of human behavior.

When Almighty God Allah reveals a word, or what is called Divine Revelation, that unearths secrets of Himself and His creation, that man and the wisest of men had not discovered up until that time. No matter how high the wise have gone with their wisdom and their ability to communicate their wisdom, when God so chooses to raise an individual and give that individual Divine Revelation, that is akin to putting the highest wattage of electricity in the head of that human being.

The human being that comes at the end of the world does not only have a high wattage but he is compared to the light of the sun, which carries light, life, energy and warmth, to all of creation. Therefore, no creature can live without the energy of the sun. Nothing of life would survive without such energy. This one that comes at the end of the world that says he is the light of the world, his brain is filled with the highest form of energy. Then transmission of that light to those who walk in darkness or to those who function on a low level has the power to raise their level of conversation, their level of thought and their level of activity.

When such a person is communicating to somebody that is dead then the person who is considered dead, is functioning on the lowest level of human behavior and human conversation or communication. They have not received that which would raise them in thought and in action from where they are. When a man like that appears, a Messenger of God, the Messiah; then to feed on his word that comes directly from God is to feed our brain the best food; the highest form of food.

Now when we go out to purchase an automobile that is a high performance automobile it is counterproductive to put a cheap source of energy in a high performance engine. The human brain is a high, exceedingly high, creation that functions best when it is fed from the highest energy source. Man's connection to God is life itself, and his disconnect from that source of the highest energy, is death.

When we are blessed with a man who has received Divine Revelation and we breathe in or inhale such wisdom, the brain cells begin to operate at their highest level of efficiency. And even though toxins may be there, even though poisons may be there, even though dull thought may be there, once there is a connection to that highest form of energy, that is contained in Divine Revelation the brain begins to oscillate, vibrate, function at its best level. The more it feeds from that source, the stronger the brain becomes. The greater its sight; the greater its hearing; the greater its ability to think and plan and bring into existence what it plans.

So Satan then recognizing that this is the end of his world; when the dead receive the life giving word contained in Divine Revelation, Satan must enter the equation to cause the person not to think on, not to dwell on, not to conversate on the Divine Revelation. So Satan's job is to turn the mind away from the high thing, and turn it toward sex; turn it toward material acquisition; turn it toward low things then Satan has a chance to take that mind where he wants to take it in contravention to where God wants to take the human being.

"Ye are all gods. Children of the Most High God.". Well what is the food that Gods feed on? They don't feed on cheap grass. They feed on the highest wisdom that is in creation. And by feeding on that They become what They feed on.

And so, I remember when we first heard the words of the Honorable Elijah Muhammad, we stayed up all night long. We had no recollection of time and we had a job to go to the next morning but we were so energized because our conversation revolved around the wisdom of the Divine Revelation of God that we went to work the next day not feeling tired because the cells of our brain and the cells of our body were so energized by our focus on the Revelation of God.

And so the highest form of communication is to speak on, ask questions about, argue over what God has revealed to His servant. Perfecting our understanding of what God reveals increases the level of energy. Hearing it, knowing it, and believing it, is one level, but understanding it and applying it, is the highest level of activity.

So this is what the Believers need to do. We need to feed on Him in our hearts. We need to feed on His word in our hearts. We need to take that word as the central food to make a god. And don't add cheap food to good food. The more you feed on the pure essence of the revealed word of God, the faster you rise into Him. Need I say more?

Jabril Muhammad: That's it. That's the whole article.

Minister Farrakhan: ... Could only be because I fed on something that caused me to rise above their level of scholarship, not in arrogance, but the eagle sees more than a dove. The eagle sees more than a sparrow and the eagle certainly sees more than the beast and the snake.

So when God reveals to a servant He gives him the wings of an eagle that he can fly high above the scholarship of the world. And this is why the scriptures says, that He will make the wisdom of this world foolishness with God.

I imagine when an eagle sees a robin flying around at its level, well that looks pretty cheap to the eagle. So, most of the governments, that have aspired to greatness have always used the symbol of an eagle. But they are low flying eagles, because they were not flying on the high octane energy of Divine Revelation—

Jabril Muhammad: That's wonderful!

Minister Farrakhan: That's high energy of Divine Revelation.

Every time I do something like this I reflect on the words of the Honorable Elijah Muhammad to me, when he was impressing upon me that he didn't make me and I couldn't understand why he would say a thing like that because I know that whatever I am it's because of him. But he said "No. I gave you the same teaching that I gave every one else. But only Allah could have shown you how to put the teachings together in the manner that you do. No Brother, I did not make you. Allah made you for me."

This, is why Jabril, *The New Testament* and the Qur'an as well, as well as *The Old Testament*, you keep hearing the words in *The Old Testament* hearken, hearken, listen, give ear, lend me your ear, because the ear is the instrument by which the highest form of energy will be transmitted. And that's why the company that we keep is so important to how high we rise or how low we fall.

So the Believer should not have a disbeliever for regular company. Because the disbeliever will not conversate on the same level as a Believer unless the Believer is introducing the disbeliever to the word and they begin to question, debate and talk about that word, then there's lifting.

But when the Believer is found having fellowship with the dead, and finding comfort in such fellowship, that Believer has fallen to the lowest level, because the dead can only bury their dead and bury the living who wants to die.

From this point through the last interview you will notice that they are not placed in chronological order. Instead I attempted to place them according to subjects. This could not be done perfectly because a few of the interviews contain more than one subject.

As you notice this section of the book started with Minister Farrakhan's answer to my question regarding conversation, in addition to the reason that I gave for starting this section with that interview, I'm also expressing my hope that his beautiful and wise answer stimulate the highest order of conversation on every subject on which we engage. But especially regarding this book, it's my hope that the readers of this book engage each other with the best kind of conversation concerning the Honorable Minister Louis Farrakhan, whose person and works merit conversation on the highest level.

INTERVIEW OF THE HONORABLE MINISTER LOUIS FARRAKHAN,
BY JABRIL MUHAMMAD,
PHOENIX, ARIZONA
JUNE 11, 2006

JABEZ

On June 10th the Honorable Minister Louis Farrakhan told me that he turned to a religious channel and heard a preacher speaking of a man, in an interesting way named Jabez. He asked me if I had ever heard of him. I said "No sir."

After some discussion I told him I would do some research on him. The next day I gave him I Chronicles 4:9-10.

The Bible has this on Jabez.

I Chronicles 4:9-10, "And Jabez was more honorable than his brethren, and his mother called his name Jabez saying, 'Because I bore [him] with sorrow.' "And Jabez called on the God of Israel, saying, 'Oh that thou wouldst bless me indeed, and enlarge my border and that Thy hand might be with me, and that Thou wouldst keep me from evil, that [it] may not grieve me!" And God granted him that which he requested."

This is the comment that the Honorable Minister Louis Farrakhan made on him the next day, June 11th.

This is what I wanted to say about Jabez: That the different variations of interpretations or translations of scholars.

Minister Farrakhan: She bore him in sorrow and she bore him in pain. His prayers that pain will not afflict him. God answered his prayer, he was spared from that. It's not quite proper in the translation.

But my mother bore me with pain and sorrow, because she tried to abort me three times. Because she was living with my brother's father but my father whom she married and never divorced came back into her life momentarily and she became pregnant with me. So all the time she was carrying me, she was in sorrow, because she tried to kill me, and then she decided to have me.

You don't do that unless you are in pain. And the pain and fear of what the child would look like that he who she was living with, my brother's father, would become aware that her husband had slipped back in and had an affair with his wife who had left him but was living with my brother's father. So she bore him in sorrow.

She bore him in pain and she bore him in fear and she bore him in great insecurity. And she therefore, became very committed in prayer that God would save her—her life; her relationship with the man. So she was prayerful out of great insecurity. But I think the prayer of Jabez was not that he shouldn't be afflicted with pain.

But that in his life, whenever he did something that was not right or proper, that he would be delivered from the consequences of his actions that he took, that in his heart, he believed was not right and the prayer of relief from affliction; but he's afflicted.

It's not seeking relief from affliction; it's not seeking relief from the pain that accompanies the mission but it's seeking God's blessing on him that when he does that which in his own mind he thinks is not correct that God would deliver him from the pain of the consequences of whatever it was that he thought was not correct.

I remember when I was the minister in New York; they had a lot of charges, different charges on me. And one day the Messenger, I was told got tired of hearing talks about me. And he said to them, "Brother a man that preaches like that has no sins."

I don't know what they thought about that, but when I heard it, it is not that he doesn't have sins, but the goodness of his work and his heart and his intentions is such that it is as though he has no sins, because God would not bring upon him the consequences of his sins.

That's coming back to Jabez and those of us favored by God. We live in a world where no one can get through a world like this without sin; no one. And yet He holds His prophets guiltless; sinless. But if we did not have sin what would be the need for Allah to have the attribute of mercy, or say that He is the Oft-returning to mercy, the Forgiving?

Well if His servants the Prophets stand in His grace; stand as recipients of His mercy and as recipients of His forgiveness, this is the path of favor that we are asked to pray for, "Oh Allah guide me on your straight path, the path of those upon whom you have bestowed favor." What greater favor is that that He would enlarge; expand your territory and keep you free from pain or affliction, because of any inadequacies that you may have.

I felt great kinship with Jabez and I know it's not there accidentally. It's there because of a prophet, the messenger of God, the Messiah His helper and helpers and people that are to be the recipients of God's mercy and we are coming to Him through pain; through great affliction; great suffering even though He has chosen us and we have chosen Him, yet we have fallen short of the glory of God.

We stand in need of His mercy; His grace; His forgiveness. And we pray that He will not afflict us with the pain that we deserve for our errant ways. So the prayer that the Messenger asked us to pray, "Oh Allah, punish us not if we forget or make a mistake. Don't lay on us the burden that thou dids't lay on those before us."

That's the comment that I wanted to make on Jabez and how I relate to him, the prayer that he prayed, the pain of his mother, and the meaning of his name. What did they say that name meant?

Jabril Muhammad: Sorrow.

Minister Farrakhan: Sorrow. Well I did say he was acquainted with grief. A man of sorrow, acquainted with grief. Isn't it the way it reads?

Jabril Muhammad: Yes.

Minister Farrakhan: So he's well aware of that part.

Jabril Muhammad: Brother Minister, how old were you when you first saw the picture of Marcus Garvey on a wall in your uncle's home?

Minister Farrakhan: I was 11-years old. What was strange about my uncle's house was the difference from my mother's home. All the men on the wall over the mantle piece in my mother's home were white. She had Jesus; white. She had King George, Queen Elizabeth; white.

When I went to my uncle's house I saw a big picture of a Black man on his wall. I asked him, "Who is that man?" He said, "He's a man that came to unite Black people."

Well that sounded like the man I was looking for. It was up kind of high on the wall. I was like the fellows we would call today, a "shorty."

I asked him to get a chair, and I stood on the chair to literally drink in the features of this great one who had come to unite our people. I asked my uncle "what was his name?" My uncle told me, "His name was Marcus Garvey." I said, "Where is he that I may go and meet him?" He said, "He's dead." The tears welled up in my eyes. I wept, because I thought I had come so close to the man I was looking for only to find out that he was gone.

My search continued until I heard that God had raised a Messenger for us. Of course, you know the statement that I made earlier, that I made many years ago when I learned that God had chosen this man before I was born. Then my only aim was to go and meet him and serve him.

Jabril Muhammad: This history must be properly understood. Researchers and writers must not twist or misuse or place it in the wrong context, lest they mislead the public—momentarily—and disgrace themselves.

INTERVIEW OF THE HONORABLE MINISTER LOUIS FARRAKHAN
BY JABRIL MUHAMMAD;
PHOENIX, ARIZONA
JUNE 28, 2006

Jabril Muhammad: Dear Brother Minister, to reiterate, I don't remember the exact date when you and your party were in Cuba when I had an experience that I have mentioned to you twice. It seemed like it was very short. I woke up ***in*** it. It was maybe 5:30AM when I woke up, when I knew I had just seen the Honorable Elijah Muhammad as clear as day. In the scene he was more to my left. I saw you. You were somewhat less clear and a little below the middle of the scene and somewhat towards the right. Almost simultaneously I heard what seemed to me to be a contingent, I wouldn't say troops, but a small contingent or body of troops coming from over towards the upper right. That's where their sound came from.

Then the Honorable Elijah Muhammad said to me, "They are coming for me in him." Immediately, I knew he was referring to you. I woke up and the scene was still there. I thought to call you, but I said no that would be very improper. Moreover, I probably couldn't reach him anyway. But it had an impact on me and then of course, when I got a chance I shared it with you.

About four days later I had another experience that did not directly involve our father or you. But there was a point of similarity. I intend to get to that another time.

Be it the Will of Allah I intend to mention it, if Allah pleases, in a follow-up series of questions, I have in mind and answers from the Honorable Minister Louis Farrakhan, Allah willing, which will be volume two.

Now, Brother Minister, I would like for you to tell me what you think about that experience.

Minister Farrakhan: First, it's a very profound experience that answers many questions for me personally and probably for others as well.

I would like to start by going back to the time when I was with the Honorable Elijah Muhammad and he said to me, "Brother I want your mind. I want you to line your mind up with my mind so that there will be one mind." If that is not the perfect recall of his words, it's 99 and 9/10% correct.

Then later on he said to me, "Brother, I'm going away. I'm going away to study. I'll be gone for approximately three years. Don't change the teachings while I'm gone. And if you are faithful when I return, I will reveal the new teaching through you."

Now, of course, Brother Jabril, his words have great impact on me, but understanding them takes time. Then of course, in 1975, February 25th, ten past nine New York time, ten past eight Chicago time, I get a call from my son Joshua, who was at the hospital (Mercy Hospital) where the Messenger was, saying to me that the Honorable Elijah Muhammad had expired.

Coming to Chicago, seeing a casket with one that looked like my father and teacher, only about twenty to twenty-five years younger; participating in a funeral; carrying the casket to the cemetery; for me, at that time, the Honorable Elijah Muhammad had expired. None of the things then that he said to me made sense.

As you know I tried to follow W. D. Muhammad as he told me he knew the direction that the nation should take after the alleged demise of the Honorable Elijah Muhammad. And so I told him that I would serve him, as I've served his father, as long as I could see that he remain faithful to his father.

As you know there had been difficulty between him and his dad. I did not wish to divide the nation, nor did I feel confident that I could lead in the absence of the Honorable Elijah Muhammad, particularly if he were dead. I could hold the teachings if he were gone and I knew he was coming back. But he already taught us that you don't come back from death.

In that case I didn't believe that I could lead the nation, though he sat me in his seat; though he said many things that would lead me to believe that he wanted me to take his place in his absence. I didn't feel confident. So if the Imam or W. D. Muhammad felt that he could, and knew the direction, then I would help him as I helped his father.

Thirty months later, I came to the conclusion that, that was not best for me—maybe even less time than that. I saw things that of which I disagreed and I did not wish to upset the house. So I decided to leave (quietly) and try to resume my music career, which was a complete failure. The God took away everything from me musically. I almost had nothing left.

I met you on that wonderful day in September of 1977. You gave me a book to read and on the third day of reading that book you came to the hotel room. And I told you, "Your eye operation was successful. The scales have been removed from my eyes." And then the long journey began.

You gave me something to read. You told me even at that time that, "The Honorable Elijah Muhammad was yet alive." And I, in my heart said, "Oh my poor Brother. He loves the Honorable Elijah Muhammad so much he can't bear the thought that the

Honorable Elijah Muhammad is deceased." And I said to him, "Well whether he's alive or not, he's not here Brother. So the work is on us to do." And I gently passed it off.

He (Jabril) gave me what I would call a commentary or something that you would add to a book that's not in the book and he gave it to me to read on the Honorable Elijah Muhammad possibly being alive. And I didn't even want to waste time with something like that. Because at that time I said, "Oh poor fella, you know, well we're going to go on and rebuild the work of the Honorable Elijah Muhammad."

One day, almost two years later, he was in my Lincoln Continental in Chicago, and he saw what he had given me, kind of ground up a little under the front driver's seat. So he took it out and smoothed it out, like one would do a wrinkled coat or shirt and knew that it wasn't destroyed. And he put it back in my hands.

I finally decided I'll entertain him. I'll read it. And as I began to read what he wrote, the words of the Honorable Elijah Muhammad began to make sense. They couldn't make sense if he were dead. But, if he escaped a death plot, then the words that he shared with me made almost perfect sense.

I say, almost, because he told me he would be gone for three years, approximately. And he was going away to study. Now it was approximately three years. It was actually 30 months. I was up; ready to take on the Herculean task of attempting to rebuild his work.

Now what you saw in your experience crystallizes all of this for me, because he now was in me; growing in me. But there were certain experiences that I had to undergo for him to fully grow in me and for me to fully grow in him. So Elijah did come back. He came back in the person of Louis Farrakhan. He came back in me because my love for him; my adoration of him; my surrender of myself to him.

Going back to my first hearing that God had raised a man for us. And knowing that I had searched for a man like this all my life, then I surrendered myself to him completely, so he was able to put himself in me. And when he left us in 1975, he knew that what he desired to do had been done, it only needed time; watering; circumstances; events for him to grow again in me.

Now with your experience I realized that when he told me, "Brother you may sit in my seat as the father over the house when I am gone." At another time he said, "Brother Allah made me to take His place among the people and I am making you to take mine."

In reality, he's growing me up to sit in his seat, as the father over the house, to fulfill the work of Elijah and the work of Elisha, and the work of many that are written in the book.

This also caused me to reflect on the Jesus figure, when one of the disciples wanted to see the father that the Jesus was always talking about. And he said to that person, "I have been among you this long and you have not seen him?" Then he went on to say, "When you see me, you see the father for I'm in the father, and the father is in me. Me, and my father are one."

Coming back to your experience, when you heard his voice saying, "They are coming for me in him." That suggests to me that oneness with him has been accomplished and he now has my mind. And my mind is now lined up with his in more ways than I probably at this juncture fully understand, but will grow to manifest it more and more.

It also signifies a great, great deal of power. It also signifies the fear of the enemy who put in *Esquire* magazine a cartoon with the former late president of France, Charles de Gaulle who said, speaking of white people, that it was Charles de Gaulle, Moshe Dayan and others from Israel and other places, "Were it not for this man, we would have a glorious future."

If they're coming for him in me then my presence ends their presence and destroys their future. So they have come to the decision; to the determination that I and we must be destroyed for them to have a future. The feet that you heard represents many troops; the many minds; the many forces that are lock-stepped now in agreement to get him in me and to get us out of the way.

We knew that such a time as this would come. And we knew that this is the only way that God can prove His presence; His

Cartoon depicting Charles de Gaulle and the Most Honorable Elijah Muhammad as it appeared in *Esquire* magazine, August 1964.

choice of a people; His power. In those footsteps of the many conspirators; hypocrites; devils, under the direction of Satan himself, they will be defeated totally and completely and then the Kingdom of God will be established.

It also brings us to fulfilling the writings of Paul in the book of Acts and most of his writings; the understanding of them; the fulfillment of them when he comes to the end of a term, where he is arrested; imprisoned and he tells the apostles and the disciples that, "I have kept the faith. I have fought the good fight. I have finished the course. Now is laid up for me a crown and I go to receive it."

Well, Paul was killed eventually, by the enemies of Jesus. But the actual meaning of that is the fulfillment of his promise: "If you are faithful, when I return, I will reveal the new teaching through you." But also it tells me that he was telling me, not about himself, but about my future. He was telling me that at a certain point I will be taken.

At a certain point I will be going away and I will be gone for approximately three years. And I will be going away to study. And for him, if I had been found faithful or worthy to begin (I think he's already given me the full word of such a book) but now the book, if it's not already planted in my heart, he will give it to me in our second meeting.

During that absence for three years, the power of the enemy will be broken in war. The seals of the book cannot be opened while the enemy still has power, as he taught us. That expression that you shared with me, which was so very short, but yet so powerful; so profound that it confirms what I thought. It confirms what I believed and translates belief now into the sure truth, or the certainty of knowledge.

Interview of the Honorable Minister Louis Farrakhan
by Jabril Muhammad,
Phoenix, Arizona
June 5, 2006

There were some days when we did not do interviews at all. This was a day when Minister Farrakhan felt better than most of the days he was here in Phoenix.

Jabril Muhammad: You've said that you were 19-years-old when you first heard that God had chosen a Messenger for our people?

Minister Farrakhan: I was standing on the corner of Massachusetts and Columbus Avenue (in Boston, Massachusetts). I heard that God had raised a Messenger for our people. I started walking because I was a little sad. I questioned God and I said, "God, why didn't you choose me? You know I love my people."

As I walked, I think I had tears in my eyes, and I said to myself, when this happened in 1931, I wasn't even born. So the sadness went away right away and I knew I had to go and meet this man and offer him my help. That's what happened.

Jabril Muhammad: Please tell us a little of your mother's efforts to fill you with love and concern for our people through the kind of material she gave you to read.

Minister Farrakhan: My number one remembrance was *The Crisis Magazine*. In it was the writing of W. E. B Dubois. She would always bring home Black newspapers, *The Afro-American*, *The Pittsburg Courier*—those two especially.

In those papers there were stories of lynching and mistreatment of our people. Of course, that deepened my desire to see someone who would come along who would free our people.

That's what led to my questioning my Sunday school teacher, that if God had raised Moses for his people and He always sent some prophet, or somebody, to deliver people who were oppressed, why hasn't God sent somebody to deliver us?

Jabril Muhammad: How old were you then?

Minister Farrakhan: About seven or eight.

Jabril Muhammad: How old were you when you stood on the chair, in your uncle's home and saw the picture of Marcus Garvey?

Minister Farrakhan: 11-years-old.

Jabril Muhammad: What were you thinking the first time you looked at the Honorable Elijah Muhammad?

Minister Farrakhan: I was a little frightened that he seemed to know what I was thinking. But then he told me "Don't pay any attention to how I'm saying it, you pay attention to what I'm saying and then you take it and put it in that fine language that you know. Only try to understand what I'm saying."

The rest of the afternoon his teaching was on the birth of a Savior. Now I enjoyed what I heard, but I wasn't overwhelmed to the point where I was going to get up to join.

When he asked for acceptance, Khadijah [her name was Betsy, at that time] got right up and went to the back but my uncle came over to me and said, "You see. Your wife got up and gone. Get up man. Get up." I didn't want to disrespect my uncle and tell him I'm not quite ready yet. I'm not fully convinced yet. But out of respect for my Uncle I got up and went and got my form.

We went back to our hotel, which is at 49th and Drexel, and Betsy [his wife's name at that time] and I started writing our letters. I had excellent penmanship in school. It was no problem for me to write my letter. We wrote it and mailed it in to 5335 South Greenwood Avenue and gave our address in New York, Long Island. We never got any answer to our letters. See there's somebody that was interfering with the mail even then because I got no answer from Chicago.

I went back to New York. This was February. I went back [to the meetings] maybe sometime—and March, April, May, June went by and in July, I visited the Mosque.

I think the first time I went may have been on a Friday night. Brother James 7X was teaching. But on that Sunday, when I went back then I heard Brother Malcolm, I got up and took my form out again.

This was in July 1955. August, September went by and around the 5th of October I got word that I had received my "X". I got my Student Enrollment on that Sunday and five minutes after I had it in my hand I memorized the ten answers to the ten questions. So that next night I was ready to recite. After I recited, they said well Brother, you're now Brother Louis 2X. Then I went to the class.

At the end of the class they called up the new converts. When they called me up to welcome me into the F.O.I. The love that I saw in the eyes and in the faces of the Brothers toward me was such a new and beautiful experience. It was something that you longed to see in Black people. As I started to speak I broke down. But in that short little talk I said "I was going to take this teaching to every nook and cranny, or corner, of the United States of America." Those were the words I spoke in October 1955.

Jabril Muhammad: What were your thoughts of the language of the Honorable Elijah Muhammad when you first heard him?

Minister Farrakhan: I, being a student of English, and verb and subject agreement, heard him speak in a manner that a public speaker who was familiar with English wouldn't do. So in my head I said, "O this man can't even talk."

When I said that he looked right at me and said, "Brother, I didn't get a chance to get that fine education that you got. When I got to the school the doors was closed. Don't pay any attention to how I'm saying it. You pay attention to what I'm saying and then you take it and put it in that fine language that you know."

As I said, I was a little frightened because he seemed to know what I was thinking. But looking back I see that he literally gave me my assignment the first day that he laid eyes on me.

Jabril Muhammad: Brother Minister in 1971, I interviewed Captain Yusuf Shah. Included in that interview were details that Brother Malcolm had spoken to the Honorable Elijah Muhammad about you even before you attended your first meeting. He told me of the arrangement that was made to seat you relative to Captain Shah so that the Honorable Elijah Muhammad could recognize that you were the person that Malcolm had referred to.

Do you have any thoughts that he may have kept the Honorable Elijah Muhammad up on your progress during your early years in the Nation of Islam?

Minister Farrakhan: Brother Malcolm knew me only as a musician. But when I became a follower in Mosque No. 7, of course he gradually saw me differently. Wednesday night was "bearing witness night." I remember at the end of the lecture, Brother Malcolm called me up to bear witness. I don't remember what I said but I remember that the reaction of the Mosque was electric.

At this point Minister Farrakhan continues his thoughts with what is a reasonable assumption about what Brother Malcolm may have said to the Honorable Elijah Muhammad, who may have been watching his progress.

Evidence of this can be seen in the light of what I learned from Captain Yusuf Shah, which is described later on in this book. It concerns the fact that an arrangement was made as to where to seat Minister Farrakhan so that the Honorable Elijah Muhammad would be able to see the face of Minister Farrakhan. Please keep reading and this significant event will become clearer when we get to that section.

In some of my Farrakhan The Traveler articles I've touched, and only touched this subject. With Allah's help I intend to write the little I know from certain things the Honorable Elijah Muhammad said, and what I know of scriptures in the light of his wisdom, that there were certain people whom he expected to come into his life. The most prominent was Minister Farrakhan. Let's continue Minister Farrakhan's words.

I assumed that he told the Messenger that the young man who was the musician, he accepted the teachings and he is in the Mosque. He has become a registered Muslim. When I called him up to bear witness he spoke and the Mosque was, Temple as we called it then, was electrified. I think I asked him to join the ministry class and he did.

Then shortly thereafter the letter came, that all musicians had to get out of show business or get out of the Temple. I wasn't in the Mosque when the letter was read. The letter was read on a Sunday, but I was playing at *The Village Barn* in Greenwich Village.

After my show I would come up to the Temple No. 7 Luncheonette at 120th Street and Lenox Avenue. They had bean soup. I don't remember who it was who told me as I was sitting down having my soup. He said, "Man the Messenger sent a letter and everybody in show business had 30 days to get out of show business or to get out of the Temple." I finished my bowl of soup and I got up and walked out of the front door of the restaurant to the corner, and as you know there weren't many steps from the restaurant to the corner.

Then I walked up 120th Street and I made up my mind right then, "I'm going to give it up." I came back in and sat down. Captain Shah came in. He was angry with the Brother who told me. I don't remember who it was. But I told Captain Shah, "Brother, I made up my mind that I'm going to give it up." I'm only assuming that Captain went back and told Malcolm and Malcolm told the Messenger that "the minute he heard it, he gave it up."

Jabril Muhammad: How much time was it afterwards that you have that vision?

Minister Farrakhan: It was the last day, the 30th day or just about December 26th, or the 27th when I had this engagement at the Nevele County Club. Nevele is eleven spelled backwards. It was a Jewish resort. I just said I'm going to get it all out of my system. I sang ballad. I sang some classic. I sang the blues. I played classical violin. I played jazz violin. I told jokes. And that was it.

I went back to my dressing room and this kind of handsome looking Caucasian came in the dressing room. I called his name about a month or so ago but I don't remember it right now. When he told me he was the manager for Pearl Bailey and Billy Daniels he asked me a question if I had a manager. I told him no. He said he would like to be my manager and he would book me into the same clubs in which Billy Daniels and Pearl Bailey sang. I would start at 500 dollars a week. We were supposed to meet the next day in Manhattan to sign a management contract.

I went home to go to sleep. In the night, I saw these two doors. One had *success* written over it and a mound in the floor that came up, maybe as high as this table. It was almost like a pyramid of diamonds and gold. But the other door had *Islam* over it with a black veil over the door. I was told to choose. And I chose Islam.

The next day I'm supposed to go down town and sign the contracts. I never did.

The test came when I went to Boston. I was working for $45.00 a week picking up bolts of cloth and putting them in racks. We were just barely making it. I got a telegram from the Golden Slipper Night Club, Jewish man; I think either Goldman or Mr. Synder, his partner. He offered me $350.00 a week if I would come back to the Golden Slipper $350.00 a week looks better to me than $45.00 a week. Of course, I turned this offer down.

Now as the Messenger is raising me, and teaching me and cultivating me, as we get closer to the time of his leaving he let me play the violin for him. He called me to play again, "Don't you know something new?"

I didn't pick up. How could I know something new? When I'm not doing that anymore. But he knew that the sacrifice that I made of my musical self killed a part of me, and that part that was killed needed to be resurrected in order for the breast to be expanded for the other part of the assignment.

All praises are due to Allah, for everything that has happened in my life, has been for a very, very good reason. I thank Allah that

He has really ordered my steps.

Now in the twilight years of my life he gives me my music because it has something to do with getting all his people.

Jabril Muhammad: Do you recall when you had the vision of the two men and your form?

Minister Farrakhan: I can't give you date or time, right now. I was still in New York City. I rather think it was early in my acceptance, October, November, December in 1955—all around in there.

In fact, it was very early after my acceptance of the teachings, because I had written my form. The two men were discussing my form. One said, "Turn it over." There was cursive writing on my form. As I was trying to see what it was the voice on the right said to the voice on the left, "Turn it over, it's not time for him to see this yet."

Jabril Muhammad: Yes sir.

Minister Farrakhan: When they turned it over, like it was the front of my letter, and the back was empty. There was writing on it. Then when the man on the right said to the man on the left, to "turn it over it isn't time for him to see it yet," there was the Arabic writing on it.

I went to the Temple on that Sunday, and I know I was in the ranks because I was in the back, not sitting near the front where a visitor would be, Malcolm wrote "Allah" on the black board in Arabic and then he wrote "Muhammad" on it in Arabic. I saw this Arabic writing on my form in this vision. From this, then, I was being told that I was Muhammad. But the consciousness of it, I didn't know.

When I was with the Messenger, when we were driving in his little gold Cadillac, in 1957, I was telling him about the experience that I had with my form and the writing on it and it was said to "turn it over, it's not time for him (me) to see it yet."

I asked him about this because I wondered what it meant. He didn't down play it. He let me know that there was something to it but he wasn't going to say what it was. I don't know that I told him the name Muhammad. But the significance of that has been dawning on me, especially now.

That was 1955 and then 1985, or thirty years later comes and I'm up on the Wheel. Then this thing comes down and there's this cursive writing on it. I leaned forward to read it. Then the Honorable Elijah Muhammad speaks and whatever was on that screen disappears. I never consciously knew that I read it.

INTERVIEW OF THE HONORABLE MINISTER LOUIS FARRAKHAN,
BY JABRIL MUHAMMAD,
PHOENIX, ARIZONA
JUNE 12, 2006

This was a day and a afternoon during which Minister Farrakhan did not feel at all very well. He did not look well that day as he got out of his car and begin walking to my door. He did not have a smile on his face. However, I clearly remembered that after he sat down he said to me that he looked forward to what I was going to ask him.

Jabril Muhammad: Brother Minister, you have shared with several of us, quite a few years ago of a vision that Allah blessed you to have that involved two doors. It's obvious you are a person of great talent. Great musicians have acknowledged that, especially during the last few years, as you have worked on this album.

In the vision if you had gone through one door, it was this that meant fame and wealth. The other door was unknown to you. The question is, since you've demonstrated such enormous talent, if you had not gone through the door of success over it, what kind of future might Allah have blessed you with, if you had lived to enjoy? Where might you think—and I know that you may not be able to answer this directly, but indirectly; think wealth and other wise, would you be, in this world, fame and wealth, wise and in terms of world wide recognition?

Minister Farrakhan: What was written over the door was the word success. What was seen in the door was a mound about three feet high, almost in a pyramid form of diamonds and gold. Success in my chosen field of music would have meant that I would have reached the goal that I had intended to reach with my music and having reached such a goal of success. What would accompany that would be great wealth; great prominence; great fame. Fame, prominence, and wealth, as an artist in the field of music rather than in any other field, that's what that door means to me.

Jabril Muhammad: The reason I'm even raising this question is two fold. The wicked writers mock you when they refer to your musical past, not in terms of the way it really was, back at that time but they refer to it in a mocking fashion. There is always the suggestion of you being improperly motivated.

The fact that you turned *that* down and lived in poverty, when you could have been wealthy. All of us who know you, know this. That speaks to your motives and which is indicated in a certain way, even when you stood on the chair and looked at Marcus Garvey as a child or even when you were seven, you raised the question that you raised in Sunday school. This gets to my point.

Minister Farrakhan: Let me say that as a child I was always trying to find my purpose for being. I had a godmother who suffered from asthma who lived in New York in the Bronx on Union Avenue. As a boy I visited her. One day she had an asthma attack. It was so brutal watching her suffer. My thought, at that young age, was that I wanted to become a doctor so that I might heal her and others so afflicted.

In the early years of my life the idea of serving people who were ill and restoring them to health was a part of my seeking for my purpose.

When I was ten years old in the fifth grade my teacher asked me, "Louis what would you like to become when you grow up?" I said I want to become a doctor because I want to heal people. She said, "Oh Louis if you became a doctor my people would never come to you and your own people wouldn't trust your medical skill. But you play the violin beautifully."

The aim of the teacher was to turn me away from a field that would bring me to science and bring me to service in a meaningful way and to turn me toward a profession that was non-threatening.

As I waxed stronger, in playing the violin, and singing in the choir, my voice stood out among a forty-voice men and boys choir. But I didn't know that I had a voice at sixteen. When I began singing ballad and was known in Boston as a very popular ballad singer then I introduced calypso to the ballad singing.

When I looked and saw that God had given me so much talent in the field of music, then I thought that my purpose in life was to serve humanity by giving them music to lift their spirit. But at the root of it all at the time, was the desire to serve; to heal, to lift the spirits of the people through music. Of course, it was not until I met the Honorable Elijah Muhammad that I really discovered my purpose for being. It was all of that and then some.

Even before he took me, Allah was taking me through something in preparation for my meeting with him.

Jabril Muhammad: Yes. That's definite.

Minister Farrakhan: You know, no matter what gifts a person may be blessed to have, it is out of the heart that the real issues of life are formed and the real meaning of the person's life gets found. It is not in the talent. It is the heart. The heart of a servant of God, is formed by God. It is not formed by a mother, or a father, or circumstances. It is formed by God and is manifested through circumstances.

The reason I say it like that, Jabril, is because in looking back at my life, as a child, I was impressed by the beauty of God's creations. I loved looking out my window when mother wouldn't let me out to play, and seeing the blue sky, the clouds.

I remember as a child of three walking in Bermuda and the smell, the beauty of the smell of sweet grass, the blueness of the sea or the ocean, nature. I remember the sadness that I would feel as a child listening to the talk of the suffering of our people. So my heart was forming back then.

Of course, my mother had a lot to do with the forming of my heart because she bore me in sorrow and in pain and because she was so insecure during my formation in her womb she was constantly seeking God. So I came to birth from her womb, as all creatures do, insecure but seeking security.

I remember going to bed every night pulling the cover over my head and forming the pillows in a way and believing I was incased in steel and nothing could get to me. I had a little peephole where I could look out but nobody could get to me. As I go back and think of how I went to sleep at nights my whole being was hungry and thirsting to be made secure.

Well I understood that security was in my mom, but from a very early age, I don't know the exact year, but I knew that security was beyond my mother and it was found in God.

From a little boy I remember running down in the street which was like right around the corner of my house, or apartment, and I felt the spirit of God just something on me where I was extremely joyous. I was just running and I knew that spirit from a child, that it was God on me. In that moment feeling that overwhelming sense of joy, peace, and complete security in Him.

When I would find myself faced with a difficulty it was not to my mother to whom I resorted. It was to Him. As my heart was being fashioned, as a young boy talented, I always wanted to share what came to me with my friends, but I saw that in sharing the good that came to me with my friends, it made what I didn't know at that time, was envy. Some of them began to speak against me.

In my nightclub life I was sixteen then, I would talk to this woman who took sailors in and whatnot. I asked her why friends of mine would talk about me because I was a growing star and people would ring the block to get into this or that night club to see me perform. She said "Oh," (they called me) "Gene." She said "Oh Gene, they talked about Jesus, so you cannot escape their talking about you."

That stuck with me. So there was never a spirit of retaliation toward those who spoke evil against me.

I remember when I was playing in the night club and I was the star of the show. I brought four young men in to surround me as members of the band. The Jewish owner of the nightclub, Mr. Eddie Levine, called me upstairs to his office. I was making $65 a week. He said "I will give you $125.00 a week if you get rid of those four that are around you. He said, because, I mean, they're not the show. It's really you." And I told him "I came here with them. I'll leave with them."

He tried to induce me to get rid of my support for money. He didn't realize money was not my objective. But one day, when I went up in my dressing room, one of the young men in the group spoke out very evilly towards me. It seemed as though there was an evil spirit in the group that this discontent had permeated. So I fired the whole group. I told him well "You all feel this way, well I didn't come in the world with any twin. So I'll get along without you all. You're dismissed."

I fired them.

I went home and I told my mother. Over days, she asked me to reconsider and bring the group back together. But I was pained to do that but as God is my witness I didn't go to my mother for guidance. I went to the Bible. I picked up the book of Psalms. I began reading and I was comforted and I was strengthened.

I cannot remember what Psalm, but the words made me to know that I should put my trust in God and go forward, which I did. I never brought those Brothers back around me again except at my wedding to Khadijah. They were the ushers in my wedding. We played again for the last time at my wedding.

These are things that formed the [me] heart that was only desirous of serving, of healing, of uplifting others through the gifts that God had given me, and not harming people.

It was an Easter Sunday I was 13; my mother had bought me a new suit. I went out with some of my friends after church. I went into a park called Franklin Park. There was a little white boy fishing. There was a bridge and he had his little pole. He pulled this pole back and he didn't have anything on the hook. But some little drops of water got on my new suit. I was showing off for my friends. I took a bracelet that I had and I put it around my hand and I went over to that boy and I struck him and I ran.

When I got home there was such an aching in my heart because even though he was a white boy, a member of a race that had inflicted so much pain on my people, he was doing nothing to bother me. In spite of the evil of his people toward our people, I felt pain—a deep pain—for doing to that young man what I did when he gave me no cause.

These are incidents in my life—there are two more that I will bring out probably in my memoirs—that are indelible on my heart, that make me to know that the [my] heart was forming for justice, not for revenge, but for justice and truth and feeling the hurt of others.

By the time I was 19, and I heard that God had chosen a Messenger, at first I was sad because I felt that He was with me all my life. I felt His spirit on me. I felt His protection around me.

I raised the question, "Why didn't you choose me?" You know I love my people." Those are the exact words. I'm crying because I'm sad that the relationship that we had from a child that, you chose somebody else. Right then, I said, "Oh when He came, in 1930, I wasn't born." So that dismisses that thought. Let me go find this man.

I'm saying that Jabril that my heart was already formed for Him and for our people, from the womb of my mother. See this is why the scriptures say, "He formed you in the womb of your mother." I think I read that somewhere. I never applied it to myself, but at this moment I know that He formed me in the womb of my mother. He allowed the circumstances surrounding my mother to give me that total insecurity that would make me see Him and Him alone as my Protector.

Jabril Muhammad: Wise God.

Minister Farrakhan: So you know, Jabril it's a wonderful thing to be favored by God. You don't know what you did to deserve such wonderful favor. I didn't do anything really, but He formed me for His glory. I see that. He formed for His number one choice (the Honorable Elijah Muhammad) but I was in His mind all the time.

He knew the boy [me] because I was two going on three when the Messenger—I was three when He was leaving him, 1935, but He knew me. He knew me. That's why, you know, Jabril, see when you say God came in the person of Master Fard Muhammad, but there was a God setting things up for Him. There was an Allah Who was fashioning things for Him to come in and manifest what was in Him from the formation in His mother's womb.

The Messenger closes the *Muslims Wants and What The Muslim Believe* with "We believe that Allah (God) appeared in the Person of Master W. Fard Muhammad, July,1930; the long awaited "Messiah" of the Christians and the "Mahdi" of the Muslims." Then he pauses and wrote: "We believe further and lastly that Allah is God and besides Him there is no God and He will bring about a universal government of peace wherein we all can live together in peace."

Well, He's paying recognition to that eternal force, that eternal mind, that eternal spirit out of which all of this comes, that Master Fard Muhammad manifests.

You know, we are in a very blessed state. I thank you for asking me such questions that brings forth from me things that—some things I thought of, other things I never thought of—of the forming of the heart and those kinds of expressions, that I never had a chance to even say such words before. But your questions help me to go back and see how I was formed. More importantly why I was formed the way I was formed.

This leads, of course, to the ultimate, *that* crucifixion—what will you give to see the devils brought into hell? "I will give all that I have and all within my power." Those are his words. He proved it in forty-four years even to the death plot that he knew and said of, "If I didn't know how I would escape I would have no hope at all."

But God gave him hope by telling him how. He said to you. "Oh I could tell you but you ... ." See, he knew. I may not know how but He knows. See, so it's *that* scene again now, on a lesser level that his complete trust in his Master is absolutely necessary to get him through.

I close this with this. In that final week, you know, it was like he was agitated, and the first violent act that was attributed to him was throwing the moneychangers out of the Temple. "You have made my house a den of thieves." He was agitated. He was irritated and then he retired to the Mt. Olive or the Garden of Gethsemane—troubled over the things of the future.

But when they laid their hands on him, he was in a certain calm; a certain knowing. "You say that you are the Messiah?" You say. "Are you the king, the leader of all Black people." You say. But this *Messiah talk* is what gets him in trouble with Caiaphas.

The devil has to do it's utmost to take me out of the hearts of the people to strip me of followers and whatever. All that He formed in me from a child to put my trust completely in Him will be put to the test. I believe He has fashioned me to pass such a test. Then the rest is history.

Jabril, nobody questioning me for my autobiography would raise questions like you have to elicit answers *like* this. This is why in the forming of a book, that talks about a man *like this*, the book would be a body without spirit, if it doesn't get to the core of the man's being, out of which he expresses what he expresses.

I don't know that those persons who will write and research can write and research, unless they have something like this book as a basis. Without this they can't write about me.

So these kinds of questions and answers will have to be a part of my autobiography.

In my autobiography the world must be shown my heart; a heart formed by God for them. If the book does not show that, then it is not an autobiography of me. It's something else. It has to be my testimony. That will begin to cause people to see God's interaction with a man who was made *for* them and it will help them to see our father.

Jabril Muhammad: Exactly. I have asked you, what I have for years now, for the benefit of others who intend to write on you.

INTERVIEW OF THE HONORABLE MINISTER LOUIS FARRAKHAN
BY JABRIL MUHAMMAD,
PHOENIX, ARIZONA
JUNE 13, 2006

This day began like the previous day and afternoon. I'm now going to skip to the afternoon. He slowly got out of his car and acknowl-

edged me with a slight smile. He walked up to my door and entered my home slowly. I knew the question I intended to ask him would emotional affect him. But I knew that so many of us need to know how to better handle our trials as our trials are a necessity and an essential factor in our growth into our divinity.

I intended to ask him to go deeper into himself which meant asking a man, who I love to go deeper into years of pain while he is in pain. So I began.

Jabril Muhammad: Brother Minister, I would appreciate it, for myself, and everybody who reads this book, that you take us *sequentially* through your trials. What are trials?

The Honorable Minister Louis Farrakhan: Well first, what is a trial? A trial is that which brings forth from the person being tried what is hidden of both good and evil.

Trials make manifest what is within. This is why Allah says that He will try the Believers at least once a year—severely. Trials make manifest. The manifestation of defects leads to the perfection of the human being.

In the world of God and righteousness trials are as necessary to the perfection of the human being as water is to the growth and development of life; and sunlight and air is to the nurturing, preservation and origination of life.

Having said that, my first trial inside the nation came after I accepted to follow the Honorable Elijah Muhammad. I believe I received my "X" on the fifth of October. Within that same month of October, or early November, the Honorable Elijah Muhammad sent a letter to Mosque No. 7 asking all who were in music or in show business that they had thirty days to get out of show business or leave the Temple.

I was then working at a place called, "The Village Barn" in Greenwich Village, New York. I was not there when the letter was read on that Sunday because I had a matinee. I came to the restaurant that evening after my matinee to get a bowl of soup. A Brother gave me the content of the letter. I did not wait for an official to tell me. I got up from the table and walked, maybe about forty or fifty paces, outside of the restaurant and made up my mind right then that I could live without music but I could not live without the truth. So I decided to give up music. That was my first test thirty days inside of the nation.

Then sometime in December, I had my last engagement, which was within the thirty days. It was at a country club in the mountains in New York—I can't remember the name of the mountains—but it was the Nevele Country Club. It is in the borsch circuit which means Jewish people went there for enjoyment; relaxation, etc.

That night I decided to get all my music out of my system. So I sang ballad; light classic. I sang blues. I sang calypso; mambo. I played classical violin; jazz violin. I danced. I told jokes. I did everything that I knew I could do.

In the audience was a man who came to my dressing room and he was the manager of Pearl Bailey and Billie Daniels. The world of music knows these two as great super stars in the 40s, 50s and 60s. He wanted me in the "stable" of these two and he offered me five hundred dollars a week to start.

Well I was making—say a hundred and fifty, or sometimes, for a performance, I would get seventy-five to a hundred and fifty dollars. But five hundred dollars a week in 1955 is like five thousand dollars a week in 1995 or 2005.

That was a trial. But I laughed and turned it down immediately and of course, I told you that that night I got that vision of show business and Islam. That was the second trial.

The third trial was I had been in the Mosque and Brother Malcolm invited me into the ministry class. Captain Shah asked me if I would be a lieutenant. I told him, "I knew nothing about how to be a lieutenant." He said, "Do you know how to obey?" I said, "Yes sir." He said, "Then you can become a lieutenant."

Within nine months my economic prospects, by giving up show business in New York, looked pretty bad. My first job was selling storm windows. I made thirty-five dollars a week and commissions but I received no commission. So I was just getting the thirty-five.

Since I wasn't selling much storm windows and doors then I got released from that job.

The Brother who married Anna Louis—he was a cook—he had a job downtown cooking in a restaurant.

Jabril Muhammad: His name was "Brother Bernard 2 or 3X.

Minister Farrakhan: Yes. He got me a job washing dishes. I didn't do that so well. They had me mopping floors, taking coffee and donuts, and whatnot, to the various offices in the area. Then they had me peeling potatoes, which I had never done in my life.

They could see that I wasn't good at that kind of work. They worked me the first day for 12 hours. I overslept. I called the job to let them know that I had overslept. They told me "That's alright. I didn't need to bother. Just come in and pick up my days pay."

He was disappointed in me because he was the one that got me the job. I failed at that job. I failed at pretty much every day jobs that I had but I was determined that I wasn't going backward. I was going forward and since I grew up in Boston, I decided to go back.

Well my next trial was coming up because Brother Malcolm had sent me - when I told him I was going back to Boston -- the Mosque was in a terrible state. The ministers there—there were two—were arguing with each and it had split the Mosque. Then he sent me with the thought in mind that I would become the minister.

Shortly after I got there, Brother Malcolm came (I thought) to make me the minister. But when we sat down in Minister Ulysses' home, with Brother Minister Lloyd, Brother Malcolm informed Brother Lloyd that he was to leave Boston to be the Minister in Springfield. He made Minister Ulysses the Minister of Boston and then said to me, "Brother Louis you will be the captain."

Well of course, he set my mind up that I was going to be minister and then he told me I am to be the captain. I, of course, had to adjust my mind to a new reality.

Once I understood that that is what was wanted of me I threw away the idea of minister and set my mind to be the captain of

Minister Ulysses. I served him well as a captain and he was as gracious and kind as a minister could be for he knew of my gift of speaking and so he would allow me sometimes on a Wednesday to speak or a Friday and some Sundays even, when he had to work, he would allow me to teach.

There was no time that I taught that those who were there for the first time, the majority, would get up and join. The Mosque then gradually became full. I, as a captain served him; served the men; went out selling the papers in the storm, or whatever it was that we as F.O.I. had to do. I did that.

Later I learned that Brother Malcolm discussed my being the minister of Boston. He said the Messenger told him, "Put him under authority. If he can work well under, then he will be qualified to go over." So that was a test that I really didn't know was a test until later. But Allah blessed me to pass that test.

As a captain I really enjoyed the love of the F.O.I. and the believers and the Mosque grew, grew, and grew. We out-grew the little Mosque that we had and they found an old building; an old Jewish synagogue. They were willing to sell it but it was in bad shape. The brothers took me there with flashlights and showed me the building but I had no vision, they did, as to what could be done with such building. So I agreed with the older more mature Muslims that we should try to purchase that building.

I was captain and then as a captain, I came out to Chicago for Savior's Day and the Messenger had the captains to speak on that Saturday, February 1957. I spoke and the Messenger was sitting right behind me. In the pictures that I saw there, he had this beautiful smile on his face. As I spoke as Captain Louis that night he invited me, for the first time, to come to dinner with him.

That night I remembered him doing something that I've never seen him do since then. At the end of the dinner he went around the table shaking everybody's hand. When he got to me and shook my hand he came close and whispered in my ear, "You remind me of David." Then he went back to his chair and of course, dismissed us. That was in February.

By May of 1957, because of problems with Minister Ulysses

and the need for funding and money to keep up his quality of life, he had to work in a foundry or his job had took him away from the Mosque; so the Messenger decided in May of 1957, to make me the minister.

Then other trials began. You know the trial of extreme poverty. I remember working in the garment district in Boston making forty-five dollars a week. They would take ninety cents out for FICA; Social Security and whatnot, and I would come home with forty-four dollars and ten cents; with my wife and three children. But I always found each week, money to donate to the Temple and of course, my charity to the Messenger and encouraged the believers to do the same. But that trial was extreme poverty.

When I finally got up to sixty-five dollars a week working days; I studied during my lunch hour. We didn't each lunch. We ate one meal a day. So I would just have a cup of coffee and write my subject out to preach.

I remembered the Honorable Elijah Muhammad said, "Well, you have gotten the Mosque up." The believers were sufficient in number to support me. So he said that I should come away from the day job and concentrate fully on the resurrection of our people. He said that I could get one hundred dollars a week. This was 1958.

Not one time in nine years did I ever get a hundred dollar. The most I ever got, as I can recall, was sixty-five to seventy dollars. But the actual charity was between thirty and forty-five dollars per week. For nine solid years I was not able to buy a new suit until the ninth year, when I was leaving. The believers gave me a new suit. I would wear suits from the pawnshop that my brother, from New York, would bring to me.

The believers would bring old cloths and put it on the steps of the house. My wife would take them in and wash and iron them and my children would have cloths to wear. We use to buy dresses at the Salvation Army and slips and things like that.

I remember going on Saturday nights to the market place in Boston, K Market Square, where the end of the day when the merchant didn't sell all of his produce. They would throw them in the street. My wife and I would get our shopping bags and go down and pick up food out of the street and fill our shopping bag and come back and feed our ever growing family.

At no time did he tell me that I could get a hundred dollars a week, if it did not come into the administration charity that was to support the minister. I would not go into the rent treasury or the general treasury or other treasuries to make up the hundred dollars. I made my family and I suffice for whatever the believers gave me.

Trial. The trial of poverty.

As the Mosque grew, I was blessed to be able to introduce music but on an Islamic base using the teachings of the Honorable Elijah Muhammad. So a play that I had written in 1956 in New York, I added to it other scenes and things and it became "Orgena"—a negro spelled backward.

I used the talented believers of Mosque No. 11 and they were so highly spirited and the Mosque just grew and grew and grew. So I remember I was invited to Chicago and the Messenger came in the living room. He told me that one of the sisters had accused me of stealing her play and I was getting all this honor for my play when in fact I had taken the idea from a play that she had written. So the Messenger asked me, "Is that true Brother?" I said, "No sir, dear Apostle." So he said, "Oh, ok, well I'll deal with it at the dinner table."

That night at the dinner table I was surrounded by Sharrieff. I didn't know when they put Sharrieff to sit next to you, who was the Supreme Captain of the nation, that that was the sign that you were about to go on trial. If you did not respond well to the trial, you will be removed, not only from the premises, but removed from your post, etc.

I got the soup down. Then he raised the questions. He was questioning me, from my vantage point, as though I was actually guilty of stealing the sister's play. And like a prosecuting attorney he went after me. Every time he would say, "And didn't you do such and such?" I said, "No sir, dear Apostle." He said, "Well didn't Brother Malcolm come and show you her play and then you?" I said, "No sir, dear Apostle."

My voice was getting softer and softer and his voice getting sterner and sterner. Then Mother Clara Muhammad burst in and said, "Well he said he didn't do it." In other words, "Will you leave him alone?" You know, she saw that I was a good little minister and she felt that I may not pass such a test. So she was going to step in and he was just going after me.

Then I got tired of saying, "No sir" like I'm arguing and disagreeing with him. I said, "Well dear Apostle, it's whatever you say I did that's what it is." He said, "Well alright then." He threw his handkerchief down on the table. Then I'm dazed. I'm like a man that's been hit with combination punches and I'm reeling on the rope and the bell rings. They have to come and get me and take me to the corner and throw water and ice to revive me.

He let it stay, you know, like that for a few seconds, it seems. Then he said, "Brother I was defending you all the time." I didn't understand that kind of defense. So he said, "Brother when did you write your play?" I said, "1956." He said, "Well the sister didn't come in the Temple until 1958." He said, "I was trying to get you to say that she stole her play from you." I said, "Dear Apostle I couldn't say any such thing as that, because I'm sure neither she nor I knew anything about the history of John Hawkins until we heard you. So in reality all that she and I did was take your teaching and put it in a way that is familiar with those of us who are in some form of show business or something like that."

He looked around the table as if to say, you see, here's a man that I'm trying to set-up to charge somebody else with what they charged him with and he said he could never do that because all of us got this teaching from him.

Wallace D. Muhammad was at the table that night. When it was over the Honorable Elijah Muhammad said to me, "You and my son Wallace go and mop up the wilderness." It was probably in 1960—1959 or 1960 right in there. Trial.

Now I go back to Boston. I do my work as best I can. The next time of trial I believe was when my Brother Malcolm in December of 1963 spoke and mis-spoke at the Manhattan center in New

York.

The Honorable Elijah Muhammad sat him down for ninety days and told him that he should be quiet. The first Sunday that he was quiet I was sent to New York to speak. Brother Malcolm did not come to the Temple but he came after the lecture and picked me up and brought me to his home.

Sister Betty cooked the meal. He and I were sitting alone in the dining room at his house at 2311 97th Street, which later became my home. But after we had the bean soup he began to tell me of the personal life of the Honorable Elijah Muhammad. He said, "I could get these sisters on the telephone.

They won't know that you are on the other end of the line. I would trick them into speaking about their personal life with him." I told him then that, "That would not be necessary." I believed what he was saying but I did not wish to involve myself with the sisters and some trick to get them to speak against him or about him.

As we were going, he was driving me to the airport. He said, "Don't tell anyone what I shared with you tonight." I looked at him and said, "No sir. I'm not going to tell any one but the Messenger." I saw him jump. He didn't say anymore.

I went home and couldn't sleep that night at all. At time for prayer the next morning at five, I received a call from him. He said, "Before you tell the Messenger could you give me time and I would write him to explain why I said what I said to you." I said, "It would take me some time to fix my mind to write such a letter to him. So if you can get your letter off in that time that would be fine." But I would not agree to just hold up my letter for him.

But I knew I had to write him but I wanted to write in such a way where I wouldn't be insulting to him. Then I told Brother Malcolm, "I don't want to be caught in the middle between two powerful men." He said, "Well there's only one powerful man and that's the Messenger." I said, "I realize that." But, in my life now, there were two powerful men—Malcolm, as my superior on the East Coast and the Honorable Elijah Muhammad as the superior. So he and I hung up the phone.

I went in to my study and I opened the Qur'an to the 33rd Surah of the Qur'an. I saw in the footnotes where the orientalists due to his having wives—the Prophet had wives—they accused him of debauchery and ugly things. I saw in that a defense for the Messenger.

I called Brother Malcolm back and I said, "I was reading the Qur'an and I found something. I would like to discuss it with you." He said, "Well come on." I jumped on the Eastern Airline shuttle, which was, I think, at that time, twelve or fourteen dollars. I went over to see my Brother. He met me at the airport. When I told him what I had read in the Holy Qur'an, he said, "I already know that Brother. But you can't handle this. You let me handle this." In that stern way of Brother Malcolm as my superior and my teacher, I said, "Yes sir." He took me back to the airport. I got on the plane and left. Trial.

The man that taught me; the man that was such a great example for me; the man that gave me an opportunity to express a gift that I never knew I had and a man that helped to polish that gift; a man that I looked at as the greatest helper of the man I love--the man I searched for all my life that I would give my life for Brother Malcolm so that he could continue to help the Honorable Elijah Muhammad, now I had to write my leader a letter of something that Brother Malcolm did that was improper.

A trial—the love between your supreme teacher and your superior teacher. Of course, I had to favor the man I had looked for all my life over a man that I met as a result of seeing the man that I looked for all my life.

That trial again I passed. The way I wrote the letter, the Honorable Elijah Muhammad called me on the telephone, he said, "I understand." In that language that I used—the delicate language that I used—he said he got the message and he understood. That comforted me. He told me that, "If Brother Malcolm would accept this, [I] would bring him back and place him over the businesses and gradually bring him back to his post."

I knew that he said that to me so that I could say that to [Malcolm]. But I wanted to see what was in my Brother. I did not offer him that olive branch that the Messenger offered him through me. Whether that is a failure on my part, but my motive was, I want to see you; how you respond to [the Messenger] without an olive branch to see what is in your heart for him.

Well Malcolm failed that test. I remember sitting with him and he said to me, "Those who would be my enemies ..." He named them. He seemed to know that I was going to ascend to the position that he held with the Messenger.

He said these very telling words to me, "I wish that it was you being an example for me rather than me being an example for you." I knew then that he did not love me as much as I loved him. For if he loved me he would not want me to be in an ugly position that he could learn from my example. I don't think I misread that but ultimately every thing that he told me came to pass.

He told me about these enemies that would be in the bush. I told him, "Like David, I'm not worried about what is in the bush because God will take care of that." So I'm not going to be around looking in the bush for my enemy. I'll let God look in the bush for them. He always saw me as more spiritual and himself as more political. I never made such a comparison but he did.

Anyway, then my captain, Jabba—I named him Jabba as it was Clarence—he got a letter from a laborer saying that Malcolm was the big dog. But I was the little puppy and we got to watch this puppy because he would respond to the call of the big dog. Clarence's wife saw the letter and read it and brought the letter to my door for me to read it. I told this Sister, "I cannot read a letter that was not sent to me. That letter was sent to your husband. You take it back to your husband."

But she told me the content of the letter. So that let me see that headquarters did not know how I was going to respond to the growing hypocrisy of Brother Malcolm so they set my own laborers against me in Boston.

I wrote an article defending the Messenger. Somehow one of the secretaries read it and showed it to the Messenger. He was so impressed with my defense of him, because he said he had people who had been with him for thirty-five years who were not able to defend him.

When these revelations came out from Wallace and Malcolm they seemed at a loss as to how to defend the man that they had known for thirty-five years. A man removed from him by a thousand miles; a man that only saw him once a year, sometimes twice a year at a laborers meeting, knew him better than those who had been around him, some of them all their lives.

After I defended him he praised my defense of him and thanked me. I wrote another article in defense of him.

Then he moved me to New York. He called me at my home in Boston and said, "I'm appointing you to be the minister of Temple No. 7." To this day, I don't know whether I accepted it. I was in shock. When he said, "As Salaam Alaikum" I said, "Wa Alaikum Salaam, dear Apostle."

I never said a word to my wife; to nobody. I went out of the house, got in my little car and I drove and cried and drove and cried and went to a spot where I would park my car and sometimes just read the Qur'an and the Messenger's articles. I wept over my Brother because I never wanted his place. I always wanted to help him to be successful as the National Representative of our father. Now I am being offered his place.

It took a little while for me to accept that. I remember teaching in the Mosque about the sperm of a prophet and how God is not prodigal that when the wife of the prophet—as I mentioned Abraham—was barren. But here was the friend of God with a living life germ. His wife is barren.

His promise is not only with Himself, the promise is with his seed. That seed then had to be sown. He allowed Abraham to go into Sarah's handmaiden. As I was saying, that what Malcolm said is the truth, but his interpretation of it is foul. I interpreted it correctly.

My captain hearing that I had said that what Malcolm said was the truth, and many believers thought that Malcolm had lied. Well in essence he did lie because he did not tell the truth as the truth should had been told. So that gave me the opportunity to tell the truth as the truth had been told.

Sometime in July, I was made the minister of Mosque No. 7. I packed up my family and drove down to New York. The house that Malcolm lived in was fire bombed. When they re-did it, they re-did it as cheaply as they could do it. When I moved into the house it had carpet on the floor that was maybe an eighth of inch thick with rubber backing on the carpet. They had a chandelier in the dinning room with plastic things from the chandelier. My family then of seven and I moved in to that house.

But other trials began from his laborers. You know, those things I don't want to go into except to say, that the things that laborers do against a person who is helping, can either destroy that person or help that person to be who that person should be.

During the rebuilding of Mosque No. 7, Maceo Haziz became very close to the Messenger.

He did things in New York; getting monies and loans and whatnot. I'm not clear on all the things that he did, but he endeared himself to the Messenger. Many times at the end of the month when we would bring the labor out to Chicago, he would always accompany me. I would go out once a month and Maceo would be with me and we would listen to what the Honorable Elijah Muhammad said at his table.

Three or four more trials—sequentially. I'm trying to get to each of them. He made me his National Representative. After making me his National Representative and giving me the name Farrakhan, which I didn't quite like, because I had seen the name Muhammad and I thought, surely, if he were giving me a name it would be Muhammad. But he gave me the name Farrakhan.

When he gave it to me in 1965, September, through the newspaper, when I came out and sat at the table, he said, "Well Minister how do you like your new name?" I didn't want to tell him, dear Apostle, I didn't like it because I saw the name Muhammad. I said, "Oh it's nice dear Apostle but what does it mean?" He said, "Oh, I has the meaning upstairs. It has very many good meanings. It is a modern up-to-date name of God. Has many good meanings Brother but I will give you the meaning in time."

That was 1965. He left in 1975, never telling me the meaning of the name. Since he told me that he would give me the meaning of the name I would not press him for its meaning. I waited for him--not realizing that that too was a test. You wait on the Lord. Lord have mercy.

Then, Brother, there was this program with Tony Brown: "Is it too late?" There was to be a nationally televised program of all of the top Black leaders to discuss: "Is it too late?" I don't remember when this was but the riots and things were taking place and it was upsetting.

He brought me out and he said, "Brother I want you to go and do this program for me." I said, "Yes sir, dear Apostle." He brought me out again and he's instructing me on how I should go and he's telling me, "Now Brother, you don't have to fear nothing from no neuter gender, because what I have given you is superior to anything that they have. You stand up on what I taught you," in words you know. It's like he's setting me up, and preparing me to meet with the leaders on this nationally televised thing.

Well, I take Brother Akbar (then Larry 4X) three days before the program I check into a hotel and I'm studying, fasting and praying--preparing. I sent my friend and Brother companion, Brother James, now known as Muhammad Ali, to buy me a new suit to wear. I was preparing.

On the morning of the show there is a dress rehearsal; getting everybody in place. They wanted me there at a certain time. I wanted to call the Messenger to see if there are last minute instructions or anything. I called him and he comes to the phone and I ask him, "Are there any instructions, dear Apostle?" "Instructions for what?" "This is the program where all the leaders coming together, is it too late?" He said, "Well you do what you want to do, say what you want to say" and hung up the phone. "Huh?"

I called back. He wouldn't come to the phone. They said he had a diabetic coma and he was in a coma. So I sat with the Brothers, Akbar and James and I said, "What should I do?" He said, "Call him back." So I called back. He said, "Is this a program for the leaders Brother?" I said, "Yes sir, dear Apostle." "Well when did you become the leader of the Nation of Islam Brother?" "Well what do you want me to do, dear Apostle?" "Do what you want to do." Then he said, "What do you want to do?" I said, "Well I want to be with you." He said, "Well come on then" and hung up the phone.

I got on the plane and flew. It was a helicopter at O'Hare. I got on it and it flew me to Meiges Field and Brother Albert picked me up and brought me to the house. It was late. Dinner had already been served. When I got there, one of the sisters, when he opened the door and brought me in the sister said, "He's here dear Apostle." I walked in to the dinning room and the house looked like it was empty. Mother Clara was there. I don't know who else was there. He sat me down right in my usual chair, right next to him on the left. Mother Clara, right in the front, right across from me.

I said, "I'm very happy to see you, dear Apostle." He said, "Well I hope so Brother." He started with his pen. "We have ten minutes dear Apostle before the show." They were testing this and that because he was the only one that was going to be by phone. So he says, "What is the name of this program Brother? "Is it too late?" " Then he started writing.

Then the program started. I'm sitting there and when it came time for him to speak, he started speaking and I said, "Go ahead dear Apostle." I was bearing witness for him, you know in my usual way, and sometimes, a little too loud.

When it was over he said, "Sharrieff"—"Brother, you must be tired"—take him downtown. Put him in the finest hotel down town Brother Sharrieff and you come and see me in the morning for coffee." But as I was going out the door he said, "Brother you passed a great test tonight." I said, "Yes sir, dear Apostle." I went out the door. They took me to a fine hotel and put me up for the night. I went back to New York the next day. That was one trial. Three more and we can close this—although I could mention more.

In 1970, Tony Brown did his program on national T.V. on me and Muhammad Temple (as it was called then) Number 7. It was on how I went out in the street talking to our lost found brothers and sisters and the junkies and there was so much love that they had for me.

Then in 1970, there was the Congress of African People. He called me to Chicago. He was sending me down there to make a speech. He said, "Brother, I want you to go down there and mock those leaders, conferencing around, wasting time when God has given me a program for them. So you just mock them Brother."

That wasn't in my heart. I'm thinking, I don't want to—I thought maybe I could win them over with another kind of speech. But, to go down there and mock them? So he looked at me, he said, "Brother, I sit at this table and I order things for you all, all around the earth like a god." He said, "If I buy farm land for you not even seeing it, I ask a question, I say, "That's the one you buy there." "If I can do all of that don't you think I know how to tell you to go to Atlanta and make a speech and become the winner?" I said, "Yes sir, dear Apostle."

I threw my idea completely out of my mind. I got my pen and took notes on what he wanted me to say. Unknown to me he sent for Minister Rahman. He said, "Brother Rahman, I told Brother what I want him to say. I want you to see if he says it just like I told him. Because if he says it like I told him, he will be written in the history of forty nations."

Minister Rahman took me to the place and I delivered the message. To this day nationalists who hated me because of Malcolm fondly refer to that speech. Brother Conrad Worrill talked to me about that speech just the other day. It's a speech that launched me nationally and internationally. Because he said, "You will be written of in 40 countries."

Then after I did what he told me to do and I obeyed him, he brought me out to Chicago, and he says, "Brother that one speech, that speech, it mean more to me than a truck load of diamonds and gold." That came after I obeyed him and delivered that message.

Now that's 1970. Now Maceo and I come out, "I want you Brother to come out once a month." "Yes sir, dear Apostle." But Maceo comes out every week. Now I'm his National Representative. Seems like that honor to be out there with him every week should be mine. So unknown to me he's watching how I'm reacting to my secretary. He's asking the secretary, "How's the Minister?" I don't know this, but I'm assuming this.

I never bothered Maceo about what the Messenger said. Because if he didn't invite me to his table I can't bug you about what he said at the table because if he wanted me there he would have asked me to be there. But Maceo would come back and share with me some of the spiritual things that the Messenger said. I always received him and it with great joy.

I never so much as one time was displeased with him for sending for Maceo and not me. At no time was there ever anger or jealousy or envy toward Maceo for being in that favored place with him. Then he was choosing an assistant to himself in Chicago. We sat around the table and he talked about his choice of Brother Yusuf Shah to be his assistant at #2 and why. Part of his reason was because he is very familiar with the Bible. He's watching me react. I'm happy. This is your choice dear Apostle. Trial.

I disagreed with Captain Shah and I wanted to fire him. Come time for a trial and the Messenger asked me, "Well where is your evidence?" "Well its back in New York. I didn't bring it," "What? You come to a trial with no evidence. Case dismissed." I jumped to my feet and saluted Yusuf. If he is your choice, then he is my choice. I never, as God is the witness of my heart, no matter what I felt toward Yusuf, he said, "I'm not going to get rid of my Captain on such flimsy evidence that you say you have, but did not bring it." "Well if you won't get rid of him, I'm through with it." I salute him and we go back to work. Trial.

Now this is not sequential now. He calls me out and he starts beating up on the West Indians and how they came in the Temple and they fought against him. He made mockery of the way they speak in such manner and, "We're never even going to let West Indian people in the Temple." He was watching me. I said to myself, "Why is he doing this? He knows that my people are from there." I don't say nothing; I don't do nothing. I leave. I go back to New York. I drive my car down under the bridge near the water to look over at the watchtower across the east river. I'm crying. "Why dear Apostle are you talking to me like this?" I have a broadcast to make on Sunday because I'm broadcasting to the whole city.

In my Sunday broadcast I talk about a crescent that starts from the Caribbean like this to North America. I said to them that, leaders from the Caribbean have come to try and awaken the Black man of America. Now God has come, not from this end of the crescent but God came to North America to choose the Black man of America. Now as they came this way from the crescent up to North America, now it is our responsibility to bring the message back through that crescent to them.

I said, "If God told me—" (The Minister begins to weep.) See, I didn't know that it would be this reaction because there is pain involved in trial. There are choices that you make in trials that can take you up or down but it's pain inflicted by God to make manifest what is hidden. He beats up on the West Indians, knowing that he's inflicting pain on me. "Well how are you going to react to that Brother?" Because he had already told me when he made me his representative that, "I will never teach another minister like I taught Malcolm until I have thoroughly tried him." So this is part of the thorough testing.

I say if God said to me at the end of my work that you cannot enter the paradise of the Black man of America that was preserved for him because your parents are from the Caribbean I said I would say to God, "Let me be the bearer of the throne of the Black man of America to carry him into that paradise." They sent that tape off to my father. He said, "Look at this boy." There is more to this.

Then, of course there's the trial of choosing Brother Lonnie Shabazz, and you, to be the radio spokesperson. I didn't know he was trying me. Because the first time you went on and spoke he sent for me. The first time Brother went on and spoke he sent for me. "What did you think of that Brother?" I said, "I enjoyed it very much." Why did I enjoy it? Because if they're bearing witness to the man I love, why would not I enjoy them? I don't have nothing to say negative about that. But he's weighing me. I don't realize that I'm being weighted.

Then I go out in 1973, I think, to California and I visit with Huey Newton. Well let's go before that. Because before that in 1972 he purchased the Mosque on Stony Island and the lecture series of *Theology of Time* begins. He starts his lectures, and I ask him, "Dear Apostle, may I come out?" "For what Brother? You has your assignment in New York and I has mine."

I stay in New York. The believers would come out and hear the lecture and come back. I would ask them, you know, about the lecture and they would be telling me what the Lamb said. I would be sitting like a student listening. For them to tell me the word of my father who barred me to come, after maybe six weeks, somehow we're on the phone and I either asked him again, I said, "You know believers are coming back and telling me the wonderful lectures and I'm reading it in the paper." He said, "Yes Brother. I wondered why you was not out here." I didn't want to remind him that, "You told me to stay." But I said, "I want to be there." He said, "Well come on."

Now I think I'm on the outs with him. So when I come the ministers are seated on the side. I sit in the back row and he starts preaching and he hears me bearing witness. "I hear my minister back here." Then he brings me and sits me—they made a room for me on the front row. "What is he doing back here? He should be down front here." They get up and make room. Then when they make room on the front row he looks over at me and say and he points to his seat. Then I gingerly get up and go sit in his seat. I could feel the daggers from the minister in the back of my head even though there is marble that hides my head. I could feel those daggers, Brother. Ok. I'm sitting in his seat.

Now I come out the next week. I don't go sit in that seat. But now he wants to see "So since I sit you there once, you going to sit there every week? That's my chair Brother." I go right back in the back—they brought me to sit on the front row with the ministers. I wouldn't go back and sit there unless he sat me there again. But for that Sunday he made me to sit in his seat. Of course, I later read that in the scriptures with Solomon. Ok. That's 1972.

Now after that I go to California and I'm speaking and I want to meet Huey Newton. He asked me to come to his apartment. I go with Rasheed, Captain Edward Sherrill and they said, "Well you can't come in unless you're searched." So I didn't see no problem. We search everybody, you know, so hey. I submit to a search. Captain Edward and the rest of them submit because I did.

But man, whatever they said to the Messenger, now the trial comes. He sends for me. He sits me between two captains. I think Sharreiff on one side and Junior on the other. And Edward Sherrill is there, his top laborers—and he starts beating on me. "You're going out there wearing out your knees to that neuter gender. Why did not you not tell him that we is the ones that started searching and you know that it is in our teachings that we carries no weapons? Why did not you tell him that, "No sir, Brother. We will not submit to no such thing when you know we don't carry no weapons? But no, you second only to myself, wear out your knees to such a man as that. Why Brother I put you in a million dollar house, not for you to go to them but to make them come to you like I does.

The Mayor of Chicago wants me to come down to the City Hall and I tell him my address. The president of the United States invites me to the White House and I told him where I live. He's welcome at any time. And here you second only to myself, you go to that neuter gender panther—when I defended them they said to me that they didn't want no defense from me; they wanted nothing written of them in my paper. You submit yourself to that?"

The more he talked I never offered no defense for myself. Then after whipping the hell out of me, and I am sitting like that, never saying a word; never offering no excuse; no nothing. He said, "I know why you did it Brother. I know why you did it." "You has fallen off the log. When a man falls off the log he can't get back up by himself. He needs help. You has fallen off the log."

He's whipping me in the presence of all of those who dislike me. But he's telling them at the same time, in the nation I'm second only to him. So he's lifting me and beating me and teaching me and trying me because now I'm a big man in the nation, see.

But can you take a whipping in front of people that don't like you? When he told me he understood why I did it, I was fine. But they were happy to see me get this beating. They were missing the point.

The last trial that I had before then was my secretary Mary 43X became friendly with Bayyinnah Sharrieff and Velora Najieb. She would ask me from time to time could she go out to Chicago on the weekend to be with Bayyinnah and Velora? I said, "Sure. Fine." She would go out. She would have dinner with the Messenger. Then Velora told the Messenger that I was sending my secretary out there to spy to get information about what is going on in his house. So he sends for me.

This is a trial now. He brings Velora in front of me and he states the charge. I said, "Dear Apostle, there are two secretaries that work for you and grew up under me in Boston, Judith Allah and (somebody Ali)." I said, "When I come to this house and I see them I give them the greetings. I ask about their parents and I ask them nothing else. You may question them and they will tell you that what I've just said is the truth. I would never send my secretary to get any information about your household."

He wanted Velora to hear that because Judith Allah came out from me from Provindence Rhode Island. I recommended her to him and the little young girl, her name now is Naseem Ali, got her doctorate degree. I sent her from Boston to him.

He said, "Case dismissed." The last time I was in front of him like that when I threaten to kill Captain Joseph, if he interfered with me running that Temple after he and Maceo had run it into financial difficulties. When they ran the Temple into financial difficulties and I came out and had no money to give to the Messenger from No. 7, he said, "Well Brother who is the minister there at No. 7? I said "Me, dear Apostle." "Well then Brother there's nothing coming. I hold you responsible for that." I didn't want to tell him, "Dear Apostle when you sent me there you told me to concentrate on the teachings and let Maceo and Shah handle the business."

I could not bring his words back to him as a defense for me.

If he tells me I'm responsible, "Yes sir." I went back and took responsibility. From that point never did a check with his name on it bounce. We restored the integrity of that name in the banks. From that day to this never has a check bounced with the name Louis Farrakhan on that check.

Another test. "Brother" he says, "All of the treasuries is yours in New York, all of them Brother." I responded, "Yes sir". He then said, "Anything that you want you just put a note in that you took so much and so much for such and such, so and so." I said, "Thank you, dear Apostle". No note was ever found because I never did it.

Another test. The Honorable Elijah Muhammad said, "Brother I has all these gifts that the people give to me at Savior's Day. I has them all downstairs. I can't use these gifts. Could you come and bring a truck and take these gifts from here Brother?" I said, "Thank you dear Apostle." But in my heart no thank you. "If they gave the gifts to you, why would I come with a truck and take gifts that I can't use?" That says many trials.

Oh by the way, after I think I passed the West Indian test, he told me, he says, "Brother what it takes the Black man of America six years to learn, the Black man in the Caribbean could learn it in six months." I later came to see, our Beloved Savior, Master Fard Muhammad, to Whom praise is due forever, had a white mother and a Black father. I know that the mother had the power of a mother in nurturing that child. But He left the family of the mother to go after the family of the father—not that mercy would not yet come back to the family of the mother but His first commitment was to the people of His father.

I said this is what he's teaching me, that my commitment—he wanted to see whether my heart was more for the people of my mother; my father; my uncle than for the Black man of America, Whom God Himself had come to save. Then he learned in that test that my heart was where his heart and Master Fard Muhammad's heart was and that the Isles await his law. They would awaken. Now. I am going with his help and guidance to these islands to give them what God has revealed. That test, that's one.

Then comes the test of the radio. I had been on the radio for six years. Every week I tell them whose program it is and we expect him to return to these microphones soon. He calls me on the telephone, "Brother, I want you to announce your next broadcast that I will be coming back to take over the broadcast, As-Salaam Alaikum." Look at this. A man has been sucking on a lollipop for six years that is not his own and he know it is not his. Now he's asked by the owner, I want my lollipop back. How do you respond? I went in and worked on the speech "Hearken unto the voice of God."

So thankful that my teacher had given me such an opportunity and now he was coming back and I wanted the people to know who they were about to hear from. When he played that tape he said, "Brother you should go back and speak next week yourself."

Now Brother Jabril, you know, I've never been asked to go over the trials of my life in Islam. There are many more that may have been fostered by him or initiated or directed by him but fostered by his laborers on me. But I will close that by saying, I have never hated my father's laborers. No matter what they said against me; no matter what they did against me, as long as they loved him and worked for him on behalf of this people that I love, I never had nothing in my heart against one who believed in him and helped him do what he did and does for our people.

His trying of me, with the opposition of my brethren, never made me to act unjustly toward any of them. The proof of that is these last near thirty years of my ministry in the absence of my father, dealing with his son, Warithu Deen; his family; his ministers; his followers; never have I done to the best of my knowledge, one thing of evil against those who did so much evil toward me.

I close this by saying, this is why my Brother Malcolm, he was not of the material to sit in the seat of our father. His pride; his gangster mentally; his willingness to trade evil for evil, if he sat where I am sitting he would use the men who would love him to kill his enemies. He was disqualified from such noble seat by turning on his benefactor and desiring for the benefactor what the benefactor never desired for him, until, of course, he turned.

Now, more than ever, I realize why I was blessed, to be chosen to sit in his seat, as a mercy for us, for our people and even for the enemy.

I thank you Brother Jabril for reacquainting me with the pain of my life in trial. Probably one of the greatest trials was to see the house that our father built that we helped him to build, by his masterful direction, to see it destroyed. To see people lose their sanity; lose their lives; lose their faith; go back to the world of the enemy and Mosques that we helped sacrifice to build, just taken from us and given over to another way of thinking and yet after that, because that was the son of my father, I would never give in to suggestions to do him harm or any believer that followed him into hypocrisy, for the Messenger told me that, "We all would leave but we all would one day return." It is because of that belief in his word and my love for them and my hope for their return, it's like you keep the lamp lit on the door that shows them the way home.

Thank you.

One thing I forgot was in 1961. I brought the play "Orgena" to Chicago and we had two performances at the Dunn Bar High School. And on the last performance the Honorable Elijah Muhammad slipped into the theater, the auditorium, sat way in the balcony to see the performance. And he sent for me to be with him the next day.

In the performance of "Orgena," there's a scene where a brother plays the part of a homosexual and a sister plays the part of a prostitute that is reformed by the call of the Honorable Elijah Muhammad. In the play I do a song that was written by one of the brothers in the Mosque and I added aspect to it but my part was very small. It's called "Chains." I was in chains singing "Look at my chains."

The next morning the Messenger sends for me. I'm in the living room with him at 4847 South Woodlawn Avenue. He's real close to me like you are and he says, "Brother I was there and I saw the play." He said, "Brother, when you catch a fish you don't leave it on the banks, as it will continue to flop around until it falls back in the water." He says, "In order to play such part of a prostitute the sister would have to think like that or to play such part as the old life, they have to go back into that life in their mind in order to play and portray such part and it could lead them back into such life." He said, "Brother, I saw your performance of the chains. There wasn't a dry eye in the place as you were singing."

He says, "I was preaching one Sunday on the prodigal son and the Savior came that night and we had dinner and He asked me, "Karriem, how did things go?" Somebody that was at the Temple, said "Oh Master" (whatever they call Him—Prophet Fard they called Him) "Oh he really taught. There wasn't a dry eye in the Temple."

He said, "Brother" his face got very stern and He looked at me and said, "Brother don't make my people cry for I came to wipe away all their tears." So he said "Now Brother" he says, "You are very talented man." He said, "But your greatest talent is in the spiritual. So I want you to give up this as of today. I want your word to me that you will not do this again." I said, "You have my word, dear Apostle. I won't do this again." He says, "Thank you Brother. Thank you."

Now for the second time he's asking me to give up music. He's pointing out to me that my greatest strength is in the spiritual even though my musical talent is great. Then I sent him a tape of songs that I had sung in the studio and he was angry. "Did not I tell you—you told me that you were going to give it up Brother?" I said, "Yes sir. I did give it up, dear Apostle. But I wanted to put it in a tape so that we can have a record of it."

The Honorable Elijah Muhammad responded with: "Oh, ok Brother."

Brother Jabril: Thank you, Brother Minister.

This interview lasted one hour and fifty-five minutes. I've mentioned a few times when during this interview he weep. He actually weep about four or five times. He arose from the chair looking pained. He received no treatment that afternoon.

His doctor said that although she did not know I was going to present such a question, that the affects would prove to be beneficial for him.

There was no interview the next day. However, Minister walked with strength and said something to me in a loud voice and with a big smile that indicated he was certainly feeling well. He entered my home and began sharing with the doctor that the previous evening he did not eat. His family members thought that the treatment wasted him. But he did not get a treatment. He said he awoke very early that morning or very late the previous night and then ate his dinner. He went back to bed.

He awoke feeling much better and prepared to come by my home.

INTERVIEW OF THE HONORABLE MINISTER LOUIS FARRAKHAN
BY JABRIL MUHAMMAD;
PHOENIX, ARIZONA
JULY 12, 2006

Brother Jabril: Brother Minister, how would you advise us in this awfully turbulent world, to help our children with proper fun? Toy manufacturers, of course, are greedy and are not really looking deeply into the interest of children. What advice would you give us with regard to buying toys for our children? What is fun?

Minister Farrakhan: The question is what is fun? Fun to one person is ignorance to another. Fun to another person is what is trifling to another. The question we have to ask is what is fun with God? Does God engage in trifling things? Does He engage in things that are foolish?

So what I found as fun is the joy of learning today what I did not know yesterday. I literally enjoy my teacher teaching me things, on the violin that I didn't know, and then making a joke out of what I did wrong that I now am learning to do right.

We don't have time for trifling things. Children should not be engaged in just silly things; playing with toys that do not teach. The joy of living is the joy of learning. Since Almighty God Allah created us as a reflection of Himself, it would seem that from as early as we can think, we should find joy in the discovery of truth.

We should find fun in the discovery of things that grow us; that edify us; that evolve us toward God.

Mindless games are valueless with God because they misuse youth. Children are mischievous. Then find something that we can learn from mischief—games of learning; games that increase ones dexterity; that teach skills in doing things; games that challenge us mentally.

I was talking to Bobby Brown in Houston, a great performer. He said, "Brother, I really need your help." I pulled him close to me, because there was a lot going on. I whispered in his ear, "Brother, you don't need me. You need a closer relationship with your Creator."

In answer to your question, which dovetails into what I said to him, I said, "When you were a sperm mixed with ovum your mother wasn't conscious of this until she missed her menses that something was happening with her. But the intelligence that was in the sperm knew what it had to do. So it made contact with the egg and the first cell of life began. Mom, unaware. Dad, unaware. But you, in that stage, were aware and the Creator was aware and the Creator was present with you.

As that first cell of life began rotating, in the darkness of the womb, there was light present in it that caused it to rotate. Then you became a clot. You became an embryo. You became a fetus and God was ever present before anyone had a relationship with you.

Your duty is to create, or to make a right relationship with your Creator. I said, "When you came forth, parents looked at you and loved you, happy to see you, and mama either gave you her breast, or she gave you milk and you began to grow. You couldn't talk. You couldn't walk. You couldn't crawl. But something was going on in the brain.

Mama didn't teach you to crawl. You just did that. Mama didn't teach you to pull up on something sturdy that you can stand up. You did that. Then everyone was amazed when you took your first step. But no one taught you that. It was an intelligence that was already in you and a relationship with your Creator that was nurtured by your mother; your father; and the environment in which you lived."

Well wasn't that fun? It was fun for us on the outside watching our baby crawl. It was fun watching the baby coo, to say, "Thank you." It was fun watching you take your first step. So fun was the joy of watching growth; development. That's fun with God.

If I want to have fun let me engage in that which grows me into Him. That is real fun.

Toys and things that parents give their children should always be with careful thought. The enemy wants us to waste time. With God there is no time to waste on foolishness. Children are ready to learn if we are ready to teach. So get no mindless games or foolish things. But if there is a toy that you want to give your child, give your child that which challenges growth; development; dexterity; skills. Then you watch the child grow and watch the smile come on your face and that is not that of a comedian. That's the joy of watching the evolution of life.

In closing, the Honorable Elijah Muhammad said, "As the shortest distance between two points is a straight line." So it is in education. The child should know at six years old what its future is. What it wants to do with its life. If it engages in mindless foolishness and triviality it will not get in tune with itself to know at six where it wants to go.

The Honorable Elijah Muhammad said, "At eighteen years of age, we should have finished our doctorate degree, ready to go out into the world to practice that which we have learned in theory. So if you get a doctorate degree at eighteen, how much time do you have for mindless activity? None.

God does not waste time. Neither should we.

The first thing that I remember that my mother gave me to play with was a violin. She was not about mindless pursuits. When she brought me toys, it was like Chinese checkers, something that engaged me. Or, a puzzle, something that engaged my mind and then something to read.

I thank God Allah for my mother who never, ever, engaged me with mindless stupidity and called it fun.

Brother Jabril: Thank you Brother Minister.

INTERVIEW OF THE HONORABLE MINISTER LOUIS FARRAKHAN
BY JABRIL MUHAMMAD;
PHOENIX, ARIZONA
JULY 22, 2006

For this interview Minister Farrakhan was in high spirits. His response to my question was explosive. There is something that occurred in the course of his answer that forces me to make an extensive comment for the sake of the reader who may know little or nothing of his "more than a vision experience" that occurred on the 17th of September 1985. So first I'll leave his words as they are with an extensive comment at the end of this interview so that the reader may understand his reference with regard to his experience when he was taken up on the wheel.

Brother Jabril: Fun is what again?

Minister Farrakhan: Fun is developing the creative mind that is seen in the sperm that has intelligence to seek the egg. A light of itself in a cell that rotates and revolves in the darkness of the womb that develops that which allows it to cling to the walls of the uterus on finding a firm resting place for growth that the body will not be able to expel this strange new life within itself.

There's intelligence there that must be fed; it must be cultivated. So the child comes into the world, nobody teaches it to coo; to say thank you. Nobody teaches it to crawl. Nobody teaches it to pull up. Nobody from the outside teaches it to walk. All of this is within itself.

What is fun? Fun is us watching intelligence develop. Fun is feeding intelligence to create the creative mind that the child will be able to say like God, "Be" and it is. That's fun!

I imagine God had a lot of fun watching the working of His mind manifested in reality. There be a light and there was the sun and the earth and He separated the waters and the firmament and he said, "Ah, this is good." That means He was pleased with what He did. That's fun with God!

Pleasure comes from creativity and watching the creative thought manifested into reality. That is fun. And anything that is an impediment to that process is not fun it is destruction of the intelligence of the being that is from God.

I believe that when I was taken up on the wheel and I saw this scroll roll down (as if inside my head) with cursive writing on it and as I slightly lean forward to look at it, the Honorable Elijah Muhammad spoke and the cursive writing disappeared. But the writing that was on the outside was indicative of that which was inside of me.

You remember when we were going to New York to inaugurate Saviours' Day on October 7th—the birthday of the Honorable Elijah Muhammad at Madison Square Garden. You asked me to repeat the vision again. [As he began to rub his thigh he said:] It felt like when an area of your body is being prepared for a shot, with a needle. I don't know what it was, but I know something was put into me.

When circumstances come up, answers come out of me that fit the circumstance. I can't say I know where it comes from. But, then yes I do. It comes from Allah and the Christ. They have already put it in me. There is in me the foreword to a book that is sitting up inside me. It's the beginning of the book that I am to receive, if it pleases Allah.

The Honorable Elijah Muhammad said to me that, "I will never teach another minister like I taught Malcolm until I have thoroughly tried him. He said, "If I had not taught Malcolm so much of the prophecies he would not have been so formidable an opponent or an enemy." So he was letting me know I am not going to teach you anything like I taught him. He never took me off to the side to teach me anything of the meaning of this and the meaning of that and the meaning of the other.

I sat in the classroom with all his other students, feeding from his lips as they fed. Then he saw—but I'm sure before then—but he saw, at a certain point that Allah was feeding me.

When I had that experience on the wheel, evidently I had satisfied the requirement of trial to make me worthy to be taught exclusively by him directly. Because when I saw the scroll with its cursive writing, even as it was Jabril, when I had the vision about my "forms." On the back of it was cursive writing. When I went to read it the voice on the right said to the one on the left with a strong voice, "Turn this over. It's not time for him to see this yet." When I asked the Messenger about it later, he said, "Oh Brother, probably it's pertaining to something of your future that you will know at the appropriate time."

Now when I go up in this experience on the wheel, I see the cursive writing again. The scroll rolls down and I'm looking but I can't read. I know it's in English. I'm going forward to read it. Then he speaks and it disappears. What was that all about? He was writing on my heart. He was writing on my soul. It is written in the Holy Qur'an that Allah is He Who takes the soul of men by night.

What does He do with it? Well He does what He pleases with it. If He writes on it and returns it to you He puts something in you that will come out from you under circumstances that bring it out. That's why with the Prophet (peace be upon him) there's confusion as to whether it was twenty-three years, or in one night. Was it twenty-three years, or was it in one night? Because the Qur'an says, "The book was revealed on [the Minister says this in Arabic—Lailat al-Qadr] the night of power." Not a verse, or two, or three, but the book was revealed in the night of power.

What is the night of power? Is it a twelve-hour night? Why was the fez of the Honorable Elijah Muhammad black with star and crescent and stars? Was it the night of power over his forty-four years? Or was it one night that a man was carried to the wheel? And something was done to him and in him and will be done through him that would literally cause the world to wonder, where does this come from? Was the Minister experiencing a night of power? How can I answer questions that I never thought of before? But while you ask the question, the answer is forming.

Even when the enemy asks me questions the answer forms, not only for the question, but I'm given insight into the reason why they asked the question before the question is finished coming out of their mouths. Where does this insight come from, except that it comes from Allah.

Brother Jabril: Thank you sir.

In the interview that you may have just read, Minister Farrakhan mentions that "I was taken up on the wheel... ." I want the reader, who may not be acquainted with the more than extraordinary experience that Minister Farrakhan had on September 17, 1985, while in Mexico, to become acquainted, or at least introduced to it.

Especially, for this part of this book, I asked Mother Tynnetta Muhammad, wife of the Honorable Elijah Muhammad, to give me a statement responding to a question I asked for this book. Of course she had given this to us often, over the last twenty-one years.

I asked her: "Please tell me when and where Minister Farrakhan first spoke to you of his more than a vision, which he experienced back on September 17, 1985."

"On the morning of September 19, 1985, immediately within hours of Mexico City's worst earthquake, which occurred at 7:19 A.M. in the morning, the Honorable Minister Louis Farrakhan and his wife Mother Khadijah, left the hotel where they were staying in Tepoztlan and traveled to Cuernavaza to the home of Mother Tynnetta Muhammad. As they came up the steps into the kitchen area, Minister Farrakhan reached the top step and when turning into the kitchen, he suddenly recalled that he was taken up into the Mother Plane. As he entered the door, he began to share the experience that he had two days earlier on September the 17th.

"He appeared a little dazed as he sat down at the kitchen table. He spoke about climbing the sacred mountain called Tepozteco Mountain at the top of which is a small pyramid dedicated to the former king of Tepozteco. These histories of the Indigenous People of Mexico all ultimately lead to unveiling parts of the history of the great folk hero of all of Meso America known as Quetzalcoatle.

The Honorable Minister Louis Farrakhan on Tepozteco Mountain in Mexico, August 1984. This photo was taken by Jabril Muhammad approximately one year prior to Minister Farrakhan's "more than a vision experience."

The Minister began to describe that he was climbing the mountain, with a few companions, when suddenly a unidentified flying object (UFO) appeared upward at the side of the mountain where the pyramid is located. He then described that three metal legs appeared from the bottom of the wheel like plane. He said he heard a voice telling him " not them; just you". And that he was told to relax. He said a light came from the ship and he was carried up on a beam of light into it.

He said that when inside this spacecraft that he never saw the face of the pilot or heard words from him. It moved away from the side of the mountain at a terrific speed. He said that he knew he was being transported to the mother wheel and that the pilot knew he was frightened of seeing such a great ship (the Mother Wheel). The pilot maneuvered his craft in a way that he did not see the Mother wheel and back into it in a tunnel.

Minister Farrakhan went on to say that the pilot escorted him to a room. In the ceiling was a speaker. Then he said he heard the voice of the Honorable Elijah Muhammad clearly speaking to him.

He said that the Honorable Elijah Muhammad began speaking to him and as he did a scroll rolled down in front of him.

He said the Honorable Elijah Muhammad began to reveal to him information about a war being plan by the president and the Joint Chiefs of Staff. He said the Honorable Elijah Muhammad wanted him to deliver this message at a press conference in Washington D. C, and to reveal their plans and to tell them that he got this information from Elijah Muhammad on the Wheel He told him that he had one more thing to do and that when he did that one more thing he would be permitted to come to the Wheel and see him face to face.

"I remember that I experienced great excitement, enthusiasm and palpitation of my heart and I said to him, Brother Minister, do you realize what you're saying? And he responded by asking me what did I see in this experience. I was so overwhelmed in my response that I could only think, my God, he literally had met with my husband. He has begun to communicate with him in his journey much like Ezekiel being taken up on a Wheel within a Wheel.

"As I began to piece this experience together, in later days, I recalled the scriptures from both Bible and Holy Qur'an that mentioned Moses mystical experience in the mountain, where he left the children of Israel below and at that particular time, there were only a few elders or companions who were able to be present at the foot of the mountain. In the experience, the tablets were revealed and Moses was not able to see the face of his Lord, but was only able to see, according to the Bible, his hinder parts, his back parts, as he went by him. And again, in each instance of his highly mystical contact with God, there was a great earthquake."

Thank you Mother Tynnetta Muhammad.

A few days later Minister Farrakhan came to Phoenix, Arizona, with Mother Khadijah and Mother Tynnetta Muhammad. That's when he told me of his electrifying experience.

I have written a25,000 word commentary on both the veracity, significance and power of his experience on www.writtentestimony.com.

Here is an excerpt of it, which I hope gives the reader a better idea of the experience which Minister Farrakhan was referring to and which indicates something of his towering spirituality.

Ninety-six months after he determined that he would, by Allah's help, lift the name and rebuild the work of his teacher, and *fifty-five* months after he announced that the Honorable Elijah Muhammad was physically alive, Minister Farrakhan had a very unusual experience. In a little mountain village, in the country of Mexico, during the night of September 17, 1985, he had a vision like experience, that was far more than a vision. He didn't realize that he had this experience until two days later when an earthquake took place.

Then, on the 19th he told his experience to his wife, Mother Khadijah, and to Mother Tynnetta Muhammad.

His vision like experience took place between two significant speaking engagements. The first was in Los Angeles, California, where he spoke to about 19,000 people, on September 13, 1985. Up to that time, it was the largest live gathering ever to hear the teachings of the Honorable Elijah (Muhammad in the history of the Nation of Islam, west of the Mississippi River.

Minister Farrakhan left Los Angeles and went to Mexico, where he experienced his vision.

The next event was to take place in New York City, October 7th, where he would speak to an audience approaching 50,000 people inside two of the buildings of Madison Square Garden and on the outside.

Minister Farrakhan used Phoenix for most of the time he spent in preparation for his speech in Los Angeles. He now returned to Phoenix to prepare for his next speech which was to come in New York City.

Mother Tynnetta Muhammad and I were with Minister Farrakhan, on the first day of his preparation for his New York speech. This discussion took place at a lake called Lake Pleasant, in Phoenix. Then as we were gathering our books and papers to return to Scottsdale (a city adjoining Phoenix) Minster Farrakhan informed me of his vision like experience.

I was at the same time both immensely gratified and profoundly moved by it and struck by what seemed to me to be the casual manner in which he told me what he did. I regarded what he told me as momentous, wondrous or spectacular, or even more than that. He did not seem to realize the weight and significant of what he was telling me.

It was a few days later, while he and I were on a jet, our way on a route that would take us to New York City, that I asked him to please go over his vision like experience again with me.

I wanted him to put his experience on tape because I wanted his every word of his experience carefully preserved. To me what he experienced was something that would powerfully reverberate around the earth.

As he spoke into the tape recorder he began to break down. He said he was realizing that something very unusual had happened to him which he could not explain. Tears began to roll down his cheeks as he spoke to me. It was evident to me that he was experiencing more fully the reality of his vision like experience, even as he spoke. He said he felt as if he had been inoculated with something and now he was feeling the effects.

To me, his reaction accounted for the way he seemed to me when he first told me of his more than a vision. When he first told me of his experience, he did not seem to recognize the enormity of what he was telling me, which he had experienced.

I was to later learn that this was also the view of Mother Tynnetta Muhammad. She told me of her impression of him when he first told her of his vision in her home in Mexico.

Now, on the jet, he was going through a stage in which the fuller dimensions of his astounding experience were dawning upon his mind.

After we finally arrived in the hotel, in New York City, we received some very fascinating information from some of his family members, including his wife, Mother Khadijah. During that same night as we were flying from Phoenix to the east coast, which is a north-east direction, we learned that sixty "baby" planes were seen moving above the city of Tucson, Arizona. They were seen traveling on the same north-east course we had traveled.

Another factor making this event so striking was that there was a heavy cloud cover over the city. Therefore, there was no way that these flying objects could be mistaken for 60 moving stars, all going in the same direction. As we all know, clouds block one's view of the stars. A total cloud cover blocks out all of one's ability to see stars, if you are on the ground. These were not flying objects with which the authorities could cope. These were, according to trained observers, "UFOs," and they were obviously flying under the clouds.

These "UFOs" generated excitement. Later I learned that there were local (in Tucson) radio interviews and several news programs which were generated by this awesome event. However, it seemed that this startling display of intelligence and power was generally kept from the country as a whole.

We wondered if we were being escorted by the "baby" planes.

Remember, there was a lot of evil and loud talk—especially from the Jewish community, and from the very highest government officials of the United States—about Minister Farrakhan. I took these planes to be Allah's way of showing them that the Minister had plenty of backup (support.)

Later on in this writing I wrote:

Four years after Minister Farrakhan received his more than a vision experience; he fully came to see that he had yet to hold *that* press conference which the Honorable Elijah Muhammad wanted him to hold in Washington, D.C. This realization was stimulated by four events, which over a four month period, in 1989, crystallized for him his decision.

Two of these events were the death of Congressman Mickey Leland (of Texas) and the other involved the traumatic events at Tiananmen Square in China.

What was referred to in America's press, as the Beijing Massacre at Tiananmen Square, began on June 4, 1989.

Representative Mickey Leland died in an airplane crash, in Gambela, Ethiopia, on August 7, 1989.

Minister Farrakhan was in Phoenix, in 1989, when these two events occurred. I noticed that both of these events seemed to have momentarily aged him as he wrestled with their meanings. He told me he knew both had something to do with him. He was in a strained state of mind as he pondered the significance of these events. The latter event, he said, had more to do with our people—especially Black youth—and yet in some way with him. But he did not know how.

After returning to Chicago, a phone call from Minister Don Muhammad of Boston, would take him further into a growing, or heightened awareness that something was going on that was big, in the biggest sense of that word. Minister Don Muhammad informed him of a gang problem in which they sought his help. He was told that the gang members were being pressured to give up their weapons. They said they would, but only if Minister Farrakhan would tell them to do so. His response was that he had not ordered them to pick them up in the first place. However, he later gave them wise and righteous advice, based on the teachings of the Honorable Elijah Muhammad, whose policies are known the world over.

Not long after he hung up the phone he was struck by what it all meant.

Out of Minister Farrakhan's understanding of the significance of these events, he made a series of extraordinary speeches. They were titled *Stop The Killing*. Among the most powerful of these talks he would make was a stupendous one which enlightened and warned Black youth as to what the slave-master's children were up to and were planning against them and us.

If you get and listen to those speeches you will see why I'm describing them as I am. One of them was delivered in Chicago, at Mosque Maryam. For more about this particular speech, see the Bibliography at the end of this book.

Lastly in September, came the fourth event, which would lead to a most profound event, fulfilling a major part of what he was ordered to do, by the Honorable Elijah Muhammad, in his vision like experience.

A Sister telephoned him to congratulate him on his anniversary. He thought her congratulations referred to the 35th anniversary of his marriage to his wife, Mother Khadijah, which was earlier that month on September the 12th. In the course of the conversation he came to see that she had the anniversary of his vision like experience in mind. The call caused him to reflect over that experience and the course of events since that time.

It then crystallized!

Minister Farrakhan decided to hold a press conference in the next month; on the day following the Saviours' Day conference in October (1989). He returned to Phoenix. Part of his preparation for this momentous event involved the preparation of his press statement. Minister Farrakhan decided to dictate the entire text, in my home, on the Friday prior to the Tuesday when he would deliver it at the press conference. Sister Marguerite X McCray did the typing.

About an hour after the text was typed and proofed he and I headed for the airport to catch a plane for the East Coast. We went to New York City.

On the next afternoon, as we neared the capital, through a circuitous route, these words from his vision like experience came forcibly to my mind: "With great speed it brought me back to earth and dropped me off near Washington where I then proceeded into this city to make the Announcement." I then thought back to the trip we had made a little better than three years earlier the day before he made his statement to the press on February 4, 1986. We had also landed at that time just outside of the capital due to fog, as I explained earlier. I thought to myself, "That experience pointed to this one. This Saviours' Day is a cover for this press conference."

I voiced this thought to Minister Farrakhan.

The fact was that we were about to go to a place (arranged for by Minister Akbar Muhammad) "nearby or close to Washington, D.C." We were about to "land," so to speak, just as he did in his vision like experience," near Washington." It was quite a feeling.

I had a copy of the text of the statement that he dictated to Sister Marguerite just the day before. I was with him, continuously, from that time until he delivered it to the public; before the media on that Tuesday. The point of this is that I am a witness to the fact that he did not change one word of the text he dictated, from the previous Friday, when he dictated it, to the following Tuesday when he delivered it.

This is related to the profound correspondence between something he dictated in his statement for the press and an event which was a definite confirmation of the announcement that he had made to the press. It involved what many call "UFOs."

Minister Farrakhan did not know how God would confirm his statement, in the ordinary way we obtain information. As we'll see in a moment, from his prepared statement to the press, Minister Farrakhan declared:

"Before you will be able to establish your mockery of me (if that is what you wish to do) for what was revealed to me in the

Wheel, you will see these wheels... ."

The next day a "little" wheel appeared over the white house. It was repeatedly highlighted on T.V. for three straight days. It shook up a lot of people. It was obviously and clearly a so-called "UFO" or one of the baby planes of which the Honorable Elijah Muhammad taught us.

Now, here is the full text of Minister Farrakhan's statement to and through the press, to America and the world.

THE ANNOUNCEMENT
Text of press conference delivered on October 24, 1989 at the J.W. Marriott Hotel in Washington, D.C. by The Honorable Louis Farrakhan

Ladies and Gentlemen of the Press, Brothers and Sisters, we are honored by your presence here this morning.

I am a man who has great respect for the Press and the electronic media and I also have respect for myself, and my mission. As you know, I do not readily submit to interviews, nor am I frequently seen on the television; for I am not before you of myself, nor do I do what I do to be seen of men.

Therefore, I have never tried to abuse, or misuse the Press to seek advantage for myself, or the Nation of Islam. So, in calling this press conference, I am calling you because of the serious nature of the Announcement that I am about to make; an Announcement on which hangs the future of this nation, its leaders and the people of America.

It is written in the book of Ezekiel,

"When I say unto the wicked, You shall surely die; and you give him not warning, nor speak to warn the wicked from his wicked way, to save his life; the same wicked man shall die in his iniquity; but his blood will I require at your hand.

"Yet if you warn the wicked, and he turn not from his wickedness, nor from his wicked way, he shall die in his iniquity; but you have delivered your soul."

It is in this spirit that I make this announcement.

In a tiny town in Mexico, called Tepotzlan, there is a mountain on the top of which is the ruins of a temple dedicated to Quetzacoatl—the Christ- figure of Central and South America—a mountain which I have climbed several times. However, on the night of September l7, 1985, I was carried up on that mountain, in a vision, with a few friends of mine. As we reached the top of the mountain, a Wheel, or what you call an unidentified flying object (UFO), appeared at the side of the mountain and called to me to come up into the Wheel. Three metal legs appeared from the Wheel, giving me the impression that it was going to land, but it never came over the mountain.

Being somewhat afraid, I called to the members of my party to come with me, but a voice came from the Wheel saying, "Not them; just you." I was told to relax and a beam of light came from the Wheel and I was carried up on this beam of light into the Wheel.

I sat next to the pilot, however, I could not see him. I could only feel his presence. As the Wheel lifted off from the side of the mountain, moving at a terrific speed, I knew I was being transported to the Mother Wheel, which is a human-built planet, a half-mile by a half-mile that the Honorable Elijah Muhammad had taught us of for nearly 60 years.

The pilot, knowing that I was fearful of seeing this great, mechanical object in the sky, maneuvered his craft in such a way that I would not see the Mother Wheel (Plane) and then backed quickly into it and docked in a tunnel. I was escorted by the pilot to a door and admitted into a room.

I shall not bother you with a description of the room, but suffice it to say that at the center of the ceiling was a speaker and through this speaker I heard the voice of the Honorable Elijah Muhammad speaking to me as clearly as you are hearing my voice this morning.

He spoke in short cryptic sentences and as he spoke a scroll full of cursive writing rolled down in front of my eyes, but it was a projection of what was being written in my mind. As I attempted to read the cursive writing, which was in English, the scroll disappeared and the Honorable Elijah Muhammad began to speak to me.

He said, **"President Reagan has met with the Joint Chiefs**

of Staff to plan a war. I want you to hold a press conference in Washington, D. C., and announce their plan and say to the world that you got the information from me, Elijah Muhammad, on the Wheel."

He said to me that he would not permit me to see him at that time. However, he said that I had one more thing to do and when that one more thing was done that I could come again to the Wheel and I would be permitted to see him face to face.

He then dismissed me. I entered the small wheel and the pilot whom I still could not see, moved the craft out of the tunnel and took it up to a terrific height and maneuvered his craft that I might look down upon the Mother Wheel. I saw a city in the sky.

With great speed it brought me back to earth and dropped me off near Washington where I then proceeded into this city to make The Announcement.

After I awakened from the vision, it seemed to vanish from my mind. However, on the morning of September 19, 1985, a great earthquake struck Mexico City and it was felt in the little town where I was staying. That earthquake brought the vision forcibly to my mind and I spoke it, later that morning for the first time to my wife, Khadijah Farrakhan, and Sister Tynnetta Muhammad, in the city of Cuernavaca.

The full transcript of Minister Farrakhan's 1989 Press Conference, he held in Washington, DC, and more references to this powerful experience are available online at www.noi.org/statements/transcript_891024.htm.

Interview of the Honorable Minister Louis Farrakhan
by Jabril Muhammad
Phoenix, Arizona
July 15, 2006

I remember that this day Minister Farrakhan got out of his car stepping in a I might call it, a "so so manner." He greeted me with a lovely smile saw the doctor and then entered my living room for me to ask him a question.

One of my primary purposes for what I was about to ask him was to get a response from him that I could turn into the increase of attention on an sales of a vitally important book that he had written titled, A Torchlight For America.

I deliberately put a copy of his book on my coffee table.

Brother Jabril: Brother Minister, about thirteen years ago, you wrote and published *A Torchlight for America.* Why did you write it?

Minister Farrakhan: In studying the Honorable Elijah Muhammad, there were times when his language was very condemning of the government of the United States, the white people of America and the world, for their evils done and planned to do against the rise of Black people universally. Then there were times when the Honorable Elijah Muhammad spoke a gentle word to Pharaoh, as the Qur'an teaches, that perhaps he would mind.

Thirteen years ago, when I began to see deeper into the irrelevance that the government of the United States saw in Black people, and their desire to get rid of us—which they deemed as a useless piece of property, I wrote *A Torchlight for America* to try to stay their hand from carrying out a plan of mass destruction of our people by showing them that among us is a light; is a guide for them that could save America from the destruction that Allah and the angels had planned for this nation.

I also sought to show them that among these so-called useless Black people were a group that God had raised as a bearer of warning and good news. Therefore, *A Torchlight for America* was written with that thought in mind. As Allah did say to Moses, you know, in other words, "Don't be so hard on Pharaoh just yet. Speak a gentle word to him, perhaps he may mind."

A Torchlight for America is a gentle word that offers solutions to the many, many problems that America is facing, that Black people are facing and in some cases, that the world is facing, so that he, Pharaoh—the government of America—might say, "Well wait a minute. There is utility in this people and perhaps we'll put this plan of destruction for them on hold." And that's my motive.

Brother Jabril: Thank you.

One of the ideas that you placed in the book was a possible solution to a very vexing problem, plaguing America, was with Black prisoners, which is a tremendous problem. Would you touch that please?

Minister Farrakhan: Recognizing that prisoners in many cases are useless to a society. Behind bars they are ill-treated and they ill-treat themselves and one another out of their utter frustration with their inability to cope with the problems that life brings to us in our evolutionary development. I recognized that this great nation was started by the release of prisoners from Europe, England, Australia—another sovereign nation and power in the world—was started by the release of prisoners; New Zealand too.

Well since we are filling the jails and the prisons, yet God has a purpose for us, I ask why not let the prisoners do their time doing something constructive? I would reach out to Africa for land that is fertile and minerally rich, with an outlet to the sea. I would ask if Africa would set aside territory and allow these prisoners to work off their time, building a new reality for Black people, supported by the funds that are given to support State and Federal penitentiaries.

I also wanted before that happened, to allow us the freedom to go in the prisons to teach our people freely and begin the process of civilizing them because Africa would be afraid to accept a criminal population from the United States.

If we were given three years to work, with the help of the government, to civilize our young men and women, then they can be released to work in Africa to build a new reality on that continent for Black people. I thought that what Abraham Lincoln had desired in the Lincoln-Douglas debate, that our sojourn in America could be a blessing for Africa. Lincoln suggested that separation of the races was a solution to the problem. He mentioned that we could be repatriated to Africa, or to some country in Central America, and with help from the U.S. government, we could build a new reality.

Of course, having robbed Black people of the knowledge of self and the love of self and having inspired in them a dislike for their roots in Africa, the more learned of our people rejected such a suggestion by Abraham Lincoln. So here we are one hundred and fifty years later, or more, with the same racial problems. Now we have over two million in jail, sixty-five percent of them, or more are Black; young people that are being wasted away.

I thought that this would bring relief to the prison population. It would bring relief to the prisoners who are sitting in prison, having time to think about themselves, their families and their future. I thought that if they felt there was a degree of hope for them, to create a new reality for their people, given the history of how prisoners were used to build the new world, their desire to want to build a new world reality for themselves and their people would give them hope and inspire them to want to study and do all the things that they should do, or could do, in those three years to develop themselves into a group of people that Africa would be willing to welcome home.

Brother Jabril: Brother Minister, one of the most vexing problems in America, and in varying degrees throughout the earth, especially in this country, is the problem of education. What were among the ideas that you presented in this book for more educators and government to ponder in order to alleviate this vexing problem?

Minister Farrakhan: Education is an evolutionary process. Since no discipline and the scholarship of that discipline, is absolute, there is much room for growth and improvement in every field of human endeavor; mathematics, biology, chemistry, science, technology, geopolitics. Everything is evolving. But the educational system is not. It is stagnant. As a result of stagnation, and people feeling that a Ph.d degree has ended their search for higher knowledge, or understanding, of their discipline, then the education becomes a tool for enslaving the mind, rather than freeing the mind.

We saw from the teachings of the Honorable Elijah Muhammad that this system of education has run its course. As the Honorable Elijah Muhammad taught us, education is the torchlight for civilization. If that torchlight is going out and you find the educational system in revolt against itself, then the civilization spawned by that educational process is on its way out as well.

Minister Farrakhan personalizes a copy of his book, *A Torchlight for America*, circa 1993.

The American people and Black people in particular, need a new educational experience. That new educational experience must start with the most priceless and precious of all knowledge, which is the knowledge of self and the knowledge of God.

When you deny God in the educational process, you deny the respect and honor that is due to the real Head Master or Chancellor of all education. So this disrespect of the Creator that is found in the public school education has led now to a break down in respect for teachers; in respect for parents; in respect for law and order in this society. So now, the seeds sown by an ineffective educational system are growing now into a destructive weed that is choking the life of the civilization and the mental desire of human beings to know more and more and more and more and more.

We find the children fascinated by the growth of technology. Fascinated, and fascinating to their parents in how quickly they grasp the technology; how quickly they move in the games that they're playing. Then they go to school and they find the slowness of the pace of learning is such that they're active minds—created by information and technological age--becomes now destructive to the order in the classroom.

It is not that the students are bad. It's that the teaching; the methodology, the philosophy under girding it, have run its course. It's time for something new and better. This is why the drop-out rate is terrific. You can't get children to stay in an environment where they are not challenged. Little children stay in front of the computer with games for hours and hours. They bother nobody. They're not involved in mischief. They're at their game, just playing away.

Well if education were as attractive as technology is, in making computers and games for children, then the children would love school as we did, when we were young. But time has passed and the educational system must now give way to something new and better. I believe this is why Christ comes at the end of this system of things to declare to the world, "Behold I make all things new." It is this scrambling of those who were the architects of the old system to try to make something new that doesn't fit the requirements of the time that causes now a total break down.

In *A Torchlight for America*, we talked about a new educational system.

In closing on this point, the Honorable Elijah Muhammad said to me, "As in geometry, the shortest distance between two points is a straight line. So, it is in education." He said, "Why don't you start the course where you intend to finish. You'll be surprised how quickly the children are able to grasp the end of the course.

And you are wasting valuable time leading up to something that they could grasp if you had the mind to teach." He said that, "At six years old, we should know what we want to do with our life."

There's no time for foolishness, when you look at life and the requirement and purpose of life." So he said looking at Yakub, the father of this world, "That he finished all the schools of his day at eighteen years of age." So the Honorable Elijah Muhammad said, "The children should be graduating with a Ph.D. degree at 18 years of age." Which means waiting until a child is six to go to school is absolutely wasting the most precious years of a child's life; and filling those six years with foolishness and untruths and cartoons that make animals speak and whatnot.

The Honorable Elijah Muhammad said, "You should deal with truth from the very day that the child can begin to think and learn; you deal with truth, not lies. Bears don't speak. Pigs don't speak. Tigers don't speak. Bunny rabbits don't speak. So let the children see humans doing what humans do. Don't confuse them.

Well a new educational system is what is required and unfortunately this world will not offer it. But Allah and His Christ is offering it, and will offer it continuously until the old dies and the new takes precedent over the old.

Brother Jabril: Brother Minister, has this book had—to any degree, any—a positive response from anyone, anywhere to the ideas you offered on a better social welfare system, in this book?

Minister Farrakhan: I'm sorry. Not that I know of. I don't think the book is studied. I don't think it's known. There's resistance to that which challenges us to think outside of the proverbial box that western education puts our minds in. There is intellectual cowardice that we want to say and do the thing that is safe; that will not provoke our former slave-masters and their children.

In that regard, we're not interested. But there are minds today that are thinking beyond because they know that our survival depends on thinking beyond what our former slave-masters and their children have put before us. But even they are not familiar with *A Torchlight for America.*

Brother Jabril: By the help of Allah, we are going to do something that will help spread it as fast as we can, in the short time we have left.

In the back of this book—in the last chapter—you have a very interesting and concise picture of the significance of the seal of the United States. Why did you put that in the book?

Minister Farrakhan: I can't remember.

[I gave it to him, turned to the last chapter. He then read it. It's only six pages. He smiled and said:]

Sometimes the Honorable Elijah Muhammad would be sitting in his dinning room listening to a tape of himself and he would get carried away and start applauding. While we were watching it was so intriguing to me because he was applauding as though he was not listening to himself. But he was listening to the intervention of God in that which he was saying to us.

As I was reading the last chapter of this book, you know, it's hard for me to say that I wrote such words. I'm applauding the intervention of God and His Christ in the words that He blessed me to put in black and white for the world to see my mind; my heart; my spirit; my soul.

If one would study, *A Torchlight for America* although I wrote it for America highlighting the diseases of a great nation, subliminally I wrote it for the Nation of Islam and the diseases that could, would and have affected us as a people. Sometimes when we see America, we say, "Oh that's for them." We miss the point. It was written with a double meaning; for America *and* for us.

The Honorable Elijah Muhammad told us *when* we study the history of Israel, in the scriptures, under that, we're also studying about ourselves. And so we should pay attention to what happened to Israel; her many rebellions; her many chastisements and yet the God was merciful to her. Well that's good for us to study and see and know that God is no respecter of persons—that He will punish; chastise us because He loves us. And if that is the only way to get us to think and act properly, then the chastisement is over due, but it is on its way.

Have we really read it to understand what the Minister was saying to America openly *and* to the nation subliminally? If you did understand it, or do understand it, why then is there seemingly no desire to push a book that so represents not just the thinking of the Minister but the heart; mind; soul and spirit of the Minister.

You can't read these penetrating words and see him as the world now sees him. This is not autobiographical. This is the Minister elaborating on that which he has learned from his teacher, the Honorable Elijah Muhammad. If the student has put such wisdom in a book for Pharaoh, *as well as for us*, it would seem to me that such a book should be in every Muslim home *and* we should want it in the home of every Black person who may want to understand more about Louis Farrakhan and the Nation of Islam.

Then we discussed the next edition with a new cover on it that brings out my idea better. A part of what he said was: "A Torchlight for America, *white and Black, you know. You could have the two Americas, you know; one with the Black, Brown, the Native, the non-white and then white America.*"

When you asked me about the seal, the true nature of this nation is found in the seal. And the six nations, out of which America was peopled, represent what the Honorable Elijah Muhammad said, "What is the meaning of American?"

In the old dictionaries it was those of European extraction, not the aboriginal people of the earth. In the mind of those who rule America they have never changed from the original perception and conception of the founding fathers. To this very moment, they are of the same mind. This is why a genocidal approach now is being taken to the Blacks and soon the Brown. The Native Americans are already a decimated group.

People of color will—according to their view—never rule in this land. This is also why, even though, we have the right to vote legally, all kinds of machinations are put in place to rob us of the power of the vote. They seek to and do corrupt our leaders, and trap them through entrapment schemes orchestrated by the government to destroy in us even the desire to vote for our own people.

All of these evil acts are a part of that mind-set that is reflected in the seal of the United States of America that is in the ruling class: the Rockefellers, the DuPont's. All of that group of minds that represents the ruling class of this nation—they have not changed. They will not change. Their idea is the destruction of the mass, if the mass looks like it will oppose what is represented in that seal and in the thinking of the founding fathers of this nation.

This is why Paul said, "We war not against flesh and blood, but against principalities and powers and the rulers of the darkness of this world and spiritual wickedness in high places."

It's a myth that America is pluralistic. It's a myth that America is for all. That is food for the sick desire of others to want to be American. But at the top they know what America is. It's what they envisioned America to be and why our presence and the multiplication of our seed is threatening and why every scientific method of destruction of us is now put into force that if we do not find a way to separate from this people, within the next ten years, there may not be Black people in America.

INTERVIEW OF THE HONORABLE MINISTER LOUIS FARRAKHAN
BY JABRIL MUHAMMAD
PHOENIX, ARIZONA
JULY 15, 2006

As the reader may recall I asked him, in the previous interview, about what he had written in the last chapter of his book on the United States seal. He honestly responded that he had forgotten. He had read the six pages during the previous interview. So I decided to ask him a question related to what he wrote.

That day was his morning session with the doctor. That morning he was in excellent spirit. But as you notice his answers are always uplifting and extraordinarily informative. To me, his answers emanate from the same spirit.

Brother Jabril: Brother Minister, earlier I asked you what was the purpose of the point that you made in the last chapter of the book, *A Torchlight for America*, on the seal; the purpose of mentioning what you did at the very end of the book?

Minister Farrakhan: Well the seal is a very important symbol of the United States of America. There was an awful lot of thought that went into the formation of that symbol by some of the founding fathers and some of those who were the signatories on the Declaration of Independence. So these men knew what they were seeing. They were God-fearing men but their God-fearing mentality did not necessarily include what was in the best interest of the Native Americans or the Blacks that were here as slaves.

They wanted to give to their posterity in that seal and that symbol that America was formed for white people, by white people, for the benefit of white people, not necessarily for any of the darker people of the world. I know that they did not foresee that America would become a melting pot. I know that they did not foresee that in the year 2006 that the demographers would say that, "By the year 2050 America would be a Brown country rather than all white country."

This means then, that those who carry the vision of the founding fathers would either have to alter the original concept of the founding fathers to make it inclusive of all of those that had come to America to become citizens of America, nominally, but not in fact.

Now the rulers of this country—the real rulers—would have to decide whether America is going to be pluralistic, inclusive of all those that make up the country, or would they pursue the vision of the founding fathers and become genocidal and destructive to the darker people of the this nation.

It appears as though the rulers have opted for the destruction of the darker people, particularly, the descendents of slaves. So the appropriate vision that went into the seal with Pharaoh with a sword in his hand. Why a sword? Because Pharaoh in the Red Sea was pursuing the children of Israel with the intent to kill them all in spite of all that God had shown him through the nine or ten plagues that Egypt had suffered. But his recalcitrance, his rebellion was so intense that he decided that he would not let the children of Israel go, but that he would punish them with death.

At the same time there's a chariot overhead that wasn't present during the time of Ezekiel's vision. That was not present at the time of the founding fathers. But they saw this wheel-like object in the sky and a beam of light coming out of it on the face of Moses which it signified to me that what was on the wheel had empowered Moses to part the waters for the children of Israel to go through and he also had the same power then, to drown Pharaoh and his army.

In that seal is a significant warning to the present government and rulers—the ruling powers—of America and the ruling powers of the present world. That should they continue with the sword against the people of God, then the destructive power that is above their head will be brought to bear on them. And as Pharaoh lost both his life; his army and the power of a great nation, so would America lose her life; her power and her authority to rule. All of that is in the seal.

I put it in the last chapter of *A Torchlight for America* to say what the founding fathers saw and what they put in the seal that they may not have fully understood its implications, but God permitted such to be placed there for us to read the seal back to them and give them two signs that they could choose—life or death. They could choose to obey God and let the new children of Israel—the Black people of America—go to become a great nation under the guidance of God. And save themselves and their nation in the process, or they could continue with the sword. But the power that is above them will destroy them completely for carrying that thought into practice

Brother Jabril: Does that argument right now in Congress revolving around civil rights indicate to you that really Black people are not citizens?

Minister Farrakhan: Yes. I had a conversation with my Chief of Protocol, Sister Claudette Maria Muhammad, who had just spoken with the Sister that I call the Mother of the *Million Man*

March and the *Million Family* March, Doctor Dorothy Height. She's in her nineties. But she said, according to Sister Claudette, that she had to go and lay down because she was in the chamber listening to the debate. She was so aggrieved over the arguments that were coming up from some of the Congresspersons against the continuation of the voting rights bill.

Well, the House of Representatives passed it with thirty-three rejections or nays the majority of course, with it to extend it for twenty-five more years, but it has to go to the Senate where the argument will become much more intense. It does say that since no other people in this country needed a voting rights bill, but as a citizen the right is guaranteed and protected.

But as Black people, we had to have something special before the Congress to guarantee us the right to vote and to protect that right once given, giving the Federal government oversight over the states in how they acted with respect to Black people's right to vote. That says so much. It says that we are not really citizens. The argument says that they don't want this for us. It is another sign of Pharaoh letting us go.

I remember the Honorable Elijah Muhammad saying to me once: There is a scripture in the Bible, I don't exactly know where it is, that the sea will give up its dead. The Honorable Elijah Muhammad said, "Whenever the sea takes a body down it then brings that body at some point to the surface, where those who are the family of such deceased can claim the body. If there is no claim then the sea destroys that body."

America now is giving us up on the surface and God is now claiming us, but the sea is now raging in anger over the fact that God has come to claim this that this sea has killed. Now the sea wants to destroy even the evidence of its killing of this corpse. So now God is at war with the ruling powers of America and this is why the scriptures says, "Shall the prey be taken from the mighty and the lawful captive delivered."

So, we are now a lawful captive, but a prey in the hands of our tormentors. Now God is after us and the sea has brought us to the surface but does not want to give us up. It is interested in the destruction of this that it has already killed.

Now, God wants the body. He can revive it. He can give it life. He can restore it to its original position and condition. So He's fighting the sea. The sea here represents the powers that rule America and their people who are in agreement with those powers that the Blacks, the Native Americans must be destroyed.

Brother Jabril: So this more than includes the answer. It engulfs the truth that you're speaking. It engulfs many other little truths. I shouldn't say little at all—big fields in the course of bigness, that includes what the Messenger wrote in 1961 in reaction to the charge about us being not American and he explained it thoroughly. So in the course of your answer just now you covered that...

Minister Farrakhan: Well we can go right back to what he said because what he said is as appropriate and true today as it was when he wrote it forty-five years ago, that we are the aboriginal un-Americans. And we have to come to that understanding that we can never be Americans. And even though the government of the United States lost by one vote in the Senate, a bill to make it a constitutional thing that no one should burn or abuse the American flag.

The Honorable Elijah Muhammad taught us well. And not one of his followers would ever burn or abuse the American flag because we see it as a symbol of a free and independent people and nation, which we hope one day to become. And we also know the significance of that flag with its six white stripes and seven red stripes and fifty stars in a sea of blue.

The scientist who made such flag for this people understood very well its meaning. And it is not an accident that such flag is before the world today and is fulfilling to the letter the meaning of such flag. So we look at the flag. We understand its meaning and we respect it as the flag of an independent people.

We hope one day to be able to fly the flag that Master Fard Muhammad gave us: the sun; the moon and the star, as a symbol of the freedom, justice, equality and universal nature of the government that Master Fard Muhammad and His Christ, the Messiah, are bringing in—a government that truly is representative of the sun and its meaning; the moon and its meaning; the star and its meaning and the laws that govern the three.

The American flag literally describes its meaning perfectly; its actions perfectly, and therefore, we have no quarrel with that flag. We see it as the symbol of white supremacy.

Interview of the Honorable Minister Louis Farrakhan
by Jabril Muhammad;
Phoenix, Arizona,
June 26, 2006

Brother Jabril: Brother Minister, Why does Allah show mercy on Yakub's made man; even at the end of his time and past that time?

Minister Farrakhan: I would like to see them save themselves if they could, you know. I did not have the bitter experience as some of our people but I felt their horrific pain. But I have grown to see that in all of the evil that they inflicted upon us, they were doing what God permitted and allowed them to be made to do. So how do you blame the clay?

Then you must understand what was in the mind of the potter. We must grow to see that and this that is going on now in the world was a drama going on inside of God and inside of the original people that has given us trouble for sixty-six trillion or more years.

The service that Yakub did for God and for us was to discover in us the germ that was a problem to us even though the germ for the most part, was under control. There were times that it was out of control and it wreaked havoc on the original man and even among the Scientists—the gods.

For Yakub to take that, that was going on; that struggle that was going on within ourselves, and give it form and expression, so that we could see in global terms what was happening to us as a nation for trillions of years was a great service to God and a great service to humanity.

If it were not for what God permitted Yakub to do, and what

white folk did following the wisdom of their God and Maker, we would not have come to a more perfected knowledge of self and of God, which then brings Master Fard Muhammad into existence to heal the internal and/or eternal struggle, by getting rid of such germ, and setting into motion a brand new order for Himself as well as for His creation.

How then, even though we've suffered such terrible evil from such people, how we deny them the access to mercy when they did such a great service for us and for God in the evil that they did to us that we are now beating them in doing to self, all over the world. We have proved that we are not better than the wicked one. We have become them. This is what forced Master Fard Muhammad to use those six great words: "Accept your own and be yourself."

Well, whose self have we been being? We have been the manifestation of the evil of ourselves. What would cause Black men to rape on the scale that they are raping in Darfur and kill on the scale that they're killing in Darfur, in the Congo, in Somalia, and in other places; cutting off the limbs of children? This horror was (and is being) done by Yakub's grafted man. This was, (and is being) done, by the original man, acting on the worst of himself.

Then you look inside America and you see who is killing whom today. It is we who are now the drive-by-shooter; the gang bangers; the rapers; the robbers; with so much hatred of self even after hearing the word of God containing His will for us, as well as for others.

I am not of the mind and spirit to destroy them, except that they reject the mercy of God and then seek to destroy that mercy. Then if you, out of the evil of your father, seek to destroy what God has raised as a mercy for you, then you have sentenced yourself and your people to that punishment of death and total annihilation.

This is the argument that Jesus had with the Jews, when they say that, "God is our father." He says, "Wait a minute. If God were your father you would love me for I proceeded forth from God. No now you seek to kill me; a man that has told you the truth."

In a parenthetical sense my teacher and I have offered you the absolute mercy of Him Who is the Most Merciful of those who show mercy. So now he not only sought to kill that Messenger but he seeks to kill the Minister of the Messenger because of his great anger at being revealed. He's earning the destruction of the Merciful God Who raised the Messenger and the Minister.

Brother Jabril: This reminds me of what you said when you were nineteen years old, to a Brother who came to you, with a powerful statement that showed your future.

Minister Farrakhan: Rodney Smith, my dear—dear childhood friend. He was the first one from Boston that I know who became a Muslim. I admired him as a Brother. He was a little older than I. He was more my Brother's age than mine.

He knew that I was hard on the white man for his evils done to our people. But we were on the same street Mass Avenue. We were walking and he said, "Gene—" He had heard these teachings from Brother Malcolm and he told me, "Man, you know, the white man he's the devil."

I didn't readily fit that name to white people. I knew of their evil. But I said to him, "Well if I go home and my wife is in bed with another man and I pick up a gun and murder my wife and that man, my wife has committed adultery; the man may have committed adultery, or fornication and then I commit murder. Where is the devil in that scenario?" He could not answer me. So that kept me from just going to the Temple out of my dislike for what white people had done to us. I would not yet give them credit for all of the evil that is going on in the world.

I could not agree with him fully. I knew this man's evil, yet I was not at that time prepared to give him credit for all of the evil that was being practiced in the world.

Even at another time, Yakub taught the devils to do this devilishment, which is lying; stealing and how to master the original man. Then I looked at my children. If, they went in the cookie jar and took cookies without permission and mother or I would ask them, "Who took the cookies?" Then they would start lying.
Well I knew Yakub wasn't in the room. Yakub did not teach my

children to lie. The lie came out of a natural fear of a consequence of having done something wrong. So to avoid punishment the lie came. So there is a natural part to lying but what Yakub was guilty of was lying about God; telling a lie on God—"Those who forged a lie against Allah." It is that kind of lie that has destroyed the vital connection of man to God.

These little lies that people tell to escape punishment for failing to carry out a duty. I know. I've done it myself. "Did you do such and such?" Oh yes. I did that." But I know that I didn't do it. But why did I lie? Because the embarrassment of having had a duty and not performing that duty. So was Yakub in that?

These are the things that God allowed me to see that are not holes in the teaching, but it allows you to see that there is a deeper; broader; wider; taller aspect to the word then just fastening on that one thing and then going crazy with it. So when the Honorable Elijah Muhammad told me that, "I don't want you to use the language devil. Use the word enemy. Use the word the slave-masters children; Satan. After thinking on it, "Why Dear Apostle would you take me away from language that you so eloquently and brilliantly brought to us and defended. But now you don't wish for your student to use such language, but to use the word Satan?"

I'm not the most brilliant or fastest person to understand. I just said, "Yes Sir. Yes Sir, Dear Apostle." But over time you think on the things that your master and your teacher have taught you to try to understand the why of it. In that is where your growth in understanding comes.

In 1960, he sent me over to the West Side to open up for him. I was just blasting the Caucasian, you know. The Honorable Elijah Muhammad came in. I sat down. He spoke. I don't even remember what the lecture was about. But when we got in the car and he was driving me to his house, he said, "Brother, do you know of any man in whom there is no good at all? I said, "No Sir, Dear Apostle." We had come to a stop light and there was an old white man walking across the street and he said, "Well there he is Brother."

Then I looked at this old man who didn't look like he could harm, in the colloquial sense, a fly. He looked absolutely innocuous, harmless. But the Honorable Elijah Muhammad pointed him out and said, "There is no good in him at all." Then he let that sink in. Then he said to me, "Brother, you can't fathom the depth of Satan." He didn't use the word devil. "You can't phantom the depth of Satan." He never said another word.

Well when I had time to think on his words, anything that you can't fathom the depth of, you're not qualified to deal with. One of the mistakes that Brother Malcolm made and others who are half-learned, is that we think we can handle Yakub's made devil who is a god and the ruler of his own world.

In thinking that, you set yourself up for failure. Because if this man is wise enough to deceive the holy wise Scientists of Islam, then what would make us think that we could handle such a man whom it took God to come to reveal and for God to prepare a man and give him the necessary power to handle such a creature, in the person of the Honorable Elijah Muhammad

Then the second part of that was when he told me, "Don't use the term devil," then I realized he was bringing me face to face then with Satan. That I would at a certain point, have to confront Satan and reveal Satan, and go to war with Satan. But he would have shown me how unqualified I was to deal with Satan. So as I'm dealing with Satan—I'm going back to your last question—I'd be hiding myself in the bosom of Him Who alone can handle Satan so that I would never get out my place.

I remember in New York I was preaching one day and I took on the Pope. He told me, he said, "Brother you leave him alone. You leave him to me." You stay, you know, on ground that you can handle. This is a little much for you.

Then later, of course, I understood that the reason he wanted to go after Satan is because Satan is the factory that produces devils. If you can reveal Satan, you give all the little devils that were made by Satan, a chance to escape the fate of Satan. But that's the final war. That's like *Raiders of the Lost Ark*—just when you think you're getting your hand on the thing you're after then this big awful thing comes out that you got to fight.

So Jabril, you know, that's your Brother's heart in a sense for the Caucasian.

The last part of that was this: Master Fard Muhammad the Great Mahdi, the Savior of the Honorable Elijah Muhammad, and our Savior, had a white mother--there was a saying – I don't know whether I heard the Messenger say it, but I heard that he said that "One day Master Fard Muhammad's mother was going to host a banquet and invite his servants to this banquet." That's a big statement.

Can you turn down Master Fard Muhammad's mother and tell her that she is less than who she is because of the color of her skin? "I ain't coming to such a banquet. Hell no." You mean if the Savior invited you to a banquet provided by His mother, you would act like Iblis and say, "I am better than she. For I am made of fire while she is made of dust." You'll reverse the Iblis of yesterday" So He would ask, you know, "Well what hindered you when it was I Who commanded you?" Ok. So then in that, it bears witness to the Qur'an's teachings that evil is a bad name after faith.

Well in *Message to the Blackman,* the Messenger said, "We are not brothers by nature but we can be brothers in faith." Well if he's your brother in faith would you call him a devil when he has submitted his will to do the will of God? That language is improper to refer to any human that is in submission to God.

There is an awful lot that we need, I think, to delve in more deeply. That's what would make me want to teach a subject called, *The Extreme Value of the White Man* to the events of our time and to the preparation of God for the Hereafter. He was and is extremely valuable in this process.

By his being valuable he earns the mercy of God, as much as the Arabs, who have deviated from the Sunnah and the Qur'an, yet they kept the Qur'an in a pure state that we could receive it. This earns them, in spite of their error, the mercy of God and the chance for forgiveness, reconciliation and returning them to the great position that they once held.

The God Whom we serve is a God that takes everything into

account when He judges and before He punishes.

Only you could question me in this manner because of the love that you have for these two books and the God Who ordered the writing of such books and the placing of such in the hands of human beings. And out of your love for Master Fard Muhammad, the Honorable Elijah Muhammad and your Brother, He gives you the mind to question me, in such a way so as to reveal, with great clarity the innards of a man that many see but don't see; many hear but don't hear; many think they know but don't know very much about that man at all--from the inside out. That's why these questions are valuable.

Brother Jabril: What you just said reminded me of something he said. You may have already heard him say it too.

He said when you come into his presence he has one ear on your mouth and the other ear on the prophecy to see where you fit. His words connect with what you just now said, and it also connects with why one of the main reasons he wanted to make you a lead wire, or a lead minister. Please comment.

Minister Farrakhan: Well the thought that first comes to my mind is the Scientists, who get up the history. They sample the thinking of the present population. They multiply that thinking with a multiplier and then they can produce the thinking in another generation, two, three, four, ten, twenty—up to twenty-five thousand years.

If you put that in a book and you give it to your servant, and then you teach your servant the understanding of the book, not just to interpret a word. You're giving him the understanding of the root thinking that produced the thing that you're reading about.

So no type is out of that equation, because we're all apart of what they wrote. He's not just talking (or teaching) the book, as we know Bible, or Qur'an. He's talking (or teaching) of that which makes the book the value that it is. When you stand in his presence and start opening your mouth, which reveals your way of thinking, he has got you. He can almost size up what you are going to turn out to be in a little while.

Well they tell me when Malcolm came he told his son, "Oh,

he'll be with us about ten years." Now what did he see coming out of a man's mouth that one ear on the man's mouth and an eye on the book? Then he fit this man into characteristics that manifest in all kinds of sequences throughout the scripture.

Well, if we're the ones that are going to fulfill prophecy and he has an understanding of prophecy, he just listens to your mouth. Then he looks at what the prophets predicted would come and then he fits you where you belong in the final outcome of things. That's not lightweight man. That's so heavy. That's why when you open your mouth you're really on display to a wise man. Even a fool sometimes, will pick up on you with just a few words.

Brother Jabril: This is good for the believer to read; others too.

INTERVIEW OF THE HONORABLE MINISTER LOUIS FARRAKHAN
BY JABRIL MUHAMMAD
PHOENIX, ARIZONA
JUNE 29, 2006

Brother Jabril: What is it about Black people, here in America, that despite our extraordinarily wretched condition, attitude and disposition, that makes us so precious, or so valuable, in the sight of God, according to what the Honorable Elijah Muhammad preached for forty-four years and that you have preached now going on twenty-nine years, absent his presence?

The Honorable Minister Farrakhan: Whenever a scientist desires to produce something he has to look for the right material. There is no creative act that does not involve some form of material. Sometimes you try one piece of metal and it doesn't work, you try another. But you're always looking for the right material to produce the right result that's not in the mind of the material it's in the mind of the creator, or the person that has an idea in mind for the material. The material doesn't matter until the idea of the carrier of the idea, wants to use the material for a purpose.

Having said that, the last fifty thousand years of the tribe of Shabazz's struggle, the tribe of Shabazz's history, has made us into a useful material for a purpose that involves infinity.

Our father Shabazz, who was one of the major Scientists,

desired to produce a people close to nature; a people who could conquer the jungle life of East Africa, or East Asia; as it is now called Africa. He wanted a people who would conquer the jungle life and conquer that which was/is akin to the jungle. He wanted to produce that kind of people, although the other wise Scientists disagreed with him.

The Honorable Elijah Muhammad taught me—I don't know who else heard him say this but—"It is impossible" he said, "for the Black man to destroy himself."

The Scientist, who was so upset who was so disappointed that he could not get all of the people to speak the same dialect, 66 trillion years ago, decided to destroy everybody, including himself. As the Messenger taught us, he drilled a hole into the earth, which was then called "moon" and filled it with high explosives. His desire was to destroy all life but he created something useful, the moon.

Having said that, no matter what we did to ourselves, in rebellion against the wishes of the other members of the family of Gods, in the circle of Gods, it was then over-ridden by a higher purpose and power.

We did conquer the jungle life. He did make a people close to nature. That's a very powerful statement, "close to nature." What does that really mean?

Close to nature would mean, to me, close to the very essence of the power of God, to create out of His nature, *nature*. So, close to nature means to me close to the essence of God in His ability to create whatever He creates out of His nature. A people like that are the material who cannot be destroyed, because you cannot destroy nature, nor can you destroy the God Who produced nature.

This people, then, were put through many extreme trials to fashion the material; to harden the material; to shape the material. So the thousands of years in the jungle and then being captured by Sir John Hawkins; being brought on a westerly course, many could not survive the journey that was producing special material. Those who survived were the strongest of the strong.

The material—being tested; the material—being fashioned,

into that, which could never be destroyed.

After four hundred years of servitude slavery and the worst form of slavery that human beings ever had to endure, with the birth of Master Fard Muhammad, and the rise of Master Fard Muhammad into the knowledge of Himself and into the knowledge of the idea of a new creation; a new sun; a new moon; a new star; a new heaven and a new earth--then out of the material of the darkness seventy-eight trillion years ago, God formed Himself, and out of the material of the darkness *came that which we now see.*

Well now, out of this material, fashioned by time, He (Master Fard Muhammad) then saw that which He needed to make what He had in His mind. The material didn't matter until an idea to put it to use came into existence. This material then was precious in His sight, though not precious in the sight of others. This was a material rejected of men, because they had no use for it. But He knew its value to Him, because it fit His purpose.

The essence of the brown germ in the original man had no use; no purpose until Yakub saw purpose for it. Then it became valuable.

It's the purpose of God, is what makes us precious. The purpose of God is what makes us valuable.

Any time an enemy sees that if you get your hands on a certain material, you could become dangerous to his aim and his purpose, he plans to destroy it.

Today, the Bush administration does not want the Islamic Republic of Iran to get its grip on nuclear knowledge. Why? What do you fear from that? They say, "So let's marshal our forces to keep Iran away from what could threaten us."

It is the same today. We are precious in the sight of God; not because of our righteousness; not because of any good that we have done. We're precious in His sight because time and circumstances has made us into the material that He desires to use as the foundation of an eternal government of peace.

The enemy now recognizes the material that God deems as precious in His sight for His aim and purposes. He recognizes the purpose that God has for the material. So the enemy's desires is to keep God from the material, and even destroy the material, so that which God wants to use the material to bring into existence which will supplant his power; his rule; his authority; his world. He's fighting against God.

That's what I see in the preciousness of Black people. We shouldn't be delusional, attributing to ourselves characteristics that we already have innately from our Creator. Of course, that's one of the reasons why we are of value because of the innate characteristics that we have that have been covered by the mud of the civilization of the enemy.

We're valuable. We are precious in the sight of God because time and circumstances has fashioned us into the material that can be utilized to make a government; a world that will never ever end.

Brother Jabril: Thank you.

What is the root of your and our father's teachings that we should not ever be the aggressor?

Minister Farrakhan: The God Who created us, created us after His own nature. Allah Himself has never been the aggressor. The way He has established His universe, and the nature of Himself, is that He sets a pattern and then He reacts to those who violate it. But He always reacts. He never initiates an aggression. He reacts to aggression.

He always cautions His servants never to worry about the attack of the attacker, because the moment they make the attack they have violated the nature of God and the nature of His creation. Therefore, they're already weak. When we respond appropriately to the attack He gives victory to those who function as He functions.

There is power in not being the aggressor. There is power in not initiating an attack. There is power in knowing the power that stands with those who obey the nature of God and the nature of His creation. As a result of that knowledge, whether we understand the power or not, if we are obedient and are never the aggressor, then when the aggressor aggresses, the power comes to the person[s] who is aggressed to respond appropriately with the backing of the power of the nature of God and the nature of His creations.

Aggressors ultimately always loose, and that is why history is full of the fall of powers that get overcome by their sense of their power. They deny the real power that is never in aggression, but always is coming from the nature of peace.

Brother Jabril: Surah 22:52 reads: "And We never sent a messenger or a prophet before thee but when he desired, the devil made a suggestion respecting his desire; but Allah annuls that which the devil casts, then does Allah establish His messages. And Allah is Knowing, Wise."

Whenever God intends to do something through His servants, or have his servants accomplish something, Satan runs a head and puts out something that looks right but it's not. How can the new believer in God's truths distinguish between Satan's move and the divine move?

Minister Farrakhan: The divine move is perfect. Satan's move is so far from perfection that running a head of God to try to produce something always leaves holes that create dissatisfaction, which then leads to perfection.

The Jews knew that one day they should expect the Messiah. They knew that if they followed what was commanded of them, he would guide them back to a proper place in the Holy Land. Then there are those who wanted to run a head and fulfill the vision absent the guidance of the Messiah.

They made a mess. But what they did is that they further placed the idea into existence. The idea is good but those who are trying to do it are bad. So the idea remains but the confused state of someone trying to do the idea is wiped away, as the true initiator, or the true actor; an original actor of the idea appears and brings it into being.

Well so it is with the Kingdom of God. Well, "The Kingdom of God is at hand," John the Baptists said. Well if it is at hand, that's close by. So Satan wants to produce a kingdom that, in his mind, correlates, or can replace, or can fulfill the desire of those who seek the kingdom.

I'm watching the enemy trying to make one world; one political reality; one currency; one this; one that. That is God's idea. So run a head Satan. That's the aggressive move. Run ahead and work out the kinks for Me [God talking]. Run ahead and use all your knowledge; all your science; all your technology and then fail. I'm watching you, because I put you here just to do that anyway. I'm watching you as you experiment with my idea of one world. You make mistakes and errors, but I'm recording.

After you've run the course and got a headache trying to do what you're not made to do, then I ask you, are you ready for me to do that now, sir? Like it was with the Savior; when He let everybody choose somebody to lead. Everybody that they chose was a mess-up. Then He said, "Are you willing to let me make the choice now?"

You have to let people exhaust their stupidity. When they're finally fully exhausted then they are ready for that which is perfect or Him that is perfect to do the perfect work.

It's not good to be aggressive. It's not good to try to run ahead of a wise God to put your stamp of ignorance on an idea that takes supreme wisdom to bring into existence. That's why God always asks the wicked to cast. "You cast your rod magicians." God sits back and watches. Then He said, "Alright Moses you cast." His rod ate up their lies.

He will let the devil go a head and cast whatever aspersions; whatever thing that he wishes to do against the truth. Go a head. Your move. But God is on both sides of the chess board because He is Master of the day of judgment. So the move that Satan makes God is directing it. He says, "Oh you forgot something. Checkmate."

It's just not good to be an aggressor. It just is not good to run a head of God to try to do what you are not qualified to do. But God is so wise and so patient. Go ahead.

The Qur'an ends it all by saying, as it reads in Surah 14:22 "And the devil will say, when the matter is decided: Surely Allah promised you a promise of truth, and I promised you, then failed you. And I had no authority over you, except that I called you and you obeyed me; so blame me not but blame yourselves. I cannot come to your help, nor can you come to my help. I deny your associating me with Allah before. Surely for the unjust is a painful chastisement."

These would be persons are pulling away those who would be. Making them manifest for who they really are. It's never good to be the aggressor. It's never good to assume things about yourself that may or may not be true. I think that's why the Bible says, "Wait on the Lord."

That's why the Qur'an says, "Seek assistance through patience and prayer." And if in our immaturity, we cannot wait for God to do it, then Satan's imperfect call to an imperfect thing that may have some of the characteristics of what God wants, but the essence of it will always be missing because Satan can never produce from the spirit of God because he doesn't have it. Wait. Be patient. So I think that that's how I would try to answer that at this moment.

Brother Jabril: Magnificent answer!

INTERVIEW OF THE HONORABLE MINISTER LOUIS FARRAKHAN
BY JABRIL MUHAMMAD
PHOENIX, ARIZONA
2006

Brother Jabril: Brother Minister, the Honorable Elijah Muhammad has given us prayers, using the words "seeking refuge in Allah." The Holy Qur'an speaks of that especially Surah 113 and 114, with which it closes.

What does the concept "seeking refuge" mean?

Minister Farrakhan: A place of refuge is a place where one goes to find complete security from any form of harm or danger. When one has a refuge in Allah God, one is placing oneself in the best most secure place or state of being. So that regardless to what is going on around that person, that person who not only seeks but finds a refuge in God, has found that place of the greatest peace; the greatest security; the greatest sufficiency of all needs, desires or wants.

David the Psalmist--troubled in his life--found a secure place;

a refuge in God.

When the Psalmist says, "The Lord is my strength and He is my salvation. Whom then shall I fear? Of whom then shall I be afraid? The Lord is the strength of my life." And then He talks about, "Hiding me under the shadow of His wings. And I shall not fear the arrow that flies by day or the one that cometh by night for I am shadowed under the wings, the protection of the Almighty."

Seeking refuge, and of course, finding it—and Jesus said it best, "Seek and ye shall find." So every true Believer in God will seek Him as their place of refuge. And then seeking they shall find that in Him is the best refuge.

One cannot seek refuge if one does not have faith that in seeking and finding that refuge that that place of refuge is sufficient. So faith is the prerequisite here—I believe in Allah, Who came in the person of Master Fard Muhammad. In Him do I place my trust. And in Him do I seek refuge from the enemies of truth and justice and freedom and equity for our people.

If you believe in Him then you will seek and find in Him that place of refuge. "Farrakhan, why would you believe in this Man as your Source of comfort, peace, security? Why would you place your trust in Him?"

I do so because before I knew a place of trust, I found a man who put his complete trust in Master Fard Muhammad and grew to know Him as his only place of refuge.

The Honorable Elijah Muhammad said to me, "If ten thousand enemies was standing out in front of my door I would not fear." And in one speech he said, "I feel so strong that I could go down the street dragging two lions behind me." Well where was his strength? Where did his strength come from? What sustained him for forty-four years in the midst of the worse opposition and constant threats of death?

He was sustained because he knew his place of refuge. He sought it completely and found it and stayed there. He told me—he said, "If Master Fard Muhammad left me for one fraction of a second you would see a walking fool." Well that told me that if he could not stand to be away from Master Fard Muhammad for a fraction of a second, that he would be exposed as a foolish man once knowing him as a wise man."

What am I to do as his student? I seek refuge in Allah, Who came in the person of Master Fard Muhammad. I have found Him and I cling to Him and I pray that He will never ever leave me for in Him I have found my place of refuge.

I pray that every Believer will seek and find Him as your place of refuge and security—that though you walk in the valley of the shadow of death you will fear no evil—for you are with God and God is with you.

He will prepare a table for you in the midst of your enemies. He will fill your cup till it runs over. And surely goodness and mercy shall follow you and me and us all the days of our life. And we will dwell in that place of refuge; that house of Allah God, forever.

In 1929 when the stock market crashed, rich people who made the stock market their place of refuge went out and committed suicide. What will rich people do who have made millions of dollars and feel in the fact that they have so much money that they have a refuge? What happens when the dollar collapses and has no more value, then where will you find your refuge?

There are those who have placed their stock, their hope, their trust in their ability to make money; their ability to do what they do that gives them material strength. But once that is disturbed then they fall apart. So if you put your trust in a weapon and the weapon fails; if you put your trust in your friends, your professor or you take your doctors of law or your monks for lords beside Allah and then you see them troubled and can't solve their problems, you take your leaders and your teachers as lords beside Allah and then you see them in a state of confusion, then what about you who depend on these sources for your refuge.

Then tell me how do you trouble God? How do you disturb Him? How do you defeat Him? Well since no one can, then what better place of refuge do we have than placing all our trust and confidence in that which cannot be shaken; that which cannot be disturbed; that which cannot be overcome. So if I am in that, then I am not disturbed no matter what goes on around me. I'm not shaken no matter what the circumstances are. I am not troubled by what troubles the world because I have found the greatest source of refuge—the unshakable, the invincible, the unconquerable, the Mighty, the Wise, the Lord of the Worlds.

You practice that, then every trouble that comes into your life you go to Him. He sees you through. Then He brings greater trouble. You go to Him. He sees you through. Then He gives you a greater test, a greater trial and you go to Him and He sees you through. He brings misfortune into your life and you go to Him and He sees you through. The death of a friend; the death of a loved one, you go to Him and He sees you through.

There is no Believer that has not been tried who placed their trust in Him and He saw you through with little things, then He gives you a bigger trial and a bigger trial and even misfortune in your life, even loss of property; loss of fruit; loss of life, you go to Him and He brings you through. Then what is He teaching us through all these lessons in our endeavor to serve Him? He's saying, "My servant put your trust in Me. I will see you through."

Sometimes we turn away from refuge. "Why me? Why do I have cancer? Why must I suffer? I've been good. I've been faithful. I've tried to be true." Then God watches. And from deep within yourself, the voice will say, "Yes. Why not you? Do you think that you would be left along on saying you believe and will not be tried? How dare you say that you are a servant of God? Did not you see how I tried Abraham with a son that he loved? And I told him to go up on the mountain and sacrifice that boy that you love that you sought and longed for. Abraham, did you do what I asked you to do?"

I'm sure he struggled with his emotions. "But who is greater, the gift or the giver? So if I gave you a son, am I not greater than the son that I gave you? Do I not deserve your devotion; your loyalty; your obedience; your submission? So take him up on the mountain and sacrifice him there." And when Abraham determined to obey God, God stayed his hand. He found in God a place of refuge and from that he became the friend of God.

Wouldn't you like to have God as your friend? What better

friend could we have? He's always watching the servant with what He tries him with. No prophet escaped trials. Didn't they boil Abraham in oil? Was He there with Abraham? Who was in the lion's den with Daniel? Who was in the fiery furnace with the three Hebrew boys? Who fed Elijah when Elijah was running in the wilderness?

What a friend we have in the Almighty Creator!

He's been teaching us all through life that He is our place of refuge.

But when we turn away because of a misfortune or because of an untimely death of someone that we love or any loss of property or diminution of fruit, if we turn away, then we lose the love of our Protector, for He says, "I'm going to try you."

But give good news to those who are patient and steadfast under trial.

Steadfast in what? In seeking Him as your place of refuge.

INTERVIEW OF THE HONORABLE MINISTER LOUIS FARRAKHAN
BY JABRIL MUHAMMAD
PHOENIX, ARIZONA
JUNE 25, 2006

The general public is generally unaware that Minister Farrakhan possesses unusual musical talent. He is working with musical geniuses to produce an unusual album. He has allowed me to listen to some of the music. His reasons for this music is profound.

Brother Jabril: Brother Minister, what were the circumstances under which you heard *that* song? What did it produce in your mind? Why did you decide what you decided to do with it? In some earlier conversations between us we've discussed what thoughts came to you in connection with what that song was. Please share them with us.

Minister Farrakhan: Well first I was lying in my bed and looking through the dial of the television and I heard this song coming up at the end of a movie where the credits were rolling. But the song sounded like the title would be "Remember Me."

And the song so touched me that I waited until I could find who the composer or who the performer was. I got the name and I mentioned it to Charles Veal. He knew the person. He does a lot of writing of music for movies. And he found the song for me.

At first, I thought it would be wonderful if Johnny Mathis would sing this and I would do the violin accompaniment around his voice. But when I became more acquainted with the words, I felt that I should sing this song, because, the whole album of music is titled "A Time for Meditation and Reflection."

I wanted the music of my life, classical, jazz, violin, voice, calypso, to sort of say in music something about the Minister, the abundance of talent that Allah gave him and his willingness to give it all up to follow the Honorable Elijah Muhammad. And that in the closing or twilight years of life Allah grants him the privilege to do his music again. I wanted to leave it so that the people might reflect, one: on discipleship—that Jesus said, "If any man would be my disciple he must first deny himself. Pick up his cross and then follow him.

In all three of these prerequisites for discipleship I have done. I denied myself—my career—in trying to follow the Honorable Elijah Muhammad and to believe in what Allah revealed to him. I picked up my cross and have suffered as a result of that for over fifty years. I have tried my best to follow in his footsteps.

Recognizing that I have come to the end of a term. I wanted my music to cause the Believers and those who have come to know me as a preacher or teacher of the word and those who will come to know me by means of the word to listen to the music. And the music will drive the word deeper into their consciousness.

The song "Remember" and then the words of it touched on three things. One: Prophet Muhammad. "If you follow this Qur'an and my Sunnah you will never deviate." The idea of the Prophet was that the people should hold in remembrance what he did; how he lived his life for God and what he suffered to establish this word; the word more important but his life is the witness of the word.

Then Jesus, in the last supper, asked the disciples to take the bread and the bread is symbolic of the word and then after supper he took the cup. He gave them wine. He said, "This is my blood that I shed for the New Testament." In words, he lived a life of sacrifice that enabled him to go to the father to take the book out of the hand of his father.

He wanted his disciples to see the life that he lived that earned him such a great reward. Then he said "Do this as often as you can in remembrance of me." In remembering him in this way he would never leave us. And he said, "And lo I will be with you even unto the end of the world."

In closing this answer, the Honorable Elijah Muhammad asked me one day—first he made a statement—he said, "Elisha—when he died—when they set his body down in the grave there was some bones there and the bones began to move." He said, "Brother, do you know what that means?" I said, "No sir, dear Apostle." He said, "It means that Elisha would rule the people from beyond the grave."

In this song—a beautiful song—it talks about remembering a person who was present who is now going to be absent. But he says, "Remember me." He said, "I will never leave you as long as you hold me in your memory for I am that shining star in its brightness, the last light fading into the rising sun which is Jesus again—the morning star is the last star you see and it leads you right up into the light of the sun.

He says, "If you tell my story, the icy or cold wind that has taken me from you, if you tell my story as I speak to you across the sky, you'll hear my voice," he said, "calling to you from across the sky, if you tell my story, I will never die." Which means from the perspective of Jesus, I will never leave you. I will always be with you.

Coming back to what the Messenger and the Qur'an tells us of Aaron—he will be remembered down through the generations and when his name is mentioned, the Believers or the righteous will say, "And peace be on Moses and Aaron."

That is, I guess, the answer to that question.

Brother Jabril: Thank you Brother Minister.

Interview of the Honorable Minister Louis Farrakhan
by Jabril Muhammad
Phoenix, Arizona
July 13, 2006

Brother Jabril: Brother Minister I have a few questions related to the 113th and 114th surahs of the Holy Qur'an.

These surahs deal with the same subject, with emphasis on different aspects of the same evils, which bring in the intense darkness when it comes. What I want you to do, by the help of Allah, *for us* is to comment on this and help us all focus on what we're faced with properly. What I need *for us* is your insight; your commentary on this big subject.

Minister Farrakhan: It is interesting to note that the Holy Qur'an closes with these two chapters of refuge, because, it is what is in these two chapters, that tries the mind, heart, spirit and soul of a Believer. If the Believer does what these two chapters tell us to do, we can get through the darkness into the brightness of a new day, which really is the Hereafter.

I seek refuge in the Lord of the dawn. Well, if we're going through a period of intense darkness, this chapter is telling us that the darkness is not permanent. After intense darkness, comes the dawn of a new day. So we are exhorted to seek refuge in Him, Who is the light of that dawn of a brand new day. Then you focus on the Lord of the dawn from the evil of what he -- and the Honorable Elijah Muhammad, in parenthesis said, "What Yakub created." Well he created an opposing world. He created a world of sport and play; a world of rebellion against the way; the life; the law; the word of God.

In this intense darkness this rebellion goes to its limit. This idea of his world goes to the extreme in tempting the Believer to engage in those things that would make the Believer unworthy of the dawn and to perish in the darkness. *I seek refuge in the Lord of the dawn from the evil of what he (Yakub) created.* What did he do? He made an opponent; an opposer to God.

A Yusuf Ali translation says, "I seek refuge in the Lord of the dawn from the mischief of created things." Well this that Yakub, the father of this world made, was a mischief-maker. In the closing days and hours, of his rule, he makes extreme mischief with created things.

Well what are the created things that he makes mischief with? He poisons the water. He poisons the air. He poisons the earth. He takes the natural inclination; the sexual drive in the human for reproduction and he twists it into a grotesque manifestation of filth and debauchery. He takes the atom, which is a created thing, and he makes mischief with it. He takes chemistry--which is a created thing--he makes mischief with it.

In essence, all of us—the Believer and the non-Believer—have to pass through this terrible darkness. The only way out is to seek refuge in Him, Who is the Lord of the dawn, the Master of that new day; that new life; that new word; that new law that is eternal. *I seek refuge in the Lord of the dawn from the evil of what Yakub made from the intense darkness when it comes."*

We are entering a very dark hour where all of this evil and mischief, that the enemy has scientifically produced, reaches its apex. It creates a period of intense darkness—a darkness that will not allow any one in it to see pass it, unless our hope is in the Lord of the dawn.

That Lord has given the Believer light. That light is that which we must cling to, in that hour of darkness, and the hope in the Lord of the Dawn that will get us through this darkness.

I seek refuge in the Lord of the dawn from him who cast evil suggestions in firm resolutions. The enemy will make evil look so appealing; so tempting that the suggestion of evil will be a great trial, particularly for the Believer. For the Honorable Elijah Muhammad said, "That the last great test of the Believer, that he has to go through, to get to the other side, is the fire of temptation."

Well what will the enemy tempt us with? He will tempt us with the things that we desire, or the things that we want. He's well able to offer it with, of course, strings attached. But if our hope is in the Lord of the dawn then we will pass up the evil suggestion that comes in a firm resolve and the evil of the envier when he envies.

Well there's a lot of envy in the world. But the greatest envy is the envy of the enemy of God who sees a people that he has trodden under foot supplanting his rule. So envy is the mother of hatred. Hatred is the mother of murder. It is the murder of the righteous, out of the envy of the wicked for the great position that God is giving to the righteous. Those of us who know what that position is, and are trying to qualify to be a part of what God makes new, must be able to get through the hatred; the murder and really, the overshadowing of death. *I seek refuge in the Lord of the dawn from the evil of the envier when he envies.*

All of these things contribute to the intense darkness. All of these things are used to trick and trip the Believer up; making them doubt what God is preparing him, or her, for. All of these are part of one great evil that produces the intense darkness, but these are components of that darkness.

The last chapter says, "*I seek refuge in the Lord of men; the King of men; the God of men.*" Well He's the nurturer of men. He's our only sovereign. He is the true God. So we should seek refuge in Him, from the evil whispering of a slinking devil, who whispers into the hearts of men.

Well when you're going through all that you're going through in the proceeding chapter, what comes up in your heart and mind? What whispering comes up in your own self that takes you away from the reward of faithfulness? These whisperings not only come from self, but it comes from outside of self from among the jinn and the men.

Well jinn here, as the Holy Qur'an and the scholars say, "Represents those fiery spirits." But to me it represents those who have not been nurtured into the divine. So they are very emotional beings—the fire of anger; the fire of disappointment; the fire of deception; betrayal. These are emotions that come from those who may surround the Believer.

There are whisperings from within ourselves when we don't understand, or getting weak in our faith, or whispering that comes from those around us who have not matured into the word of God. They are very emotional persons who are guided by their feelings rather than by intelligence.

Then whispering that come from men. Men, to me, meaning, more mature people. Mature in the word of God. Mature in the way of God. But the arch deceiver has affected them. As the Bible teaches that, "The dragon will take down a third part of the stars of heaven." The Honorable Elijah Muhammad said, "This is not just talking about scholars of Islam, but some of the Holy wise Scientists themselves."

If a Scientists goes down and he starts whispering into the hearts of Believers that are on the path of faith--that's a heavy, heavy, trial for us. So hold fast to that handle as the Honorable Elijah Muhammad taught, that will never break off from us unless we break off from it. The Holy Qur'an says, "Hold fast to the rope of Islam and be not disunited."

Well under a trial like the ones in the 113th and 114th surahs, it would be hard to remain united with that which becomes a victim of the darkness of the evil suggestions of the hatred; of the murder plots of the whispering. So Allah says in the Qur'an, "He will separate us and put like with like." So under such darkness the hypocrites will be with the hypocrites. The disbelievers will be with the disbelievers. And through the darkness the Believers carrying his light with him will find another Believer and remain united with those who persevere and are steadfast under such a tremendous trial.

The Honorable Elijah Muhammad gave us a prayer to say. It is a prayer of refuge. This prayer of refuge, the Honorable Elijah Muhammad asked us to say it seven times a day. "I seek refuge in Allah from anxiety and grief, from the lack of strength and laziness, from cowardice and niggardliness. From being overpowered by debt and the oppression of men."

The supplicant asks, "Suffice thou me with what is lawful and keep me away from what is prohibited. And with your grace make me free from want of what is beside you."

If we acted on this prayer, and the things that this prayer is asking Allah to give us refuge from, this ties to the last two chapters of refuge. Because when the darkness comes and so many fall, we would be full of anxiety. We may loose cherished possessions and people whom we love which bring about grief.

In that hour we seek refuge from anxiety and grief. And then, the loss of strength, which is attacking our faith, for the scripture says, "The race is not to the swift, or the strong, but to that one who can endure to the end." That is great faith. Great strength.

When you seek refuge in Allah from the lack of strength and then the lack of strength makes one lazy in the performance of duty. Because even though we're going through a dark period that does not absolve us from requisite duty; duty to God; duty to self; duty to wife; duty to children; duty to community and duty to nation. So when you loose strength then you become lazy in the performance of duty.

Then, of course, you seek refuge from niggardliness, miserliness, not willing to share what we know, or what we have with a fellow-suffering Believer.

In that hour famine may arise in the land. If the Believer has a bowl of soup and brother Believer has none, then a brother Believer has a claim on half of that bowl. But, if we're niggardly, or miserly, and want to hoard and hold, then we are doubting that Allah would be sufficient for us.

We seek refuge from anxiety and grief and from the lack of strength and laziness and from cowardice and niggardliness. Niggardliness is cowardice because it shows fear that the God will not suffice me tomorrow, as He sufficed me today. So I should be niggardly with my substance today in fear that I won't have something tomorrow.

Cowardice in the hour of trial would cause us to fall. So we must seek refuge in Allah and challenge what we fear. Allah says, "Surely I will try you with something of fear, hunger, lost of property; lost of life, diminution of fruit. So give good news to those who are patient and steadfast under trial because they seek refuge in Allah, the Lord of the dawn; the Lord of men; the King of men and the God of men.

Then, "I seek refuge from being overpowered by debt and the oppression of men." Debt is a form of slavery and oppression. So in a dark hour you don't want to get into debt, you want to strive to get out of debt because by means of debt you'll be oppressed—"I'll take your car." "I'll take your home." "I'll take whatever you owe because you don't have money to pay your note then you loose it."

Well, seek refuge in Allah.

Lastly, "Suffice thou me with what is lawful" in a season of great temptation when evil is made fair seeming. Please, Allah, suffice me. Be sufficient for me in what is lawful in your sight and make me free from any want of what is beside what you want for me and for us.

If we can do that, more than likely, we will survive the darkness into the dawn of a brand new day.

Brother Jabril: Thank you, Brother Minister.

INTERVIEW OF THE HONORABLE MINISTER LOUIS FARRAKHAN
BY JABRIL MUHAMMAD
PHOENIX, ARIZONA
JULY 16, 2006

Brother Jabril: Brother Minister, in the light of your knowledge of the word of God, through our father, and the scriptures, what is friendship?

Minister Farrakhan: The Christians have a song that they sing titled, "What a friend we have in Jesus." So to understand friendship, one must understand how Jesus lays down the true meaning of friendship in the words that he taught; in the life that he lived and the things that he did that proved that he, as the representative of God, was and is a true friend and represents the true friendship of Allah (God). So Jesus, in this way sets the standard by which we measure friendship.

Many of us are associates. Many of us have some degree of camaraderie. But a friend is far different. To study the life of the man in *The New Testament* that is called Jesus the Christ, we learned that friendships start with the willingness to sacrifice yourself to do something of value for someone whom you love. To study to prepare oneself to deliver another is a supreme act of sacrifice and friendship.

The Honorable Elijah Muhammad taught us that Master Fard

Muhammad studied forty-two years of His life to prepare Himself to come to deliver a people that didn't know Him; didn't want to know Him; didn't really care. But because He knew, He cared enough to sacrifice His life to create a bond of friendship with a people who were friendless. He came to North America by Himself. That's to tell us that a true friend is not looking necessarily for company to do something good for someone that He loves.

He says in Isaiah, "There was none to uphold Him. So His own right arm, it upheld him." So within Himself, He summoned the strength and the power necessary to show His friendship by delivering a people who needed to be delivered. That's the Qur'an when it speaks of Him, it usually uses these attributes: "Surely Allah is the Mighty, the Wise."

He comes by Himself and is not concerned about the environment that His friend or His people are in. He settles Himself in that same environment and begins the arduous task of teaching and preparing one and making an example of friendship for that one that He might make an example of friendship for us all. So He teaches. He's willing to go to prison. When He goes to prison He sends for His Servant, Elijah Karriem at the time, to show him the price that he would have to pay to help in the deliverance of his people.

He suffered persecution. All of this, He did to show what a real friend is. And then after He prepares one to represent His friendship, wherever he is, He guides; He protects that one who represents His awesome act of friendship.

The Qur'an speaks truthfully, "Only Allah and His Messenger are your friend and the true believers." Because, if we believe in Allah and His Messenger and follow that noble example, then we become friends of the Messenger and friends of each other.

Now some of us think that there is friendship when somebody does a kind act toward us. It could be. But that would depend on the motivation. In the Qur'an it says, "Take not Jews and Christians for friends for they are friends of each other."

Naturally when you talk to a Christian and you read something like that, they're very upset. Well, how come you can't take me for a friend and you just said that a true Christian is a Muslim and a true Muslim is a Christian. If we understand that no ayat or verse of the Qur'an was revealed outside of a context, then what was the context of the revelation of that verse? And you will find that though Muhammad (PBUH) had come in an act of friendship to deliver the Arabs from the terrible state of ignorance that they were in to make them worthy of eminence and greatness, but there were certain Jews and certain Christians who acted in an alliance to stop him from being a friend to the Arab people.

In that context, the Arabs could not take Jews and Christians for friends if they were in opposition to one whom Allah had raised to do a supreme act of friendship for the Arab people and through them make them friends of humanity.

Well, here we are in 2006. After 911 and the media landslide of negative propaganda against Islam, there were certain Christian leaders and Jewish leaders who came together to denounce Islam and the God of Islam as Satan. How then can you and I as Muslims take such Christian and such Jews for friends, when they are denying that which befriended us. So Allah warns us in the Holy Qur'an, "Why do you offer them love when they deny that which you believe and seek to drive you out of your places because of your belief based on an act of friendship from Allah and His Messenger."

We have to be careful today how we use such a term as "my friend." If we identify the coming of the Mahdi as the supreme act of friendship and His raising of the Honorable Elijah Muhammad and giving him the example of a friend and Elijah Muhammad sets that example for forty-four years among us, and we would do well to limit the use of such word. You can't even say that among Muslims that we are friends, because there are too many hypocrites among the believing community. So take Allah. Allah is - only Allah and His Messenger. Well, we know those Two. They have given us a supreme act of friendship. We know the Qur'an is right. "Only Allah and His Messenger are your friends and those who believe." But the question is who are they?

So, in such a time of trial as this is and the sorting out that is going on, soon we will be able to unite believer with believer and we would know that the believer is the friend of the believer.

Brother Jabril: Brother Minister in this book, *A Torchlight for America,* you have a small section about five paragraphs long, about "Put God First". How would you advise America, given what they call a pluralistic society to wisely put God first without running into all of these constitutional arguments and whatnot?

Minister Farrakhan: There is no way that America can put God first. She's gone too far. And if she had someone to lead her that would try to put her back to a right state where she could begin to solve her internal and external problems, they would be assassinated very quickly. Because there are those who wanted to reduce the sovereignty of this nation and make America a tool for a global empire, that America is not going to control. But the power of America would be used to give these, who are the architects of this power to control, by the use of the power of America.

Putting God first would destroy that aim and ambition. Because what that aim and ambition though on the front is noble—appears noble—it is satanic. Because it is Satan trying to use America and the power of America to gain global dominance over the wealth of the earth and give it to whom they please and get rid of the mass poor of their world.

God has to step in and put Himself first because the wicked will never put the God of Righteousness first. They have put god first, but it is the god of this world who is Satan himself. Now God comes to put Himself first and He will, as the Honorable Elijah Muhammad told us, set up a government of peace wherein we all can live in peace and enjoy freedom, justice, equality and the brotherhood of the human family.

Brother Jabril: Brother Minister, more and more on television there are half hour, one hour and even two hour specials—they give it different names, countdown to Armageddon, and whatnot. They deal mainly with arguments or the scientific or pseudo basis or at least the appearance of scientific presentations that we're living in the last days. Not necessarily religious orientated programs. We see this more and more on television, pastors are talking in terms of whether or not this is the end time or that it is the end time. When you see these programs what do you think of them?

Minister Farrakhan: Some of the wiser ones are trying to warn their people. It is becoming so clear that the veil of deception is being rent so that even the most foolish of the people can see that we're living in the time of trouble like there has never been since there was a time and a nation. So the question that scholars are wrestling with is: how do we get out of such a time as this? And they don't have answers. There is an answer. But they are not willing to make that determination.

As I listen to the news and I listen to the response of President Bush to the horror that Israel is putting on the Lebanese people, his response was not only inadequate but it was pathetic for a world leader of the most powerful nation to not order a nation that depends on America to restrain itself from the destruction of a nation over some members of Hezbollah going across an established blue line to kill and kidnap, either two or three Israeli soldiers and take them into Lebanon.

The president's response that, "She has a right to defend herself," of course, every nation has that right. And the fear that America is invoking in smaller nations by referring to them as the "axis of evil" as I warned President Bush, that out of fear of their own survival they will work furiously to gain weapons of mass destruction because they believe that, that is the only deterrent to what America's preemptive aggressive strike would stay. They must have the ability to respond in like fashion. Then and only then do they feel that a dialogue that has meaning can take place.

To make Syria afraid; to make Iran afraid; to make North Korea afraid; to make any little small nation afraid is to say to them as the scripture says, "Wake up the mighty men of war. And let them turn their plow shares and their pruning hooks into spears and swords" because this is a time of global war.

Their efforts for peace may be noble, but they will not come to pass until war has decimated the war-mongers. And many, many, many, many millions of human lives will be lost. But at the end of it all, God will establish His kingdom on earth

Brother Jabril: This statement covers a question that could come up in a conversation, no doubt it does come up in many households whether or not we not living through, or even ***in*** the book of Revelation?

Minister Farrakhan: Yes. We are living in the book of Revelation and we are moving quickly toward the end of that book. And this is why I tell the pastors that if you don't preach to give the people understanding of the prophecies concerning this time, then the people would not know what to do to save themselves. And as the scripture says, "If it were not for His elects sake, that He shorten these days, no soul would make it through," such a terrible time that we are now approaching or we are now in.

At this point I wish to try and give the reader what I was thinking just prior to the next question. First, I thought to ask Minister Farrakhan two last questions, one for the very next session, which was coming up shortly, and I intended to ask him the last question on the next morning.

I had not really decided whether I was going to ask him the last question, as we had been doing it over the years—without any prompting from me—or have this question typed and in my hands to give to him, when we concluded the next interview, when I walked him to his car.

The next question you'll see in a moment. The question for the following morning was typed and was read. It was, "What do you want the reader to take from this book after they've read it?" I never had to consider giving it to him in written form or verbally raising it. This was because he answered both questions at one time.

In additional to not knowing what the next question was—which he answered magnificently—he answered both the asked and the un-asked question in that one session and finished it right at the end of the tape!

Brother Jabril: Next to the last question of this book is this: Brother Minister what do you think about these questions that have been put before you by me over the last several years, and what have they allowed you to do?

Minister Farrakhan: Questions elicit answers. Answers to profound questions help people to see one: the mind of the questioner and the mind of the one being questioned. It helps the reader to see whether God is present with the answer that is being given. Since you don't prompt me that I could go home and think about an answer, but as I said to you in one of your questions to me, as you raise the question, the answer starts forming in my head.

Now either I am a voice of God, for our people and humanity, or I am not. I hate arrogant speech where people declare things of themselves that may or may not be true. I am frightened of declaring something that speaks to ego rather than to the wisdom and the will of God. So I try my best as he told me, not to worry about where I am in the scriptures, but to make his great commission known and he would represent me to the people. These questions that you ask of me cause me to represent him; make his commission known and in so doing, he's representing me to those who would read such answers.

I think I have been enlightened by the questions, because many of them I never had a thought on before. And it goes to show that what God has put within it takes a stimulus of some kind to bring it out. The Honorable Elijah Muhammad wrote, "It is one thing to know that iron ore is in the earth. It is another thing entirely to mine it out of the earth and put it into the service of others."

I don't know all that God and His Servant, the Honorable Elijah Muhammad have put within me in preparing me to sit in his seat as the father over the house in his absence. So your questions of me bring out what is within that it may be put into the service of others.

I thank Allah for these days, months, and years of questions that have brought out of me that which I did not even know was in me. And sometimes in reading back some of the answers that I have given to the questions, is demonstrative to me, that it is not I who is speaking, but it is He who is using me as His mouthpiece to our people and to the world, so that when the people read such questions, and such answers, that illuminate the questioner and the person being questioned.

They can see without a doubt, if their hearts and minds are open, that God has intervened in our affairs. That God has raised the Messiah from among a people who are no people at all. And this Messiah has taught and trained a student that God has made for him that when you read the answers of a student then that illuminates the teacher.

Who could read such answers and not know that God has visited us? Who could read such answers and not know that a strange thing has happened among this most beautiful but destroyed people? Who could read such answers and not know that a light has been placed among a people that walked in darkness? Even a light that would be a light to the gentiles if they would respond properly to that light, they too could join in the good news that, *that* light brings.

I thank Allah for putting it in your heart and your mind to question me in a manner that I've never been questioned by anyone. The reporters don't question me on the nature of God, the nature of His revealed word and the things that you have questioned me on, that illuminates my own nature, mind and spirit. They are not interested in nothing like that.

Many of my ministers are not deep enough in their study of the word to question me in such manner or if they are, they have not availed themselves of the opportunity to do such. But because you have been by my side from the first day of my awakening from the sleep and saw the scales removed from my eyes that I could see more clearly the Honorable Elijah Muhammad and Master Fard Muhammad—that I may stand up again and begin this marvelous work of strengthening my Brothers and Sisters in faith and continuing His warning to the government and people of America.

These questions have been wonderful for me and I have to tell you, I look forward to reading the book myself to see what God has given through me to others. I can't wait to see such book and I thank you from the depth of my heart for putting my answers in book form that the people who I love so much and fear for their safety in this dark hour may read such words and hopefully be guided in a time of my absence to come through the dark hour of trial and tribulation without breaking their faith in Master Fard Muhammad to Whom praises are due forever and His Servant, the Messiah the Christ, the Jesus that all of our people have longed for; hoped for; sang about; rejoiced over; that he's one from among them that the historical Jesus was a sign of, that is now being fulfilled in their midst.

If our preachers would see and know that Jesus is the right man, Jesus is the right name. It's just looking backward in time to an ancient Roman Empire while they are living in a modern Rome, where these new Sanhedrin exercise control over the Romans—the modern Romans—and now have led this nation to its ruin and now seek my death as a representative of the Jesus that we all have loved after learning of him through the Gospels. Who wouldn't love a man like that? Who wouldn't praise a man like that? And to be restored just by his name and just by reading accounts of him from Matthew, Mark, Luke and John and the Acts of the Apostles and the Apostles. How much more would we grow if we knew the flesh, blood, spirit, mind, and were baptized in the word of this Jesus?

I close this with this: to my beloved Christian family whom I love and am willing to give my life for as well as my Muslim family, that I love and willing to give my life to see the word of God established and fear removed.

Jesus is worthy of praise. And Jesus should be praised much. That is what the name Muhammad means: one worthy of praise; one praised much.

If the Muslim world could see that the Muhammad of the Qur'an of fourteen hundred years ago was a sign of the Muhammad that would come at the end of the world, and if the Christians could see that the Jesus that they look back to and forward to his coming again is not the man of two thousand years ago, that came up among a people that were no people in Nazareth, is a man coming up out of a people that is no people to fulfill the scriptures. Can any good come out of the ghettos of America? "Out of Egypt; out of bondage; out of a state of suffering have I called my son."

If we could grow beyond our emotional attachment to the past to see the present in its fullness, then we would know that Jesus is Muhammad and Muhammad is Jesus. They are one and the same. Then the Qur'an would have greater meaning for it is written that the Jesus would speak unto them all that I shall command him. And if you read the four gospels you don't read what God commanded Jesus to say, but in the Qur'an it is repeated over and over again, Muhammad say and when they do, you say. This is the answer to the unification of the family of Abraham.

May Allah bless this book to open the hearts and minds of its readers. May Allah cause this book to make clear to the world that the Muhammad that you love is alive and well today. And the Jesus that you adore is alive and well today. And this kingdom of Muhammad; the kingdom of Jesus the Christ is not only at hand; but after this war, it will be established on this earth. And these Black people of America who are the despised and the rejected, God has called to be the cornerstone of this New World Kingdom.

I thank you Brother Jabril for your questions. I thank Allah and His Christ the Messiah for the answers. And I pray that it will be a blessing to all those who read and study that which is contained in this book.

THE END

Thank You, Thank You, Thank You, and Thank You!

Several years ago, I took the time to study exactly what the words "thank you" meant. In short, this expression means to express and show gratitude for a divine favor. And so, I ***thank*** each of you, who in any way, large or small, helped me to help the Honorable Minister Louis Farrakhan get his words published in this book.

I ***thank*** all of you, in advance, who now know of this book and who will spread the news of its existence to others.

Jabril Muhammad
September 26, 2006

Atlanta, Georgia; *Min. Ava Muhammad*

Baton Rouge, Louisiana; *Sister Deeangela and Brother Ghani Muhammad*

Chicago, Illinois; *Joy and Arthur Muhammad, Sister Latonja Muhammad, Sister Kim Muhammad and Sherice Muhammad*

Cleveland, Ohio; *Min. Richard Muhammad*

Dallas, Texas; *Brother Kenny Muhammad, Min. Jeffrey Muhammad*

Gary, Indiana; *Brother Adrian Muhammad*

Houston, Texas; *Itina and Laviyous Muhammad*

Indianapolis, Indiana; *Min. Nuri Muhammad*

Jersey City, New Jersey; *Brother Aaron Muhammad, Brother Garfield Muhammad, Brother Jason X, Brother Joseph 12X, Brother Tuquwan X, Sister Willie Muhammad*

Las Vegas, Nevada; *Brother Bruce Muhammad, Min. Duke Muhammad*

Memphis, Tennessee; *Min. Anthony Muhammad*

Mesa, Arizona; *Brother Joe Muhammad*

Newark, New Jersey; *Sister Linda Muhammad*

New Orleans, Louisiana; *Brother Rashid Muhammad and Brother Minister Willie Muhammad*

New York, New York; *Brother Andrew 3X Muhammad, Brother Anthony 7X Muhammad, Brother Aubrey 2X Muhammad, Brother Author 2X Muhammad, Brother Cedric X, Brother David 7X Muhammad, Brother Eddie 4X Muhammad, Brother Edward 91X, Muhammad Brother Eric 3X Muhammad, Brother Jacques Muhammad, Brother Jermaine Muhammad, Brother Jonathan 2X Muhammad, Brother Joseph Muhammad, Brother Lewis Muhammad, Brother Marlon Muhammad, Brother Nemsen X, Brother*

Paul 5X Muhammad, Brother Phillip 4X Muhammad, Brother Captain Richard Muhammad, Brother Robert 13X Muhammad, Brother Sean Muhammad, Brother Shaheed Muhammad, Brother Vernon Muhammad, Brother Wilbur Muhammad and Brother Wilfred Muhammad

Oakland, California; *Min. Keith Muhammad*

Patterson, New Jersey; *Sister Angela Muhammad, Sister Kathy Muhammad and Sister Tanisha Muhammad*

Philadelphia, Pennsylvania; *Andrea and Bobby Muhammad, Min. Rodney Muhammad*

Phoenix, Arizona; *Brother Britian Muhammad, Brother Bobby Muhammad, Brother Carlos Muhammad, Sister Edith Muhammad, Brother Gary A. Muhammad, Brother Gary C. Muhammad, Brother Hakeem Muhammad, Brother Hannibal Muhammad, Brother Islam Muhammad, Brother James Muhammad, Sister Kimaada Muhammad, Sister Linda Muhammad, Brother Michael Muhammad, Dr. Patina Muhammad, Brother Ray Muhammad, Brother Ron C. Muhammad, Brother Steve Muhammad*

Plainfield, New Jersey; *Brother Bryant Muhammad, Brother Dave Muhammad, Brother Maurice Muhammad*

Sacramento, California; *Min. Isaiah Muhammad*

San Diego, California; *Min. Hugh Muhammad*

San Francisco, California; *Min. Christopher Muhammad*

Seattle, Washington; *Min. Milford Muhammad*

Stockton, California; *Min. Brian Muhammad*

Upland, California; *Brother Mustafa Cajeme Muhammad*

Virgin Islands; *Sister Lynda Muhammad*

Washington, D.C.; *Brother Cedric Muhammad*